Psalms of Christ

Psalms of Christ

The Messiah in Non-Messianic Psalms

Daniel H. Fletcher

WIPF & STOCK · Eugene, Oregon

PSALMS OF CHRIST
The Messiah in Non-Messianic Psalms

Copyright © 2018 Daniel H. Fletcher. All rights reserved. Except for brief quotations in critical publications or reviews, no part of this book may be reproduced in any manner without prior written permission from the publisher. Write: Permissions, Wipf and Stock Publishers, 199 W. 8th Ave., Suite 3, Eugene, OR 97401.

Wipf & Stock
An Imprint of Wipf and Stock Publishers
199 W. 8th Ave., Suite 3
Eugene, OR 97401

www.wipfandstock.com

PAPERBACK ISBN: 978-1-5326-5079-6
HARDCOVER ISBN: 978-1-5326-5080-2
EBOOK ISBN: 978-1-5326-5081-9

Manufactured in the U.S.A.

Unless otherwise noted, Scripture quotations are from The Holy Bible, English Standard Version, copyright © 2001 by Crossway Bibles, a division of Good News Publishers. Used by permission. All rights reserved.

The Bible text designated JPS 1917 is from The Holy Scriptures (Old Testament), originally published by the Jewish Publication Society in 1917. Electronic text Copyright © 1995-98 by Larry Nelson (Box 1681, Cathedral City, CA 92235). All rights reserved. Used by permission.

Quotations designated KJV are from the 1769 Blayney Edition of the 1611 King James Version of the English Bible. Copyright @ 1988–1997 by the Online Bible Foundation and Woddside Fellowship of Ontario, Canada. Licensed from the Institute for Creation Research. Used by permission.

English translations of the Septuagint are from The Septuagint Version of the Old Testament by Sir Lancelot C. L. Brenton, 1844, 1851, published by Samuel Bagster and Sons, London, original ASCII edition Copyright © 1988 by FABS

International (c/o Bob Lewis, DeFuniak Springs FL 32433). All rights reserved. Used by permission.

Scripture taken from the Modern English Version. Copyright @ 2014 by Military Bible Association. Used by permission. All rights reserved.

Quotations designated NET are from The NET Bible, Version 1.0 - Copyright © 1996-2006 Biblical Studies Press, L.L.C.

Quotations designated (NIV) are from THE HOLY BIBLE: NEW INTERNATIONAL VERSION®. NIV®. Copyright © 1973, 1978, 1984, 2011 by International Bible Society. All rights reserved worldwide.

Scripture quotations marked NLT are taken from the *Holy Bible,* New Living Translation, copyright © 1996, 2004, 2007. Used by permission of Tyndale House Publishers, Inc., Carol Stream, Illinois 60188. All rights reserved.

Quotations designated NRSV are from the New Revised Standard Bible Version, Copyright @ 1989, Division of Christian Education of the National Council of the Churches of Christ in the United States of America. Used by permission. All rights reserved.

To Hannah, Nathaniel, and Lydia

"Children are a gift from the Lord; they are a reward from him."
(Psalm 127:3)

Contents

List of Tables and Figures | viii
Preface | ix
Abbreviations | xviii

    Introduction | 1
    Psalm 1 | 16
    Psalm 23 | 26
    Psalm 29 | 42
    Psalm 30 | 54
    Psalm 46 | 65
    Psalm 67 | 84
    Psalm 88 | 96
    Psalm 100 | 117
    Psalm 119 | 134
    Psalm 127 | 174
    Psalm 137 | 196
    Psalm 148 | 216
    Conclusion | 230

Bibliography | 235

Tables and Figures

Tables

1. Psalm 23 and the Exodus | 35
2. Chiasms of Psalm 88 | 99
3. Psalm 88 and the Exodus | 101
4. Psalm 88 and the Passion of Christ | 115
5. Torah and its Synonyms in Psalm 119 | 136
6. Servant, Son, and God's House | 191
7. Creation in Genesis 1—2 and Psalm 148 | 218

Figures

1. Contrasting Polarities | 56

Preface

INSPIRATION FOR THIS BOOK came from a series of presentations I gave at the Inman Forum for Biblical Preaching at Ohio Valley University, Vienna WV, in the summer of 2015. My dear friend Mike Moss invited me to speak on preaching from the OT. I developed a newfound love and appreciation for the OT as a result of my doctoral studies at Westminster Theological Seminary, where many courses focused on the NT use of the OT. In particular, a class on biblical interpretation during the Second Temple period taught me to wrestle with the complexities of the interpretive environment of the NT writers. While the NT authors share the interpretive methods of Judaism, their *starting point* for biblical interpretation was that Jesus Christ is the summation and goal of the Jewish Scriptures. I must humbly confess this was the first time that I was introduced to the christological character of the OT, as the NT understands it (e.g., Luke 24:25–27, 44–47; John 5:39–40). I will unpack this throughout this book, but for the moment the point here is that *the NT reads the OT from a post-resurrection perspective, finding throughout its pages a comprehensive witness to the redemptive-historical significance of the life, death, and resurrection of Jesus.*

As a seminarian, I was excited to explore the exegetical "tools of the trade" of the NT use of the OT: typology, allegory, intertextuality, prophetic fulfillment as "filling up" (*plēroō*) a passage with christological meaning, adaptation, to name only a few.[1] These tools are, in part, the exegetical methods themselves that the NT employs when interpreting the OT in light of the Christ event. To be sure, these methods are not unique to the NT; they are part and parcel of first-century Jewish exegesis. The NT authors simply apply the methods of their time to the interpretation of the Jewish Scriptures in light of the salvific work of Jesus Christ. Even more than my enthusiasm

---

1. E.g., Typology (John 3:14; cf. Num 21:8–9); allegory (Gal 4:24; cf. Gen 16; 21); intertextuality (Phil 2:10–11; cf. Isa 45:23); prophecy as "filling up" (Matt 2:15; cf. Hos 11:1); adaptation (Eph 4:8; cf. Ps 68:18).

around exegetical technique, I also became convinced that the NT interpretation of the OT is less about method per se, and more about interpretive starting point. Richard Longenecker concludes after a robust examination of the NT use of the OT: "The Jewish context in which the New Testament came to birth, significant though it was, was not what was distinctive or formative in the exegesis of the earliest believers. At the heart of their biblical interpretation was a christology and a christocentric perspective."[2] In other words, the NT understands Israel's Scriptures in light of the gospel story where the resurrected Lord is the lens for a proper understanding of the OT. To be clear, what we find in the NT is a "backward reading," beginning with a post-resurrection perspective, and the faith conviction that the ultimate meaning of the OT is found in none other than Jesus Christ. In short, the NT reads the OT through a "Jesus lens."[3] Stated provocatively, the NT does not start with Genesis and work its way to the gospel, but rather the reverse: it begins with the gospel and reads backward to Genesis in light of *established* conclusions and convictions concerning the gospel of Christ. Therefore, the interpretive starting point for understanding the christological character of the OT is the NT itself.

This brief immersion into the NT use of the OT was a paradigm shift in my understanding of the Bible. Another shift occurred as a result of an elective course on Psalms in my last semester of doctoral coursework. I had always loved Psalms, probably for the same reason many other Christians do: as a storehouse of human emotions that resonates with our emotional and spiritual experiences as we wrestle with the mystery of faith. Psalms is not pop-psychology, but deep spirituality written from faith for faith, whether in the heights of spiritual jubilation or the depths of personal agony. But my affection for Psalms eventually shifted to other concerns as I learned the intricacies of the organization (or "shape") of the Psalter, its convergence with torah, its end-times trajectory, its inner-biblical exegesis (i.e., how it interprets other parts of the OT), and the messianic import of the "royal psalms." Coming to grips with the multifaceted theology of Psalms proved to me to be a counterbalance to a personal experience of its emotional expressions.

I write about these two seminary courses and their respective emphases simply to illustrate that the forum topic I eventually settled on was "Christological Preaching from Psalms." Therefore, I write this book as a personal and passionate exploration of two topics close to my heart: christological interpretation of the OT and Psalms. To be sure, this is not the first book to

---

2. Longenecker, *Exegesis*, 187.
3. For a popular-level treatment, see Williams, *Jesus Lens*.

connect NT Christology with Psalms, nor is it the first to apply a christological interpretation to the OT generally. This book shares a general outlook of interpreting Psalms christologically with Richard Belcher's *The Messiah and the Psalms*. Belcher's thesis is that all the psalms have a relationship to Christ, not just the traditional messianic psalms.[4] He examines some psalms that are quoted in the NT and some that are not. A distinguishing feature of my work is that none of the psalms studied here are quoted in the NT; for that matter, there is only minute overlap between the psalms covered in the two books (excluding Pss 46, 88, 137). The present book also converges with Patrick Reardon's *Christ in the Psalms*, which offers short summaries of the historical setting of each psalm (in the LXX) followed by brief christological reflections. Reardon's book is not research based per se, whereas the current book offers documentation of the historical analysis as it explores the ancient setting of each psalm, as well as its anticipation of NT Christology. Sidney Greidanus's *Preaching Christ From Psalms* was published during the writing of the present work. As is the case with Belcher, there is some overlap in the psalms treated (e.g., Pss 1, 23, 29, 100); yet nearly half of the psalms in Greidanus's book are quoted in the NT in some messianic sense (e.g., Pss 2, 8, 22). Therefore, his work does not have a sustained focus on non-messianic psalms. Additionally, his lectionary approach is very different from the present work. Greidanus's book is geared toward the academic discipline of practical theology (i.e., preaching and worship), while the current one is geared more toward biblical theology (i.e., the organic unity of the OT and NT), understanding that these are not mutually exclusive, at least not ideally.[5] In spite of the differences between these three books and the current one, they have proved indispensable for my work.

Far from being an exhaustive application of Psalms to Christ, the approach of the current book is quite simple: to apply the NT conviction that the book of Psalms is ultimately about Christ to select non-messianic psalms. My approach is canonical, so that when examining a psalm's christological character, I want to propose answers to questions like: What canonical connections exist as a result of a christological reading? How does this psalm evoke Christ? How does it point to Christ? How do Christ's life,

---

4. Belcher, *Messiah*, 7.

5. For Brevard Childs, "Biblical theology is by definition theological reflection on both the Old and New Testament. It assumes that the Christian Bible consists of a theological unity formed by the canonical union of the two testaments" (Childs, *Biblical Theology*, 55). Geerhardus Vos explains the organic, unfolding nature of the Bible, where revelation is not completed in one exhaustive act, but unfolds in a long series of successive acts. In other words, biblical theology asserts that revelation is an organic process, whereby a line of development is drawn from the OT to the NT, as the former grows into the latter, like a seed grows into a mature tree (Vos, *Biblical Theology*, 5–18).

death, and resurrection illuminate the psalm? Because Psalms is the book of the OT most quoted in the NT, each psalm should be read in the context of the Christian canon of the Old and New Testaments for a Christian biblical theology of Psalms.[6] I believe the main thrust of a psalm is more christological than its various verses. Therefore, I will draw attention to each psalm as a whole, and will not attempt a verse-by-verse christological application. To be sure, not every verse of a psalm is christological, but the psalm *as a whole* points to Christ, and is illuminated by his person and work. Certain verses in a psalm may resonate a christological tone more loudly than others, but the combination of a psalm's verses sounds a louder, more harmonious christological song.

This book examines the following twelve psalms from the Hebrew Bible: Pss 1, 23, 29, 30, 46, 67, 88, 100, 119, 127, 137, and 148. Why these twelve psalms? Mostly out of personal interest, but also because none of them are traditional messianic psalms, and because they span the five books of the Psalter, allowing for a more comprehensive look at the Christology of the whole. I will approach each psalm from two angles. First, I will apply what biblical scholars call "grammatical-historical exegesis"[7] in an effort to understand the psalm in its historical context in terms of vocabulary, structure, poetic parallelism, metaphorical language, historical setting, etc. For brevity, I will simply refer to this step as "History." Second, I will apply a christological hermeneutic to each psalm in order to illustrate how it points to the gospel of Christ. I will refer to this step as "Christology." Why these two steps? If the goal is christological interpretation, can we not skip the first step? No, because God is a god of history, and reveals himself within human history. The Bible did not fall out of the sky, but grew out of the soil of ancient Palestine. Vern Poythress explains, "God spoke to people in human language, in human situations, through human authors. God himself in the Bible indicates that we should pay attention to these human factors in order to understand what he is saying and doing."[8] Simply put, historical concerns matter for establishing the original meaning of a passage of Scripture from

---

6. Wenham, "Canonical," 348.

7. It is difficult to do better than the following definition: "Grammatical-historical exegesis attempts to uncover the meaning that the text would have had to its original human authors and readers. This involves a consideration of the cultural, social, geographical, linguistic, and historical background to the original situation, the usual significance of the words, phrases, and idioms used, any special circumstances or problems faced by the author or his original hearers, how the passage fits in with what the author says elsewhere, what type or genre of speech/writing this is, the purpose of the book as a whole, how the passage functions literarily in the larger text, and where the original hearers stand in redemptive history" (McCartney and Clayton, *Reader*, 120).

8. Poythress, "What Does God Say?," 98.

the standpoint of the human author and his audience. However, historical exegesis is not the be-all-end-all of biblical interpretation. While it is helpful for establishing a base meaning of the text in its historical context, it is insufficient for reaching the divine author's meaning, which ultimately concerns Jesus Christ. God elevates the human discourse to a higher plane to serve his larger redemptive purpose of the gospel.

As a brief example of how history and Christology work together to illuminate a psalm, consider Ps 27. Assuming the superscript ("of David") is historically accurate, the psalm describes an event in the life of King David.[9] It is a poetic description of God's sanctuary as a place of solace for David as he seeks shelter from his enemies.[10] The psalm does not prophesy about the future Messiah per se in any grammatical-historical sense, and the NT never quotes Ps 27; therefore, it is not among the traditional "messianic" psalms. It is about an unknown period of David's life, recounting how God sheltered David when his enemies pursued him. The story of David demonstrates that his life was in constant danger. Using the tools of historical interpretation, Ps 27 commemorates the salvation of God throughout David's life, and the psalmist recalls these past experiences for the purpose of conveying a faith message to his original audience. This is the stuff of grammatical-historical exegesis, which seeks to understand the linguistic, historical, social, and religious setting of the original author and his audience.

At the same time, God is the ultimate author of Scripture, and his meaning is primary over that of the human author. God uses the words of the psalm to transcend the specific historical circumstances described therein. Another way of stating this is that when we, as Christians, read a psalm through a canonical lens, that is, in light of the completed Christian canon of the Old and New Testaments, the psalm's meaning may extend well beyond the intentions of the human author, especially as it relates to Christology. God's later words of revelation have bearing on his earlier words, and vice versa. Therefore, no biblical text exists in isolation from other biblical texts. Poythress observes, "Any passage is to be read in the context of the entire Bible. God intended from the beginning that his later words should build on and enrich earlier words, so that in some sense the whole of the Bible represents one long, complex process of communication from one author."[11] Therefore, I will demonstrate later that the psalmists were not likely thinking of Jesus Christ, much less the church, when they first penned

---

9. I will address the "of David" superscripts in the Introduction.

10. For a grammatical-historical interpretation of Ps 27, see Fletcher, "Sanctuary," 97–119.

11. Poythress, "What Does God Say?," 91.

their psalms; however, the larger context of the divinely-inspired canon nevertheless provides connecting links between passages, where the OT and NT carry on a canonical dialogue as readers read both testaments in relation to each other. In the case of Psalms, the NT transforms our understanding of the Psalter *when we read it in light of Jesus Christ,* as it calls to mind various aspects of his life and work of redemption. There is, therefore, no need to limit interpretation to discovering the intent of the original psalmist; the divine author's meaning, which always points to Christ, is supreme. The completed canon, then, helps discover God's intent in relation to Christ for later generations as the recipients of the completed canon.

Given that the OT is about Jesus, the divine meaning establishes a christological connection not apparent on the surface level of the psalm. Read christologically, Ps 27 becomes a song of God's protection of Christ from those who sought to kill him. Indeed, God vindicated Jesus from the charge of false testimony through the resurrection. Consider 27:12–13: "Give me not up to the will of my adversaries; for false witnesses have risen against me, and they breathe out violence. I believe that I shall look upon the goodness of the LORD in the land of the living." When read christologically, this passage evokes Jesus's passion (i.e., suffering and sacrifice) and resurrection: false witnesses maliciously insulted and assaulted him, yet God delivered him by raising him from the dead. Given that the OT does not have a developed doctrine of the resurrection, the original context involves David's faith in God's deliverance *in this life,* that is, the "land of the living," in contrast to the vague non-existence of the grave.[12] For the poet, there is no life beyond the grave; salvation consists of God's preservation of life in this world. However, the "land of the living" evokes the resurrection—eternal life beyond the grave—*when read from a post-resurrection vantage point.* Church fathers like Augustine and Jerome, for example, referred to eternity in heaven as the "land of the living" in contrast to life in the fallen world as the "land of the dying."[13] Yet their understanding comes about not from an analysis of the historical setting of the psalm, but from their Christian conviction that Jesus Christ defeated death at the resurrection, and this allows them to apply the original language of the psalm in a Christian context. Much more could be said regarding the grammatical-historical exegesis of

---

12. Wilson, *Psalms,* 487.

13. Augustine contrasts men who seek to do "good" in the "land of the dying" with saints who trust that they will see good in "the land of the living" (Augustine, *Expositions* 112, §5). Similarly, Jerome's *Letter to Eustochium,* written in 404 CE, mentions "the land of the living" when speaking of the eternal destiny of Paula, a devoted Christian convert from Rome, who had recently died (Shaff and Wace, *Nicene,* §29). On "land of the living" as a reference to the afterlife in Psalms, see Dahood, *Psalms,* 170.

this psalm and its subsequent christological interpretation (e.g., "The LORD is my light and my salvation"; Jesus is the light of the world; "Wait for the LORD"; Christians eagerly await the promise of Jesus's Second Coming and the final resurrection, etc.), but the point here is that God's meaning elevates this psalm from its historical rootedness in the life of David to a witness to the eternal gospel.[14]

To be sure, we need both exegetical methods because God is not aloof from human history; yet his larger redemptive purposes transcend the original situation of the human author. Dan McCartney and Charles Clayton observe:

> Since Scripture functions in human contexts, *our access to its divine meaning can only be by way of the human authors and their contexts.* The human author's meaning and his concrete sociolinguistic situation provide the starting point for understanding God's meaning for all his people. We get to know the human author's "point" in order to fully grasp God's "point."[15]

The Bible must be read in accordance with the rules of ordinary human language. As Friedrich Schleiermacher explains, "A more precise determination of any point in a given text must be decided on the basis of the use of the language common to the author and his original public."[16] Given that Scripture was written by human beings, our entry point for understanding its content comes by way of apprehending what the authors meant based on the original linguistic context of the words they used, how their audiences would have most likely understood those words, and the cultural and religious setting shared by the authors and their audiences. In fact, this is how we understand any written text, ancient or modern. Even so, Christians believe Scripture is much more than a mere human document—it is not just another ancient writing—its authority as the word of God bears witness to the divine author who has spoken first through the human authors, but finally and fully in Jesus

---

14. I would encourage the reader to read Ps 27 twice; the first time taking note of the grammatical-historical issues, metaphorical language, parallelism, etc., and then a second time as a witness to Christ's sufferings and exaltation. This is the kind of interpretive method I will be using throughout this book.

15. McCartney and Clayton, *Reader*, 26.

16. Schleiermacher, *Hermeneutics*, 117. Similarly, Alexander Campbell sounds much like Schleiermacher: "The words and sentences of the Bible are to be translated, interpreted, and understood according to the same code of laws and principles of interpretation by which other ancient writings are translated and understood; for, when God spoke to man in his own language, he spoke as one person converses with another—in the fair, stipulated, and well-established meaning of the terms" (Campbell, *Christian System*, 3).

Christ, the Word (John 1:1; Heb 1:1–2). Scripture's pinnacle purpose is to point readers to Christ as the climactic revelation of God.

Therefore, I will follow a two-step method of historical interpretation followed by christological interpretation throughout this book. I will examine each psalm in its original historical context, and then apply a christological reading to demonstrate how the psalm points to Christ. Ultimately, I want to explore what it means to follow the interpretive assumptions of the NT, not by stepping directly in the footsteps of the apostles, only going where they go, but by following their lead, and going in the *direction* that they set for us when interpreting the OT. I want to read Psalms through a Jesus lens not to find Jesus under every rock in the OT (although 1 Cor 10:4), but to see it as an expansive redemptive-historical witness to the gospel.

This book is an introduction to christological interpretation of the OT for beginning college and seminary students, church leaders, and interested lay readers. I hope it serves as a valuable tool for preaching and teaching Psalms from a Christian perspective, offering pastors something meaningful to say about the relationship of Christ to Psalms, and its relevance to the church as a witness to the gospel. Many people in our pews have not been taught to read the OT through a Jesus lens; therefore, they remain bogged down in what appears to them to be an antiquated, bygone part of the Bible with no connection to their Christian identity, apart from a few moralisms and messianic references scattered throughout. I hope this book contributes to a robust reading of the OT that understands Jesus as its summation and goal.

Following the NT, which sets forth the *trajectory* of christological interpretation of the OT, my hope is that we can experience fresh readings of non-messianic psalms by illustrating their christological character. In other words, I want to explore the question, "What might it look like to apply christological interpretation to non-messianic psalms?" I use the term *explore* intentionally because I do not presume any christological interpretation in this book as definitive for any particular psalm. I am simply exploring the issue and proposing interpretations that I believe are consistent with the NT conviction of the christological character of the OT. The general approach of this book is to highlight christological themes in select psalms from a bird's-eye view. I do not want to sacrifice the overriding theme of the psalm at the expense of methodological minutiae. I will not, therefore, enter into the morass of theories and definitions concerning methods like intertextuality, authorial intent, and the multifaceted nuances of the NT use of the OT, but will briefly address these when applicable, and refer the reader to the notes for additional resources on the topic.[17] I have adopted a canonical approach that reads OT passages in light of NT ones, and vice versa, within the larger context of the Christian canon, in order to show how the passages may illuminate each other when read christologically. I have transliterated original language terms for the sake of readability, and have included a bibliography of the sources used for this book, as well as additional sources on christological interpretation of Psalms, NT use of the OT, and Psalms generally.

Many thanks to David Musgrave, Andy Walker, and Paul Watson for their input; their expertise has proved invaluable. To Rodney Cloud for encouraging us faculty in the Turner School of Theology to take time to research and write, while at the same time making the spiritual nourishment of the students at Amridge University a priority. To Dr. Michael Turner and the administration at Amridge for their ongoing support. To Doug Green, now at Queensland Theological College, for introducing me to the academic study of Psalms during his tenure at Westminster Seminary, and for pressing for bold christological interpretations of the Psalter. To Mike Moss at Ohio Valley University for inviting me to speak at the Inman Forum. To Lauren Daniel for her editorial efforts. To the good folks at Wipf & Stock for their professionalism during the publication process. To my wife and kids for their faithful love. And finally, to my parents, Joe and Dianne, for their eagerness to hear of the weekly progress (or lack thereof) of this book, and for their constant encouragement and exhortation in the faith, which they have so bountifully passed down to me.

---

17. Beale and Carson, *Commentary*; Beale, *Doctrine*; Carson and Williamson, *It is Written*; Fletcher, "Nicodemus," 111–32; Fletcher, *Signs*; Gundry, et al., *Three Views*; Hays and Green, "Use of the Old Testament," 122–39; Hirsch, *Validity*; Juel, "Interpreting," 283–303; Longenecker, *Exegesis*; McCartney, "New Testament's Use," 101–16; Moyise, *Evoking*; Snodgrass, "Use of the Old Testament," 209–29.

Abbreviations

ANE	Ancient Near East
Aram.	Aramaic
BIBD	*Baker Illustrated Bible Dictionary*
Eng.	English
ESV	English Standard Version
Gk.	Greek
HB	Hebrew Bible
Heb.	Hebrew
JPS	Jewish Publication Society
Lat.	Latin
lit.	Literally
LXX	Septuagint
MEV	Modern English Version
MS(S)	Manuscript(s)
MT	Masoretic Text
NET	New English Translation
NIDB	*New Interpreters Dictionary of the Bible*
NIV	New International Version
NLT	Lew Living Translation
NT	New Testament
OT	Old Testament

para.	Paragraph
pars.	Parallels
pl.	Plural
sg.	Singular
St.	Stanza
trans.	translation
Vulg.	Vulgate

Introduction

"Reading the OT anew in light of the story of Jesus' death and resurrection opens both text and reader to new, previously unimagined, possibilities."—Richard B. Hays

To be frank, I was not taught a healthy view of the OT growing up. I was not taught that the OT was an abiding witness to the gospel, but was a bygone set of rules and regulations and outmoded worship forms. Passages like 2 Tim 3:15–17 were often made to refer to the NT, not the OT:

> . . . and how from childhood you have been acquainted with the sacred writings, which are able to make you wise for salvation through faith in Christ Jesus. All Scripture is breathed out by God and profitable for teaching, for reproof, for correction, and for training in righteousness, that the man of God may be competent, equipped for every good work. (ESV)

But the OT is what Paul has in mind, and his assumption is that the Scriptures of Israel testify to the salvation of the gospel of Christ. Paul believes that the OT is all that is needed to learn the message of salvation in Jesus Christ, including the righteousness that flows from a relationship with him. Of course, this also applies to the NT today, which states even more explicitly the salvation of Christ. But Timothy lacked the benefit of the completed biblical witness of both testaments in his first-century Jewish context. Nevertheless, what he had in the Jewish Scriptures was enough for his instruction in the faith of Christ. For Thomas Lea and Hayne Griffin:

> He [Paul] was not suggesting that a part of Timothy's childhood instruction involved the New Testament. The aim of the content of the sacred writings is to relate God's saving purpose in Christ. Timothy's study of the Scriptures had grounded him in that wisdom and enlightenment that leads to faith in Jesus Christ. The Scriptures lead to salvation but only as they point

to Christ. The Scriptures themselves do not provide salvation, but they do point to the Savior who can provide it. The phrase "through faith in Jesus Christ" shows how the Scriptures make individuals wise. They enlighten them to the necessity for faith in Jesus Christ.[1]

My past experience with the OT was one of practical neglect: it had no authoritative value for the life and function of the church. The OT was part of inspired Scripture, to be sure, but I was taught that the OT was not written primarily for Christians. In fact, we often used the moniker "New Testament church" to describe our adherence and allegiance to the NT, the "constitution" of the church.[2] Granted, we studied the OT in Sunday school, seeking earnestly to digest its facts, figures, and predictive prophecies of the Messiah, but in no way was the Lordship of Christ *the* driving assumption of what the OT was really about. It was about Israel, not the church. We could count the number of messianic proof texts (i.e., various verses scattered throughout the OT), memorize them to support apologetic aims (i.e., prove that Jesus was the Messiah), and then forget about the rest of the OT for all intents and purposes. The OT did not play a major role in establishing our Christology beyond a few messianic prophecies. My colleague even told me that his mother literally cried when he told her he planned to get his doctorate in OT! While her emotional reaction may not be the norm, it reflects the practical neglect of the OT in many Christian traditions historically. Take my own Restoration Movement tradition as but one example that has attempted to more or less follow the NT church in its external forms and organization, but has largely neglected the inner workings of the Bible of the apostles, as well as its proper interpretation as a scriptural tradition that is primarily about Jesus Christ.

This book is an attempt to resurrect the OT to the place of authority it had for the "New Testament church," and to read it like the NT does—as a witness to Christ. The OT was, after all, *the* Bible of the early church.[3] It

---

1. Lea and Griffin, *1, 2 Timothy, Titus*, 234.
2. Fletcher, "Constitution," 1–17.
3. I recognize the lack of precision of using designations such as OT and NT when speaking of Scripture in the first-century CE because doing so imposes anachronistic canonical constraints on the ancients. Neither is it accurate to speak of the church's use of the "Hebrew Bible" because the vast majority of scriptural quotations in the NT come from the Gk. tradition known as the Septuagint, commonly designated LXX. Yet it is also imprecise to refer to "the" Septuagint because it did not exist as a single entity, but as a Gk. tradition composed of multiple revisions. It is more accurate, therefore, to speak of the church's use of "Israel's Scriptures," which does not impose modern canonical constraints—whether Protestant, Catholic, or Orthodox—and takes into consideration the multiple text traditions available at the time in their Heb., Aram., and

seems now to be a matter of common sense for Christian movements that seek to more or less pattern themselves after the NT church (to the extent that that is even possible 2,000 years later, or even theologically necessary to begin with), that it would also follow the apostles' hermeneutical procedure of how to read the Jewish Scriptures.

I anticipate an objection to applying apostolic hermeneutics today: "That was okay for them but not for us; they were inspired and we are not."[4] Let's trace that logic for a moment. We are expected to follow their lead at church planting, church government, church discipline, church doctrine, worship forms, etc., but not their interpretive approach to Scripture? So much for being "a people of the book." If not the NT itself, where do we as "New Testament Christians" go to learn how to interpret the OT as Jesus and the NT writers interpreted it? Moisés Silva states it provocatively, "If we refuse to pattern our exegesis after that of the apostles, we are in practice denying the authoritative character of their scriptural interpretation—and to do so is to strike at the very heart of the Christian faith."[5] Andreas Köstenberger and Richard Patterson state similarly, "One important guiding principle for the way in which we today ought to read the Old Testament is the study of how the New Testament writers themselves read the Hebrew Scriptures. If we want to be biblical in our hermeneutical practice, there is no better place to look than the hermeneutical approach of the biblical writers themselves."[6]

If we do not get our interpretive practice from the NT, where do we get it? Again, a common response is, "We follow the NT approach to the OT only in the specific passages laid out for us in the NT, but we cannot extend it to other passages because they are not explicit examples." In other words, because the NT does not interpret a passage christologically, for us to do so "goes beyond what is written." As Klyne Snodgrass describes it, we should not expect to find "new instances"—beyond those explicitly laid out in the NT—of verses applied to Jesus by using the exegetical methods of the apostles, presumably because we do not share their authoritative revelatory

---

Gk. forms. With that said, I will use the OT/NT designations because of convention and convenience. While this book primarily appeals to the Protestant canon, which is identical to the Hebrew canon except for the ordering of certain books, it will refer to the Gk. tradition at times. This study follows the numbering of the Hebrew Psalter, which consists of 150 psalms.

4. For this basic view, see Longenecker, *Exegesis*, 197; Snodgrass, "Use of the Old Testament," 223.

5. Silva, "New Testament Use," 164.

6. Köstenberger and Patterson, *Invitation*, 195.

role.⁷ Yet, are we really only to read the OT christologically in the few places where the NT does so? So much for Jesus's words that the "all the Scriptures" are about him (Luke 24:25–27; cf. John 5:39). Should we apply a "canon within the canon" approach where we read only certain OT passages christologically and practically ignore the rest; or at most, memorize facts and figures and moralize OT stories? According to this logic, if the NT does not expressly exegete an OT passage, it is "hands on" from a grammatical-historical perspective, but presumably "hands off" from a christological one.⁸ So much for Ps 23! So much for Ezekiel's valley of dry bones! So much for the book of Esther—its main point is the salvation of God's people! We can also ignore the so-called *protoevangelium* of Gen 3:15. The NT does not interpret any of these passages christologically; so, according to the traditional logic, we should not either. Again, what is one to make of Jesus's claim that "all the Scriptures" witness to him, when several OT books are not quoted in the NT messianically or otherwise (e.g., Judges, Ruth, Chronicles, Ezra, Nehemiah, Esther, Ecclesiastes, Song of Solomon, Lamentations, Obadiah)?⁹ Do these not witness to Jesus Christ?

Given the traditional reasoning, none of these texts or myriad of others carries any christological import simply because the NT is silent about them. This reduces the Christian approach to the OT to a catalog of messianic proof texts at the expense of the rest of the OT. As Dan McCartney confirms:

> If our perception of the larger divine intent in the Old Testament is limited to solely those passages for which the apostles inspiredly spelled it out for us, it seriously limits a Christian use of the Old Testament. Further, the christocentric interpretation by the apostles is itself derived from the teaching of Jesus, who appears to be the fountainhead of this whole messianic way of reading the Old Testament.¹⁰

I am convicted, therefore, that the NT writers have given us examples of how to read the OT christologically, and they expect us to apply their post-resurrection hermeneutical perspective in our own reading of the OT, and not restrict ourselves to their examples as the only "approved" ones. In short, they have given the church an *inspired interpretive trajectory* for understanding the OT rightly (i.e., christologically). To use a common—albeit

---

7. Snodgrass, "Use of the Old Testament," 223.

8. This is also defended in Longenecker, *Exegesis*, 198.

9. I admit the tenuousness of such lists because it is not always easy to decide whether a NT passage quotes or alludes to an OT one; further, quotations may, at times, be duplicates within the OT itself, making it difficult to determine which book is being cited.

10. McCartney, "Hermeneutics," para. 7.

imperfect—analogy, they have taught us how to fish, not given us a fish. As for the NT writers being authoritative interpreters of OT Scripture, I agree that they are foundational for the church as bearers of unique divine authority, commission, and revelation; yet, is this not even more reason to adopt their overall interpretive approach to the OT? It is precisely *because* of their inspired authority that our interpretations should be rooted in their use of the OT. In short, when we implement their interpretive strategy today, we are not relaying the foundations of scriptural interpretation, but are moving about freely in the house God has built for us in Christ.

I believe we have in the NT a "go and do likewise" scenario where Jesus and the NT writers give the interpretive map for christological readings of the OT, even "non-messianic" passages. Yes, they give methods of exegesis too, but these are subservient to the larger goal of interpreting the OT christologically. Put differently, there is nothing inherently "Christian" about grammatical-historical exegesis, typology, intertextuality, allegory, or predictive prophecy; these are all evident in the OT itself. But what is distinctly Christian is the hermeneutical starting point of the apostolic church: Israel's Scriptures are about Jesus Christ. They point to him; he is their ultimate goal and meaning, and the Holy Spirit enables Christians to read the OT as a comprehensive witness to the gospel of Christ.

Does this also apply to so-called "non-messianic" passages? It is fairly obvious that the NT writers have applied christological interpretation when they quote an OT passage as referring in some way to the person and work of Christ. What about OT passages not cited in the NT, or those that do not make the traditional "messianic" lists? Are they messianic too? Patrick Reardon observes:

> The correct interpretation of certain psalms comes more readily than others, and the task is rendered easier still if a psalm's meaning has already been made plain in the New Testament. The New Testament is, after all, the key to the full (that is to say, Christian) understanding of the Old. When the New Testament tells us the meaning of some passage in the Old Testament, then the matter of authentic interpretation, for us Christians, is settled.[11]

For example, Psalms[12] is quoted more often than any other OT book in the NT.[13] Reardon sees the Psalter as so perfused with Christology that "Christ

---

11. Reardon, *Christ*, 61.

12. For consistency, "Psalms" refers to the Psalter (the book of Psalms), and "psalms" refers generally to individual psalms without reference to its number, and is understood from the context (e.g., "the psalm recalls the exodus").

13. Bullock, *Encountering*, 46; McCann, *Theological*, 163; Longman, *How to Read*

walks within the psalms."[14] Psalms citations in the NT vary where some are directly related to Christ (Ps 22:1 quoted in Matt 27:46), while others are indirectly related to him (Pss 69:25 and 109:8 quoted in Acts 1: 20 as being fulfilled in Judas). It is worth noting that nowhere does the OT speak of "the Messiah" per se; the definite article "the" is always omitted.[15] Therefore, identifications of "messianic psalms" vary considerably because the scholarly community lacks objective criteria for what makes a psalm messianic. Nevertheless, a basic assumption is that messianic psalms are, in one way or another, related to the Messiah's person and work within the establishment of God's kingdom in Israel and the world.[16] But this depends on whether one is looking at it from a strictly OT perspective, NT perspective, or a combination of both as the unfolding of God's plan throughout redemptive history.

From an OT perspective, for example, royal psalms (2, 18, 20, 21, 45, 72, 89, 101, 110, 132, 144)[17] are often understood in a messianic sense because they relate to Israel's earthly king, and anticipate God's end-times king—the Messiah, the son of David. While these psalms do not refer to "the Messiah" in an absolute sense, the noun Messiah ("anointed one") occurs nine times in these eleven psalms, and twice in verbal form ("to anoint").[18] Given that the royal psalms were retained during the Babylonian exile, when Israel had no king, their existence must point beyond the immediate situation to keep alive the hope that the Davidic dynasty would rise again.[19]

There is a scholarly consensus that the postexilic community shaped the Psalter into five books, including the royal psalms, in a world that the community did not control, in eager expectation of a new order of its national identity under a future Davidic king.[20] As C. Hassell Bullock notes, "The royal psalms, once the Davidic dynasty had fallen, helped to keep alive the hope that it would rise again, although that was not likely their original purpose. And when that hope did not materialize in its historical form, it

---

Psalms, 65; Just, "Quotations."

14. Reardon, *Christ*, xvi.

15. Tesh and Zorn, *Psalms*, 71.

16. Belcher, *Messiah*, 30; Tesh and Zorn, *Psalms*, 70. I recommend Belcher's brief history of interpretation on the development of the term "messianic" in relation to Psalms (*Messiah*, 21–30).

17. The list is taken from Bullock, *Encountering*, 178. Bullock has a fine exegetical analysis of the development of messianism in the royal psalms (pp. 177–86).

18. Ibid., 182.

19. Belcher, *Messiah*, 118.

20. On the postexilic shaping of the Psalter, see deClaissé-Walford, *Introduction*, 45–57. Although, the exilic community also played a role in shaping the Psalter.

turned into a hope for the appearance of the Messiah, the Anointed One."[21] The royal psalms were therefore "reinterpreted in the expectation of a time when a new Davidic ruler would appear."[22] Brevard Childs echoes this general outlook on the messianic function of the royal psalms: "Although the royal psalms arose originally in a peculiar historical setting . . . they were treasured in the Psalter for a different reason, namely as a witness to the messianic hope which looked for the consummation of God's kingship through his Anointed One."[23] To be clear, such messianic import was most likely not clear to the original authors of the royal psalms. But again, God is the ultimate author of Scripture, and biblical texts should be understood within his larger redemptive plan. As Tesh and Zorn remind us, "This messianic significance in the Psalms may not have been understood by the psalmists, nor those who heard them, but it was in the mind of the Spirit who inspired them."[24]

In addition to the royal psalms, many have understood the psalms "of David"[25] as *de facto* messianic based on their connection to King David, not because they speak of the Messiah per se, but because David is an illustration of one who lived his life in the hope of the reign of God.[26] Due to many disappointments in Israel's history following King David—not least of which were the eventual deportations of the northern and southern kingdoms into Assyria and Babylon, respectively—a messianic hope emerged whenever the Psalter mentioned Israel's second and greatest king. Many

21. Bullock, *Encountering*, 182.
22. Belcher, *Messiah*, 25.
23. Childs, *Introduction*, 517.
24. Tesh and Zorn, *Psalms*, 73.
25. Authorship of the so-called "Davidic psalms" is notoriously difficult. The Heb. preposition *le*, often translated "of" in Eng., which is found in the superscriptions of many psalms, has a range of possible meanings—much like the Eng. counterpart. It is commonly understood to indicate authorship, as in "by David," and this may well be the case; but this cannot be established from the preposition itself, much less the superscripts of the psalms, which were added later in the Psalter's composition history. It can also indicate possession ("belonging to"), most likely belonging to a group of psalms (e.g., "of the sons of Korah"). The preposition can also indicate relationship ("about" or "pertaining to"). Or, it can mean "for" someone (i.e., on behalf of, in dedication to, or at the direction of). Thus, "of David" conveys the idea of being *related to David in some way*. The meaning of the psalms does not depend on the precise identification of their author; therefore, I will refer to the "David" of the Psalter out of convenience, and do not intend a rigid statement of authorship. For this issue, see Tesh and Zorn, *Psalms*, 45–46, 49–50; deClaissé-Walford, *Introduction*, 145–55; Longman, *How to Read Psalms*, 40–42. Aside from "of" as possibly indicating authorship, one should notice the intentional ambiguity of *Psalms of Christ*, the title of this book.
26. Belcher, *Messiah*, 25.

years of exile and a dissolved Davidic monarchy provided the catalyst for interpreting the royal psalms in an end-times fashion. Doug Green notes that a growing number of scholars now agree that the Psalter was edited in such a way that encouraged readers to interpret it no longer simply as prayers and hymns rooted in the experience of ancient Israelites, but as prophecies of events at the climax of Israel's history (i.e., eschatologically).[27] The "David" of the Psalter, then, evokes hopes for an end-times "anointed one" reminiscent of historical King David. Therefore, a christological reading of Psalms sees the "David" of the Psalter as a figure of Christ; David's kingship offers us an Old Testament image or figure of Jesus Christ's kingship.[28] Bullock observes along the same lines that the royal psalms readily lend themselves to the NT messianic view.[29] However, this is only partially true because from a NT perspective, messianic psalms extend beyond the royal and Davidic psalms to find their ultimate fulfillment in Jesus Christ. The royal psalms have not been transmitted within a specific collection but are instead scattered throughout the Psalter,[30] and this weighs against isolating them too narrowly from other psalms in a hyper-messianic sense to the exclusion of non-royal psalms. Belcher's observation is well taken: "A psalm can be considered Messianic if it deals with the person of the king. However, if only psalms that deal with the person of the king are Messianic, then the number of Messianic psalms is limited severely."[31]

The NT does not solely connect royal or Davidic psalms to Jesus (e.g., Ps 78:2 quoted in Matt 13:35); as we will see later, the entire Psalter speaks of him. I appreciate Green's reservation with the traditional "messianic" category, which limits it to psalms quoted in the NT as direct prophecies of Christ: "Instead of treating the small group of psalms that the NT 'applies' to Jesus as a special group of direct prophecies of the Messiah, I regard these psalms as the tip of a prophetic and messianic iceberg. It is not that the NT quotes *all* of a small group of messianic psalms. Rather, it quotes from a *few* of a very large group of messianic psalms."[32] Put differently, the *whole* Psalter is messianic, anticipating God's eternal reign through the long-awaited Messiah.[33]

---

27. Green, "Christ's Shepherd," 36.
28. Collett, "Christology," 393.
29. Bullock, *Encountering*, 184.
30. Childs, *Introduction*, 515–16.
31. Belcher, *Messiah*, 29. Green estimates the number of psalms that some scholars deem traditionally "messianic" to be less than fifteen ("Christ's Shepherd," 34).
32. Green, "Christ's Shepherd," 38.
33. Mitchell, *Message*. For a more concise version of Mitchell's thesis, see Mitchell, "Remember David," 528–29.

INTRODUCTION 9

The traditional list of messianic psalms is as follows: Pss 2, 8, 16, 22, 40, 45, 68, 69, 89, 109, 110, 118, 132.[34] Again, the list varies among commentators because there are some psalms that the NT quotes, but that do not make the messianic list: Pss 31, 35, 41, 78, 102.[35] My concern in this book is with psalms that the NT does not quote (but may nonetheless allude to), and my thesis is that we should read these messianically. Some might object that it is inconsistent to speak of christological interpretation of psalms that are not mentioned in the NT (the explicit examples argument earlier), but not if Jesus has anything to say about it; he declared that all the Scriptures witness to him (Luke 24:25–27, 44–47; John 5:39). I will interact in more detail with specific passages later, but suffice it to say here that at a minimum, they reveal that the OT is ultimately about Christ and cannot be reduced to a select number of messianic proof texts explicitly evidenced in the NT.

The NT basis for christological interpretation of the OT comes from the mouth of Jesus himself:

> And he said to them, "O foolish ones, and slow of heart to believe all that the prophets have spoken! Was it not necessary that the Christ should suffer these things and enter into his glory?" And beginning with Moses and all the Prophets, he interpreted to them in all the Scriptures the things concerning himself. (Luke 24:25–27)

> Then he said to them, "These are my words that I spoke to you while I was still with you, that everything written about me in the Law of Moses and the Prophets and the Psalms must be fulfilled." Then he opened their minds to understand the Scriptures, and said to them, "Thus it is written, that the Christ should suffer and on the third day rise from the dead, and that repentance and forgiveness of sins should be proclaimed in his name to all nations, beginning from Jerusalem." (Luke 24:44–47)

> You search the Scriptures because you think that in them you have eternal life; and it is they that bear witness about me, yet you refuse to come to me that you may have life. (John 5:39–40)

The first two passages are the most relevant to this study because they specifically mention the prophets and/or Psalms.[36] The first is in the context of Jesus talking with two disciples—one named Cleopas and the other

---

34. Green, "Christ's Shepherd," 35.

35. Ibid., 36.

36. Although John's christological use of the Prophets and the Psalms should not be ignored. See Brendsel, *"Isaiah"*; Daly-Denton, *David*; Manning, *Echoes*.

anonymous—on the road to Emmaus after the resurrection. Their faces are downcast; their dreams dashed because they were hoping that Jesus was the liberator of Israel. In their way of thinking, the crucifixion of Jesus proves otherwise. Yet they do not realize with whom they are talking as they travel on the road—none other than the resurrected Christ. We know better as later readers of Luke's Gospel. We know it is Jesus himself because Luke tells us so (Luke 24:15).

I sometimes think that as Christians, who have nearly 2,000 years of Christian reflection on the story of Jesus, expect everyone to understand the story as clearly as we do today. We have the benefit of a completed NT canon that provides supporting evidence to substantiate Jesus's claims about his divinity and mission. We also have the benefit of knowing that the fruit of Jesus's life, death, resurrection, and ascension is a worldwide church committed to the proclamation of the gospel story. But the disciples on the road to Emmaus have none of these retrospective insights. As a matter of fact, because they do not realize that Jesus has been raised from the dead, their perspective is vastly different from ours today, as we stake our very faith on that claim as a historic reality. We read the story with post-resurrection lenses. The Emmaus disciples still had hazy crucifixion lenses on their eyes, thinking the cross was the end of the Jesus story. They understand the story only in terms of what happened on Friday, but Jesus wants them to understand it also in connection with what happened on Sunday. Again, we suppose that they should have been able to "figure it out"; that the OT testifies to the suffering, death, and resurrection of Israel's Messiah. Jesus even says as much by noting their slowness of heart to believe the Scriptures (24:25). However, they did not understand from the Scriptures the narrative of the gospel of a crucified and risen Savior. To be sure, it is not a matter of knowing more biblical content, but of having the proper interpretive framework. For Richard Hays, "The puzzled Emmaus disciples have all the facts but lack the pattern that makes them meaningful."[37] Their knowledge of the OT was deficient regarding its relationship to the person and work of Christ.

Therefore, the resurrected Lord gives them a crash course in hermeneutics. Israel's Scriptures testify to his mission of redemption—Moses, *all* the Prophets, *all* the Scriptures coalesce around his identity. Luke's use of the word "all" in 24:27 emphasizes the comprehensive nature of the OT witness to Christ. It is worth noting that Luke does not identify any specific passages as messianic per se. While it is safe to assume that his second volume, the book of Acts, records several of these on the lips of the apostles and their associates (e.g., Acts 2:25 [Ps 16:8–11]; 2:34–35 [Ps 110:1]; 3:22–23

---

37. Hays, *Reading Backwards*, 14.

[Deut 18:15, 18, 19]; 3:25–26 [Gen 22:18; 26:4]; 4:11 [Ps 118:22]; 4:25–26 [Ps 2:1–2]; 8:32–33 [Isa 53:7–8]; 13:33 [Ps 2:7]; 13:34 [Isa 55:3]; 13:35 [Ps 16:10]), the emphasis here is on the totality of the Scriptures as a witness to Christ's sufferings and glorification. Granted, the texts in Acts do in fact span from the books of Moses[38] to the prophetic corpus, but not all the Prophets are represented, nor obviously are all the Scriptures. Therefore, it is better to understand Luke's comment as suggesting "the whole narrative of God's dealings with Israel unlocks God's purposes that culminate in Jesus's crucifixion and resurrection."[39] Lest we reduce the OT to a handful of messianic passages, we should recognize in it a larger, unified story of God's redemption of humanity. Tremper Longman III and Al Groves comprehend the OT story as a grand story pointing to Christ:

> Jesus did not arrive unannounced; his coming was declared in advance in the Old Testament, not just in explicit prophecies of the Messiah but by means of the stories of all of the events, characters, and circumstances on the Old Testament. God was telling a larger, overarching, unified story. From the account of creation in Genesis to the final stories of the return from exile, God progressively unfolded his plan of salvation. And the Old Testament account of that plan always pointed in some way to Christ.[40]

The second passage, Luke 24:44–47, is most relevant to this study. Iain Duguid calls it a "summary of Jesus's master class in Old Testament interpretation."[41] In the context of Luke 24, the scene shifts from Emmaus to Jerusalem, from two disciples to the eleven apostles (minus Judas). They are not a little confused about the events of the crucifixion and resurrection of Christ. Although Jesus has repeatedly taught them the necessity of his passion and his subsequent resurrection in Luke's Gospel (9:22, 44; 13:33; 17:25; 18:31–33), they still do not understand. One might think that seeing the resurrected Lord would be enough to give them unobstructed clarity on the teaching of Scripture regarding his person and mission, but this is apparently not the case. Luke reports that while in the very presence of Jesus they were "troubled," and "doubt" had arisen in their hearts (24:38). Jesus once again gives a lesson in biblical hermeneutics. Seeming surprised at their

---

38. There is another way to interpret this verse that emphasizes the role of Moses as the first rejected prophet of all the OT prophets. This makes good sense of the context, which centers on the sufferings of Christ. Nevertheless, the emphasis on "all the Scriptures" still stands. For this, see Tannehill, *Luke*, 356.

39. Garland, *Luke*, 954.

40. Longman and Groves, foreword to *After God's Own Heart*, ix–xi.

41. Duguid, *Is Jesus in the Old Testament?*, 10.

lack of understanding of the Scriptures and their testimony to the Messiah's mission, Jesus reminds them that he has already taught them previously during his earthly ministry about his relationship to the Scriptures: "These are my words that I spoke to you while I was still with you . . ." (24:44). In other words, this is not the first time they have heard from Jesus a scriptural description of his mission. Being Jesus's inner circle as his chosen apostles, Luke may be implying that they are (or should be) more informed than the two disciples in Emmaus. Therefore, Luke's description of their unbelief is thick with irony. He gives essentially the same hermeneutical lesson as earlier in the chapter on christological interpretation: the entirety of the OT is a witness to Christ, especially his sufferings and resurrection (v. 46). Steve Moyise notes, "It is clear Luke believes that all of the Scriptures point to Jesus, and that during his final days on earth he explained this to his disciples. More specifically, he believes that Jesus explained how the Scriptures speak of a messiah who must first suffer and then enter into his glory."[42]

While Luke is explicit about the content of Scripture—Jesus's sufferings and resurrection—it is by no means limited to these events. For Luke, Scripture also speaks to Jesus's incarnate birth (1:69–70), his inaugural ministry (4:18–19), his rationale for teaching in parables (8:10), the triumphal entry (19:38), etc. Jesus repeats in sweeping terms the pervasive witness of Scripture to himself: "Everything" written about him must be fulfilled (24:44). What is more, he uses a three-part division of Israel's Scriptures to convey the comprehensiveness of scriptural testimony concerning himself: " . . . in the Law of Moses and the Prophets and Psalms" (my trans.). Once again, the focus of his teaching was not on a few "messianic" texts here and there, but rather the entire Old Testament.[43] Adding up all the messianic passages in the OT results in only a small portion of the OT pointing to Christ. As N. T. Wright has noted, the comprehensive christological hermeneutic of Luke 24 "looks more like a way of reading the entire scriptural story, and within that the entire book of Psalms, than an attempt to pluck a few key texts out of a mass of otherwise unhelpful material."[44] What Luke has in mind here is a christological hermeneutic where the OT is a coherent and comprehensive witness to the gospel. But all is not well. The apostles, in spite of hearing the resurrected Lord's description of the pervasiveness of the gospel in the OT, are apparently still obtuse. What is needed is not more rigorous study, more precise exegesis, or more meditative introspection, but divine intervention; or, at least divine explanation. Luke writes,

---

42. Moyise, *Jesus and Scripture*, 65.
43. Duguid, *Is Jesus in the Old Testament?*, 10.
44. Wright, *The Case for Psalms*, 33.

"He [Jesus] opened their minds to understand the Scriptures" (v. 45), as he had done earlier in Emmaus. Luke does not necessarily imply that they need a supernatural infusion of divine insight to understand the Scripture, but simply that Jesus gave them new insights, which they can only understand from a post-resurrection perspective.[45] Nevertheless, for Luke, the message of the Scriptures is not self-evident; one's mind must be opened to it, and they are rightly understood only in light of Jesus's death and resurrection.[46]

We should be crystal clear about what has happened here in Luke 24. The followers of Jesus did not reason from the OT and come to the right conclusion. They tried this approach, and it ended in frustration because they did not see how the crucifixion fit the Messiah's mission. It was not clear to them until *after* they encountered the resurrected Lord.[47] Jesus gave them a post-resurrection perspective—a christological lens through which to read the story again, this time in reverse order. Not that they read the OT from the last canonical book to the first, but from the end of the story as the interpretive starting point. Starting from their experience of the resurrected Lord, Jesus himself "interpreted to them" (v. 27), "opened the Scriptures" (v. 32), and "opened their minds" (v. 45) to understand the OT. Again, we have to be honest about the reading strategy Luke teaches here. It is not "start at the beginning and you will figure it out if you try hard enough, dig deep enough with the right exegetical technique," but rather, "start from the end and then you will see clearly how to read the OT story in relation to Christ." Put differently, we must read the story backward with resurrection lenses on our eyes. Hays states it provocatively, "Jesus' exposition of Israel's Scripture will have to undertake the task of reading backwards: it will have to show *retrospectively* the pervasive presence of this theme—which had never been perceived by anyone in Israel prior to the crucifixion and resurrection."[48] In order to understand the OT as a witness to Jesus's sufferings and resurrection, we must *start* with Jesus.

Enough has been said about reading the OT with the right interpretive lenses. Luke's point is well taken: read the OT christologically in order to

---

45. Black, *Luke*, 393.

46. Culpepper, *Luke*, 486.

47. What is more, it is not clear until they share a meal with the resurrected Lord. Scriptural understanding is not just about cognition but also relationship. David Garland is worth quoting at length: "The meal after Jesus' exposition of the Scriptures on the road reveals that the proclamation of the Word is necessary for understanding, but it alone does not bring understanding. Understanding comes in the meal fellowship of the community and in welcoming and feeding strangers. Meal fellowship alone is insufficient. It needs to be accompanied by instruction related to Jesus" (*Luke*, 168–69).

48. Hays, *Reading Backwards*, 14.

understand its true meaning as a witness to the gospel. However, we are not finished with Luke 24:44–47, and now come to the most salient point for the remainder of this study: if *all* of the Scriptures point to Christ, it stands to reason that this includes Psalms—not just some of them—all of them. In fact, the Greek text of verse 44 lacks the definite article for Psalms, and a more accurate translation is "Everything written about me in the Law of Moses and the Prophets and Psalms." There are a couple of reasons for stressing this particular translation. Some have taken Luke's description as evidence of the threefold-division of the Jewish Scriptures at the time as "the Law of Moses, the Prophets, and the Psalms." While this has historical precedent in the Dead Sea Scrolls,[49] the division was normally referred to as "the Law of Moses, the Prophets, and the Writings" (Psalms being the first book in the last division).[50] More importantly, the use of a single definite article before "Prophets," yielding "the Prophets and Psalms" is hardly incidental, and suggests that *Psalms—the whole book—is prophecy*.[51] This most likely reflects Luke's conviction that the Prophets included Psalms.[52] Psalms, then, *must* be read christologically because it is a book of prophecy.

Simply stated, the Prophets and Psalms should be taken together, reflecting a Jewish assumption in the Second Temple period that Psalms is among the prophetic corpus of Israel's Scriptures. In fact, the Dead Sea Scrolls demonstrate the belief that David, the archetypal psalmist, wrote thousands of psalms through the *spirit of prophecy*: "The total [psalms/songs] was four thousand and fifty. He [David] composed them all through the spirit of prophecy which had been given to him from before the Most High" (11Q5 27.10–11).[53] Similarly, Luke states in Acts that David was a "prophet," conveying the prophetic nature of Ps 16 as a prediction of Christ: "Brothers, I may say to you with confidence about the patriarch David that he both died and was buried, and his tomb is with us to this day. Being therefore a prophet, and knowing that God had sworn with an oath to him that he would set one of his descendants on his throne, he foresaw and spoke about the resurrection of Christ" (Acts 1:30–31). Green concludes, "For Peter and other apostles, David was as much a prophet as Isaiah, Jeremiah, and Ezekiel, and the psalms that bear his name were read as predictions of

---

49. "... to you we have written that you must understand the book of Moses and the words of the prophets and of David ..." (4QMMT 96). See Martínez, *Dead Sea Scrolls Translated*, 79.

50. Culpepper, *Luke*, 967. The prologue to Sirach has "The Law, the Prophets, and the others."

51. For the Granville Sharp Rule for definite articles in Gk., see Black, *Greek*, 80.

52. Green, "Christ's Shepherd," 37.

53. Martínez, *Dead Sea Scrolls Translated*, 309.

eschatological events, now fulfilled in the story of Jesus and his followers."[54] As noted previously, we need not limit this to royal and/or Davidic psalms because the entire the Psalter should be read in a prophetic and eschatological direction.[55]

In light of this discussion, Luke 24:44 groups Psalms with the Prophets as a grand corpus of prophecy that points to Jesus as Israel's Messiah. Luke intends to highlight the Psalms as a key prophetic text.[56] Therefore, it is in light of this prophetic trajectory that I interpret the various psalms in this book in an effort to read them christologically. To be clear, the psalms covered here are neither quoted directly in the NT nor among the standard messianic psalms. Even so, Psalms as a whole is filled with imagery and ideas that point to Christ. When read in the context of the Christian canon of Scripture, and from the post-resurrection perspective of the NT writers, all the psalms are messianic, evoking various aspects of the gospel of Jesus Christ.

---

54. Green, "Christ's Shepherd," 37.

55. Ibid. David Mitchell notes that the figures whose names head various psalms—David, Asaph, Heman, Jeduthun, and Moses—were regarded as prophets from biblical times; therefore, the editor of the Psalter would have regarded the psalms bearing their names as future-predictive ("Remember David," 529).

56. Culpepper, *Luke*, 967.

Psalm 1

"Christ most certainly came in the way of sinners by being born as sinners are, but he did not stand in it, for worldly allurement did not hold him."—Augustine

History

PSALM 1 IS THE ideal introduction to the Psalter because it models the life of discipleship that delights in following God's instruction, and calls the reader to do likewise. One cannot simply read this psalm and walk away without making a decision as to the direction of one's life. As James Mays remarks, "Let the readers understand and ask in what way their feet are set."[1] In many ways, the remainder of the Psalter illustrates the difference between the "righteous" and the "wicked" and the respective paths on which they walk. This idea of two paths is pervasive in Hebrew wisdom literature, especially the book of Proverbs (Prov 2:20–22; 3:12–17), and it is in this context that Ps 1 also teaches that one's life is a journey; one chooses a particular route for existence. While the word *wisdom* does not appear in the psalm, its main point is nonetheless clear: to show the reader the wisdom of walking in the ways of God and the folly of ungodly living.[2] Therefore, Ps 1 has been classified as a wisdom psalm.[3]

While Ps 1 is a fitting introduction to the Psalter, it should not be read in isolation from Ps 2. In fact, Ps 2 immediately carries forward the distinction between the righteous and the wicked into the context of God's anointed king and those who oppose him. Nancy deClaissé-Walford rightly points out that Pss 1—2 together form the introduction to the Psalter: "Psalm 1 urges the reader to meditate upon the Torah as the oath to right living, and Psalm 2 states that, regardless of the useless plotting of earthly rulers, the

---

1. Mays, *Psalms*, 44.
2. Tesh and Zorn, *Psalms*, 85–86.
3. DeClaissé-Walford, *Introduction*, 61.

God who sits in the heavens is sovereign over the created order."[4] Psalm 1 offers a sharp contrast between those who seek God and those who ignore him. On one hand, it describes one who delights in the instruction of the Lord, which results in an intimate relationship with him. On the other hand, it sets in contrast to this one who spurns God's instruction, opting instead for a life of autonomy resulting in wickedness.

"Blessed" (1:1) describes the individual who is content to walk with God rather than the wicked. It is possible to define "blessed" as *happy* because some Hebrew lexicons offer it as the first definition among others.[5] This psalm, therefore, portrays the individual who exists in a state of happiness as an outgrowth of one's covenant obedience.[6] "Happy" may even be parallel to the "delight" that the individual has when meditating on God's "law" (*torah*, v. 2). However, words get their connotations from the contexts in which they are used and from everyday use, not from dictionaries. A dictionary gives a range of possible meanings for a word based on common usage, and not a definitive definition in every case. While the word often translated "blessed" (*ashrey*) in most English translations of verse 1 can mean happy, in some cases (possibly even this one), it is important not to understand happiness here in the sense of a mere passing emotion. In the context of Ps 1, the close relationship between the righteous one (the "blessed" one in v. 1 is also "righteous" in vv. 5–6) and God brings blessedness, and is better understood in terms of "contentment."[7] That is, the blessed one is content in life because of the intimate relationship he has with God, and as a result avoids and abhors wickedness.

The one who is "blessed" is not anyone but a specific, although unknown, individual. More specifically, it is a certain "man" who is blessed. The original language of verse 1 reads: "Blessed is the man who . . . " Patrick Reardon explains that the words here are "emphatically masculine—that is, gender specific."[8] In other words, the psalm does not pronounce a blessing on obedient people in general (i.e., humanity), but on a specific "man." The Hebrew language has two different words for "man": *ish*, which is a male/husband, and *adam* as in "humanity," which includes males and females collectively.[9] The same occurs in the Greek language where *anēr* refers to a specific man/husband and *anthrōpos* to humanity in general. Both the He-

---

4. Ibid., 64.
5. Davidson, "*Ashrey*," Lexicon, 52.
6. Longman, *Psalms*, 56–57.
7. DeClaissé-Walford, *Introduction*, 61.
8. Reardon, *Christ*, 2.
9. The Heb. *enosh* is a synonym for *adam*, and most often refers to mortal humanity.

brew and Greek versions of the OT use *ish* and *anēr* respectively, indicating that 1:1 refers to a particular man who is blessed and obedient.[10] Given the canonical placement of Pss 1—2 as a lens through which to read the Psalter, it is not a stretch to identify the "blessed man" in Ps 1 with the anointed king of Ps 2 who devotes his life to God, the true sovereign of the cosmos. The combined effect of the two psalms is that he becomes a model of covenant obedience, a true subject of the King.

While English poetry is often—though not always— known for its rhyme, Hebrew poetry is most known for its parallelism.[11] Parallelism occurs when two or three (or more) lines (sg. "colon" pl. "cola") have some kind of relationship to each other. This sometimes comes across in English translations as what seems to be more or less simple repetition. For example in 1:1, one who "walks not in the counsel of the wicked" (colon A) is basically the same as one who "stands not in the way of sinners" (colon B) is basically the same as "nor sits in the seat of scoffers" (colon C). In other words, lines A, B, and C essentially make the same point, but with slightly different wording. But there is probably more to it than mere repetition. The relationship between the parallel lines has a sharpening effect where line B often carries forward the thought of line A, and intensifies or amplifies it. As James Kugel notes, line B "goes beyond" line A.[12] Instead of a simplistic A = B approach, Hebrew parallelism conveys "A is so, and what's more, B is so."[13] Such "echoing" has the effect of line B not simply repeating line A, but heightening it. Or, as Tremper Longman notes, "The B colon intensifies, specifies, or sharpens the thought of the first colon."[14]

With this in mind, 1:1 describes the one who is blessed as avoiding evil in all its facets. What is more, there are two intensifications at work in these three lines. First, the progression of walking—standing—sitting suggest

---

10. However, as Greidanus observes, this may press the syntax too far, and should not be used to exclude righteous people in general. The word can be used in gender-neutral contexts (e.g., Gen 13:16). The thought of the two psalms, when taken together, is that the "man" is any godly person who abides by torah and walks in covenant obedience (Ps 1), and anticipates the end-times reign of God through his Messiah (Ps 2). See Greidanus, *Preaching Christ*, 56–57. Even so, exegeting OT passages according to their minute syntactical details is not out of the realm of the NT use of the OT (e.g., Gal 3:16). For the "blessed man" of Ps 1 as the Davidic king of Ps 2, see Collett, "Christology," 394.

11. We do not actually know what biblical Heb. sounded like. The vocalization of the MT was codified over a millennium after the composition of most of the psalms, and centuries after Heb. had ceased to be the vernacular of the Jewish people (Alter, *Art of Biblical Poetry*, 4).

12. Kugel, *Idea of Biblical Poetry*, 8.

13. Ibid. As Kugel observes, "B always comes after A, not simultaneously" (p. 43).

14. Longman, *Psalms*, 44.

increasing increments of association: "To *walk* with someone is to be associated with them, but not as deeply as to stand with them or *sit* with them."[15] This motion-oriented progression may be meant to communicate the idea that sin is a temptation that one first tries out (i.e., walk), later becomes accustomed to (i.e., stand), and finally becomes a habit or lifestyle (i.e., sit).[16] Second, the terms for evil become more specific and more forceful through the progression (*wicked, sinners, scoffers*); i.e., a scoffer is a specific kind of wicked person.[17] Given our classification of Ps 1 as a wisdom psalm, it is no coincidence that scoffers are in a category of their own as those who lack wisdom (Prov 9:7–12; 13:1; 14:6). The overall effect of this *A is so, what's more B is so* parallelism in Ps 1:1 is to distance the blessed one from evil so that he avoids it at every stage and scenario.

Verse 2 makes clear how the blessed one avoids evil: he delights in the "law" (*torah*) of the LORD (1:2). The Hebrew word *torah* can mean law, as in the legal requirements of the Law of Moses (Exod 24:12; Deut 4:8), but "instruction" is the better translation, despite most English translations' preference for "law." Reducing torah to a set of laws does not take into account the instructional and spiritual nature of God's commandments and ordinances. For the biblical writers, God's commands are called torah because they instruct rather than simply legislate.[18] As far as the psalmist is concerned, they are neither a burden to be borne nor an obligation to be met because the blessed one "delights" (v. 2) in living by them.[19] S. Edward Tesh and Walter Zorn note that torah is a "gift from the Creator," providing instruction on how to best live life.[20] In its literary sense, torah is the five books of the Pentateuch (Genesis—Deuteronomy), as both the history of ancient Israel (i.e., the narrative material of the Pentateuch) and the laws that God gave them.[21] Therefore, the larger function of God's torah is to

---

15. Ibid., 56.
16. DeClaissé-Walford, et al., *Psalms*, 60–61.
17. Ibid.
18. Mays, *Psalms*, 41.
19. Tesh and Zorn, *Psalms*, 88.
20. Ibid.
21. DeClaissé-Walford, *Introduction*, 61. Mays notes the probable complement to the five books of the Pentateuch in the five books of the Psalter (*Psalms*, 42). Torah is often capitalized when referring to the five books of Moses as written Scripture. However, because the Heb. term *torah* means more than written revelation, the decision to capitalize is based on the context in which the word is used, and this is always interpretive. It is virtually impossible to be consistent in every instance. I personally prefer to leave the term lower case to preserve the ambiguity of the original Heb., unless it is clear from the context that the literary Torah is in view, which most scholars take to be the case in Ps 1.

"instruct," not simply command. As deClaissé-Walford summarizes, "The Torah is the ancient Israelites' memory of God's total involvement in their life."[22] Torah gives Israel its identify as the covenant people of Yahweh.

It seems best, then, in the original context of Ps 1:2 to understand "law" as referring to God's written instruction in the Pentateuch, but I will demonstrate later when commenting on Ps 119 that this by no means exhausts the application of the Hebrew term *torah*. Besides, it is one thing to interpret a psalm in the original context of its author as a stand-alone psalm; it is another to read it in the larger context of the final (i.e., later) editorial shape of Psalter. That the book of Psalms begins with a torah psalm suggests that it serves as a lens through which to read the entire Psalter as a book of God's instruction. The eventual placement of Ps 1 at the beginning of the Psalter invites readers to read the whole book of Psalms as instruction—instruction in prayer, in praise, in God's way with us and our way under God.[23] In other words, God's instruction is not limited to the Pentateuch; it also includes Psalms.

Nevertheless, for the psalmist and his original audience, verse 2 most likely refers to the practice of "torah piety" as the "diligent adherence to the instructions found in the stories, the laws, and the prophetic words of the Torah, the first five books of the Old Testament."[24] In Ps 1, torah piety is "Scripture piety"—torah in its written form as Scripture that one can read and absorb in order to gain wisdom for living.[25] The consuming passion of the blessed one is his devotion to God's written instruction, which preserves him from the ensnaring traps of sin. While the blessed one "meditates" (ESV) on God's instruction day and night, this does not mean silent contemplation as the word often conveys in contemporary usage. For the ancients, reading was not done in silence, but aloud.[26] Verse 2 illustrates one who demonstrates devotion to the daily reading of Scripture. Taken together, verses 1–2 describe the blessed one as he who finds delight not in sin, but in reading and reflecting on God's torah. As God exhorted Joshua, "This Book of the Law shall not depart from your mouth, but you shall

---

22. DeClaissé-Walford, *Introduction*, 61.
23. Mays, *Psalms*, 42.
24. DeClaissé-Walford, *Introduction*, 61.
25. Mays, *Psalms*, 41–42. Mays also notes that torah piety is a fitting introduction to the Psalter because Ps 1 implores the reader to read the whole Psalter as instruction in prayer, in praise, in God's way with us, and our way under God (p. 42).
26. DeClaissé-Walford, et al., *Psalms*, 61. Rolf Jacobson notes that the word translated "meditate" is also used in the OT for the cooing of a pigeon (Isa 38:14), the growling of a lion (Isa 31:4), and the voice of a human (Ps 35:28).

meditate on it day and night, so that you may be careful to do according to all that is written in it" (Josh 1:8).

Next, the poet expresses the state of the blessed one with the metaphor of a fruitful tree in verse 3. This image occurs elsewhere in the OT: "Blessed is the man who trusts in the LORD, whose trust is the LORD. He is like a tree planted by water, that sends out its roots by the stream, and does not fear when the heat comes, for its leaves remain green, and is not anxious in the year of drought, for it does not cease to bear fruit" (Jer 17:7–8). Given the semiarid climate of Palestine, this metaphor is especially vivid for the residents of that region. But this is not a case of a tree that happens to grow next to a water source, as if it sprang up in such a convenient location. Instead, the tree has been *planted* by streams of water, indicating intentionality and conscious decision.[27] Therefore, the association of streams of water in verse 3 and God's torah in verse 2 is obvious. "The stream is God's instruction."[28] As Gerald Wilson observes, "Those who delight in Yahweh's *torah* are 'planted'—as by a master gardener—in the place where they can receive the nourishment they need to flourish."[29] Because of his reliance on God's instruction, the blessed one is fruitful and prosperous. As the metaphor suggests, this is not a temporary consequence, but a settled conviction and condition. Much like the earlier idea where the path on which one walks through life is about habitual and professed living, the fruitful tree planted by water conveys consistency.[30]

Verse 4 literally reads, "Not so the wicked." By placing the negative "not so" (*lo ken*) at the beginning of the sentence, the psalmist not only contrasts the wicked with the blessed one, but also does so with the strongest possible emphasis. The wicked have no such foundation as God's torah. They arrogantly believe that they can sustain themselves, yet are like "chaff," the waste product that is blown away by the wind after the wheat has been harvested. John Calvin expressed the view that a withering tree, in contrast to a vibrant one, is not strong enough for the contrast here.[31] The contrast is not about life and death but about usefulness and uselessness. Longman also emphasizes the intended contrast: "Chaff is the opposite of a tree. While a tree has an abundance of life-giving water, chaff is dry. The tree is deep-rooted and productive; chaff has no connection to

27. Ibid., 64.
28. Ibid.
29. Wilson, *Psalms*, 97.
30. Calvin, *Psalms*, Apple e-book, ch. 1.
31. Ibid.

the earth, but rolls as the wind blows it, and is useless."[32] What is more, also implicit in the contrast are the *contentment* of the blessed and the *misery* of the wicked. The wicked are not blessed because they reject the instruction of the Lord and live in a constant state of discontentment and frustration, having to rely only on themselves.

The psalm concludes with two verses on the destiny of the wicked (vv. 5–6). Although the wicked will not "stand in the judgment," this is not likely a reference to the eternal destiny of the wicked, which is a doctrine that is developed more fully in the NT than in the OT. It may simply refer to the moment in this life when God brings consequences on wicked people for their actions.[33] In other words, they have no fellowship with the righteous, and the wicked will get what is coming to them—no matter the timeframe. It is impossible at times for humanity to discern between those who are truly blessed and those who look blessed based on worldly appearances. God will not confuse the two and each will receive their due.[34] Even so, there is more happening in verses 5–6 than divine recompense; there is a subtle emphasis on the *communities* of the righteous and the wicked. The "blessed man" (sg.) has been a "one among the masses"[35] so far in the psalm. The only group per se that has been mentioned has been the "wicked ones" (note the pls. *reshaim* ["wicked"], *khataim* ["sinners"], *letsim* ["scoffers"]). For the first time in the psalm, "righteous ones" (*tsadiqim*) appears as a positive community that counterbalances the community of the wicked.[36] Community is obviously implied in the mention of the "congregation" of the righteous (v. 5). The sequence of the psalm suggests that the blessed one avoids the company of evildoers, devotes himself to God's torah, and has finally found a community to which he belongs.[37]

Finally, in the last verse of the psalm, the LORD is mentioned as the subject. He "knows" the way of the righteous. The Hebrew concept of knowledge is not as much intellectual as it is relational. "To know" (*yada*) suggests "intimate and internal care,"[38] as God and the righteous enjoy

---

32. Longman, *Psalms*, 58. There is also a contrast of poetic length devoted to the tree and the chaff: the tree occupies four cola, but the chaff only one (DeClaissé-Walford, et al., *Psalms*, 62).

33. Longman, *Psalms*, 58. Longman notes, however, that given the postexilic setting of many of the psalms, it is not inconceivable that a more sophisticated understanding of the afterlife had developed by the time of their composition.

34. Ibid.

35. DeClaissé-Walford, et al., *Psalms*, 60.

36. Ibid., 62–63.

37. Ibid., 63.

38. Ibid.

mutual relationship. Therefore, the "way of the righteous" is the object of the verb "to know" so that God closely watches over the righteous. Yet in the second colon, the way of the wicked is the subject, placing them in charge of their own destiny. The grammar shows that the wicked "autonomously" walk through life—and ultimately to their judgment—as if they are their own lords, while God guides the steps of the righteous.[39] In the context of the two paths of the Hebrew wisdom tradition, verse 6 describes the destination of each path: the psalm begins with "blessed" and ends with "perish," and these depend on which path one walks. C. Hassell Bullock concludes, "The two ways contrasted in this poem lead in two opposite directions, the one to blessedness and delight, and the other to disrepute and disappearance."[40]

Christology

John Calvin noted the importance for a disciple of Christ to have a "teachable spirit,"[41] and in a very real sense a *teachable spirit* is what Ps 1 means by being "blessed" and "righteous"—eager for God's instruction and devoted to knowing him in covenant relationship.[42] Psalm 1 describes the life of a model disciple who abhors wickedness and nurtures his spiritual health by feasting daily on God's word. While there are many fine examples of godly men and women throughout the Bible who demonstrate many facets of discipleship, none does so perfectly. However, when one reads Ps 1 through a christological lens, Jesus is "the man" (*ha ish*), and only in him does this psalm find its ultimate expression.[43] He is the man who is devoted to and delights in God's torah with a teachable spirit. Only Christ exhibits preeminent discipleship as he learns how to best live life by meditating on God's torah and calling others to follow his example. Put differently, Jesus, the model disciple, calls all people to be his disciples, to pattern his routine.

Psalm 1 evokes the discipline of Jesus's daily life as he commits himself to God's word and calls others to emulate him. The NT reminds us that from childhood Jesus demonstrated devotion to God's instruction, and

---

39. Ibid.
40. Bullock, *Encountering*, 219.
41. Calvin, *Psalms*, Preface.
42. McCann, *Theological*, 40.
43. Luther, *Psalms*, 22; Reardon, *Christ*, 2. Church Fathers like Eusebius (*Commentary on the Psalms* 1) and Augustine (*Expositions* 1) read Ps 1 christologically so that Jesus was "the blessed man" of 1:1 (Blaising and Hardin, *Psalms*, 3).

this continued throughout his life. We are reminded of his great learning at the temple at the age of twelve (Luke 2:42–52); his appeal to Scripture and trusting relationship with the Father, which preserve him during his temptation in the wilderness (4:1–12); his custom of attending synagogue (4:16), and his acceptance of his God-given mission in terms of scriptural prophecy (4:16–21). Luke reminds us that Jesus habitually practiced the spiritual disciplines of silence and solitude (4:1, 40–42; 5:15; 6:12). Simply put, this psalm calls to mind the basic spiritual habits of Christ from which he drew strength for his day-to-day ministry, not least his avoidance of sin and devotion to Scripture in the temptation narrative.

The psalmist can only imagine one who completely avoids the snares of sin, but the NT reveals that Jesus does precisely this, living a sinless life (2 Cor 5:21; Heb 4:15). Some may object by pointing out that Jesus's ministry was directed toward sinners; and it is not entirely true to suggest that he avoided evil; after all, he certainly did not avoid its appearance (Luke 5:29–31). Jesus most often fellowshipped with sinners, eating with them, healing them, and teaching them; yet he did so not to promote their rebellion, but their repentance. Psalm 1 is concerned with *participating* in wickedness, not ministering to broken sinners. The unwavering testimony of the NT centers on Jesus's perfect righteousness, that he "committed no sin" (2 Cor 5:21), and his atoning death on the cross is likened to the sacrifice of a lamb "without blemish or spot" (1 Pet 1:19). It is in this sense that only Jesus is truly righteous and that Ps 1 ultimately points to him.[44] In fact, "righteousness" and Jesus Christ are so closely connected in the NT that there is no daylight between them: "Jesus Christ, righteous" (my trans. 1 John 2:1).

Finally, his righteousness is not an end in itself; it is also for us, the messianic community—the church. We participate in his righteousness so that we are none other than the "assembly of the righteous" (Ps 1:6). As mentioned previously, the "blessed/righteous" one in the psalm is an individual contrasted against a community of the wicked, but in verses 5–6 he is part of an assembly—those who share righteousness and relationship with God. This community of the righteous evokes the NT covenant community. To be sure, the church is made of sinners, but these are also the beneficiaries of his faithfulness to the covenant, and by virtue of their identity in him, are indeed "the righteousness of God" (2 Cor 5:21).[45] The psalmist does not have in mind the fullness of the church as the new covenant community in Christ, but his language evokes it when read through

---

44. Longman, *Psalms*, 59.
45. On "righteousness of God" in 2 Cor 5:21, see Wright, "Righteousness," 200–08.

the lens of Christ's work, which includes the establishment of the church, the new covenant community. A christological reading of Ps 1 emphasizes Jesus as the blessed/righteous "man" who avoids the snares of temptation by his devotion to God's torah and whose covenant faithfulness sustains the messianic community.

Psalm 23

"As this is a lowly and homely manner of speaking, He who does not disdain to stoop so low for our sake, must bear a singularly strong affection towards us."—John Calvin

History

PSALM 23 IS PERHAPS the most beloved, well-known psalm. It is the classic description of God's protection and provision. Psalm 23 reminds the believer of God's daily care in personal, covenantal terms. The caring nature of God is an ever-present reality, especially in times of travail. I will begin by making some general observations about the psalm, and then proceed to work though the thesis that exodus imagery saturates the psalm, taking it well beyond simple metaphorical relationships between shepherd and sheep (vv. 1–4) and host and traveler (vv. 5–6), to a declaration of God's covenant loyalty to Israel.

It is ironic that the shepherd metaphor is timeless, resonating with folks throughout the world, transcending cultures, eras (from the agricultural ANE to the technological twenty-first-century West), and providing comfort to myriad of worshipers. On one hand, the metaphor is powerful because it stirs our emotions in a way that literal words cannot.[1] It is one thing to talk about God's protection and provision; it is another to attach imagery to it so we can more easily visualize it. According to Tremper Longman: "We know how a shepherd lives with his sheep, tends to their every need, keeps them from getting lost and protects them from wild beasts. All of these characteristics and more come to mind when God is called a shepherd. It would take a page of prose to communicate what the psalmist has stated in a clause, and it would do so with less impact."[2] On the other hand, much of the ancient imagery throughout Psalms is quite foreign to most modern Westerners' experiences. Using myself as an example, I am severely limited in my experience

---

1. Longman, *How to Read Psalms*, 116.
2. Ibid., 117.

with sheep, which consists almost entirely of minimal interaction at the local petting zoo. I have observed them in pasture with a shepherd only once in my life. I was riding on a tour bus in Israel on what seemed to be the most treacherous road imaginable, winding its way alongside a mountain with only a few inches separating the road from the cliff. Out the left side of the bus I saw far down into the ravine where a shepherd walked ahead of his sheep as they followed his every step. The sight, while etched in my memory, lasted only seconds until we rounded another curve, making our way through the mountains on our way to the next holy site on the tour.

To be sure, I have read many pages in books that describe the relationship between shepherd and sheep—many of them commentaries on Ps 23—but had never experienced it myself until this moment. Descriptive words on a page do not suffice for a tangible, hands-on experience. The intimate relationship between shepherd and sheep is the dominant imagery of Ps 23 (vv. 1–4), and yet most of us (esp. those of us who live in urban settings) have never actually seen the interaction, much less experienced it firsthand. Even so, the imagery sticks in our minds because it is just that—imagery, not explanatory phrases. Imagery is easier to grasp because it elicits emotion more so than cognition. In other words, we do not have to have firsthand knowledge of shepherds and sheep in order to visualize God providing necessities like food, water, rest, and safety. These are the main themes of the psalm, but putting them to paper in the form of metaphor enables them to speak louder than mere words on a page.

Psalm 23 is often characterized as a psalm of trust.[3] While the shepherding metaphor is predominant in the psalm, it is not the only one used to convey God's care and comfort of the poet. In reality, it is a dual metaphor of shepherd and king, which also adds it to the category of a royal psalm, especially as it relates to David the psalmist.[4] The portrayal of kings as shepherds was not unique to ancient Israel. The ANE frequently used this combined metaphor to express various forms of leadership, creating a sense of ambiguity where the leader ruled as sovereign over a people, but also implied pastoring them in terms of their protection and provision.[5] For example, the Babylonian Code of Hammurabi states, "I have sought for them peaceful places . . . I made the people of all the settlements lie in safe pastures."[6] Similarly, the Babylonian god Marduk is described as one "who provides grazing and drinking places."[7]

3. Longman, *Psalms*, 133.
4. Ibid., 134–35.
5. Mays, *Preaching*, 119.
6. De-Claissé-Walford, et al., *Psalms*, 241.
7. Ibid.

This ambiguity of the dual metaphor extends even to the tools of the trades: a "rod" and a "staff" call to mind the tools of a shepherd,[8] while at the same time are the symbolic equipment of a king, especially since the word for "rod" (*shevet*) is most often translated "scepter" (cf. Gen 49:10; Judg 5:14; Ps 45:7; Isa 14:5).[9] Commentators have not always appreciated this ambiguity opting for one over the other; but the two are not mutually exclusive. As James Mays notes, "To the author of Ps 23, 'shepherd' was royal as well as pastoral. The author was writing of the providing and guiding and protecting by a ruler as well as by a shepherd."[10] As previously noted, this combined image of shepherd-king occurs in ANE literature, but is also by no means limited to Ps 23 in Hebrew Scripture. In Ezek 34, the shepherds of Israel are the kings who are to pastor the people, providing care, comfort, and protection.[11] Yet in Ps 23, *God* assumes the role of Israel's sovereign pastor for the psalmist expresses his trust in Yahweh (v. 1): the Shepherd-King of Israel protects and provides for Israel's earthly king (i.e., David), as a shepherd for his sheep, sheltering David in God's "house," the Jerusalem temple—the earthly palace of Yahweh.[12] Thus, the psalmist eats at the table not in the house of a common host, but of the LORD, the Shepherd-King.

Commentators offer many different theories regarding the structure of this psalm. One would expect no shortage of ink when it comes to analyzing arguably the most famous chapter in the Bible. Nevertheless, most of the proposals derive from a very basic structure where verses 1–4 describe the shepherd metaphor and verses 5–6 the host of a banquet:

> Stanza 1   The Lord as Shepherd (vv. 1–4)
> Stanza 2   The Lord as Host (vv. 5–6)[13]

---

8. Longman notes the rod and the staff are implements that the shepherd uses to fend off predators and to goad the sheep in the right direction and toward provision (*Psalms*, 136).

9. Mays, *Preaching*, 119; McCann, *Theological*, 130; McCann, *Psalms*, 768.

10. Mays, *Preaching*, 119.

11. McCann, *Theological*, 129.

12. Longman, *Psalms*, 137. I have written elsewhere on microstructuring within the Psalter where smaller groups of psalms with common themes are placed consecutively for various purposes. Psalms 26—30 are commonly referred to as the "sanctuary psalms" because each psalm mentions the sanctuary or temple. Some have expanded the group to include Pss 23—30 for the same reasons, Ps 25 being the exception. Thus, Ps 23 fits the larger group as a "sanctuary psalm," but to a lesser degree than Pss 26—30 (Fletcher, "Sanctuary," 97–119).

13. DeClaissé-Walford, et al., *Psalms*, 239.

The shift from shepherd to host need not be seen as radically different, but a shift nonetheless. The host is not a shepherd inviting sheep into his home to sit around his table. The host metaphor (I take it as a kingly-host, given the shepherd-king metaphor) in verses 5–6 accomplishes the same purposes as the shepherd in verses 1–4: the gracious host does for the guest exactly what the shepherd does for the sheep—provides food, drink, and shelter/protection.[14] The psalmist introduces the primary themes of provision and protection in the first two verses, and these provide the lens for reading the remainder of the psalm. The first verse equates God with a shepherd, only taking two words in Hebrew (*YHWH roi,* "Yahweh my-shepherd") to express what English does in five ("The LORD is my shepherd").[15] This is equivalent to stating in mathematical terms, "YHWH = my shepherd." Not only is the equation stark, it says something about the whole psalm, where the rest of it unpacks the initial metaphor in terms of shepherding (vv. 1–4), finally changing to the royal metaphor in verses 5–6, which continues to expound on the provision and protection themes initially associated with the shepherd metaphor.

Verse 2 begins the unpacking of the metaphor in terms of not lacking anything. Because the Lord is my shepherd, he is all I need. The verb "lack" is supposed to take a direct object, yielding the sense of "I shall not lack _____," be it food, water, shelter, etc. However, the poet does not give the object of the verb; the rest of the psalm fills in the missing object of verse 2.[16] Mays summarizes the main thought of the psalm: "When the Lord is your shepherd, you do not lack the nurturing and guiding and protecting of your soul. 'The Lord is with you; he restores your soul.' The psalm is about the soul-restoring presence of the Lord."[17] What we have in Ps 23 is a poetic description of the Creator who provides all the necessities of life for his creation. Far from a "health and wealth" gospel that teaches that God provides for our greeds rather than our needs, this psalm critiques our modern materialistic notions of abundant living and declares that God provides our daily bread. From day to day, he meets our needs—the most important being himself! J. Clinton McCann notes, "For the psalmist, God is the only necessity of life, because God provides the other necessities—food, drink, shelter/protection."[18] And while the psalm's imagery, at times, conveys tranquil scenes of shepherding and table fellowship, tranquility gives way

14. McCann, *Theological*, 131.
15. Mays, *Preaching*, 118.
16. Ibid., 119.
17. Ibid.
18. McCann, *Theological*, 128.

to sheer survival as the psalm unfolds, revealing a shepherd who protects his flock in the midst of the darkest valley, and a host who hosts the traveler before the face of his enemies. Again, the imagery is usually understood in terms of tranquility, but it is intended rather to say that God keeps the psalmist alive. In fact, "restores my soul" (v. 3a) likely conveys the rescue of the sheep[19] and can be paraphrased "keeps me alive."[20]

It is at the point where the reader might expect me to give insights on the shepherding profession in antiquity, waxing eloquently on the pastoral background of the first four verses of the psalm. But given my lack of personal experience with sheep, observations along those lines would be woefully inadequate. I will spare the reader from the agony of reading an unenlightened description of shepherding from an urbanized Westerner. I will leave it to the reader to consult the commentaries for the pastoral background. I feel no burden to add to what others have already shared on the ins and outs of shepherding sheep from Ps 23. Instead, I want to discuss the underlying exodus motif that serves as the primary redemptive-historical reference for Ps 23. A closer look at the psalm reveals a strategic emphasis on God's redemptive acts on behalf of Israel throughout her history. The shepherd-sheep metaphor is just that: a metaphor for a larger, more complex Israelite tradition dealing with God as the redeemer of his people. Psalm 23 praises God for delivering the nation of Israel from Egyptian bondage as a shepherd delivers his sheep from danger. I am proposing here that the writer composed the psalm out of this tradition and has woven into the psalm allusions to the memories of the exodus recorded in other places in the OT.[21]

---

19. Brueggemann and Bellinger, *Psalms*, 123. Brueggemann and Bellinger observe, "We may picture a sheep living without water or grass, exposed to wild animals, and therefore at risk. This protective, attentive shepherd changes all of that and the sheep is given a life of well-being" (ibid.). Some commentators see the term for "restore" (*shuv*) as the language of repentance. Thus, the verse conveys returning to God in repentance for the purpose of being restored (DeClaissé-Walford, et al., *Psalms*, 241–42). While the term at times conveys repentance (Hos 14:1; Joel 2:12), Ps 23 is not a "penitential psalm," and to spiritualize the text in such a way goes beyond its original shepherding imagery. Nevertheless, the two views need not contradict each other, and, as Derek Kidner notes, may even converge, so that the rescue of a sheep pictures the deeper renewal of the person of God in his or her spiritual helplessness (*Psalms 1–72*, 110).

20. McCann, *Theological*, 128.

21. Mays, *Preaching*, 120. I use "traditions" and "memories" to refer loosely to both oral and written materials, but am conscious of not arguing for a genetic connection between specific biblical texts per se. We simply cannot be precise about the dating of Ps 23, or the other passages in their final form that I reference in this context. I think it best to assume an interpretive milieu from which the psalmist and other OT authors drew when reflecting on Israel's redemption at the exodus, and these have been woven throughout the biblical witness. I have adapted my list of passages from Mays, *Psalms*, 118.

The Lord is the shepherd of his people is a common OT metaphor (e.g., Gen 49:24; Pss 77:20; 78:52; 79:13; 80:1; 95:7; 100:3; Isa 40:11; Ezek 34), but this image does not arise in a vacuum; it has its roots in the exodus event. For example, Pss 77 and 78 are retellings of the exodus story where psalmists reflect on the redemptive history of Israel at a later time. They are recollections of history in that they retell—and in so doing, reinterpret—this pinnacle redemptive event of the OT. As both psalms recall the exodus event, they echo the shepherd metaphor of 23:1–4. After a poetically stylized recollection of the mighty act of God at the crossing of the Red Sea, Ps 77:20 concludes, "You led your people like a flock by the hand of Moses and Aaron." Similarly, Ps 78 recalls the exodus-wilderness event as the grand testimony to God's covenant faithfulness to Israel—despite its repeated rebellion—and uses the shepherd metaphor to describe God's power and persistence to deliver his people from Egyptian bondage: "Then he led out his people like sheep and guided them in the wilderness like a flock" (v. 52). These two passages are important not simply because they affirm the shepherd metaphor, but because they do so in the context of the exodus.

Psalm 23 affirms the daily provisions of the Shepherd-God so that the sheep has no want of anything in addition to God himself ("I shall not want," v. 1). Here is also an echo of the exodus as Moses reminds the people of God's faithfulness to them, recalling his provisions in the midst of the treacherous wilderness journey. Moses calls to their remembrance that God knows the plight of his people and provides for the necessities of life: "He knows your going through this great wilderness. These forty years the LORD your God has been with you. You have lacked nothing" (Deut 2:7). Again, this passage is in the context of reflecting on the exodus-wilderness event; it is not a proverbial statement about God's provisions, but is contextualized in this pinnacle redemptive event in the OT. As the psalmist has no wants beyond the day-to-day sustenance of God, so also Israel "lacked nothing" in the wilderness.

As the shepherd "leads" (*nakhal*) the sheep (Ps 23:2), so also God "led" (*nakhah*) the Israelites out of Egypt and "guided" (*nakhal*) them into the Promised Land (Exod 15:13). While the Hebrew verb for "to lead" occurs three times in these two verses, the exodus context of the latter passage is even more important as the Song of Moses, which he sang immediately after crossing the Red Sea. Again, the exodus event serves as the backdrop for both passages, placing them in identical redemptive-historical contexts.

The traditional translation, "He leads me beside still waters," evokes images of a peaceful water source from which sheep, weighed down with thick wool, can drink without fear of being swept into the currents and drowned. An alternate, and equally accurate, translation is, "He leads me to water in places of repose" (JPS). It is grammatically unclear if *menukhot* ("resting places," "rest") modifies *mayim* ("waters"), thus yielding something like "still waters," or refers to places of rest, which are conveniently near a water source, be it a stream, pond, well, river, etc. Thus, the emphasis is not so much on the stillness of the water source as the rest that comes with being led to water. The idea of being guided to a water source where God provides for the thirst of his people evokes the water from the rock narratives of the wilderness journey (Exod 17 and Num 20). Granted, the point is not the water itself (i.e., the kind of water whether flowing or not), but that God quenches the thirst of his people by providing water in abundance. As Num 20:11 states, "And water came out abundantly, and the congregation drank, and their livestock." Again, Ps 78 recalls this miraculous provision of water in the wilderness with its retelling of the exodus story: "He split rocks in the wilderness and gave them drink abundantly as from the deep. He made streams come out of the rock and caused waters to flow down like rivers" (vv. 15–16). Not that every mention of "water" in the OT evokes images of the exodus-wilderness, but when one reads 23:2 in light of the redemptive-historical backdrop proposed here, it is not difficult to hear echoes of this wilderness tradition.[22]

Psalm 23:4 affirms a lack of fear in the midst of trials. As the psalmist walks through the "valley of the shadow of death," or better, the "darkest valley,"[23] the Shepherd guards and guides him. In fact, in the midst of this crisis—the low point of the psalm—the psalmist refrains from speaking of God in the third person, opting instead for a more direct and personal second person ("you") address: "You are with me."[24] As Rolf Jacobson describes, "It is in moments of crisis that the Lord moves from an abstract concept (a *he* about whom one has memorized doctrinal statements) to a living God with whom one has a relationship (a *you* in whom one trusts, to whom one speaks, on whom one can rely)."[25] Therefore, absence of fear in this context is not based in the power or prowess of the psalmist—whether David the warrior-king or

---

22. *Menukhot* is a feminine pl. noun and *mayim* ("waters") is a masculine pl. noun. This may point away from the traditional translation "still waters" (where "still" functions as an adjective modifying "waters") to "resting places," which happen to be near a water source. Not to put too fine a point on the grammar, but I am conscious of a possible objection to seeing a connection between *still* waters and the *flowing* water from the rock.

23. "Valley of the shadow of death" is the traditional translation, and is often preached in funerals as a note of confidence as the deceased passes from life in this world to eternal life in God's presence. Of course, this idea is profoundly true, but the main idea of the psalm is that God protects the psalmist from all kinds of dangers associated with "darkest valley"; death, per se is not mentioned, but is implicit as but one of the dangers of the valley (Longman, *Psalms*, 135–36).

24. DeClaissé-Walford, et al., *Psalms*, 243.

25. Ibid.

someone else—but in the protective presence of God ("For *you* are with me"). Similarly, Moses, upon entering the Promised Land, repeatedly exhorts the Israelites against fearing the occupants of the land. Their lack of fear comes not from their own might, but from the protective presence of God: "When you go out to war against your enemies, and see horses and chariots and an army larger than your own, you shall not be afraid of them, for the LORD your God is with you, who brought you up out of the land of Egypt" (Deut 20:1). Echoing the same sentiment at the commissioning of Joshua, Moses exhorts his young servant: "It is the LORD who goes before you. He will be with you; he will not leave you or forsake you. Do not fear or be dismayed" (31:8). Once again, as Ps 78 recalls the exodus narrative, the psalmist connects God's presence with a lack of fear: "He led them in safety, so that they were not afraid" (v. 53). While the Bible is full of general admonitions against fear in varying contexts, 23:4 echoes the exodus tradition by grounding the psalmist's confidence in the relational presence of God.

As noted earlier, in addition to the shepherd metaphor, the twenty-third psalm also uses that of a gracious host (23:5–6), which continues the themes of protection and provision. God provides hospitality by preparing a table before the psalmist (v. 5). This also has exodus connotations. Once again, 78:19 recalls the miraculous provisions of God in the wilderness and asks a rhetorical question: "Can God spread a table in the wilderness?" The obvious answer is "yes" when one considers the manna and quail (and water) with which God fed the Israelites during their desert travels.

In the face of an onslaught from his enemies, the psalmist affirms that the Lord's "goodness" and "mercy" pursue him (23:6). To be sure, it is not his enemies that pursue him—as is often the case in Psalms (e.g., 7:5; 69:26; 71:11; 109:16)—but these attributes of God.[26] The Hebrew verb *radaf* has a more active sense as "to pursue" than the traditional English translation "to follow."[27] The traditional translation may give the misleading impression that as the psalmist journeys through life, he charts his own path and is the master of his own destiny, and God's attributes simply *follow* as convenient helps on the way. However, the original language is much stronger so that the divine attributes of goodness and mercy are pictured as incarnate forces, which will not rest until they have tracked down and provided a safe harbor for the endangered psalmist.[28] Indeed, goodness and mercy *pursue* the psalmist throughout his life. What is more, the personified attributes

---

26. McCann, *Theological*, 131.

27. Ibid. Hence, the NET translation, "Surely your goodness and faithfulness will pursue me all my days."

28. DeClaissé-Walford, et al., *Psalms*, 244.

of goodness (*tov*) and mercy (*khesed*) are covenant attributes that speak of God's faithfulness to his people, and notably these are often mentioned in exodus contexts.[29] For example, in response to Moses's request to see God, he tells Moses that he would allow his "goodness" to pass before him (Exod 33:19). Additionally, *khesed* lies at the heart of God's character as the word appears twice in his self-revelation to Moses (34:6–7). Similarly, Deut 7:9 praises God as one who "keeps covenant and steadfast love (*khesed*)." Thus, the main theme in Ps 23:5–6 is *khesed*, which is the very character of God as declared to Moses at the exodus.

The final exodus reference that I will mention occurs in the final colon of the psalm: "I shall dwell in the house of the LORD forever" (v. 6).[30] This reference to the house of God may not appear at first to refer to the formative period of Israel's history at the exodus, but rather to the monarchy period over 400 years later when the temple was constructed by Solomon (2 Sam 7:13; 1 Kgs 6—8). Yet Moses predicts this future dwelling of God among his people: "You will bring them in and plant them on your own mountain, the place, O LORD, which you have made for your abode, the sanctuary, O Lord, which your hands have established" (Exod 15:17). The specific language of "house of the LORD" is an obvious reference to the Jerusalem temple, and adds to the psalm's emphasis on God as the King.[31] Therefore, the references to hospitality in verses 5–6 are not simply referring to hospitality in general; they signify a royal banquet in the house of the divine King of Israel. The temple is where God makes his presence known to the people; thus, the psalmist proclaims that he will live in the light of God's presence for the duration of his life.[32] Once again the psalm uses a metaphor; the temple represents God's presence. In other words, no one actually lives in the temple, but its very presence indicates God's dwelling among his people. McCann notes that "the final line of the psalm is another way of affirming that 'you are with me' (v. 4), as the immediately preceding line

---

29. The Heb. word *khesed* is exceedingly difficult to translate into Eng. with only one word. Translators often translate it "steadfast love," "covenant loyalty," "covenant faithfulness," "covenant mercy," "lovingkindness," "covenant of love," "faithful love," etc. Therefore, many reference works simply transliterate it as *khesed* and do not translate it. The pairing of "goodness and mercy" is by no means limited to exodus contexts (Pss 100:5; 106:1; 107:1; 118:1; 136:1).

30. A literal translation for "forever" is "length of days," which signifies the duration of the psalmist's life. The OT lacks a developed doctrine of the afterlife, which gains momentum in the intertestamental period, and becomes even more fully developed in the NT (Longman, *Psalms*, 137).

31. Brueggemann and Bellinger, *Psalms*, 124.

32. Longman, *Psalms*, 137.

has also proclaimed (v. 6a)."[33] Jacobson summarizes the psalm's ultimate destination as the presence of God:

> The point of the metaphor is that the destination that one reaches after being led along *the paths of righteousness*, the destination one reaches at the end of *the days of my life*, the destination toward which one is shepherded and indeed toward which one is harried by God's pursuing *goodness* and *hesed* is none other than God's very self. God is the psalmist's destination.[34]

In light of this discussion, which is by no means exhaustive, we can summarize the psalm's allusions to the exodus event in the following table:

Psalm 23	Exodus Traditions
"The LORD is my shepherd"	"You led your people like a flock" (Ps 77:20)
	"Then he led out his people like sheep and guided them in the wilderness like a flock" (Ps 78:52)
"I shall not want"	"You have lacked nothing" (Deut 2:7)
"He leads me beside still waters"	"You have led in your steadfast love the people whom you have redeemed; you have guided them by your strength to your holy abode" (Exod 15:13)
	"And water came out abundantly, and the congregation drank, and their livestock" (Num 20:11)
	"He split rocks in the wilderness and gave them drink abundantly as from the deep. He made streams come out of the rock and caused waters to flow down like rivers" (Ps 78:15–16).
"I will fear no evil, for you are with me"	"You shall not be afraid of them, for the LORD your God is with you" (Deut 20:1; 31:8)
	"He led them in safety, so that they were not afraid" (Ps 78:53)
"You prepare a table before me"	"Can God spread a table in the wilderness?" (Ps 78:19)
"Goodness and mercy shall pursue me"	"I will make all my goodness pass before you" (Exod 33:19)
	"Abounding in steadfast love" (twice in Exod 34:6–7)
	"Who keeps covenant and steadfast love" (Deut 7:9)
"I shall dwell in the house of the LORD"	"You will bring them in and plant them on your own mountain, the place, O LORD, which you have made for your abode, the sanctuary, O Lord, which your hands have established" (Exod 15:17)

Table 1 Psalm 23 and the Exodus

33. McCann, *Theological*, 132.
34. DeClaissé-Walford, et al., *Psalms*, 245.

Space does not allow for a more thorough interaction with each of the exodus traditions above, but hopefully enough has been said to illustrate the most salient points of contact between them and Ps 23, and to offer another lens through which to read this beloved psalm in addition to the traditional shepherding background.

Christology

It may come as a surprise to many readers to learn that Ps 23 has not traditionally been considered a "messianic" psalm, nor does the NT quote from it. Even so, it probably alludes to it, and the psalm evokes some of the most basic recollections of the person and work of Jesus Christ. The quote by John Calvin at the beginning of this chapter identifies the principle objective of shepherd metaphor: the humble descent of God into the affairs of humanity. Put differently, the metaphor illustrates the self-humiliation of God as he enters into the world on behalf of humanity to identify with and care for it on the most personal level. Given that God evidences his affection for humanity by "stooping low" (à la Calvin) to care for its basic needs, the shepherd metaphor in Ps 23 anticipates the incarnation of Christ in the NT. It is difficult to do better than C. Hassell Bullock:

> The theology of this psalm arises out of the practice of life, the practice of the lowliest of occupations, shepherding sheep. In the broad outline of biblical theology, it is not an exaggeration to say that this imagery is a hint of the incarnation of God in human flesh, in Jesus of Nazareth. That God would condescend to the level of a shepherd is remarkably assuring, affirming his love for humanity.[35]

Granted, there are other images of God in the OT that convey various aspects of his relationship to his people (e.g., king, creator, father, fortress, rock, etc.), but none captures the meekness of God like the shepherd image. The incarnational theme of God as shepherd comes into even sharper focus in Jesus Christ as the good shepherd (John 10:1–30). Shepherding is such a prominent motif in Scripture that it is difficult to be precise as to which OT passage John has in mind. The two most likely candidates are Ezek 34 and Ps 23, and these are not mutually exclusive because they both speak of God as the shepherd-king of his people. In the former passage, God condemns Israel's kings for failing to pastor the nation (Ezek 34:1–10). They have fleeced the flock, and have failed to protect it from being scattered and devoured. In

---

35. Bullock, *Encountering*, 171–72.

short, they have not reflected the shepherd heart of God. As a result, Ezekiel prophecies a time when God *himself* will tend his flock, bind its wounds, and care for it in a way reminiscent of the divine shepherd of Ps 23 (Ezek 34:11–31). In John, Jesus, like Ezekiel, pronounces judgment on the Jewish leaders for duplicating the failed shepherding of Ezek 34.

While Ezek 34 is likely the most immediate scriptural background to Jesus's discourse, there are also obvious echoes of Ps 23, the paradigmatic passage describing God as the shepherd of his people. John echoes the relationship between the divine shepherd and his sheep in Ps 23 when Jesus declares that his sheep know his voice and follow him rather than a stranger (John 10:3–5). In short, they "know" him. He, too, knows them and calls them by name (10:3). He is also the entry point through which they must pass to find pasture (10:9). John summarizes this closeness of relationship between the shepherd and his sheep when Jesus affirms: "I am the good shepherd. I know my own and my own know me" (10:15). Finally, the good shepherd lays down his life for his sheep (10:11, 15, 17), undoubtedly a reference to his vicarious sacrifice in John's Gospel.[36] The life of the psalmist that is nourished by green pastures, refreshed by waters, and protected from life-threatening dangers reaches its full end-times invigoration when the good shepherd provides "eternal life" to his sheep (10:28).[37] He renders powerless the ever-present dangers of the darkest valley in Ps 23 so that his sheep "will never perish" (John 10:28).

It is beyond the scope of this chapter to discuss all the comparisons of the "Good Shepherd discourse" in John 10:1–30 with the divine shepherd of Ps 23. The associations are so numerous that it is not a stretch to refer to the twenty-third psalm as the "Good Shepherd Psalm."[38] In fact, Beauford Bryant and Mark Krause note, "The early church remembered Jesus as its shepherd (Matt 9:36; 26:31; 1 Pet 2:25) and applied OT passages to him that pictured God as shepherd (particularly Psalm 23)."[39] Similarly, given that the Good Shepherd discourse culminates by proclaiming the unity between the Father and Son ("I am the Father are one," John 10:30), Christians should be quite comfortable paraphrasing Ps 23:1 like Augustine of Hippo: "Since my shepherd is the Lord Jesus Christ, I shall not lack anything."[40] Jacobson,

---

36. O'Day and Hylen, *John*, 106.

37. "Eternal life" in John does not wait until the last days; it is available now through Jesus (ibid.).

38. Reardon, *Christ*, 43.

39. Bryant and Krause, *John*, 233. Reardon also notes that Jesus as the good shepherd appears in the catacombs of Rome, a second-century work called *The Shepherd of Hermas*, and in Polycarp's *The Martyrdom of Polycarp* 19:2 (*Christ*, 43).

40. Augustine, *Expositions* 23, in Blaising and Hardin, eds., *Psalms*, 178.

too, aptly summarizes the incarnate shepherd: "When the New Testament names the one who lays down his life for the sheep as the Good Shepherd, the New Testament is faithfully confessing the incarnation in Jesus of the same divine shepherd whom the ancient psalmist trusted."[41]

As Ps 23 evokes the NT image of Jesus as the good shepherd, it also evokes the image of Christ as the host of a banquet, the so-called "messianic banquet."[42] Given the emphasis on table fellowship in the early church, especially the Lord's Supper, it is not difficult to hear echoes of this sacrament in the words of the psalm when interpreted christologically: "You prepare a table before me" (Ps 23:5). As in Ps 23, where the images of shepherd and host relate to each other as metaphors of God, they come together again in Mark 14. The context is Jesus's last Passover meal, which prefigures the Lord's Supper. It is at this meal where he is the host who prepares a table for the twelve apostles (14:22–25). We can fairly speak of Jesus as the "host" of this meal because he is the one who blesses the bread, breaks it, and distributes it to his guests, along with the cup (vv. 22–23). He also offers the words of institution about the new covenant and the role that this reconstituted meal would have in the kingdom of God (v. 24). Further, the pericope that immediately follows this host scene speaks of a shepherd: "I will strike the shepherd and the sheep will be scattered" (14:27; cf. Zech 13:7).[43] What is more, an earlier pericope shows Mary of Bethany anointing Jesus's head with oil (Mark 14:3–9), which was a common sign of hospitality in the ancient world, calling to mind Ps 23:5b, "You anoint my head with oil." To be sure, Mary does more than she realizes: what for her was a sign of hospitality was for Jesus a prophetic action, preparing him, as the God's Messiah, for his burial (Mark 14:8). The psalm, then, is the testimony of the Lord's Anointed One when read in a Christian context.

Mark 6 also brings the two images of shepherd and host together in the person and ministry of Christ. All four Gospels recount the story of Jesus feeding the crowd of 5,000 (Matt 14:13–21; Mark 6:30–44; Luke 9:10–17; John 6:1–15). McCann notes that the story has "obvious eucharistic overtones," evidenced in Mark's use of eucharistic verbs to describe how Jesus "took" the bread, "blessed," "broke," and "gave" it to the disciples (Mark 6:41; cf. 14:22).[44] Here is another meal that prefigures the Lord's Supper, yet also

---

41. DeClaissé-Walford, et al., *Psalms*, 245–46.

42. Reardon, *Christ*, 44. Reardon refers to the messianic banquet as an "altar," symbolizing Christ's sacrifice on the cross where the bread is his body and the cup is his blood; but I see this as the pinnacle moment of *fellowship* among Christians, and think of it more in terms of a table. See Hicks, *Table*.

43. McCann, *Theological*, 135.

44. Reardon, *Christ*, 44.

looks back to the shepherd's provisions in Ps 23. While each of the four Gospels records the same story, only Mark notes that Jesus had the crowd sit on the "green grass" (Mark 6:39), a detail that recalls the twenty-third psalm's "green pastures" (Ps 23:2).[45] Similarly, only Mark gives Jesus's motivation as *pastoral* compassion and care: "He had compassion on them because they were like sheep without a shepherd" (Mark 6:34; cf. Ezek 34:4–5).[46] Both Mark 6 and 14 share the images of shepherd and host with Ps 23, and early Christians perceived these images as integrally linked in Jesus Christ.

Psalm 23:4 affirms the presence of God in the life of the believer ("You are with me"). Further, God's presence may lie behind the reference to the temple in verse 6—that is, the temple is the symbol of God's presence. McCann observes that the final line in the psalm is another way of affirming that "you are with me" (v. 4).[47] The metaphors of shepherd and host serve this larger affirmation that God's protective and sustaining presence is a constant companion to the psalmist, whether in the calm countryside, the darkest valley, or at table. The NT reaffirms God's presence among his people not in terms of mere metaphors, but in the man, Jesus of Nazareth. Matthew 1:23 calls Jesus "Immanuel" ("God with us") at the beginning of his Gospel and affirms the same at the end ("I am with you always, to the end of the age," 28:20).[48] This emphasis on Jesus Christ as the divine presence in the world serves as the bookends for Matthew's Gospel. Given the connection between God as shepherd and host in Ps 23 and Jesus as the good shepherd and host in the NT, it seems obvious to add to these the divine presence. As McCann concludes, "In New Testament terms, Jesus is shepherd, host, and Emmanuel."[49] When thinking of Jesus as shepherd, host, and "God with us," Christians read Ps 23 as pointing to God's end-times Messiah who ultimately fulfills the manifold imagery of the psalm.

We can add yet another angle to the traditional identification of Jesus as the shepherd of Ps 23. In light of the NT conviction mentioned previously that the Scriptures are ultimately about the Messiah's suffering and resurrection (Luke 24:46), Jesus fulfills the role of the psalmist, the sheep under God's guidance and care. Additionally, I noted earlier that the Psalter was shaped during the postexilic period so that the "David" of the Psalter became the

---

45. McCann, *Theological*, 135; Reardon, *Christ*, 43. Matthew 14:19 mentions only "grass," Luke does not mention grass at all but that the place was "desolate" (Luke 9:12), recalling God's provisions in the wilderness; John 6:10 mentions that there was "much grass" in the place.

46. McCann, *Theological*, 135.

47. Ibid., 132.

48. Ibid., 135–36.

49. Ibid., 136.

highly anticipated king, the Messiah, the end-times expectation of the Psalter. With this in mind, Doug Green proposes a fresh reading of Ps 23 in an article whose title captures the essence of this alternative christological interpretation: "The LORD is Christ's Shepherd."[50] Given the end-times shaping of the Psalter, "David" (see superscript for Ps 23) is no longer the historical King David, but rather "eschatological David"—the Messiah.[51]

The movement within the psalm parallels the life of Christ at nearly every turn. In other words, when one follows the journey of the psalm in light of Christ's life, death, and resurrection, it "now predicts that Yahweh will be faithful to his promise to protect and preserve his Messiah at every point in his life's journey."[52] The journey of the psalmist travels from rest (vv. 1–3), to the threat of death (v. 4), and finally to restoration and abundance (vv. 5–6). This journey is multifaceted, for it describes not only that of the psalmist, David, and his Shepherd in its original context, but also that of Israel who went from rest in the Promised Land to the darkest valley of the exile, and eagerly anticipates the restoration of the temple in Jerusalem at the time of the Psalter's final shape (i.e., postexilic period).[53] However, it ultimately refers to God's Messiah, whose life tracks with the journey (or pilgrimage) of the psalm. Green's christological reading mirrors the gospel narrative in six short verses: "Psalm 23 establishes the outline of Messiah's story. His final destiny will be glorious: a return to the abundance of Eden in the Lord's temple, with (defeated) enemies arrayed before him (v. 5). Before this climax, however, Messiah must pass through the valley of the shadow of death—perhaps a brush with death, or some deathlike condition."[54] The astute reader knows that the psalmist does not actually die in the psalm, so how can it prophetically speak of Christ who dies on the cross? A Christian reading of 23:4 transposes the psalmist's near death experience into the actual death of Christ by reading the psalm in light of the gospel story.[55] In other words, a grammatical-historical interpretation does not permit an actual experience of death by the psalmist, but a christological interpretation that reads the psalm in light of Jesus's story does in fact result in the

50. Green, "Christ's Shepherd," 33–46.

51. Ibid., 40.

52. Ibid., 41.

53. This is essentially the view of McCann (*Theological*, 130). It represents an allegorical interpretation of Ps 23 in the exilic and postexilic periods. Green also notes the movement of Israel from pasture to wilderness to temple ("Christ's Shepherd," 40).

54. Green, "Christ's Shepherd," 41.

55. Ibid., 43–44. Green (44n27) uses Ps 16 as a similar example where the original context speaks of the psalmist's *protection* from death, while Peter interprets it as a prophecy of the Messiah's *rescue* from death via the resurrection (Acts 2:25–31).

death of the Messiah. Additionally, because Ps 23 follows Ps 22, which the NT ties inextricably to the cross of Jesus Christ, the canonical placement of the two psalms recalls Jesus's journey from suffering to salvation. In order for Christ to fully rest in the peace of Ps 23, he must first pass through the daunting road of Ps 22.[56]

It is beyond my purpose here to engage all the exegetical observations of each verse of Ps 23 to Christ, the sheep.[57] But when read in light of the gospel, the twenty-third psalm speaks of Christ's journey—his life, death, and resurrection—where the LORD is his shepherd who provides for his daily needs and restores his life by delivering him from death, and exalts him into the presence of the LORD in the heavenly temple (Heb 8—9).[58] Psalm 23 is a summary of the gospel in the OT. A Christian reading of the psalm proclaims that its fullest meaning rests in the relationship between Christ and his Father, evoking the passion and new life of Jesus, as well as the gifts of the Lord's Table.[59] Suffice it to say here that both views—Jesus is my Shepherd and The LORD is Christ's Shepherd—coalesce as christological interpretations of Ps 23, a psalm about God's Anointed One.

---

56. Eaton, *Psalms*, 124.
57. See Green, "Christ's Shepherd," 38–46.
58. Ibid., 41.
59. Eaton, *Psalms*, 124.

Psalm 29

"We worship the Creator who has revealed himself as the Redeemer."—Dietrich Bonhoeffer

History

THE HEBREW SCRIPTURES BEGIN with the story of creation, and creation themes permeate the OT. Sometimes the psalmists reflect on the creation narratives of Gen 1—2 (e.g., Pss 8; 24:1; 33:6), while at other times on God's providential maintenance of the natural world (e.g., 19:1–6; 29; 104; 148). The Psalter declares that God's glory is evident through the things he has made, and the world is the theater of his glory.[1] Psalm 29 has been classified as an enthronement psalm[2] or a hymn of praise,[3] and these two are not mutually exclusive for God's enthronement calls forth praise. In Ps 29, both his enthronement and resulting praise stem from the manifestation of himself in nature, specifically the thunderstorm. Psalm 29 affirms God's sovereignty over creation, as well as his providential care of it.

The ancient Hebrews had a strong perception of the distinction between the Creator and the creation. They were not pantheists who saw nature itself as divine. The biblical doctrine of creation implies a greater-lesser relationship between God and his natural creation. In the words of C. S. Lewis, "To say that God created Nature, while it brings God and Nature into relation, also separates them. What makes and what is made must be two, not one. Thus the doctrine of Creation in one sense empties Nature of divinity."[4] The Israelites were creationists who believed that Yahweh was the creator who stood apart from his creation, while at the same time infusing it with his glory so that it continually testifies to his majesty. Again, Lewis summarizes the relationship

---

1. Mays, *Preaching*, 45.
2. McCann, *Psalms*, 792.
3. Longman, *Psalms*, 155.
4. Lewis, *Reflections*, 80.

between the Creator and the creation: "Nature and God were distinct; the One had made the other; the One ruled and the other obeyed."[5] God's sovereign rule over creation permeates Ps 29 as he uses nature to reveal his glory in the heavens above and on the earth below.

Psalm 29 may be the oldest of the psalms.[6] Its structure reveals the following three divisions: the call to worship and testimony (vv. 1–2), the appearance of Yahweh in the storm (vv. 3–9), and the acknowledgement of Yahweh's enthronement as king (vv. 10–11).[7] Its imagery evokes ancient Canaanite theophanies (i.e., appearances of a god to humans) of Baal, who was often symbolized by a thunderstorm. In fact, it was common in ANE religions to associate various gods with the power of the storm. The Egyptian god Amun was the great storm god who provided rain for crops and animals.[8] In Canaanite mythology, Baal was the "rider of the clouds," and is often pictured wielding thunder in one hand and lightening in the other.[9] Baal worshipers said that the voice of Baal was heard in the thunderstorm.[10] Therefore, the imagery, linguistic forms, and rhythmic patterns shared between Ugaritic poetry and Ps 29 invite comparative analysis. However, scholars debate whether or not a Canaanite hymn had influenced the psalmist. One view sees Ps 29 as an adaptation of an older Canaanite hymn where the name Yahweh is substituted for Baal, making it a polemic against Baal and appealing to the power of Yahweh in the storm. However, no specific Canaanite hymn actually exists, so this view rests on a flimsy hypothetical document at best.[11] To be clear, it is not as if a hymn to Baal is known to us, but there is a wealth of extant Ugaritic poetry that predates Ps 29 and that shares stylistic similarities with it.[12] Another view sees the psalm as an original production of the Hebrew psalmist, whose style and phraseology reflect that of the Canaanites. In other words, the psalmist has used terminology and modes of expression common to his ANE context.[13] It can be said with a significant measure of confidence that "thematically it

---

5. Ibid., 77.
6. McCann, *Psalms*, 792.
7. Wilson, *Psalms*, 503.
8. Ibid., 509.
9. DeClaissé-Walford, et al., *Psalms*, 285. See the Aqhat Epic where Baal is referred to as the "Rainmaker" and the "Rider-of-the-clouds." For an Eng. translation, see Margalit, *Ugaritic*.
10. Brueggemann and Bellinger, *Psalms*, 148.
11. Tesh and Zorn, *Psalms*, 240.
12. For the similarities, see Longman, *Psalms*, 155.
13. For this brief survey, see Tesh and Zorn, *Psalms*, 239–40.

is clear that this Israelite poem borrows from its Canaanite environment."[14] Such borrowing was likely polemical or apologetic to teach Israel that it was not Baal who was the power of the storm, but Yahweh.[15] It is worth noting that the LXX superscript for this psalm associates it with the last day of the Festival of Tabernacles at the end of the dry season: "On the occasion of the solemn assembly of the Tabernacle." A storm would be a welcome relief, as well as a forecast of God's provisions for another season.[16] Psalm 29, then, is a potent polemic against any notion that the pagan god Baal was responsible for the refreshing rains.

The thunderstorm is no mere natural phenomenon; it is Yahweh's work and does his bidding, resulting in his praise and glory. The fact that the covenant name of God, Yahweh, occurs eighteen times in Ps 29 underscores the anti-Baal polemic. If the Israelites were tempted to associate Baal's voice with the thunder and lightening of the storm, the psalm makes it clear with the sevenfold repetition of the "voice of the LORD" that only Yahweh speaks through the storm. Patrick Reardon believes the psalm uses onomatopoeia—a poetic device in which a word imitates the thing to which it refers—in its repetition of the "voice of the LORD" where the word "voice" (*qol*) is pronounced with the full glottal shock of the Hebrew letter *qoph* (which sounds like a strong k or kh in Eng.). Put differently, the word mimics the sound of a repeated thunder roll.[17] With seven being the number of completeness or fullness in the Bible, the point is that the thunderstorm reflects Yahweh's all-powerful strength.[18] These poetic devices—onomatopoeia and repetition—illustrate God's voice as a reverberating thunder roll.

The psalm's polemical thrust begins with the address in 29:1 to "heavenly beings" (*bene elim*, lit. "sons of gods"). This verse is notoriously difficult to interpret. Some English translations struggle to capture the literal sense of *bene elim*, and tend to soften it to "mighty ones" (NIV) or "heavenly beings" (ESV) because it, along with the plural noun *elim*, refers to gods in ANE literature. Therefore, translators may be reluctant to admit the possibility that Israel may have acknowledged the existence of other gods

---

14. DeClaissé-Walford, et al., *Psalms*, 281. Rolf Jacobson likens Israelite "borrowing" from the Canaanite religion to Christianity's use of a pagan tree as a symbol for Christmas, or the pagan name "Easter" for its festival of the resurrection.

15. Longman, *Psalms*, 155.

16. Tesh and Zorn, *Psalms*, 244. For this reason, Jacobson calls it a festival psalm (DeClaissé-Walford, et al., *Psalms*, 281).

17. Reardon, *Christ*, 55. Although this is possible, it is impossible to know what biblical Heb. sounded like. McCann (*Psalms*, 792) notes, nevertheless, that the noun translated "voice" in Ps 29 is sometimes translated "thunder" in the NRSV (cf. Exod 19:19).

18. McCann, *Psalms*, 792.

alongside Yahweh.[19] Gerald Wilson notes that we cannot rule out the possibility that some of the early Israelites were polytheists, especially given the biblical data that records many instances where Israel ran after other gods. The biblical portrait demonstrates Israel's repeated efforts to worship pagan gods in the polytheistic milieu of the ANE. Wilson comments that this propensity to worship other deities eventually led to the exile where idolatry in Israel was ultimately stamped out. In other words, only *after* the exile were the Hebrews considered to be absolute monotheists.[20] Psalm 29, therefore, does not reject altogether the existence of other gods, but rather puts them in their proper place—beneath Yahweh in subordination to him, and who worship Yahweh themselves (29:2).

When warning Israel against worshiping other gods, the OT does not unilaterally call into question their existence, but their worthiness to receive worship. These other gods worshiped by the pagans pale in comparison to the all-powerful and authoritative creator, Yahweh. What we appear to have in the biblical record of the belief system of ancient Israel is henotheism, in which many gods are thought to exist, although only one (i.e., Yahweh) has claim on one's absolute loyalty.[21] Yahweh is the "most high God," sovereign over all other heavenly beings, and is to be "exalted above all gods" (1 Chr 16:25; Pss 95:3; 96:4; 97:9; Dan 11:36–37). The first commandment speaks of having "no other gods before me" (Exod 20:3); that is, Yahweh holds first place among whatever gods are thought to exist.[22] Of course, these passages and others like them can be interpreted metaphorically so that their rhetorical purpose is to magnify the glory of Yahweh at the expense of pagan deities.[23] Either way, Yahweh is king of the cosmos. Psalm 29:1–2, therefore, is the template for interpreting the psalm as a polemic against foreign gods.

19. Wilson, *Psalms*, 508. The OT also uses both *bene elim* and *elim* to refer to gods: (Exod 15:11; Job 41:25; Pss 29:1; 89:6; Dan 11:36). Some commentators align with the softer translations and interpret "sons of gods" as "angels" (Tesh and Zorn, *Psalms*, 241; Longman, *Psalms*, 156). I would argue that angels, as created heavenly beings, are part of the divine council; but limiting Ps 29:1 to angels dilutes the psalm's polemic against Baal as the power of the storm.

20. Wilson, *Psalms*, 508.

21. Ibid., 509.

22. Ibid. Even Israel's great affirmation of monotheism, the Shema ("Hear, O Israel: the LORD our God, the LORD is one") has been interpreted as a statement of God's (1) uniqueness and incomparability, (2) singularity (i.e., God is wholly different from other gods, and does not have multiple manifestations and forms like the Canaanite gods, esp. Baal), and (3) integrity (i.e., God is not inwardly divided; there is no divine schizophrenia; he has a unity of will and purpose). Thus, the Shema is not an abstract statement of monotheism in the sense that no other gods are thought to exist, but rather emphasizes that Yahweh alone is Israel's covenant God (Wright, *Deuteronomy*, 95–98).

23. Wilson, *Psalms*, 504.

The scene portrays the divine council that meets in the heavenly throne room of Yahweh where he summons divine beings to acknowledge (lit. "ascribe to") his glory and strength.[24] While angels may be present at this council of "heavenly beings," the psalm's polemic points to the council as the deposed gods of the Canaanite pantheon.[25]

The polemic is strengthened in verse 2 where the heavenly beings are invited to worship the LORD by ascribing to him the "glory" due his name. The heavenly throne room scene evokes the image of a palace where the king's court has been hailed to hear an authoritative word from him. The heavenly beings are called to appear before the throne in order to pay homage to the Lord and to worship him. By acknowledging his glory, they confess the majesty of Yahweh above all gods. Here, as in verse 1, "glory" is the organizing motif of this heavenly worship assembly. The initial summons features the term "glory" (vv. 1–2), and it also occurs at the beginning and end of the proclamation of the voice of the LORD (vv. 3, 9).[26] Mays defines the term in the context as a summary for the divine attributes of the LORD as king and as a description of the manifestation of God's divine royalty in the world.[27] Additionally, God's glory is specifically expressed through the storm in the context of Ps 29. While not an exhaustive portrayal of God's glory, the rhetorical effect is to invite the onlookers to see his glory on display in the storm. The heavenly court that testifies to the glory of God does so "in the splendor of holiness" (lit. "splendid holy attire," v. 2), which is either a reference to Yahweh's royal robes that signify his rank as king, or to the court apparel given to those who appear before a king in his throne room.[28] We need not decide between these two views as they both make the same point: Yahweh's kingly majesty calls forth worship, and the pagan deities themselves ascribe to him glory and strength and humbly bow in worship when they are summoned before his presence.

The body of the psalm describes various effects of God's all-powerful strength—the voice of the LORD (vv. 3–9). The phrase "voice of the LORD" moves the psalm along a progression, like a storm, from beginning to end. This voice of the LORD not only resounds in the context of the storm in Ps 29, it also answers the call for God to not remain silent in Ps 28:1.[29] This

---

24. McCann, *Psalms*, 792. For the divine council, see Gen 1:26; 1 Kgs 22:19; Pss 58:1; 82:1; 89:7; 103:19–21; 148:1–2.

25. Ibid.

26. Mays, *Psalms*, 136.

27. Ibid.

28. Wilson, *Psalms*, 504; Tesh and Zorn, *Psalms*, 242. Cf. 2 Kgs 10:21–22.

29. Wilson, *Psalms*, 504.

is another instance of "microstructuring" within the Psalter where some psalms have been intentionally placed adjacent to one another due to connecting, similar, or overlapping content. Verses 3–8 describe the track of the storm as it develops over the Mediterranean Sea and heads eastward toward Palestine, hitting land at Lebanon in the north and extending far to the south to the wilderness of Kadesh. There is certainly more to this "track" than mere geography. Given the polemical nature of the psalm, the "waters" and "many waters" of verse 3 reflect the ANE mythological mindset that views water as a chaotic force that endangers creation. Waters need to be tamed, and only the gods can do so. In the context of Ps 29, Yahweh rules over the chaotic waters so that they do his bidding. What seems an untamable and destructive force is in full submission to the voice of the LORD. This harkens back to the creation narrative where darkness was over the face of the deep and the Spirit of God hovered over the waters (Gen 1:2). The ancients saw the waters as barriers to God's creative agenda, but he was the great victor who subdued the abyss and transformed it from a life-threatening force to a life-giving servant. Walter Brueggemann and William Bellinger reiterate how "waters represent the powers of chaos and disorder that oppose YHWH's creation."[30] Similarly, Mays notes the larger mythological worldview where the divine victor who was victorious over the counterforces of chaos resulting in the creation of the world and manifests the reign of the deity.[31] Psalm 29:4, then, reiterates God's victory over the forces of chaos and propels the psalm forward as the storm makes landfall in verses 5–9, which describe various effects of the storm—metaphorically the voice of the LORD—as it passes over land.

The mighty wind gusts and thunderous voice of God pierce the forested region of Lebanon (v. 5), which was known in the ANE for its cedar trees. They were the largest trees in the region, and associated ANE accounts claim that the great monster Huwawa guarded them.[32] The polemic of the verse is clear: Yahweh's theophany decimates the great forest, and no foreign god can withstand his torrent. What is more, the entire mountainous regions of Lebanon and Sirion (or Mount Hermon) jump in fright at the piercing sound of the voice of the LORD (v. 6). The imagery conveys booming thunder and blinding flashes of lightening so fearsome that what seem to be immoveable and unshakeable mountains jump like a young wild ox ("unicorn" KJV), which is renown for its strength and aggression (cf. Num

30. Brueggemann and Bellinger, *Psalms*, 148.

31. Mays, *Preaching*, 45.

32. Wilson, *Psalms*, 505. Wilson notes that Solomon imported cedars from Lebanon when building his palace as well as the Jerusalem temple (1 Kgs 5:6–10; 7:1–12).

23:22; 24:8; Deut 33:17; Job 39:9–12). Again, the track of the storm is massive; it comes ashore in the northern regions of Lebanon and extends to the southern regions to the desert of Kadesh (v. 8), and everything in between.[33] The final effect of the voice of the LORD is that it "twists the oaks and makes the forest bare" (v. 9 NIV). Verse 9 is notoriously difficult to translate due to textual discrepancies in the manuscript tradition; an equally plausible translation of the first colon reads: "makes the deer give birth" (ESV). The idea is that the thunder associated with God's voice is so terrifying, it causes animals to give birth prematurely.[34] The first option (i.e., "twists the oaks") best fits the context and parallelism of the verse.[35] It gives the impression that the storm continues on its track and nothing can withstand its power. The theophany signifies that the power of the LORD is unobstructed, truly terrifying, and yet it brings the refreshing rains.

I noted previously the "glory" theme of the psalm, and verse 9c brings this theme to a climax as the power of the thunderstorm inspires worshipers in the temple to cry "Glory!" Here at the peak of the storm worshipers fulfill the opening call to "Ascribe to the LORD the glory due his name" (v. 2).[36] It is unclear if this is the heavenly temple (or throne room) of God, or the earthly temple in Jerusalem. Perhaps the ambiguity is intentional and fuses heavenly and earthly worshipers together in one grand chorus shouting the praises of Yahweh. Put differently, heavenly worship is echoed in the worship of the LORD in the temple in Jerusalem.[37]

Many psalms draw to a close with a statement summarizing the main theme of the psalm, and Ps 29:10 is a good example of this literary device. What the psalmist implies at the beginning of the psalm, he expresses more fully near the end: the LORD reigns! The throne room scene of verses 1–2, where the gods bow before the royal presence of Yahweh, comes to full expression in verse 10. The storm begins to dissipate with a summary statement of the kingship of God who "sits enthroned over the flood" (v. 10). The thunderstorm of verses 3–9 is but a mere manifestation (however

33. DeClaissé-Walford, et al., *Psalms*, 286. It is possible to view the wilderness of Kadesh as the territory east of Lebanon and just south of Damascus (Longman, *Psalms*, 155; Wilson, *Psalms*, 505n6). This fits well the track of the storm in Ps 29 as it makes landfall. However, given the reference to the temple in v. 9, and given the polemical nature of the psalm as an exhaustive rebuke of Baal worship, the desert of Kadesh in the south adds to the psalm's rhetorical effect. The storm is enormous, extending beyond the borders of Palestine to areas "controlled" by pagan deities.

34. Tesh and Zorn, *Psalms*, 243.

35. Ibid. For discussions of the text and translation of v. 9, see ibid.; Wilson, *Psalms*, 506.

36. Wilson, *Psalms*, 506.

37. Brueggemann and Bellinger, *Psalms*, 148.

magnificent) of the cosmic reign of Yahweh. One can say that verses 3–9 illustrate the reign of God, while verse 10 definitively declares it. In other words, let there be no doubt about who tames the abyss—Yahweh, not Baal. The reference to the "flood" (*mabbul*) probably carries a two-fold sense referring to the Mediterranean Sea where the storm developed, and also to the chaotic waters of the flood in Gen 6—9. In fact, the latter is the only other place in the OT where the same term appears, and it does so twelve times.[38] Psalm 29:10 declares God's reign over the very powers that threaten to destroy creation. This essentially parallels the thought in verse 3, where the voice of the LORD was over the waters, yet it is not merely a restatement of that thought, but an amplification of it. It is the grand declaration of the reign of Yahweh in the psalm, and it is because of verse 10 that Ps 29 is often categorized as an enthronement psalm.

Again, the parallelism of verse 10 is not synonymous in the sense that colon B ("the LORD sits enthroned as king forever") merely restates colon A ("the LORD sits enthroned over the flood"). Instead the B colon heightens the A colon: "The LORD reigns over the flood; and what is more, the LORD reigns forever." Put differently, the first colon is spatial and the second is temporal, although both are universal.[39] To be sure, one is not greater than the other, but they are different from each other. Nevertheless, in the ANE worldview, the most turbulent, violent, untamable force known to humanity rests in submission beneath the feet of God. Wilson captures well the psalmist's awareness of Yahweh's reign in verse 10: "This exercise of divine authority and control over the chaotic forces threatening to undo creation and human existence established once and for all that Yahweh is the cohesive power that holds the universe together."[40]

With this declaration of God's universal reign, the psalm ends as quickly as the storm began, and the result is precisely what one expects once the storm passes—peace. Reardon observes that most of the psalm is loud and active, but decidedly peaceful at the end.[41] Calmness occurs once the whipping winds, torrential rains, blinding lightening and booming thunder of a violent storm has ended. Psalm 29 ends with this sense of peace, but it is more than simply the absence of the thunderstorm. The Hebrew concept of peace (*shalom*) is wholeness, harmony, and completeness.[42] In the context of Ps 29, Yahweh is the provider and sustainer of his people; he gives the

---

38. Wilson, *Psalms*, 507.
39. DeClaissé-Walford, et al., *Psalms*, 286.
40. Wilson, *Psalms*, 507.
41. Reardon, *Christ*, 56.
42. Tesh and Zorn, *Psalms*, 244.

refreshing rains for their crops, herds, and livelihood. As I noted earlier, the LXX superscript to this psalm associates it with the final day of the Feast of Tabernacles, which was in part an agricultural feast that celebrated Yahweh as the one who quenched the dry and thirsty land. The final verse of the psalm, then, commemorates the provisions of God who sends the rains and meets the needs of his people.

The last line of the psalm may be a prayer ("May the LORD bless his people with peace"), or it may be a declaration: ("The LORD blesses his people with peace").[43] Either way, this verse is the psalm's pinnacle polemic against Baal worship: Yahweh, not Baal, provides for Israel, and the strength of Yahweh, not Baal, is manifested in the storm and imparts strength to Israel. The larger ANE cosmic themes of the psalm reach down to a practical level in verse 11 where God's glory and strength bring peace upon Israel. Mays notes that the very power that creates the universe "offers the people of God the coherence and constancy of *shalom*."[44] Similarly, Dietrich Bonhoeffer affirms the psalm's practical import: "Psalm 29 lets us wonder at the frightful power of God in the thunder, and yet its goal lies in the power, the blessing, and the peace which God sends to his people."[45] Thus, Ps 29 ends with a summons to Yahweh, who harnessed the chaotic waters of creation and the flood, and who manifests his glory in the storm, to channel his power toward Israel for its wholeness and wellbeing.

Christology

Although not a traditional "messianic psalm," Ps 29 lends itself quite naturally to christological connections. It evokes several instances in the life and ministry of Jesus. When placed in the context of the larger biblical canon, Ps 29 echoes various aspects of Christ and his work, and points to him as its ultimate canonical expression. For example, keeping in mind that Ps 29 is an enthronement psalm, it shares both imagery and terminology with the royal birth announcement of Jesus in the Gospel of Luke. Immediately after an angel announces to shepherds that Jesus, the anointed Christ, is to be born in the city of David, the angel is joined by "a multitude of the heavenly host praising God and saying, 'Glory to God in the highest, and on earth peace among those with whom he is pleased!'" (Luke 2:13–14). This is reminiscent of the enthronement theme of Ps 29 where heavenly beings ascribe to the Lord "glory and strength" and the "glory due his name" (29:1–2). This

43. McCann, *Theological*, 164.
44. Mays, *Preaching*, 46.
45. Bonhoeffer, *Psalms*, 29.

royal theme reaches its peak in verse 10 where Yahweh's kingship is affirmed twice: enthroned over the flood and enthroned forever.[46] When the hosts of heaven combine their voices into a cosmic chorus of praise to God for his glory, they are proclaiming the enthronement of the King. What is more, the angelic announcement in Luke culminates with a declaration of shalom, as does Ps 29. As McCann notes, "The proclamation of the heavenly beings in Luke 2 is essentially the same as that in Psalm 29—glory to God, the correlate of which is peace among God's people."[47] Both passages share the same movement: a heavenly host praises God for his glory, announces his kingship, and proclaims his peace among his people.

One who is familiar with the stories from the Gospels of Jesus stilling the storm (Mark 4:35–41; Matt 8:23–27; Luke 8:22–25) can hear a loud echo of the raging storm of Ps 29, which dissipates into shalom. While attempting to cross the Sea of Galilee in the evening, Jesus and his disciples are caught in a sudden windstorm. The waves are crashing into the boat, filling it with water and threatening the lives of everyone on board. Yet Jesus is asleep on a cushion in the stern. After the frantic disciples wake him, he rebukes the wind and says to the sea, "Peace! Be still!" (Mark 4:39). As the storm in Ps 29 concludes with an affirmation of God's "peace" (29:10), the wind of the storm on Galilee "ceased, and there was great calm" (Mark 4:39). Mark's account ends with a puzzling question from the disciples to which the reader—who knows the many biblical instances where God tames chaotic waters—already knows the answer: "Who then is this, that even the wind and sea obey him?" (v. 41). Psalm 29 provides the answer: it is God, for only he commands the waters to do his bidding, and they obey; and only God brings "peace" to his people. Jesus has demonstrated the identical sovereignty over wind and waves attributed to Yahweh in the OT.[48]

Even the description of Jesus asleep in the stern has divine connotations. Sleep is a symbol of divine rule in the ancient world, and Jesus demonstrates here his power to command the waters; his sleep is a sign of divine sovereignty.[49] Similarly, the Gospel accounts of Jesus walking on the water (Mark 6:45–51; Matt 14:22–33; John 6:15–21) give expression to the declaration of Ps 29 that God is enthroned *above* the waters. The motif is, of course, very similar to the calming of the storm: God controls the chaotic waters. But here, Jesus is literally "above" the water; he walks on it, demonstrating his mastery of this seemingly untamable force. The scene has many

---

46. McCann, *Theological*, 164.
47. Ibid.
48. Blomberg, *Matthew*, 150.
49. Garland, *Luke*, 356.

affinities with the calming of the storm: the disciples are in a boat, there is a storm, the boat is battered by the wind and waves, Jesus saves, etc. But this time, Jesus is not *in* the boat. Instead, he appears during the height of the storm walking on the Sea of Galilee. In response to the fear of the disciples, who think they have seen a ghost (Matt 14:26), Jesus identifies himself with a phrase that inextricably unites him with the God of Israel in the OT: "I am" (*egō eimi*, Mark 6:50; Matt 14:27; John 6:20). This phrase, although translated for clarity in English, as "it is I," is used repeatedly in the LXX in direct reference to Yahweh (Exod 3:14; Deut 32:39; Isa 41:4; 43:10–11, 25; 45:18; 46:4; 48:12; 51:12). It is in these contexts where God identifies himself as the sole creator, sustainer, forgiver, and redeemer of his people. Jesus adopts this same phrase when identifying himself in the Gospels, especially in John (John 4:26; 6:20, 35, 51; 8:12, 24, 28, 58; 10:7, 11; 11:25; 13:19; 14:6; 15:1; 18:5–6, 8). Again, as in the calming of the storm earlier, Jesus is one with Israel's God. The God who sits enthroned above the waters in Ps 29 walks on the Sea of Galilee in the NT. What is more, the conclusion of Ps 29 is similar to the end of the scene in the Gospels. Where the psalm concludes with the dissipation of the storm and the resulting peace of God, the Gospels recount that upon entering into the boat, "the wind ceased" (Mark 6:51; Matt 14:32). In light of Ps 29, these accounts demonstrate that Jesus is the anointed king who dominates the waters that represent chaos.[50]

As God's thunderous voice is a dominant theme in Ps 29, it reverberates again in John 12:28–29, although in a very different context. Jesus has just predicted his "glorification," the Johannine language of crucifixion, resurrection, and exaltation as one complex event; that is, the "uplifting" of the Son of Man. After some Greeks come to see Jesus, he concludes that his hour has come to be lifted up on the cross, beginning his journey back to the Father (12:20–23). Jesus says of the Father, "Glorify your name" (v. 28). Verse 29 states, "A voice came from heaven: 'I have glorified it, and I will glorify it again.'" John then records that the crowd that had gathered nearby heard the heavenly voice, but some thought it had "thundered," while some thought it was the voice of angel. Reardon perceives that the thunderous voice of Ps 29 "is the same thunderous voice" in this scene in the Gospel of John.[51]

Finally, Jesus's death, resurrection, and exaltation signal his triumph over the forces of evil. The cross, far from being the tragic end to a noble and sacrificial life, is the very means through which God defeats his enemies—sin and death. The cross, which is meant by Rome to mock Jesus's claims

---

50. Longman, *Psalms*, 157. Along similar lines, Longman notes how Jesus as King of kings and Lord of lords defeats the beast that rises out of the sea (Rev 13:1–10; 19:11–21).

51. Reardon, *Christ*, 56.

of kingship, is his actual coronation, his glorification (John 12:23; 13:31). Those with eyes to see and ears to hear recognize it as the crowning of the Messiah, a son of David, who shepherds, serves, and sacrifices his life for humanity. John's Gospel records in plain terms the charge of Jesus's "crime" that is written and placed above his head on the cross: "Jesus of Nazareth, the King of the Jews" (John 19:19). Andreas Köstenberger and Justin Taylor note John's intended irony: "Pilate was executing Jesus for actually being the King of the Jews . . . Jesus was not just a king; he is *the* king, and he will return one day to finally and fully establish God's kingdom on his newly created heaven and earth."[52] Granted, the cross event is not in view in the original context of Ps 29, but enthronement is. The NT, then, gives a finer expression to the glory motif of the psalm by revealing the sacrificial heart of the God whose kingly glory is manifest in the storm. While he is king of all gods, and while his voice shatters the storm-swept landscape, he brings peace to his people ultimately by means of his self-sacrifice on a Roman cross (Col 1:20). Jesus is the incarnate manifestation of the power and glory of God in the NT. Thus, the Hebrews writer reminds us of Christ's enthronement at the cross and ultimately at the ascension: "Looking to Jesus, the founder and perfecter of our faith, who for the joy that was set before him endured the cross, despising the shame, and is seated at the right hand of the throne of God" (Heb 12:2).

---

52. Köstenberger and Taylor, *Final Days*, 155.

Psalm 30

"We weep only until that morning of resurrection gladness, looking to the joy that blossomed in advance in the early-morning resurrection of the Lord."—Augustine

History

PSALM 30 HAS ONE of the most mysterious superscripts in the Psalter: "A psalm of David. A song at the dedication of the temple." "Temple" (ESV) is interpretive because the Hebrew literally reads "the house" (*ha bayit*), which may refer to the king's royal palace.[1] Given the language of "dedication" (*hanukkah*), a term most often reserved for the dedication of the altar at the temple (Num 7:10, 11, 84, 88; 2 Chr 7:9), it makes more sense to see this as a reference to the dedication of the Jerusalem temple, the house of the LORD.[2] However, this creates a problem because the superscript seems to associate David with the dedication of the temple. I have already addressed the issue of Davidic authorship in relation to the possible meanings of the "of David" title in the superscripts. In short, David likely wrote many psalms, even though "of David" does not necessarily refer to authorship. In other words, David may not have written this psalm, and the historical problem of associating him with the dedication of the temple is solved. Yet some ambiguity still remains because the content of the psalm seems to have nothing to do with the temple's dedication.[3] It may be the case that the superscript to Ps 30 is really the colophon (i.e., an inscription at the end of a book) to Ps 29 where God's glory is declared in the temple (29:9).[4] Even so, because the superscript refers to *the* house, Ps 30 likely concludes a

---

1. Wilson, *Psalms*, 514.
2. The Aram. Psalms Targum translates "house" as "sanctuary" (Tg. Ps. 30:1), attempting to remove the ambiguity of the Heb.
3. Longman, *Psalms*, 158.
4. Ibid.

smaller grouping of "sanctuary psalms" (23—30) that emphasize the house of Yahweh.[5]

A few scenarios may shed light on the superscript as it relates to the temple. First, the words "a song at the dedication of the temple" may be a later addition to the original superscript that simply read "a psalm of David."[6] Thus, the psalm in the original context had nothing to do with the temple or David's relationship to its construction and dedication. It was simply a psalm of thanksgiving that was in some way associated with David. Second, although David did not build the temple, he acquired the materials for its construction (1 Chr 22:2–19), and may have penned Ps 30 with the intention of having it sung in the future when Solomon builds and dedicates the temple (2 Sam 7:13; 2 Chr 3—7, esp. 6:14-42). Scripture mentions the role of music in the dedication ceremony (5:11–13a; 7:6), which may have included this psalm among others. Third, the temple reference in the superscript may not be to the Solomonic temple, but the dedication of the postexilic temple of Zerubbabel (Ezra 6:16–18).[7] Finally, rabbinic literature associates Ps 30 with the rededication of the temple during the Maccabean revolt in 165 BCE (b. Sop. 18:3).[8] After the Seleucid king Antiochus IV "Epiphanes" desecrated the temple by sacrificing a pig to Zeus on the altar of burnt offering, the Maccabees, led by Judas Maccabeus, waged a three-year guerilla warfare campaign against the armies of Antiochus, took back the temple, purified it, and dedicated it. This dedication ceremony, described in 1 Macc 4:52–59 and 2 Macc 10:1–9, is commemorated in the Jewish feast of Hanukkah ("dedication"). While certainty is elusive regarding the historical scenario of the superscript, the content of Ps 30 is equally as mysterious because it seems to have nothing to do with the temple, describing instead the psalmist's deliverance from a life-threatening calamity.

Because of the poet's experience of salvation, Ps 30 has been called a "classic thanksgiving song,"[9] which commemorates the psalmist's journey from disorientation to reorientation, from distress to deliverance, from trial to thanksgiving. In one sense, it recalls the deliverance of an individual who God has delivered from some kind of calamity. This is evident in the psalm's use of the first person in verses 1–3. Yet a wider audience is also in view, given the address to the worshiping community in verse 4: "Sing praises to

---

5. Wilson, *Psalms*, 514. For the sanctuary psalms, see Fletcher, "Sanctuary," 97–119.

6. DeClaissé-Walford, et al., *Psalms*, 289.

7. Ibid.

8. Mays, *Psalms*, 140.

9. Longman, *Psalms*, 157–58.

the LORD, O you his saints, and give thanks to his holy name." Structurally, the communal invitation to worship is followed by a narrative of the events surrounding God's deliverance of the singer in verses 6–12, which harkens back to the initial declaration of praise in verses 1–3. Given this twofold emphasis on personal and public praise, the structure of Ps 30 is more or less straightforward:

> Summary of need-rescue-thanks (vv. 1–3)
> Interlude: communal call to praise (vv. 4–5)
> Narrative recollection of need-petition-rescue-thanks (vv. 6–12)[10]

How this structure coheres is more complex. The psalm presents a series of opposites, or "polarities" that when taken together contribute to its thematic unity of thanksgiving. These polarities convey the negative and positive experiences and emotions of the psalmist as God takes him from trial to triumph. The pairing of contrasting polarities is a poetic device that serves as the psalm's "building blocks."[11] The following figure illustrates the negative and positive polarities that form the structure of the psalm:

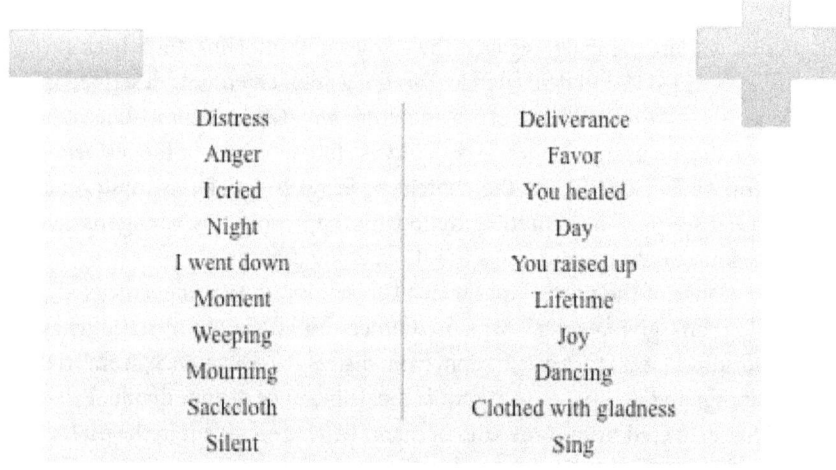

Distress	Deliverance
Anger	Favor
I cried	You healed
Night	Day
I went down	You raised up
Moment	Lifetime
Weeping	Joy
Mourning	Dancing
Sackcloth	Clothed with gladness
Silent	Sing

Figure 1 Contrasting Polarities

Verse 1 is a typical introduction for a psalm of thanksgiving where the psalmist praises God for his beneficence on behalf of the psalmist. It provides the lens for interpreting the rest of the psalm. Although the heart

---

10. Adapted from Brueggemann and Bellinger, *Psalms*, 151–52.
11. DeClaissé-Walford, et al., *Psalms*, 290.

of the psalm expresses the psalmist's "disorientation" in the face of calamity (30:5–10), the opening verse expresses his "reorientation," hinting that the calamity was but temporary. The psalm begins with a picturesque metaphor of drawing a bucket up from a well (v. 1), which represents God's rescue of the psalmist from distress.[12] It is not clear who the psalmist's "foes" are; if the psalmist is King David, he had many.[13] The idea behind this opening verse is that when those who trust in God are caught in times of duress, their enemies jump at the opportunity to gloat in their misfortune. But the precise identity of the psalmist's enemies does not matter for understanding the driving sentiment of the psalm: God delivers from distress. The type of distress is only hinted at in verses 2–3 with such phrases as "you have healed me," and "brought up my soul from Sheol," which is amplified and somewhat clarified by "restored me to life from among those who go down to the pit." Again, note the interplay of the polarity: "brought up my soul . . . go down to the pit." This appears to refer to God's healing of the psalmist from some sort of physical illness, and this is more or less the standard view among commentators.[14] For the poet, this illness meant certain death. He was as good as dead. The use of Sheol, the Hebrew term for the realm of the dead, which is parallel to "pit,"[15] drives home the point that the illness placed the psalmist within reach of the grave. In contemporary parlance, the psalmist "had one foot in the grave." Thanks be to God who plucked him out of the line of those currently waiting to enter Sheol.[16]

As mentioned previously, the psalmist's thanksgiving is not a private matter. He goes public with the news of his healing before the worshiping community of saints (v. 4). The word translated "saints" (*khasidim*) comes from the Hebrew word used to convey the idea of "enduring covenant loyalty" (*khesed*).[17] Those who are called to join in the psalmist's praises are none other than his fellow covenanters to whom Yahweh has pledged his covenant

12. Longman, *How to Read Psalms*, 145.

13. Wilson, *Psalms*, 515.

14. John Calvin was less sure of this view, opting instead for a spiritual condition that stems from the confessional language of vv. 6–7 (*Psalms*, Apple e-book, ch. 30). McCann (*Psalms*, 796) notes that the language may be figuratively used for various trials and sufferings of life (Ps 147:3; Hos 6:1; 11:4; 14:4; Jer 3:22; 33:6). I appreciate the observation of Rolf Jacobson: "The generic language allows believers in every generation to pray and sing this psalm anew, using it to reflect on the myriad crises that humans pass through in life and using it to deflect toward God any credit for having 'made it'" (DeClaissé-Walford, et al., *Psalms*, 289).

15. McCann, *Psalms*, 796. McCann notes the terms Sheol and pit sometimes occur together (Ps 88:3–4; Isa 38:18).

16. Wilson, *Psalms*, 516.

17. Ibid., 516n8.

faithfulness. Tremper Longman understands these saints to be the psalmist's "fellow worshippers, and his story of deliverance is intended to incite them to praise God."[18] Walter Brueggemann and William Bellinger capture well the public aspect of the psalm: "The summons of praise is addressed to the congregation of the faithful, the assembly that joins the individual voice of thanks. Now the entire community celebrates the particular transformation of the individual petitioner."[19] Therefore, verses 4–5 signal a redirection away from direct address to God and toward the covenant community, presumably those assembled at the temple for worship. In addition to the invitation to the community to join in praise and thanksgiving for the psalmist's deliverance (v. 4), the singer exhorts the community with an affirmation of the transient nature of the "anger" of God (v. 5). As of yet, the psalm does not describe the cause of God's anger, but simply declares its impermanence in contrast to the staying power of his favor. As J. Clinton McCann eloquently states, "God's commitment to life (v. 3) and lifetime commitment of favor mean that the ultimate end of human suffering is not 'weeping' but 'rejoicing.'"[20] God's favor is longer and stronger than his anger.[21]

Verse 6 suggests the cause of God's anger: the arrogance of the psalmist. Seasons of prosperity often silence the humble recognition of God's goodness and blessings on behalf of his people (Deut 6:10–12; 8:11–18). The arrogance of the psalmist is the root cause of his suffering at the hands of God. Put differently, God's anger and abandonment are manifested in the psalmist's suffering, and in this case may be physical illness. While Scripture does not systemically spell out the connection between sin and illness, OT theology allows for a connection in some cases where sickness is viewed as divine punishment for sin.[22] For example, Ps 30 is strikingly similar to Hezekiah's prayer for healing, which implies a link between his illness and his sin, although no specific sin is mentioned (Isa 38:17; cf. 2 Kgs 20:1–11). God's punishment of the Egyptians with the plague of boils is another instance of physical illness as divine punishment (Exod 9). Similarly, God punishes Israel with a plague because of David's census (2 Sam 24; 1 Chr 21).[23] Even the NT raises the issue of the relationship between sin and sickness, suggesting a connection in some cases (John 9:1–2, 34). Jesus's disciples express a

---

18. Longman, *Psalms*, 159.
19. Brueggemann and Bellinger, *Psalms*, 152.
20. McCann, *Psalms*, 796.
21. DeClaissé-Walford, et al., *Psalms*, 294.
22. Wilson, *Psalms*, 178.
23. For other Jewish sources on divine reciprocity of sin and sickness, see, 2 Macc 4:38; 9:5–6; 13:7–8; LAB 44:9–10; 4Q181 1, 1–2.

common view that various physical ailments *can* be the result of sin.[24] They ask Jesus of a man blind from birth, "Who sinned? This man or his parents, that he was born blind?" Jesus does not offer an exhaustive explanation, but simply clarifies that in this instance neither "this man" nor "his parents" sinned, resulting in his blindness (cf. 5:14). It is beyond our scope here to dive into this complex theological relationship, but suffice it to say that the psalmist sees a direct connection between his arrogance and the life-threatening divine punishment of God in Ps 30.

The psalm-singer describes divine punishment in terms of God hiding his face (v. 7). Hebrew thought often describes being in someone's presence as being before his or her "face." In other words, face is a metonym for *presence* and often describes interpersonal relationships.[25] The usage here goes beyond mere presence and includes the favor and protection of God.[26] When the psalmist speaks of God hiding his face, the situation is dire: God has withdrawn his presence, beneficence, and protection from the life of the psalmist, leaving him utterly alone. For the poet, his arrogance caused God to hide his face so that the poet was dismayed. With such confidence in his own abilities, what need does he have for God? To be clear, this is not divine ignorance or oversight of the psalmist's plight, but an intentional withdrawal of protection that leads to a period of distress for the psalmist.[27] Yet given the larger context of this psalm of thanksgiving, the withdrawal of God's face is only temporary and for the larger good of the psalmist. In other words, in the withdrawal of God's face, the psalmist experienced the "redemptive abandonment" of God. God's withdrawal was ultimately for the psalmist's good: the feeling of divine absence caused the wandering psalmist to run back into the arms of God.[28] This is not unlike God's temporary withdrawal from Israel during the Babylonian exile: "For a brief moment I deserted you, but with great compassion I will gather you. In overflowing anger for a moment I hid my face from you, but with everlasting love I will have compassion on you, says the LORD, your Redeemer" (Isa 54:7–8). For the psalmist, absence makes him long for God's healing power and presence, and he indicates this by his prayer for deliverance, which is the substance of verses 8–10.

The psalmist's plea is ultimately for his salvation from the current crisis, be it illness or some other life-threatening situation. His greatest fear

---

24. Thompson, *John*, 206.
25. Longman, "Face," 563.
26. DeClaissé-Walford, et al., *Psalms*, 295.
27. Ibid., 295–96.
28. Longman, *Psalms*, 159.

is death (v. 9). The manner in which he calculates his own demise as a potential threat to the praise of God is one of the most complex theological expressions in the OT. He reasons in verse 10 that his death would bring no praise to his God: "What profit is there in my death, if I go down to the pit? Will the dust praise you? Will it tell of your faithfulness?" This may be taken in two ways, which are not mutually exclusive but have different emphases associated with each view. The first view states the matter in negative terms: loss of the psalmist equals loss of praise. God has a vested interest in preserving the life of the psalmist who may then testify to God's faithfulness.[29] In the absence of a clear notion of the afterlife, the poet calls for God to consider the potential hit to his own reputation as a result of failing to deliver the psalmist who cannot praise God from the grave. In other words, if he dies, God would be deprived of a worshiper (6:5; 88:10–11).[30] James Mays captures the psalmist's intertwining concern for his own life preservation and praise for God's faithfulness: "At issue is there being someone to proclaim the faithfulness of the LORD. Praise has a theological basis as well as an anthropological one. Praise is the way that the faithfulness of the LORD becomes word and is heard in the LORD's world."[31]

Psalm 116:15 similarly affirms the costly value of the lives of God's saints ("Precious in the sight of the LORD is the death of his saints"),[32] and breathes the same air as Ps 30: God's saints are costly to him because he loses a witness to his glory in the world when they die. It costs God greatly when they die. Psalms 30 and 116 are similar songs of deliverance that testify to the theological and anthropological basis for worship. As noted before, this concept (i.e., death as the silencer of humanity's glorious praise for God) should be seen in the OT context of the absence of a clear notion of the afterlife. For the ancients, praise stopped at the grave.[33] The OT does not envision an eternal life with God when his saints will worship in his presence for eternity (cf. Rev 22:1–5). As previously stated, the grave or pit is Sheol, the realm of the dead, and the rationale of the psalmist is that dead people cannot lift their voices in praise of God's faithfulness. The psalmist will soon pledge that he will not be silent in the face of God's deliverance (Ps 30:12), but here in verse 8, the threat of his silence looms as a consequence of God's abandonment. The silencing of praise as an appeal to God's self-

---

29. Brueggemann and Bellinger, *Psalms*, 151.

30. Tesh and Zorn, *Psalms*, 248.

31. Mays, *Psalms*, 141.

32. "Precious" should be understood in the sense of a "precious jewel." The word "costly" is perhaps a clearer translation when considering the larger argument in Ps 116: God delivers his saints from calamity, and they, in turn, praise him for his mercy.

33. DeClaissé-Walford, et al., *Psalms*, 296–97.

interest is but one way of interpreting the psalmist's concern and prayer for his deliverance.

An alternate view expresses the matter more affirmatively: the meaning of life itself is praise. Put differently, the psalmist's question about praise is a question about life because to live is to praise God, and to praise God is to live.[34] The psalmist prays to live because he sees praise as the purpose of life, and this awareness calls forth thanksgiving (v. 4), worship, and dancing (vv. 11–12). The appeal in verse 9 dovetails with the final verses of the psalm, which indicate that the appeal achieved the desires effect—deliverance. Verse 9 is not as much an appeal to God's self-interest as it is the psalmist's embrace of life as a God-given gift that reflects his faithfulness; and, being clothed with joy (v. 11) and thanksgiving to God forever, the psalmist's whole life becomes praise (v. 12).[35] The silence of the grave is finally eclipsed by the singer's refusal to be silent in light of God's gracious help (vv. 10, 12).

When God delivers people it is cause for celebration. Whether deliverance is from enemies, famine, or illness, God's people declare his praises in the midst of the community of faith assembled at the temple for worship. Psalm 30 exalts God for his redemption of the psalmist in the face of certain death. However, the psalmist's praise is not a private matter, but a communal affair, as it resounds throughout the temple in the presence of the worshiping community.

Christology

What appears on the surface to be the psalmist's struggle with a personal calamity, be it physical illness or suffering in general, becomes a passage that has very strong christological undercurrents when read in light of the gospel. As we have seen with other psalms, aspects of Ps 30 are applicable to both Christ and the church. In terms of the psalmist's healing from physical illness, the Gospels reveal Jesus as the great physician who heals the infirmities of his people (Luke 4:23). Jesus's healing ministry testifies to his identity as the Son of God, and demonstrates his compassion and care for the outcasts of society, which include those with physical illnesses. What is more, given the psalmist's deliverance from certain death, the Gospels witness to God's ultimate victory over both sin and sickness, even if the two are not always directly correlated. As Paul proclaims in 1 Cor 15:26, death is the enemy of God, and will be defeated once and for all at the return of Christ. The bodily resurrection is not an isolated event, but the firstfruits of God's

---

34. McCann, *Psalms*, 796.
35. Ibid., 797.

plan to redeem the fallenness of our physical bodies and save us from the grave (15:23). Thus, Ps 30, the model prayer for those who have been healed from serious illness, points ultimately to the physical and spiritual healing that Christians receive as a result of Jesus's victory over death. The psalmist's experience of healing and deliverance is our experience in Christ. Put differently, the flow of Ps 30 from plea to praise is analogous to the church's journey of redemption, which culminates in the resurrection.

John Eaton captures the similarity between the psalmist's deliverance and that of the church: "The later church related the psalm to her times of penitence and re-dedication, times when the grace of God drew her up from the abyss of death, healed her, clothed her with gladness and led her to a time of dancing, celebrating afresh the resurrection from which her life first sprang."[36] In other words, the psalm may function as an allegory for the church's redemption from death. Again, Paul proclaims the victory of the resurrection over the effects of sin, namely death: "Death is swallowed up in victory. O death, where is your victory? O death, where is your sting?" (15:54b–55). Not only does the prayer remind us of our healing in Christ, it is also a model prayer of thanksgiving *to* Christ, our great physician, and praises him for our deliverance. Longman reminds us of the call to praise, resulting from Paul's reflection on the gospel's transforming power over fallenness: "Jesus Christ is the one who 'has destroyed death and has brought life and immortality to light through the gospel' (2 Tim 1:10). How can we neglect to render our thanks to our Lord Jesus Christ?"[37] Additionally, this corporate prayer of thanksgiving by the church is consistent with the historical setting of the psalm, which includes the rescue of the nation of Israel following the exile. Based on the function of the psalm in the context of temple worship, deliverance is not only for the individual psalmist but also the entire worshiping community. Mays concludes that the poetry of salvation in Ps 30 "can be and was read as a rendering of individual or national experience."[38] The corporate experience of salvation in Israel lends itself to application in the later Christian community.

Not only does the Ps 30 function as a metaphor for the church's redemption in Christ from sin, sickness, and death, but also as an abbreviated narration of the gospel of Christ's suffering for sin and rescue from death. Psalm 30 is a prelude to the passion of Christ, and Christians have interpreted it in this light for centuries. The quote by Augustine at the beginning of this chapter suggests that the psalmist's deliverance from death

---

36. Eaton, *Psalms*, 143.

37. Longman, *Psalms*, 160.

38. Mays, *Psalms*, 140.

anticipates Christ's resurrection. Verse 3, for example, echoes the resurrection experience of Christ: "O LORD, you have brought up my soul from Sheol; you restored me to life from among those who go down to the pit." As discussed previously, it also anticipates the general resurrection of Christ's followers at the end of the age. Jerome read Ps 30 in light of the mutual redemptive experience of Christ and the church: "This psalm is about the time of the passion, the resurrection and the consummation of the age."[39] Thus, the structural flow of the psalm as a whole evokes events of Jesus's passion where "the time of suffering is followed by the morning of the paschal deliverance."[40] Jesus experienced God's anger for a moment on the cross, but his favor for eternity in the resurrection. Granted, Jesus did not display the prideful arrogance of the psalmist, but the crucifixion was an atoning death whereby Jesus bore in himself the sins of the world, thereby incurring the wrath of God (2 Cor 5:21; 1 John 2:2). Patrick Reardon captures the christological essence of the psalm: "The dark hour of the Passion gave way to the dawn of victory."[41] So the psalm's language of rescue and deliverance from the grave, while not originally referring to resurrection per se, awaits the Christ event for reinterpretation.[42] Jesus's rescue from death at the resurrection provides the lens for interpreting Ps 30 in light of Christ.

Even Jesus's prayer for deliverance in the Garden of Gethsemane harkens back to that of the psalmist: "What profit is there in my death, if I go down to the pit? Will the dust praise you? Will it tell of your faithfulness? Hear, O LORD, and be merciful to me! O LORD, be my helper" (Ps 30:9–10). Anticipating the agony of the cross, feeling crushed under the weight of the sins of the world, which thereby leads to God's intentional withdrawal, Jesus prays for his Father to spare him from drinking the "cup" (Luke 22:41–44). Andreas Köstenberger and Justin Taylor convey the essence of Jesus's prayer for salvation in that he "knows he is about to bear God's judgment for sin as a substitutionary sacrifice for the sins of the world. 'Cup' was a common metaphor for God's righteous wrath poured out on sinners."[43] Lest we forget that God did *ultimately* save Jesus from the separation of death, the Hebrews writer reflects on his prayer in the garden: "In the days of his flesh, Jesus offered up prayers and supplications, with loud cries and tears, to him, who

---

39. Jerome, *Brief Commentary on Psalms* 30, in Blaising and Hardin, *Psalms*, 221.
40. Reardon, *Christ*, 57–58.
41. Ibid., 58.
42. Mays, *Psalms*, 141.
43. Köstenberger and Taylor, *Final Days*, 92. On "cup" as a metaphor for God's wrath, see Isa 51:17–23; Jer 25:15–18; Lam 4:21; Ezek 23:31–33.

was able to save him from death, and he was heard because of his reverence" (Heb 5:7).

When all of this is taken together, the narrative of Jesus's passion and resurrection evokes the psalmist's proclamation: "For his anger is but for a moment, and his favor is for a lifetime. Weeping may tarry for the night, but joy comes with the morning . . . You have turned for me my mourning into dancing; you have loosed my sackcloth and clothed me with gladness" (Ps 30:5, 11). In light of these reverberations with Jesus's passion and resurrection, Ps 30 is traditionally used during the season of Easter.[44] Even more to the point, the "David" of the psalm is a biblical type of Christ, where Jesus is the "deeper, truer voice in this psalm," who thanks God for delivering him from the grave.[45] The prayer of the psalmist is ultimately the prayer of Christ. The prayer of the psalmist is also that of the church in recalling her journey from sin to salvation.

---

44. McCann, *Psalms*, 797.
45. Reardon, *Christ*, 57.

Psalm 46

"Have no fear, then, be not disturbed, having an invincible Master as we do, to whom all honor and glory is fitting, together with the peerless Father and his vivifying Spirit, now and forever, and for ages of ages."—John Chrysostom

History

THE WORLD IS AN unstable place. Ever since the fall in the Garden of Eden, the world has been plagued by both natural and man-made disasters. Where do God's people turn when they feel the weight of opposing forces closing in on them? How do they keep from feeling overwhelmed by the chaos that surrounds them on a daily basis? Psalm 46 answers these questions by reminding God's people of his presence among them. The world is full of powers of chaos, evil, and war. Yet God is present with his people, and tames those principalities and powers; he is a refuge of peace for his people.[1] In times of insecurity and instability, the hope of the people is the stability of God and the security that comes from his presence among them.

Psalm 46 declares that the power and presence of God are with his chosen people during times of crisis. Military imagery saturates the psalm as a formidable enemy surrounds and threatens the city of Zion (i.e., Jerusalem), the geographical location of the presence of God. The psalmist even uses ANE cosmic imagery to illustrate the chaos of the moment. While the exact historical scenario behind the psalm is unclear, some scholars have attempted to reconstruct the scene in terms of Sennacherib's attempted invasion of Jerusalem in 2 Kgs 19:32–36.[2] God prevented the Assyrian king from entering Jerusalem, killed 185,000 Assyrian troops, and drove Sennacherib back to Nineveh, where his sons eventually murdered him. However, this is only a tentative reconstruction because the battle language is non-specific

---

1. Brueggemann and Bellinger, *Psalms*, 219.
2. Tesh and Zorn, *Psalms*, 334–35.

and may reflect any number of battles in ancient Israel's war-laden history. Nevertheless, interpretation of the psalm does not depend on identifying the specific scenario behind it. The psalm transcends any local situation, and ultimately proclaims the universal deliverance of God on behalf of his people.[3] This is the psalm's timeless message.

The superscript of Ps 46 is full of information, yet the details remain mysterious to modern readers: "To the choirmaster. Of the sons of Korah. According to Alamoth. A song." Tremper Longman observes that over fifty psalms have the title "To the choirmaster," who was probably the individual to whom the psalms were entrusted and who was in charge of Israel's worship at the sanctuary.[4] "Alamoth" may refer to the type of accompaniment such as voices, instruments, or both (cf. 1 Chr 15:20).[5] Additionally, Ps 46 is a song of the sons of Korah.[6] The role played by the sons of Korah at the temple is interesting to note, although it is unclear what role, if any, they played in the composition and compilation of the psalms that bear their name (Pss 42–49; 84–85; 87–88).[7] Korah was the great-grandson of Levi who led a rebellion in the wilderness, and who was swallowed up by a hole in the earth; but his sons were spared (Num 16; 26:11; cf. Jude 11).[8] Their descendants supported David who gave them responsibilities at the temple as a guild of singers when he revised its liturgy and personnel (1 Chr 26:1–10). They continued to be gatekeepers of the temple in the postexilic era (1 Chr 9:17–19; Neh 11:19); they also baked the sacred bread (1 Chr 9:19, 31).[9]

A common feature of the Korah Psalms is the repeated references to "the city of God," sometimes called "Zion." To be clear, Ps 46 is not a psalm about Jerusalem; it is about God's protection of his people and his presence among them in the city of Jerusalem, the location of the temple. God's ability to safeguard the stronghold of Israel's faith, Jerusalem, is the theme of the psalm.[10] The inhabitants of the city declare together that salvation belongs to their God, who acts on their behalf. Therefore, the psalm is aptly described as a community hymn or a communal psalm

---

3. Ibid., 335.
4. Longman, *Psalms*, 30.
5. Ibid. For a more in-depth discussion, see Kidner, *Psalms 1–72*, 40–41.
6. "Song" (*shir*) underscores the musical nature of the poem (Longman, *Psalms*, 29).
7. DeClaissé-Walford, et al., *Psalms*, 399n1.
8. Bullock, *Encountering*, 74.
9. Ibid. See also, Longman, "Korahites," 1021.
10. DeClaissé-Walford, et al., *Psalms*, 421.

of confidence.[11] To be sure, this does not dilute God's deliverance of the individual (e.g., "The LORD is my light and my salvation," 27:1), but his deliverance throughout the Scriptures benefits both the individual and the covenant community. Put differently, God delivers individuals in community, not in isolation.[12] As we will see, this communal dimension is prominent in Ps 46.

The psalm has a simple structure of three stanzas, separated by three *Selah* notations:[13]

St. 1 God, a Shelter and Refuge (vv. 1–3)

Selah

St. 2 The City of God (vv. 4–7)

Selah

St. 3 Behold the Works of the Lord (vv. 8–11)

Selah

Its placement in the Psalter indicates that it should not be read in isolation from the collection of the first Korah Psalms (Pss 42—49). Psalms 47—48 echo the prominent declaration of the sovereignty and protection of God of 46:1. Therefore, it is best to read Pss 46—48 together for a fuller emphasis on God's protective presence than either psalm alone.[14]

The psalm begins with the foundational premise that permeates the entire psalm: God rules the world and is sovereign over every threat to the stability of his people (46:1).[15] This resonates with the conviction in Ps 23 that God is the protective shepherd of the psalmist. Unlike Ps 23, which describes God's care of the individual, Ps 46 describes God's providential care of the covenant community—the people of Israel. Yes, the Lord is *my* shepherd (23:1), but he is also *our* refuge and strength (46:1). The grammar of verse 1b is difficult, especially as it relates to the function of the verb *matsa* ("to find"), which is often left untranslated by many English versions. For example, the ESV renders the phrase, "A very present help in trouble." Thus, it is a declaration of God's goodness in general terms without any specific temporal reference to his actions in the past. A very wooden translation might also read, "A help in distress he [God] has been found to be exceedingly." John Calvin stresses that

---

11. Ibid. Given the place of Zion in the psalm, deClaissé-Walford also sees it as a "song of Zion."

12. Tesh and Zorn, *Psalms*, 336.

13. Slightly adapted from deClaissé-Walford, et al., *Psalms*, 421. On *Selah* as an unknown notation, possibly an interlude, see Longman, *Psalms*, 31.

14. Tesh And Zorn, *Psalms*, 335.

15. McCann, *Theological*, 137.

the past tense of the Hebrew verb gives the sense of a repeated occurrence: God has been found *repeatedly* to be a help in distress for his people and will continue to be so now.[16] In other words, this is not wishful thinking where the community hopes for the very first time for God's deliverance from the current distress. Instead, they have repeatedly experienced God's deliverance in the past, which gives them an earnest expectation in the present that he will prove faithful and deliver them again. I prefer the rendering of the MEV: "A well-proven help in trouble."[17] This is not the first occurrence of God's deliverance; he has always been faithful to his people and will deliver them from the present crisis.

What is more, the proven help of God is the basis for the community's confidence, and this is suggested with an emphatic "therefore" in verse 2.[18] Put differently, verse 1 is the presupposition of verse 2 so that the safety, security, and stability of God is a communal conviction based on God's well-proven reputation. Yes, the Lord is the refuge and strength of his people, but from what, or who? What calamities does the psalmist have in mind that would spur the community to declare their confidence in God? The imagery of verses 2–3 may suggest natural, cataclysmic disasters, like a violent earthquake that rattles the earth's tectonic plates and reduces mountains to rubble as they crumble into the sea. Indeed the image is terrifying because to the ancients, mountains were secure, stable, and immoveable, and waters were forces of chaos.[19] Alternatively, the waters that "roar and foam" may call to mind the raging seas of a storm that threatens the landscape as it passes onto shore.

The imagery of verses 2–3 evokes the combination of a category-five hurricane and an earthquake measuring a ten on the Richter scale.[20] Yet most Psalms scholars do not believe that the psalmist is describing natural events here, but rather adopts ANE terminology, which speaks often of the strength and stability of mountains and of the chaotic nature of waters, to describe the present crisis in truly terrifying terms. Waters that "roar and foam" (v. 3) are obviously not tranquil, and ANE poetry uses this terminology as a metaphor for chaos.[21] To be clear, the threat is not simply to the people of God, but to the entire created world. According to J. Clinton

---

16. Calvin, *Psalms*, Apple e-book, ch. 46.

17. The ESV provides this as an alternate translation in a footnote, but I prefer it as the primary translation.

18. Tesh and Zorn, *Psalms*, 336.

19. Longman, *Psalms*, 204.

20. McCann, *Theological*, 137.

21. DeClaissé-Walford, et al., *Psalms*, 42.

McCann: "In the ancient Near Eastern understanding of the universe, the mountains were the foundation that both anchored dry land in a watery chaos and held up the sky. The worst possible scenario would be for the mountains to "shake" or "tremble," for dry land would be threatened from below by water and from above by the sky falling.[22] As discussed in Ps 29, God tamed the chaotic forces at creation. In Ps 46, however, chaos threatens to reassert itself and destroy the order of creation.[23] In spite of the threat of chaos, however, the psalmist declares that the sovereign God who calmed chaos at creation is the refuge and strength of his people.[24] There is no reason to be afraid of the impending cosmic crisis, however terrifying it may be at the moment.

The chaotic waters of verses 2–3 give way to the calm waters of verses 4. The turbulent seas that roar and foam, endangering the covenant community, yield to a peaceful, tranquil river whose streams gently flow through the "city of God," that is, Jerusalem. The scene is reminiscent of the Garden of Eden (Gen 2:10).[25] The reference to the river and its streams in Ps 46:4 is probably metaphorical because there is no river in Jerusalem.[26] The ancient city's water supply came from springs (e.g., Gihon), aqueducts, and underground tunnels. In fact, the lack of a consistent water supply was an ever-present danger during a prolonged siege.[27] Without water, what prevents the city from becoming a parched and dreadful place? From where will the people draw their strength in times of adversity? The psalmist explains the meaning of the metaphor in verse 5: God is the river! He is "in the midst" of the city. He sustains his people with his abiding presence. Scripture often uses gentle flowing waters, like rivers and streams, metaphorically for the God's Holy Spirit who quenches the spiritual thirst of the covenant community in a dry and barren world (Isa 44:3; 55:1; Ezek 36:25–27; 47:1–12; Zech 14:8; Joel 3:18; John 3:5; 4:10; 7:37–38; Titus 3:5; Rev 7:17; 22:1–2). Here, God's presence brings help, blessing, and peace in the midst of cosmic

---

22. McCann, *Theological*, 137. Gerald Wilson notes that chaotic waters threaten to destroy even the gods in ANE parallels; the gods "cower in fear" at the approaching floodwaters. Thus, the point in Ps 46:1–3 is that Yahweh reign supreme, and the waters are no threat to him (*Psalms*, 716).

23. Brueggemann and Bellinger, *Psalms*, 217.

24. Ibid.

25. Belcher, *Messiah*, 63.

26. Brueggemann and Bellinger, *Psalms*, 217.

27. Longman, *Psalms*, 205. Longman also notes that if Jerusalem had a river or other water supply, this would blunt the force of the psalmist's proclamation that God's presence is like a river. Theoretically, the people could rely on the water supply for their sustenance rather than the presence of God among them. God's presence, not a literal river, enhances the security of the city.

calamity.[28] Other ancient civilizations shared the symbolism of rivers that flowed from the sacred dwellings of the gods, especially mountains.[29] Such sacred places represented divine presence.[30] As Walter Brueggemann and William Bellinger explain, "The streams of water flow from the divine presence and bring nourishment and hope to the community. The refreshing cool waters coming from the divine presence bring joy to the city and thus to the community of faith."[31] Water symbolizes the refreshing presence of God in the midst of the city.

The theme of divine presence continues in verse 4b as the psalmist describes the presence of God in Zion—the location of his "holy habitation" (i.e., the temple). The reader should not overlook the royal imagery of God sitting on his throne in the temple in Jerusalem where his presence nourishes his people. The kingship of Yahweh and the choice of Zion/Jerusalem as the place of divine dwelling are theological affirmations that undergird the entire psalm, even if the royal palace imagery is limited to verse 4.[32] The city has no need to fear the cosmic instability because God has chosen to make his dwelling there among his people. Whatever the present crisis, it is only temporary, for God will help the city the very next morning (v. 5). As with mountains above, sacred places were often thought of as cities of the gods, which the psalmist echoes in verse 4. In the Babylonian creation epic Enuma Elish, the hero of the story, Marduk, builds a city immediately after conquering Tiamat, the goddess of the sea and her army of sea monsters.[33] This progression is much like Ps 46 where God protects his people against the roaring and foaming waters, followed by a reference to the city in which he manifests his presence. In Ps 46, the city is safe because God's holy dwelling is within its walls. He lives there and nourishes it as a river nourishes a city, securing and sustaining it. Even so, the point is not to encourage trust in the city, but in God. As James Mays states eloquently, "The song does not invite trust in a place but in a Presence who wills to dwell with his people."[34]

28. Belcher, *Messiah*, 62.
29. Mays, *Psalms*, 185.
30. Brueggemann and Bellinger, *Psalms*, 217.
31. Ibid.
32. Ibid., 218.
33. DeClaissé-Walford, et al., *Psalms*, 422–23.

34. Mays, *Psalms*, 185. In fact, God may withdrawal his presence from the city if the sinfulness of its inhabitants warrants it; this was the case in the Babylonian exile (Ps 74; Jer 7; Ezek 9—11).

The psalm-singer restates the cosmic devastation of verse 3 in human terms in verse 6, notably war.[35] But the exact relationship is unclear: the cosmic dissolution of verses 1–3 may be symbolic of human destruction (i.e., war) in verse 6; they may be two separate events altogether; or, they may be general descriptions covering a range of calamities from which God delivers his people—from cosmic instability to historical war. Whether the very foundations of the earth are in danger of collapse, or the threat of war from the enemies of God's people, God's presence brings peace and security to the community. God is present to defeat the forces of chaos and war in the world and is a refuge and peace to his people.[36] He brings hope and safety in the midst of crashing seas and warring nations.[37] To be clear, the threat is no longer cosmic forces, but the perpetual warring of the "nations" (v. 6). Military imagery saturates the remainder of the psalm and serves to underscore the chaos of the nations. The psalmist uses the same vocabulary about the nations and the cataclysmic events, underscoring the parallelism: the nations "rage" (*hamah*) as the waters "roar" (*hamah*), and the kingdoms "totter" (*mot*) as the mountains "move" (*mot*) into the heart of the sea. Nevertheless, the city "cannot be moved" (v. 5). The rest of the psalm contrasts international instability with the stability of God as the beginning contrasts cosmic chaos with the sovereignty of God.[38] As nations wage war against the people of God and each other, God is the divine warrior who fights for his people.

The divine warrior is a pervasive biblical concept, especially in Psalms where it occurs in seventy-five percent of the psalms in the Psalter.[39] This metaphor "provided the ancient Israelites with a powerful picture of protection and defense in the midst of the chaos of the natural and political world in which they lived."[40] Verses 7–11 bring this idea to the fore in Ps 46 as Yahweh brings an end to the wars of the nations. The divine-warrior theme depicts Yahweh as a warrior-god who fights for his people against forces that threaten them. These can be cosmic forces like

---

35. McCann, *Theological*, 138.
36. Brueggemann and Bellinger, *Psalms*, 219.
37. Ibid., 218.
38. McCann, *Theological*, 138.
39. DeClaissé-Walford, et al., *Psalms*, 424–25n9. With this all-too-brief discussion of the divine warrior motif, I do not intend to delve into the challenging topic of God-sanctioned violence in the OT. I am limiting my discussion of the divine warrior to the cosmic, not physical, dimension; the latter, while important, is beyond the scope of this book. For violence in the OT, see Boyd, *Cross Vision*; Enns, *The Bible Tells Me So*, 29–70; Seibert, *Violence of Scripture*; Sparks, *Sacred Word*, 30–44.
40. DeClaissé-Walford, et al., *Psalms*, 425.

the chaotic seas, which are home to mythic sea monsters, like Leviathan (74:12–17) or flesh-and-blood enemies, like the Egyptian armies at the exodus (Exod 15:1–3). He can even fight against Israel in judgment of its violation of the covenant (Lam 2:5).

The title that the psalmist uses for the divine warrior in Ps 46:7, 11 is "LORD of hosts" (lit. *YHWH Sabaoth*). This title is significant for two reasons. First, it is the covenant name of Israel's God, Yahweh (written in English translations as "LORD"), who is also the God of Jacob; hence, the refrain "The LORD of hosts is with us; the God of Jacob is our fortress" (46:7, 11).[41] Yahweh, the God of the patriarchs, enters into covenant with his people and pledges as a stipulation of the covenant to provide for and protect them. Second, he has an entire army of "hosts" (*tsabaoth*) at his disposal. This may refer to the armies of the nation of Israel, heavenly beings or angelic hosts, hosts of sun, moon, and stars, or a combination of these.[42]

What is more, the God of the patriarchs is a "fortress" for the covenant community in times of crisis (v. 7). The fortress metaphor links with the opening salvo on God's stability and security where he is a "refuge and strength," and a "well-proven help" for his people in troublesome times (v. 1).[43] The metaphors of refuge and fortress reinforce the rock-solid reputation of Yahweh. The larger context suggests that God has at his disposal an innumerable host of armies to defend the cause of his people. Not only is he capable of defending his people from the onslaughts of the warring nations, he does so by bringing an end to war altogether (vv. 8–9). The psalm describes how God ends war in two ways. First, the psalmist invites his readers to consider the "marvelous" or "appalling" (*shammoth*) works of Yahweh that end wars. This probably refers to his acts of judgment on warring nations. For example, recall how God decimated the Assyrian army that encamped around Jerusalem in 2 Kgs 19:32–36.[44] God rallies around his people and decimates their enemies. Second, he has the power to stop wars by destroying the weapons of war, like bows, spears, and chariots (Ps 46:9).[45] He makes wars cease, and as a result ushers in an era of peace and universal shalom (cf. Isa 2:4). John Eaton describes this as a vision of

---

41. The refrain in vv. 7 and 11 and may have originally followed v. 3 in conjunction with the three occurrences of *Selah* (Tesh and Zorn, *Psalms*, 337).

42. Brueggemann and Bellinger, *Psalms*, 218.

43. Wilson, *Psalms*, 718.

44. Tesh and Zorn, *Psalms*, 338.

45. Belcher, *Messiah*, 63. Longman notes that the word for "chariot" may also be translated "shield" (NIV); the point remains the same (*Psalms*, 205n6).

"beautiful destruction" as weapons lie in piles across the earth, broken up and burned—for the Lord has ended wars, as only he could.[46]

Psalm 46:10, one of the most quotable verses in the Psalter, serves as a culmination to the battle scenes of verses 8–9. The poet quotes God directly: "Stop your warring!" In the battle context of verses 7–11, "Be still" is not an invitation to contemplative spirituality—though there is nothing wrong with that per se—but a command to cease making war. There are two additional caveats to interpreting the verse. It may be a command to the warring nations to "cease their rebellion and bow before God" and acknowledge his sovereignty.[47] Or, a better alternative is to see it as a command to both the foe and faithful alike as the voice of the triumphant divine warrior who breaks into the scene, calling "all combatants to stop their fighting and pay attention. Only when they stop their struggles can they acknowledge that Yahweh is God."[48] I appreciate the paraphrase of Tesh and Zorn: "Stop! Be quiet! Stop your babbling and warring! Know that I am the one and only God!"[49] The addressees should trust not in their military solutions for peace, but in the sovereignty of God, the divine warrior, who, ironically, does battle to defeat war and the weapons of war.[50] The foe, then, whether willingly or unwilling, will "exalt" Yahweh and confess his kingship over the earth (v. 10). The refrain in verse 11 concludes the psalm like a resounding battle cry, repeating the community's confidence in Yahweh's power and presence as forces of security and stability in the midst of chaos. Clearly, Ps 46 functions as a communal affirmation of confidence in the divine warrior's ability to safeguard his covenant community.

Christology

Psalm 46 inspired Martin Luther's famous song "A Mighty Fortress is Our God," the "battle hymn" of the Reformation. The song echoes the theme of the psalm, emphasizing God's presence among his people in the midst of chaotic circumstances. Luther interpreted Ps 46 christologically where Jesus is the divine warrior, Lord of hosts, whose presence safeguards his people. The Christology of the song is most apparent in the second verse:

---

46. Eaton, *Psalms*, 191.
47. Belcher, *Messiah*, 63.
48. Wilson, *Psalms*, 718.
49. Tesh and Zorn, *Psalms*, 338.
50. Brueggemann and Bellinger, *Psalms*, 218.

> Did we in our own strength confide,
> Our striving would be losing,
> Were not the right Man on our side,
> The Man of God's own choosing.
> You ask who that may be?
> Christ Jesus, it is he;
> Lord Sabaoth his name,
> From age to age the same;
> And he must win the battle.[51]

Therefore, the Christian reader of the psalm finds confidence in Christ's presence as the divine warrior.[52] Luther is certainly not alone in his christological interpretation of the divine warrior. The NT takes up the OT motif and applies it to Jesus Christ. Due to the vastness of the divine warrior motif itself, not to mention its manifold application in the NT to Jesus Christ, I can address its christological application only briefly here and refer the reader to other sources that give it more sustained treatment.[53] The NT applies the motif to Christ in several ways, but I want to address two primary uses for the sake of brevity: Jesus's ministry as a new exodus, and his ultimate victory over the enemies of God's people at the Second Coming.

First, his ministry is described as a new exodus for the people of God, notably in the Gospel of Mark (although not limited to Mark). I showed previously that Exod 15:1–3 portrays Yahweh as a warrior who rescues his people at the exodus, destroying the Egyptian armies, and eventually leading Israel into the Promised Land. Jesus's ministry in the Gospel of Mark builds on the new exodus expectation of the OT, which anticipates a future time of deliverance for God's people reminiscent of the first exodus. Mark begins with a blended scriptural reference to Mal 3:1, Exod 23:20, and Isa 40:3, and suggests a progression in the wilderness through which the divine warrior will march to his sacred mountain, defeating his foes, delivering his people from oppression, and establishing his sovereign reign: "Behold, I send my messenger before your face, who will prepare your way, the voice of one crying in the wilderness: 'Prepare the way of the Lord, make his paths straight'" (Mark 1:2–3).[54] Beginning with John the Baptist's announcement

---

51. Martin Luther, "A Mighty Fortress is Our God," lines 10–18.
52. Longman, *Psalms*, 206.
53. Notably, Longman and Reid, *Warrior*.
54. Ibid., 92.

of "one more powerful than I" (1:7), the Gospel suggests a warrior figure who will initiate an epochal event in redemptive history.[55]

After the divine warrior is anointed at his baptism and tested in the wilderness (note the exodus symbols of water and wilderness), he proclaims the arrival of the kingdom of God; i.e., the realm in which God reigns and that has broken into human history in the person of Jesus of Nazareth, the Son of God (1:15). Implied in Jesus's proclamation and throughout Mark's Gospel is the immanent victory of God over the demonic forces that are currently ruling this age (cf. John 12:31), manifesting themselves in physical enemies, disease, death, and idolatry.[56] Mark's narrative centers on Jesus as the divine warrior who battles and defeats his enemies—cosmic forces of evil who persecute his people—who take multiple forms like demons and raging seas. Jesus repeatedly casts out demons as evidence of the immanent victory of the kingdom. What is more, demons know exactly who he is and that he has the power to rebuke and destroy them (Mark 1:24–25). That Jesus "casts out" (*ekballō*) demons shows that he forces them to submit to his authority as the Spirit-anointed messianic king. Yet Jesus is not the only one who defeats demonic forces; his twelve apostles join him as a miniature army of the kingdom—symbolic of the twelve tribes of Israel who fight for the Promised Land—to cast out demons and proclaim the reign of God (6:7, 13). In the OT exodus and conquest narratives, the twelve tribes may be regarded as twelve military divisions prepared for battle under the ultimate leadership of Yahweh, the divine warrior.[57]

Jesus, as the divine warrior, also subdues other cosmic foes of God, like the chaotic waters. When he stills the storm on the Sea of Galilee (4:35–41), he demonstrates his dominion over the abyss in ways reminiscent of Yahweh in the OT. As I discussed in both Pss 29 and 46, waters were regarded as cosmic enemies within the Baal myths, and Israelite traditions echo this sentiment in similar ways, portraying the sea as a cosmic foe of Yahweh (Job 26:11; 38:8–11; Pss 65:7; 74:13–14; 89:9–10; 107:23–25; Isa 51:9–10; Hab 3:8, 15).[58] Jesus rebukes the wind and commands the waves, "Peace! Be still!" (Mark 4:39). What is more, the original language of "rebuke" (*epitimaō*) and "be still" or "be muzzled" (*phimoō*) is identical to Mark's first account of Jesus's casting out a demon (1:25), suggesting an underlying

---

55. Ibid., 93.

56. Ibid., 98, 102.

57. Ibid., 103. Similarly, the seventy-two disciples in Luke's Gospel are given authority to "tread on serpents and scorpions, and over all the power of the enemy" (Luke 10:19). Serpents and scorpions were synonyms of demonic powers in the literature of the period (p. 104).

58. Ibid., 114.

identity between these two phenomena: they are complimentary episodes of the divine warrior vanquishing his foes.[59] Therefore, the use of exorcism language provides a cosmological context for the story of Jesus stilling the storm.[60] Even the terminology of "storm" (*lailaps*) in 4:37 carries overtones of demonic power.[61] With Jesus's victories over demons and the sea, Mark clearly intends to illustrate how the divine warrior plunders the cosmic forces of evil.

The psalm also evokes the book of Revelation, which offers a glimpse at the cosmic, end-times battle where Jesus, the divine warrior, conquers the enemies of God's people. Specifically, Rev 19:11–21 gives a particularly vivid—even if symbolic—description of Jesus's final battle against evil. It is beyond the scope of this book to get into the hotly debated interpretive issues of Revelation. Suffice it to say here that my assumption is that the symbolism throughout the book is just that—symbolism—and need not be taken literally or allegorically to make sense of this complex piece of literature. In other words, the symbols themselves are not the message; they simply embody and carry the message. Nevertheless, its main point, while cast in apocalyptic images, centers on the ultimate victory of the divine warrior and the consummation of his eternal kingdom.

Contrary to popular opinion, which tends to use the Bible's apocalyptic literature like an ancient telescope, focusing its lenses on the most dazzling news headlines of the future—notably those in the Western hemisphere where prophetic speculation runs rampant among many authors and televangelists—apocalyptic literature always addresses the immediate trials and tribulations of persecuted peoples. It does not give a precise chronology of future events waiting to be decoded by a wildly imaginative, modern-day "prophet" with a calculator. Rather, it interprets earthly events, especially the struggles and persecutions of God's people, as manifestations of the heavenly warfare between God and the forces of evil, and depicts the coming victory of God over those forces by means of symbolic images.[62] The images give hope for divine deliverance of the faithful in the face of intense persecution, resulting in the resurrection of the righteous and judgment of the wicked. The comforting message to persecuted peoples is that God will vindicate his saints, judge the disobedient, and triumph over all powers of evil.

---

59. Ibid., 114–15.
60. Perkins, *Mark*, 580.
61. Williamson, *Mark*, 101.
62. McCartney and Clayton, *Reader*, 240.

The images of Revelation often depict scenes of divine warfare, reminiscent of the mythic imagery associated with divine conflict in the OT.[63] For example, Isaiah describes a scene in which Yahweh, the divine warrior, wears a robe that looks as if he has stomped grapes in the winepress (Isa 63:2–3). The reader soon learns that it is not wine that has stained God's garments red, but the blood of his enemies, namely Edom: "I have trodden the winepress . . . I trod them in my anger and trampled them in my wrath; their lifeblood spattered on my garments, and stained all my apparel" (v. 3). This passage anticipates the OT motif of the Day of Lord—a future time when God will "intervene powerfully and decisively in human history to bring about his promised plan," which includes enacting judgment on the enemies of his people.[64]

John echoes this staggering scene from Isa 63 and applies its imagery to Jesus in Rev 19:11–21. The vision begins with Jesus, the "Word of God" (cf. John 1:1), riding onto the battlefield on a white warhorse; his eyes are blazing with fire, and his robe has been dipped in blood (Rev 19:11–13); not his own blood shed on the cross, but that of his enemies who he has trampled during the battle.[65] The context of 19:11–21 is not redemption, but retribution. Jesus appears in the vision as a blood-soaked warrior intent on finishing the cosmic battle. What is more, he has a sharp sword protruding from his mouth, symbolizing the word of God, or the gospel of the kingdom, which is both a word of salvation for God's people and a word of condemnation for his enemies.[66] The "armies of heaven," who may be the saints, angelic hosts, or both, accompany him to the battle, evoking the "Lord of hosts" in the OT (e.g., Ps 46:7, 11). We need not be precise about the identity of the divine warrior's army in Revelation because as we will see, they do not participate in the battle; they do not fight. Instead, John focuses on the achievement and glory of Christ alone.[67] The enemies of the divine warrior are the beast, the false prophet, and the kings of the earth and their armies (Rev 19:19), each symbolizing those who are persecuting Christians in Asia Minor toward the end of the first-century CE (i.e., the Roman Empire), as well the great dragon, the ancient serpent, who is the devil and Satan (20:2).

In anticipation of the final battle, an angel calls for vultures and other scavenging birds to gather over a battlefield of soon-to-be dead bodies in

---

63. Longman and Reid, *Warrior*, 180.
64. Longman, "Day of the Lord," 407.
65. Poythress, *Retuning King*, 174–75.
66. Davis, *Revelation*, 346.
67. Poythress, *Returning King*, 175.

eager excitement of the "great supper of God," the so-called "gory supper," at which they will feast on the dead corpses of the divine warrior's enemies (19:17–18; cf. Ezek 39:4, 17–18). This is a grotesque image to be sure, but it functions as the counterpart of the blessed and beautiful messianic banquet of the Lamb in Rev 19:9, serving as a visible victory over the persecuting powers. Next comes the battle itself. Shockingly, John recounts no battle at all. Perhaps it is assumed, but the subsequent verses describe no "clash of arms" between the divine warrior and his armies and the enemy.[68] In fact, the armies of the Messiah never draw their weapons.[69] In fact, the only fighting that occurs is when the sword coming from the divine warrior's mouth kills the enemy armies after he has captured the beast and the false prophet and thrown them alive in to the lake of fire (19:19–21), symbolizing how Christ simply declares his enemies vanquished by his authoritative word, and it is so. As Christopher Davis states, "The final judgment is no contest."[70] The battle is swiftly won.

As a final note of conquest, John recounts yet another vision of the divine warrior's victory as he captures the dragon and his armies who had surrounded God's people, the "beloved city" (20:9), a scene that is reminiscent of the nations surrounding the city of God in Ps 46. Once again, John recounts this final episode in the briefest of terms: "But fire came down from heaven and consumed them" (20:9).[71] The war is over. The end result of the divine warrior's victory is the renewal of the heavens and the earth (21:1). This victory is so exhaustive and final that the sea, the ancient enemy of the divine warrior in the OT, and archetype of cosmic evil, has no place in the renewed cosmos: "Then I saw a new heaven and new earth, for the first heaven and the first earth had passed away, and the sea was no more" (21:1).[72] The divine warrior has finally and fully conquered all the forces of evil so he can dwell among his covenant people in the renewed cosmos (21:3), where they are liberated from every trial and tribulation (21:4). God does not simply deliver his people from oppression, but also dwells with them. What is more, they can finally drink freely from the peaceful river of life (22:1), which echoes Ps 46:4 and the river that flows through the city of God, symbolizing God's presence. Indeed, Jesus is the full revelation of the

---

68. Davis, *Revelation*, 349.

69. Ibid. Davis aptly notes that there is no literal "Battle of Armageddon," as popularly conceived.

70. Ibid., 349.

71. Longman and Reid, *Warrior*, 187.

72. Ibid.

divine warrior from the OT who executes judgment against all the enemies of God and his people.[73]

While it is tempting to get caught up in the war imagery of Revelation, the imagery serves the larger goal of encouraging the discouraged—to give God's people the earnest expectation that he will set the fallen world to rights, which includes not only their own redemption, but also divine retribution on those who persecute them. The warfare scenes of Rev 19—20 are about nothing less than the eradication of evil. While these scenes, especially the gory supper, may be challenging to many Christians who view Jesus as the Prince of Peace (Isa 9:6), the good shepherd (John 10:11), or the great physician (Luke 4:23), their function is to provide hope for his people who endure intense persecution. Put differently, to the messianic community he *does* bring peace between God and fallen humanity, to Jesus's flock he *is* the gentle and good shepherd, and to those who have suffered ailments of every kind—both spiritual and physical—he *is* the great physician. But he is at the same time the divine warrior who fights for his people, and it is also through this image that he brings wars to an end, defends his flock against its enemies, and defeats disease and death. As Vern Poythress observes: "The Bible as a whole, as well as Revelation, indicates that the Second Coming is for the purpose of salvation and renewal of the world (Rev 21:1–8), as well as destruction. But 19:11–21 focuses on the destructive aspects. Evil must be destroyed, not only for the sake of God's justice, but for the sake of the purity of the new world (21:27)."[74]

Again, we must be careful not to miss the *symbolic* nature of divine warfare in Revelation. It is not, and will not be, a literal war between Christians and flesh and blood enemies, but a spiritual war between the forces of good and evil. Remember that for ancient Judaism, cosmic forces of evil lay behind earthly forces of evil, so this remains a spiritual battle, not a literal one. The beast, the false prophet, the wicked kings of the earth, and their armies, symbolize the forces of evil and chaos.[75] This, when combined with the fact that the armies of Christ do not actually fight in the final battle, should caution Christians who would interpret this passage as a call to arms, and as a summons to holy war on earth against the "enemies" of Christianity now or in anticipation of the Second Coming. After all, it is only Jesus who "makes war" in Revelation, but he does so by dying on the cross. It is through his sacrifice that he conquers the kingdom

---

73. Andreas J. Köstenberger, et al., *Cradle*, 861.

74. Poythress, *Returning King*, 175.

75. Davis, *Revelation*, 348. Recall that in Rev 11: 7 and 13:1 the beast arises from the sea, which further connects Revelation's symbolic world to that of the OT, esp. the divine warrior's taming of the chaotic waters (Longman and Reid, *Warrior*, 188).

of Satan (5:9–10), and it is through his sacrifice that believers participate in his ultimate victory: "And they have conquered him by the blood of the Lamb" (12:11). Davis has rightly concluded, "Christians have no need to take a weapon at the time of the final judgment. The struggle is over and their victory is already secured."[76] The NT affirms that he is indeed the Prince of Peace; he has come to establish peace between God and sinful humanity (Eph 2:11–17), which will one day manifest itself in the ceasing of all wars.[77] In light of Revelation's vivid and violent divine warrior motif, ironically, Jesus commands all warring peoples: "Be still and know that I am God" (Ps 46:10).

In the analysis of Ps 23, I noted one of the dominant themes of the psalm was God's presence with the psalmist: "For you are with me" (23:4). The dwelling theme reaches its christological culmination in Jesus who promises to dwell with his people forever (Matt 28:20). The same theme of God's presence is evident in Ps 46, arguably even more so than in Ps 23, especially in the twice-repeated refrain "The LORD of hosts is with us" (46: 7, 11). But there is a subtle difference between the two psalms: Ps 23 speaks of God's presence with the individual psalmist (i.e., "with me"), while Ps 46 speaks of his presence among the community (i.e., "with us"). In terms of the community dimension of Ps 46, we see the theme of divine dwelling come to its fullest expression in Jesus Christ in Matthew's Gospel, which goes to great lengths to demonstrate that God's presence dwells within the messianic community in the person of Christ. As Matt 1:23 affirms, "They shall call his name 'Immanuel' (which means, God with us)." The two-fold refrain in Ps 46 affirms that God is "with us"; the Hebrew is *immanu*, and a close look at the word shows that it is almost identical to the name given to the Messiah in Matthew's Gospel—"Immanuel" (with the addition of *el*, which is Heb. for "God"). God's protective, providing, and peaceful presence in the psalm finds its most complete expression in Christ Jesus our Lord, abiding in our midst all days, even to the end of the world.[78] In additional to Matthew, John speaks of God's dwelling among mortals as being inseparably linked to Jesus Christ, who has "dwelt among us" (John 1:14).[79] John adopts the imagery of the tabernacle and temple traditions of the OT, using the verb "to dwell" (*skēnoō*), which is related to the noun *skēnē*, which is used of the tabernacle in the LXX.[80] The divine presence in 1:14 echoes

---

76. Davis, *Revelation*, 350. See also, Keener, *Revelation*, 456–59.
77. Belcher, *Messiah*, 64.
78. Reardon, *Christ*, 90.
79. Mays, *Psalms*, 185.
80. Belcher, *Messiah*, 64.

the sentiments of Ps 46 from a christological perspective: Christ is the reality of the manifestation of God's presence with his people.[81] Indeed, Jesus fulfills the psalmist's proclamation that God is with us.

As we have seen above with other psalms, notably Pss 1 and 23, the OT anticipates the messianic community—the people who belong to the Messiah—the church. This is especially true of Ps 46, which I have described as a communal hymn of confidence. The first person plural pronouns make it especially suitable for a community of faith that is gathered for worship. Psalm 46 speaks of the "city of God," Jerusalem, the location of the temple. However, the psalm's emphasis is less about the place and more about the presence of God among his people (e.g., "God is in the midst of her," v. 5). God dwells in the city, and this is the theme of the psalm as illustrated by two-fold refrain: "The LORD of hosts is with us; the God of Jacob is our fortress" (vv. 7, 11). From a Christian perspective, this sounds an ecclesiological note in the psalm where the church is the holy city—the place of God's dwelling.[82] For Dietrich Bonhoeffer, "What Mount Zion and the temple were for the Israelites the church of God throughout the world is for us—the church where God always dwells with his people."[83] Reardon states the matter succinctly: "The voice in the psalm is that of the church, the dwelling place of God."[84] The church has no fear when the earth is full of chaos, or when its enemies advance against it because believers are the dwelling place of God's Spirit, both corporately (1 Cor 3:16–17) and individually (1 Cor 6:19). In spite of the tumult of the world, the church of God remains secure and stable. Thus, the first three verses of the psalm reflect God's protection of his church in the midst of the conflict and instability of this world.[85] What is more, this is no modest or underestimated theme in Scripture—God's people as a holy city.[86] Along with the long-awaited Messiah, Jewish messianism also anticipated an end-times Jerusalem, which would provide the center from which God's reign would expand throughout the world.[87] After the Babylonian exile, prophets like Ezekiel anticipated the restoration of the people, land, city (i.e., Jerusalem), and temple (Ezek 37—48; cf. Jer 3:17; Zech 14:11).[88]

---

81. Ibid.
82. Reardon, *Christ*, 89.
83. Bonhoeffer, *Psalms*, 40.
84. Reardon, *Christ*, 89.
85. Ibid., 90.
86. Ibid., 89.
87. Wilson, *Psalms*, 720.
88. Ibid.

It should come as no surprise, then, that the dominant image of humanity's eternal home with God in the book of Revelation is a city, the "new Jerusalem" (Rev 21:1—22:5). What is a temporal and tentative dwelling place for God in the OT is a permanent place for his presence among his people in Revelation, and the latter is the fulfillment of the former. Even the river that symbolizes God's presence in Ps 46:4 finds its ultimate fulfillment in the new Jerusalem: "To the thirsty I will give from the spring of the water of life" (Rev 21: 6). And "Then the angel showed me the river of the water of life, bright as crystal, flowing from the throne of God and of the Lamb through the middle of the street of the city" (22:1–2). The cumulative effect is the "city of God" of Ps 46:4–5 anticipates its fullest expression in the new Jerusalem, the "holy city" (Rev 21:2). Again, as in Ps 46, the emphasis in Revelation is less about a place and more about presence: "Look! God's dwelling place is now among the people, and he will dwell with them. They will be his people, and God himself with be with them and be their God" (Rev 21:3 NIV). Divine presence is the most prominent theme in all of Scripture, which uses a variety of expressions that build on one another, culminating in the new Jerusalem: God dwelt among humanity in the Garden of Eden (Gen 2:7, 16; 3:8), in the tabernacle in the wilderness (Exod 25:8; 40:34), in the temple in the holy city (1 Kgs 8; Ps 46:4–5), and above all in Jesus Christ (John 1:14). God pours out his Spirit so that the church may be the dwelling of God (1 Cor 3:16; 6:19). The new Jerusalem is the culmination of these as the pinnacle and peak of God's presence among his people.[89]

Revelation's description of the holy city, while vivid, centers on God's dwelling among his renewed creation, and evokes the theme of divine presence of Ps 46.[90] Whatever threats, whether natural or man made, are behind the words of the psalmist, they are eliminated completely in the new Jerusalem when God wipes away every tear, having conquered death, mourning, crying, and pain (Rev 21:4). In other words, Zion represented God's presence among his people because the temple was located there. But the presence of sin made his dwelling provisional and tentative. God could withdraw his presence due to the sinfulness of the people. Because he defeated sin and death and the crucifixion and resurrection respectively, the

---

89. Poythress, *Returning King*, 186.

90. It is beyond the scope here to get into the nature of the new creation. I share the assumption of Poythress that it is a renewal of the old creation, not a new creation from scratch: "Some have thought that the new universe will be an entirely new one, having no connection with the old. But Isaiah 65:17–25 and Romans 8:21–23 indicate that a transfiguration of the old world is in view. . . . Everything is new (21:5), but the result is the redemption of the old, not its abolition" (ibid., 185). See also, Hicks, et al., *Embracing Creation*.

new Jerusalem is a more perfect dwelling of God's presence with humanity. Stanley Grenz summarizes, "The greatest statement we can make is that the eternal community will be a place where God is present. It will mark the completion of the promise that runs throughout the entire Bible, namely, that God will be present among his people."[91] Psalm 46, then, is a communal hymn of confidence in the securing and sustaining presence of God, symbolized by the river that flows through Zion. The psalm anticipates Jesus Christ as the flesh and blood dwelling of God among humanity, the divine warrior who delivers his people from their enemies, and the new Jerusalem as the eternal dwelling of God among the messianic community.

---

91. Grenz, *Community*, 842–43.

Psalm 67

"Because one had fallen, it rose again with many; one grain of wheat has fallen into the ground and a fruitful harvest came of it."
—Jerome

History

PSALM 67 MAKES A grandiose boast for such a small psalm. In only seven verses, the psalm proclaims God's universal sovereignty as the provider and sustainer of both Israelites and non-Israelites. The distribution of vocabulary hints at the main message of the psalm as "God," "us/our," and "peoples" are repeated six, seven, and seven times respectively, illustrating the sovereignty of God over Israel and all other nations. In short, "the peoples/nations"—OT terminology for Gentiles—will join with Israel to extol God for his abundant provisions.

That the Gentiles would sing praises to God for his blessings is not what one might expect upon reading the OT. Throughout the OT, the Gentiles are often hostile to God's covenant people, portrayed as idol worshipers and pagans, and are the epitome of impurity and uncleanness. However, this is only half true; in fact, the OT reflects attitudes about the Gentiles that range from hatred to full acceptance.[1] The Psalter itself evidences this range of attitudes. Some psalms speak of the hostility of the nations against Israel, which makes the nations unfortunate recipients of the wrath of the divine warrior who destroys them on behalf of Israel (Pss 2:1–3; 33:10; 46:6–10; 48:4–6; 76; 97:6–7). Other psalms are much less hostile and speak of God's kingship over the nations, calling them to acclaim their rightful and righteous king (7:7–8; 22:27–31; 47:8–9; 82; 86:9; 96:10–13; 99:1–5).[2] Christopher Wright observes that various psalms "not only soar into the presence of God in adoration, confession, thanksgiving, praise and protest,

---

1. Gowan, *Eschatology*, 42.
2. Ibid., 45.

they also take wings and fly to the ends of the earth and bring the nations of the world into the scope of their vision."[3] Therefore, Ps 67 goes further than a simple affirmation of God's kingship, for it declares God's providential care of the nations in addition to Israel. The attitude of the poet toward Gentiles is not only "nonadversarial,"[4] but also downright missional.[5] This missional spirit is especially evident in Israel in the exilic and postexilic periods; and it is likely no mere coincidence that the Psalter was shaped during these periods. Isaiah, notably among OT prophets, prophesies about the salvation of the Gentiles in terms of both Israel (Isa 60:2–3) and the Servant of the Lord (49:6) as being a light to the nations. Similarly, Isa 40—66 speaks of the immanent fulfillment of the promise of blessing to all the families of the earth through the offspring of Abraham (cf. Gen 12:3).[6] What is more, while God only calls Israel "my inheritance," the nations also occupy a special place in his heart, referring even to the ancient enemies of Israel, the Egyptians and Assyrians, as "my people" and the "work of my hands" respectively (Isa 19:24–25).

There is some debate as to whether postexilic Israel actively sought proselytes or simply stood as a testimony to God's glory by being willing recipients of his grace.[7] The former is an active method of outreach that *seeks* proselytes while the latter is passive that *accepts* them. John Calvin takes the missional mindset of Ps 67 in the passive sense: "Every benefit which God bestowed upon his ancient people was, as it were, a light held out before the eyes of the world, to attract the attention of the nations to him."[8] Either way, the goal was not for Israel to hoard the blessings of God, but to praise him for distributing them also to the nations. To be clear, the focus of the psalm is neither Israel nor the nations per se; instead, *God* is the focus because he distributes his blessings throughout the earth. John Eaton summarizes the theocentric nature of Ps 67:

> The sight and sound of strong rain made the people of the Psalms think directly of blessing from heaven; the rising green of earth told of the shining face of God, bright with favour. Good crops and flocks and herds spoke of his passing through the earth, the victor over chaos, the Creator who wrought the miracle of life.

---

3. Wright, *Mission*, 74. E.g., Pss 22:27–28; 47:9; 67; 72:17; 86:9; 87; 96; 102:15, 21–22; 117.

4. Wilson, *Psalms*, 925.

5. Tesh and Zorn, *Psalms*, 447.

6. Gowan, *Eschatology*, 52.

7. Ibid.

8. Calvin, *Psalms*, Apple e-book, ch. 67.

But the joy of all the earth was to be not so much in the gifts themselves, as in him, the savior, "God, our God." The glad song was a thanksgiving, a testimony to the ruler and guide of all creation. And to him, at every stage of the year's growth, prayer was raised, as to the one who alone could so give and sustain life.[9]

Eaton illustrates the common belief that Ps 67 may have originally been sung during a harvest festival, notably the Feast of Tabernacles, given the reference to the earth that has "yielded its increase" in verse 6.

The genre of Ps 67 is related to the Gentile issue above, but it is complicated by the translation of the main verbs in verses 3–5. If the verbs are translated as imperatives, the psalm is a prayer-wish (i.e., "Let the peoples praise you . . ."), and if translated as imperfects (i.e., "The peoples will praise you . . ."), the psalm is a prayer of thanksgiving.[10] We need not decide between these two because they both convey the same idea: the Gentiles acknowledge the reign of God and praise him for his bountiful provisions. As for the placement of Ps 67 in the Psalter, it follows Pss 65—66, which evidence similar themes that God's blessings upon his people will be extended to "all flesh" (65:2) and "all the earth" (66:1–4).[11] Therefore, the subset comprised of Pss 65—67 is another instance of microstructuring within the Psalter.

The structure of Ps 67 is at first glance very simple, consisting of three short stanzas separated by a refrain: a communal benediction invoking divine blessing and salvation (vv. 1–3), a prayer for universal praise of God for his just rule and sovereignty (vv. 4–5), and confidence in the universal blessing of God (vv. 6–7).[12] Upon closer inspection, however, the psalm has a chiastic structure, focusing on God's sovereign care of the nations:

> A Request for blessing and the global result (vv. 1–2)
>   B Refrain (v. 3)
>   C The confession of God's care of the nations (v. 4)
>   B1 Refrain (v. 5)
> A1 Another global result of the blessing (vv. 6–7).[13]

Psalm 67 begins with a rewording of the Aaronic (or Priestly) blessing of Num 6:24–26, which reads: "The LORD bless you and keep you; the LORD make his face to shine upon you and be gracious to you; the LORD lift up his

---

9. Eaton, *Psalms*, 246.

10. DeClaissé-Walford, et al., *Psalms*, 538n2. I will follow the ESV here in translating the psalm as a prayer-wish.

11. Wilson, *Psalms*, 925; DeClaissé-Walford, et al., *Psalms*, 539.

12. Wilson, *Psalms*, 926.

13. DeClaissé-Walford, et al., *Psalms*, 538.

countenance upon you and give you peace." The poet's first substantial change to the blessing involves a shift in the terms used for God. The original blessing in Numbers uses the covenant name of Israel's God, Yahweh.[14] However, Ps 67, consistent with many psalms in Book 2 of the Psalter (esp. the so-called Elohistic Psalter comprised of Pss 42—83), opts for the more general "God" rather than the divine name, possibly because of the universal tone of Book 2.[15] As to be expected, the original blessing applies only to Israel as God's covenant people, and this context invokes Yahweh's name and the blessings associated with Israel's covenantal relationship with its God. Because "face" is often a metaphor for presence in the OT,[16] the implication is that Israel's covenant with Yahweh is an intimate relationship where God abides by the terms of the covenant to bless Israel with his divine presence for their safety and sustenance. Yahweh "blesses them by granting them an intimate relationship with himself and a harmonious one with other people, as well as providing material benefits such as abundant crops and large happy families" (Deut 28).[17] What is more, throughout the Psalter, the shining of God's "face" or "light" is regularly coupled with the anticipation of deliverance, redemption, or salvation.[18] The totality of the face-metaphor shows that God delivers his people and dwells with them. Psalm 67:1, therefore, reflects the original intent of the Aaronic blessing with the use of "us" as the recipients of God's covenant blessings, namely Israel.

Even so, verse 1 should not be read in isolation, but must be coupled with verse 2, which expands the original blessing to include "all nations." The amplifying effect of the parallelism should not be missed. God blesses Israel and causes his face to shine upon them (v. 1); what is more, he does this not only for the benefit of Israel, but also for those outside of Israel (v. 2). In other words, verse 2 is dependent on verse 1 and gives the reason why God blesses Israel: so that God's way and salvation may be made known among the nations.[19] Thus, the poet's second substantial change to the original blessing involves its expansion to include non-Israelites. He does not ask for God's mercy upon Israel alone, but that non-Hebrew nations might also come to a knowledge of God and his salvation.[20] A consequence of the blessings to Israel is that the life-giving power of God will be known beyond

---

14. Tesh and Zorn, *Psalms*, 448.
15. Wilson, *Psalms*, 929.
16. Longman, *Psalms*, 256.
17. Ibid.
18. Wilson, *Psalms*, 927.
19. DeClaissé-Walford, et al., *Psalms*, 539.
20. Tesh and Zorn, *Psalms*, 448.

Israel in the world.[21] For the psalmist, God's blessings upon Israel are also distributed to the nations so they too may "know," that is, experience, the same blessings as Israel as a result of an intimate relationship with God. Therefore, God's "way" in verse 2a is none other than his sovereign and mighty provision for humanity, which the poet describes as God's "saving power" (v. 2b). God's abundant blessings on Israel serve as a challenge to the nations to recognize and seek him.[22] Verse 3 completes the first stanza by carrying forward the thought expressed in verse 2, namely, that the Gentiles may know the power of God.

Verse 3 functions as the "central confession" of the psalm, which the poet repeats twice as a refrain (vv. 3, 5).[23] Where verse 2 uses the terminology of "nations" to describe non-Israelites, verse 3 uses the synonym "all peoples" as an ethnic descriptor (i.e., Gentiles).[24] Not only will the peoples recognize God's kingship, they will praise him for his sovereign provisions. The cumulative effect of the first three verses reinforces the fact that God's covenant with Abram was *so that* his offspring would be a blessing to the Gentiles: " . . . so that you will be a blessing . . . in you all the families of the earth shall be blessed" (Gen 12:3). God's covenant with Israel does not secure their isolation from the Gentiles as the haves and have-nots. Israel does not monopolize God's blessings, but is a conduit for the Abrahamic blessing to the nations.[25] Therefore, the psalmist reinterprets the original Aaronic blessing so that it extends also to the Gentiles, which is part and parcel to God's covenant with Abram. The eventual blessing of the Gentiles is built into the fabric of God's promise to Abram. In other words, the psalmist has taken the Aaronic blessing of Num 6:24–26 to its logical conclusion based on the very substance of the original covenant of Abraham. As Wright notes, "Whatever God is doing in and through Israel itself must ultimately impact the nations, for that is the reason for Israel's existence in the first place."[26]

Not only is God's saving power an occasion for God's praise among the nations, so also his judgment (v. 2). This may sound strange to modern readers, especially Christians who tend to think of God's judgment solely as his punishment of sin. For many, the Day of Judgment is to be feared above all, like in the opening line to the song "That Day of Wrath" by Thomas of

---

21. Brueggemann and Bellinger, *Psalms*, 290.
22. Tesh and Zorn, *Psalms*, 448.
23. McCann, *Psalms*, 940.
24. Tesh and Zorn, *Psalms*, 448.
25. Longman, *Psalms*, 256.
26. Wright, *Mission*, 74.

Celano: "That day of wrath, that dreadful day . . ."[27] C. S. Lewis notes that the psalmists do not share this fearful sentiment, for judgment is an occasion of "universal rejoicing."[28] What is more, the different outlooks between the ancient psalmist and the modern-day Christian is because the former viewed God's judgment like a civil court case with himself as the plaintiff; whereas, the latter views it like a criminal case, with himself or herself in the dock.[29] The former hopes for resounding triumph with heavy damages; the latter acquittal.[30] The Jews eagerly anticipated the "Day of the Lord" as the moment where God would set the world to rights, vindicate the suffering of the righteous, eradicate all injustice, coronate the messianic king, and yes, judge the sinful acts of the enemies of Israel. But even this last divine action (judgment of Israel's enemies, Isa 13:1–22; Obad 15) is frequently combined with prophecies of the restoration of both Israel and the nations (Isa 11:10–12; Joel 3:14–18), which includes the outpouring of the Holy Spirit on all people (2:28–31).[31]

God's judgment is not a negative event for the psalmist, for it holds great promise that "God comes, not to destroy but to set the world right and bring all into God's kingdom."[32] Indeed the governance of God over the affairs of the world is the only assurance of equity (Ps 67:4). As a consequence of God's equitable governance, he "guides" the nations upon the earth (v. 4c). This phrase intensifies the previous one by describing *how* God governs the peoples. The term for "guide" (*nakhah*) is the same verb used in 23:3 for God's shepherd-like guidance of the psalmist: "He *leads* me in paths of righteousness."[33] God guides the nations in Ps 67 in the same way as Israel: conducting them in the right way, toward a predetermined destination, a desired goal as they share his blessings and trust in his governance.[34] It is because of this righteous reign of God over the nations that the psalmist repeats the refrain from verse 3 again in verse 5: "Let the peoples praise you, O God; let all the peoples praise you!" This refrain identifies the main point of the psalm: the hope or expectation that all the peoples of the earth will join in the praise of Israel's God.[35]

---

27. Thomas of Celano, "That Day of Wrath," line 1.
28. Lewis, *Reflections*, 9.
29. Ibid.
30. Ibid.
31. See Longman, "Day of the Lord," 407–08.
32. DeClaissé-Walford, et al., *Psalms*, 540.
33. Tesh and Zorn, *Psalms*, 449.
34. Ibid.
35. Wilson, *Psalms*, 927.

Most commentators see the original setting of the psalm as some kind of harvest festival because of the reference to the earth yielding its increase in verse 6a. When taken with the universal scope of the psalm, the idea of a fruitful earth is that a world united in the worship of God and in harmony with his ways will be a productive world.[36] What is more, the fruitful earth is God's blessing upon "us" (vv. 6b–7), which in verse 1 refers to Israel, based on the Aaronic blessing. The psalm, however, expands the blessing to include the nations so that "us" at the end of the psalm includes both Jews and Gentiles. The rhetorical effect of the psalm, therefore, draws the nations into the blessed "us."[37] Israel does not to monopolize the gracious gifts of God, but uses them as a beacon to draw the nations to him. Psalm 67 paints an idyllic picture of Israel not as mere consumers of God's blessings, but as distributers of them; and this is built into the very fabric of God's promise to Abraham, as well as the Aaronic blessing.

When God cut a covenant with Abraham in Gen 12:1–3, the substance of that covenant was *blessing*, in that he would be both blessed by God, as well as a blessing to the whole world. There is a fivefold use of the Hebrew root for "bless/blessing" (*barakh*): "And I will make of you a great nation, and I will *bless* you and make your name great, so that you will be a *blessing*. I will *bless* those who *bless* you, and him who dishonors you I will curse, and in you all the families of the earth shall be *blessed*" (vv. 2–3). Blessing is clearly the central theme of these verses. Abraham and his descendants will be the special recipients of God's covenant blessings and will eventually be a channel of blessing to all peoples. The first half of this blessing is more or less easy to grasp from the OT. Israel was God's special possession among humanity. There was to be a separation between Israel and the nations where the former displayed God's holiness and powerful presence for the latter to see. There was to be zeal for God's holiness and a passion for his righteous ways, which stood opposed to the uncleanness of the pagans. In one sense, God had chosen Israel to be his special privileged possession: the unique recipients of his redemption who walked intimately with him in covenant. James D. G. Dunn perceives that the "corollary of the axiom of Israel's election is, of course, the non-election of the other nations (Gentiles) . . . God's choosing Israel to be his own was that Israel should keep itself apart for Yahweh alone. *Separation to God* (being holy) necessitated *separation from other peoples*."[38] But this cannot be taken in isolation from Israel's larger function as a blessing to others, which is rooted in the Abrahamic

---

36. Tesh and Zorn, *Psalms*, 450.
37. Brueggemann and Bellinger, *Psalms*, 291.
38. Dunn, *Theology*, 101.

covenant. Even the Aaronic blessing of Num 6:22–27 with its initial focus on Israel as the covenant people of God, implies the extension of covenant blessings beyond the boarders of Israel. The Aaronic blessing reiterates the great covenant blessing of Gen 12:1–3.[39]

The Aaronic blessing is also called the "priestly" blessing not only because God initially gave it to Aaron and his sons, the first of Israel's priests, but because it describes the role of priests in the first place: to serve as the conduits of God's blessings to the people. To be clear, the priests do not bless the people; the blessing comes solely from the Lord; the priests' function is to channel it.[40] The ministries that a priest carries out on a daily basis are for the sake of others, not himself. He lives to bring blessing to Israel.[41] Yet God exhorted the people that they were to him a kingdom of priests (Exod 19:5), and this, too, implies not only that they were to live lives of holiness and separation from the unclean nations, but that they also did so for the benefit of their neighbors.

There is a dual function involved in Israel's priestly identity; Israel as a priestly kingdom lives for the sake of the nations; Israel is to be totally devoted to God's service and to model in its corporate life allegiance to the true God and the life of blessing that God meant for all.[42] Wright summarizes, "The priesthood of the people of God, then, is a *missional function*, which stands in continuity with their Abrahamic election and impacts the nations. Just as Israel's priests were called and chosen to be servants of God and his people, so Israel as a whole is called and chosen to be the servants of God and all peoples."[43] What is more, "blessing" especially in Numbers, is pervasive; it extends into all areas of life, including numerous descendants, fruitful land, good health, long life, protection from enemies, and God's abiding presence.[44] Therefore, the use of Aaronic blessing in Ps 67 points back to its origin in God's covenant with Abraham, extending it beyond the borders of Israel. For R. Dennis Cole, "Yahweh's blessing upon his faithful people Israel was in turn to be an instrument of blessing upon the nations of the world (Gen 12:3; 22:18). From the children of Abraham, Isaac, and Jacob, to their children's children, and to the ends of the earth, the purpose of

---

39. Cole, *Numbers*, 129.

40. Milgrom, *Numbers*, 50. Milgrom notes the threefold use of the divine name in the blessing formula itself (Num 6:24–26), as well as the literal wording of v. 27 as "and it is I" or "I Myself," which reflects the emphatic placement of *ani* ("I") in the Heb.

41. Goheen, *Light*, 38.

42. Ibid., 39.

43. Wright, *Mission*, 121.

44. Cole, *Numbers*, 129.

Yahweh's blessing of Israel was a worldwide mission of blessing and hope."[45] The blessings that God showered onto Israel as a consequence of his faithfulness to the covenant were also available to the Gentiles, according to the psalmist's interpretation of the Aaronic blessing in Ps 67.

Christology

Psalm 67 anticipates an era of universal allegiance to God where both Israel and its neighbors sing the praises of God for his provision and protection. Creation will worship as one family—comprised of Jews and Gentiles—its Creator who shows no favoritism. Calvin rightly views Ps 67 a "clear prophecy of that extension of the grace of God by which the Gentiles were united into one body with the posterity of Abraham."[46] The NT affirms that Jesus Christ is the fulfillment of the psalm's hope that all peoples will be drawn to God as the recipients of his blessings and grace.[47] Furthermore, the NT describes in more detail Israel's role in blessing the nations. Paul's argument in Gal 3, for example, goes to great lengths to explain that Jesus Christ is the offspring of Abraham who has blessed both Israel and the nations, making them one family of God. Paul's logic is not always easy to follow, but his close reading of God's covenant with Abraham moves him to conclude that Jesus is the summation of God's promises to unite Jews and Gentiles into one family. When arguing against the Galatian agitators who insisted that Gentiles become Jews in order to be saved, Paul draws an analogy between Abraham's faith and that of the Galatian Christians (3:7). Those who exhibit faith like Abraham, the "man of faith" (3:9), are his true children. Therefore, for Paul, God's promise of offspring to Abraham is more than physical descendants, but includes spiritual descendants as well; that is, those who mirror Abraham's faith, whether Jew or Gentile, are his family. What is more, the scriptural record of God's promise to Abraham—that all nations would be blessed through him—was a prophecy of "the gospel" (3:8); namely, membership in God's family extends beyond the borders and rituals of Israel and includes all those who, like Abraham, demonstrate faith in God's promises. The Gentile mission of the NT fulfills the expectation of Ps 67 and flows out of God's covenant with Abraham. It did not constitute a departure from Israel's election, but was actually a fulfillment of Israel's own mission.[48]

---

45. Ibid., 130.
46. Calvin, *Psalms*, Apple e-book, ch. 67.
47. Longman, *Psalms*, 257.
48. Dunn, *Theology*, 113.

Even more to the point is through whom God has brought about this plan of salvation: Abraham's "offspring," Jesus Christ (Gal 3:16). Paul reasons that God's covenantal promises to Abraham concerning his offspring (Gen 12:1–3, 7; 13:14–17; 15:5, 18; 17:4–8; 22:16–18; 24:7; 26:2–5) literally refer to a singular physical descendent of Abraham, even though the word for "offspring" (*sperma* in Gk., *zera* in Heb.) is often a collective singular, like "nation" in English, which implies many people. Surely, Paul is well aware that the collective noun can indicate a plurality of descendants (cf. Gal 3:29), as well as a single descendant.[49] He appeals to both senses in the larger context of Gal 3. On one hand, Paul clarifies that God's promise does not primarily concern many "offsprings," but a single "offspring" (3:16). This offspring is none other than Jesus Christ in 3:16. On the other hand, Paul expands the argument to include also the messianic community, those who are "in Christ," so that they, too, are the "offspring" of Abraham: "And if you are Christ's, then you are Abraham's offspring" (3:29). Paul understands that Scripture points to Christ as the singular offspring of Abraham, while at the same time anticipating multiple descendants for Abraham. This is an instance of corporate solidarity where Christ is the preeminent offspring of Abraham who represents a larger group of offspring.[50] Therefore, those who are in Christ are Abraham's offspring and heirs according to God's promise.[51]

By stating that Christ is the offspring, Paul interprets God's promises to Abraham in a Christian manner, and reveals that the Abrahamic covenant climaxes in Christ and those who believe in him.[52] Hence, the main theme of Gal 3:7—4:7 is oneness, Christian unity, which is implied in our solidarity in Christ.[53] Paul's exegesis throughout the argument may seem a flagrant violation to the original grammatical sense of the collective singular "offspring" in the Abraham narratives, but it is thoroughly consistent with the rabbinic exegesis of his day. What is different for Paul is his hermeneutical starting point (i.e., Christ is the summation of the promises to Abraham), which applies a christological interpretation on the OT text.[54] Paul reads the promises in Genesis as direct prophetic figurations of Christ.[55] Richard Hays summarizes Paul's christological and corporate exegesis: "Christ is the

---

49. Bruce, *Galatians*, 172.

50. For a more precise definition, see Virkler and Ayayo, *Hermeneutics*, 184–85.

51. Dunn, *Theology*, 116.

52. McKnight, *Galatians*, 167.

53. George, *Galatians*, 248.

54. Moo, *Galatians*, 230. Moo cites Gen. Rab. 22:9 as a similar example of a collective singular, which speaks of Abel's shed "bloods" as a reference to his descendants (p. 244).

55. Hays, *Galatians*, 264.

one true heir of the inheritance promised to Abraham, and Christ's people share in this inheritance only by becoming incorporated into his life."[56] It is ultimately through Christ that God's promises to Abraham are fulfilled, which includes, of course, the blessing of the nations, uniting both Jews and Gentiles under the Messiah as one family of God. All of this is built into the fabric of Ps 67 with its use of the Aaronic blessing, which reiterates God's covenant with Abraham. The universal commitment to God envisioned in Ps 67 results from the work of Christ as the blessing of Abraham (Gal 3:7–9).

The missional spirit of Ps 67 not only concerns Israel's mission to bless the nations, but also provides the missional directive of the church as the messianic community. Wright pointedly observes that because we are in Christ, "we not only share in the blessing of Abraham, we are commissioned to spread the blessing of Abraham."[57] In other words, the psalm not only points to Christ as the fulfillment of the Abrahamic blessing, but also to the church's share in that blessing as a priesthood and a holy nation who declares the excellencies of God (1 Pet 2:9). Therefore, the mandate for ancient Israel to be a blessing continues in the contemporary church. Again, Wright reminds us, "In Christ we inherit Abraham's blessing, we also inherit Abraham's mission—that is, to go and be a blessing, to be the means by which God's blessing comes to others."[58] It is no secret that the earliest Christians in Acts are missional, spreading the good news of Jesus's kingdom from Jerusalem, to Samaria, and to the ends of the earth (Acts 1:8). But it would be a mistake to ground the church's missional identity solely in Acts or even the Great Commission (Matt 28:19–20) without considering its participation in the blessing of Abraham in the OT. As stated earlier, both Christ and the messianic community are the "offspring" of Abraham. The church does not owe its origins to Pentecost alone, but also to Abraham, and its missional mandate stems from God's mission in Abraham to be a blessing to the nations.[59] Many Christians like to think of themselves as "New Testament Christians," eschewing directives from the OT as being indicative of their Christian practice, but the earliest Christians did not think of themselves this way. After all, the "New Testament church" did not actually have a New Testament to inform them of their mission. Instead, the OT Scriptures provided the motivation and justification for their outreach efforts.[60] Their Bible was the OT, and the stories of Abraham and Israel provided for them

---

56. Ibid.
57. Wright, *Mission*, 72.
58. Ibid., 81.
59. Ibid., 73.
60. Ibid., 29.

their missional calling whereby they participated in God's mission to redeem, restore, and reconcile humanity.

In an era in which Christianity has become largely focused on one's personal relationship to Jesus Christ, we need to hear the message of the church's mission in relation to that of Abraham and ancient Israel: to bless all peoples. The blessing of the church is for the salvation of the nations, so that they, too, may know God and experience his covenant blessings.[61] The message of the early church is not primarily "accept Jesus so you can go to heaven when you die"; instead, it implies a missional *application* of salvation in the present that is intensely practical, impacting the lives of others in addition to one's personal salvation both now and for eternity (Acts 2:42–47; 4:34–35). Once people pledge their allegiance to Christ through baptism, being invigorated by the Holy Sprit, they begin to live redemptive lives by sharing God's blessings with others. In our present era of racial friction, socio-economic separation, and gender inequality, the message of God's reconciliation of humanity—the substance of the Abrahamic blessing, the Aaronic blessing, and Ps 67—is especially relevant.

---

61. Mays, *Psalms*, 225.

Psalm 88

"See how these verses manifest the actual circumstances of the passion and the resurrection."—Cyril of Jerusalem

History

THE BOOK OF PSALMS expresses the full range of human emotions, from jubilant celebration to dark despair. Readers can open the book and find themselves in the words of the psalmists as they praise God for his mighty acts of deliverance, or cry out to him in the anguish of their souls. Whether we are joyful at the prospects of God's care for our lives as Creator and King, or whether we "take him to task" for his seeming absence and apathy toward our plight, Psalms is a treasure trove of human emotions. No other book of the Bible reflects the vastness of human nature like Psalms. It arouses our emotions, directs our wills, and stimulates our imaginations and intellect.[1] John Calvin called Psalms "An Anatomy of all the Parts of the Soul."[2] It lays bare the intellectual and emotional innards of humanity and puts them on display, so we may know ourselves more deeply. This is what makes the book so appealing and accessible to readers throughout the ages. It captures the essence and complexity of all facets of humanity as the special recipients of God's image among all creation.

The lament psalms reflect the darkest corners of human emotion. They express sadness and pain, frustration and anger, anxiety and fear, and they are addressed to the only one who can do anything about it— God. Kathleen Billman and Daniel Migliore describe biblical lament as that "unsettling biblical tradition of prayer that includes expressions of complaint, anger, grief, despair, and protest to God."[3] Never do the psalmists complain about the plight of their dismal situation to other human

---

1. Longman, *How to Read Psalms*, 75
2. Calvin, *Psalms*, Apple e-book, Preface.
3. Billman and Migliore, *Rachel's Cry*, 6.

beings because the worst problems of life are beyond the sphere of human influence. For Dietrich Bonhoeffer, "Even in the deepest hopelessness God alone remains the one addressed."[4] The psalmists lift their complaints to God because whatever situation they find themselves in belongs to God's sphere of influence. He can, and often does, deliver them from the calamities of life. Behind the lament psalms lies a confession of the kingship of Yahweh and an ever-present trust in him as the Sovereign of life. Put differently, lament psalms stem from faith, even if that faith is shaken. They are honest expressions of "authentic faith"[5] that address God from the context of a covenantal relationship.

The apostle Paul writes from his own context of afflictions and persecutions that his lament to God stems from the same spirit as the psalmist in Ps 116:10: "I believed, and so I spoke" (2 Cor 4:13). Simply put, the reason that the psalmist and Paul lift their laments and cry to God for deliverance is because they believe in his power to save. John Mark Hicks explains that laments are "prayers of faith because they express the questions of faith to the God whom faith trusts. They ask God the questions that only he can answer."[6] But expressing our anger, frustration, even exasperation with God is not easy because it makes us uncomfortable; we fear crossing an imaginary line (that only God knows) that divides honest expressions of grief from condemnation of God. As James Mays notes concerning lament, "Its insistent boldness in holding up all of life's worst, with its vehement demands for God's responses, is a devotional strategy that makes us distinctly uneasy."[7] To be clear, while the language of some biblical laments is often accusatory of God's seeming absence and apathy in the midst of the psalmist's suffering—sometimes even accusing God of sleeping on the job (Ps 44:23)—the fact remains that they flow from hearts that seek God. They declare his ability to deliver; they affirm his strength and sovereignty; and in the context of Holy Scripture, they are written *from* faith and *for* faith. That is, biblical laments are not warnings of what not to say to God in the midst of a trial, but are inspired examples of how believers may express their bitterness, anger, and frustration to God. God knows our hearts anyway; he knows how we feel because he created us. We might as well pour out our hearts to him because he knows us inside and out. Suppressing our feelings is not being honest with ourselves, or with God.

---

4. Bonhoeffer, *Psalms*, 47.
5. Brueggemann and Bellinger, *Psalms*, 381.
6. Hicks, *Trust Him*, 185.
7. Mays, *Preaching*, 108.

Suppressing lament as a form of prayer makes the other elements of prayer—praise, thanksgiving, confessions, intercession—ring hollow.[8] Billman and Migliore ask some pointed questions that should encourage people of faith to be brutally honesty with God: "How can praise be free and joyful if the realities of broken human life are not named and lamented? How can heartfelt thanks be given for healing if the wounds are denied?"[9] The prayers of lament acknowledge the goodness of God, but not all that happens in his world is good. This is especially relevant in terms of the covenant between God and ancient Israel, which is a covenant with both blessings for obedience and curses for disobedience. Consider the faithful Israelite woman who lives in covenant with God and expects that God will uphold his end of the covenant, based on the terms of that covenant, to bless her for seeking his will and loving her neighbor as herself. Yet she struggles to understand why her child died, why her husband was cheated out of what little money they had, why her son was rushed off to war, or why she has become captive to a debilitating disease. She is truly the innocent sufferer, who does not deserve the fiery ordeal that engulfs her. This is the stuff of the lament psalms. They ask questions of God because they see a disconnect between the righteousness of the individual (or the nation) and the turmoil of life. If God is faithful to his covenant, why do the wicked prosper and the righteous suffer? There are no easy answers to the kinds of questions lamenters ask, and there is no easy resignation to suffering.[10] Lament psalms are honest appraisals that something is not right with the world, and they bring the fallenness and brokenness of the world into the throne room of God and question him about it.[11] Over half of the Psalter is composed of lament psalms.[12] This says something about the world in which the psalmists live; namely, that it is broken. It is off kilter, and often does not reflect the goodness of God. The preservation of the lament psalms for thousands of years is a testimony to the continued fallen state of God's creation, which was originally "good," but now needs redemption.

This brief introduction to lament brings us to Ps 88, arguably the darkest of the lament psalms. Before engaging the psalm itself, a few cursory comments about the "building blocks" of biblical laments are in order to better understand the structural elements and theme of Ps 88. Lament

---

8. Billman and Migliore, *Rachel's Cry*, 19.
9. Ibid.
10. Bonhoeffer, *Psalms*, 47.
11. Hicks, *Trust Him*, 200.
12. Ibid., 198.

psalms typically contain several elements that highlight the fallen state of creation, while at the same time affirm God's sovereignty over every form of evil and suffering: invocation, plea for help, complaint, confession of sin or an assertion of innocence, curse of enemies, confidence in God's response, and a hymn or blessing.[13] Granted, not every lament psalm has each of the seven elements, but they usually have most of them. However, Ps 88 only has three of these traditional elements: invocation (v. 1), plea for help (v. 2), and complaint (vv. 3–18). What is more, these elements are not equally balanced throughout the psalm because the invocation and the plea take up only a very small portion of the overall prayer.[14] It is one long complaint, and unlike most laments, lacks a resolution to the crisis or a final note of praise for God's faithfulness. The psalmist's desperate cry is met with silence—Yahweh's silence. Structurally, the psalm is built on the themes of darkness and death, the former term occurring in each section of the psalm (vv. 6, 12, 18),[15] and the latter comprising the centerpiece of the chiastic structure of the first and last sections:[16]

Section one (vv. 1–9)	Section two (vv. 10–12)	Section three (vv. 13–18)
A Invocation and plea for help (vv. 1–2) B Troubles (v. 3) C Pit (v. 4) D Dead (v. 5) C1 Pit (v. 6) B1 Wrath (vv. 7–9a) A1 I call (v. 9bc)	Rhetorical Questions	A I cry (v. 13) B Why? (v. 14) C Death (v. 15) B1 Wrath (vv. 16–17) A1 Darkness (v. 18)

Table 2 Chiasms of Psalm 88

Additionally, the psalm possesses a range of vocabulary associated with death: Sheol (v. 3), pit (vv. 4, 6), dead/death (vv. 5, 10, 15), grave (vv. 5, 11), dark/darkness (vv. 5, 12, 18), deep (v. 6), shades (v. 10), Abaddon (v. 11), and land of forgetfulness (v. 12).[17] The last word in the psalm is "darkness," which further underscores the lack of resolution to the lamenter's crisis. Two final notes on the sheer darkness of the psalm involve the volume of the psalmist's cries and the duration of the crisis. The

13. Longman, *How to Read Psalms*, 27.

14. DeClaissé-Walford, *Introduction*, 95.

15. McCann, *Theological*, 98.

16. The chiastic structure of section one is from Zorn, *Psalms*, 148, and that of section three is my own.

17. McCann, *Theological*, 98.

psalmist exhausts the vocabulary of lament in verses 1, 2, and 13 with three different Hebrew words for "cry" or "call" (*tsaaq, rinnah, shava* respectively).[18] As for duration, the crisis is ongoing as indicated by the time stamps "at night" (v. 1), "every day" or "all day" (v. 9), and "in the morning" (v. 13). As McCann summarizes, "Every possible approach, at every possible moment, has been tried, and the result is 'darkness,' literally, the final word of the psalm."[19] For the lamenter, his suffering has gone unnoticed and unanswered, and he has reached the breaking point. The most natural reading of the affliction in Ps 88 is that the psalmist has suffered a prolonged illness that has caused his friends to abandon him and that has brought him to the point of death.[20] While the language may describe suffering in general terms and not necessarily an illness per se, most commentators see the references to death, Sheol, and the grave as indicative of the threat of physical death from a terminal illness.

We saw in Ps 23 that the psalmist uses language associated with the exodus from Egypt to illustrate God's shepherding care of his people. The same phenomenon occurs in Ps 88, although to a lesser degree than in Ps 23. The cries of the psalmist evoke the exodus experience both in terms of salvation and affliction, creating an empathetic experience between himself and the Israelites in Egyptian bondage. He even draws an analogy between his own suffering in the depths and the drowning of the Egyptians. This echoing effect creates an "exodus lens" through which to read the psalm and illustrates the psalmist's belief that God has traditionally responded when his people "cry out" to him (Exod 3:7, 9; Deut 26:7; Josh 24:7; Pss 9:12; 77:1; 107:6, 28).[21] As God rescues the Israelites from Egypt upon hearing their cries, the psalmist pleas for God to do the same now and rescue the psalmist from his current crisis. The table below illustrates echoes of the exodus in Ps 88:[22]

---

18. Ibid.
19. McCann, *Psalms*, 1027.
20. Longman, *Psalms*, 319. Richard Belcher cautions against limiting the psalmist's suffering to a physical illness; the language may be metaphorical, describing other distressing situations (*Messiah*, 72). Belcher's caution is duly noted, but most scholars interpret the language as describing physical illness; this seems to be the most natural meaning of the psalmist's pleas, which repeatedly cry out for deliverance from the grave.
21. McCann, *Psalms*, 1027.
22. I have compiled Table 3 from McCann's exegetical insights (ibid., 1027–28).

Psalmist's current crisis	The exodus experience
My salvation (*yeshuah*, v. 1)	My salvation (*yeshuah*, Exod 15:2)
I cry out (*tsaaq*, v. 1)	Their cry (*tsaaq*, Exod 3:7, 9)
Deep (*metsolah*, v. 6b)	Depths (*metsolah*, Exod 15:5)
Go out (*yatsa*, v. 8)	Brought out (*yatsa*, Exod 18:1; 20:2)
Affliction (*oni*, v. 9a)	Affliction (*oni*, Exod 3:7)

Table 3 Psalm 88 and the Exodus

In addition to the afflictions of the psalmist in Ps 88, the placement of the psalm near the end of Book 3 (73—89) is significant. While most scholars agree that Ps 88 is an individual lament, it flows quite naturally into the national lament of Ps 89, which concludes Book 3 of the Psalter. Book 3 may be seen as a response to the message of Book 2, especially Ps 72, which is "to," "for," "about," or "by" Solomon. Book 2 and its concluding psalm, Ps 72, should likely be read as a prayer for God to uphold his covenant promise to David to establish his throne forever (2 Sam 7:16).[23] Book 3, then, reflects the historical reality of the dissolution of David's throne, at least in the minds of the psalmists. Sadly, Book 3 reflects events that occurred during Israel's divided kingdom, the subsequent obliteration of the northern kingdom in 722 BCE by the Assyrians, and finally the destruction of the southern kingdom by the Babylonians in 586 BCE.[24] Many of the psalms in Book 3 are community laments, which reflect the desperate situation of the people of Israel following the deaths of Kings David and Solomon. Psalm 89, which concludes Book 3, begins as a community hymn of praise, recalling God's covenant loyalty to the Davidic dynasty (vv. 1–37), but ends in exasperation for the apparent loss of that dynasty (vv. 38–52). The crisis of Ps 89, like that of Ps 88, does not come to a resolution because the Babylonian exile effectively extinguished Israel's monarchy. Thus, the nation of Israel, with a Davidic king, was no more.[25] The reader of Book 3 comes face to face with the dissolution of the Davidic dynasty upon reaching Ps 89, and this is not disconnected from the dark message of Ps 88.

Psalm 88, while an individual lament, has also been read historically as a metaphor for the community's afflictions in the midst of the exile. For example, the targumist interpreted the psalmist's prayer for himself ("Let my prayer come before you," v. 2) as a prayer on behalf of Israel and the national crisis facing the community: "Let my prayer *for your people, the house of*

23. Zorn, *Psalms*, 39.
24. DeClaissé-Walford, *Introduction*, 85.
25. Ibid.

Israel, come before you" (Tg. Ps. 88:3).[26] Therefore, the communal nature of Book 3, which is composed largely of community hymns and laments, sheds light on the afflictions of the people of Israel that culminate in the despair of exile (Ps 88) and the loss of the monarchy (Ps 89). It is important to keep in mind that Ps 88 does have a communal dimension, even if the individual dimension receives the most attention in most literature on Psalms, including this one. While many scholars hold that Book 3 speaks to national crises of exile and a dissolved monarchy, it would be a mistake to limit its application to ancient Israel at the expense of communal and personal calamities today. Book 3 speaks to every time throughout the ages when the fallenness of the world and the sovereignty of God seem incompatible with each other. As Beth Tanner observes, "Book Three is a poetic rendering of theodicy, and its themes fit as well today as they did in its ancient context."[27] The same can be said of the applicability of Ps 88 as an example of floundering faith for those who are in the throws of intense suffering of every kind.

According to the superscript, Ps 88 is associated with "Heman the Ezrahite." Scripture speaks of a wisdom figure during the time of Solomon by this name in 1 Kgs 4:31, as well as a Levitical musician named Heman in 1 Chr 6:33. The Heman of Ps 88 may be one of these two men or another person altogether.[28] It is perhaps noteworthy that the Heman of 1 Chr 6 is associated with Asaph and Ethan the Ezrahite, the latter possibly associated with Ps 89. Although it is a Korah Psalm, it is unclear if Heman the Ezrahite had any association with the Sons of Korah.

The opening petition is the first and only flicker of faith in Ps 88 as the psalmist pours forth his plea to Yahweh, the covenant God of Israel. For Tanner, the opening line, "O LORD, God of my salvation," is the "first and last line of the psalm that is not one of anguish."[29] In spite of the dark tone of the psalm, this direct address to Yahweh assumes a foundation of faith, though shaken. Walter Zorn describes the psalmist's faith as being like a faint heartbeat that has not ceased altogether.[30] "Yahweh" is the first word in the psalm in the original Hebrew, indicating that the lamenter appeals to the only one that can remedy his situation—the Lord of the covenant.[31] This immediately places the psalmist's predicament in the context of a cov-

---

26. Targum translation in italics. On the Psalms Targum, see Evans, *Ancient Texts*, 197–98.
27. DeClaissé-Walford, et al., *Psalms*, 583.
28. Ibid., 668n5.
29. Ibid., 671.
30. Zorn, *Psalms*, 149.
31. Eaton, *Psalms*, 314.

enant relationship with Yahweh, and the assumption is that Yahweh is a God who is faithful to his promises to bless his people as they live in covenant with him. He has proved faithful in the past, delivering his people time and again.[32] This is the foundational assumption of the poet's plea: God is not simply the savior of the nation of Israel, but of the psalmist himself (i.e., Yahweh, God of *my* salvation," v. 1a). The implication is that the psalmist has experienced God's salvation in the past and pleads once again to the God of the covenant to hear his ongoing prayer as he cries out "day and night" (v. 1b) during the current crisis.

The psalmist bemoans that he has reached the peak of his ability to endure suffering in verses 3–5. The English translation "For my soul is full of troubles" (v. 3) renders the Hebrew idiom "my soul is satisfied with," which often communicates the fullness of something good (63:5; 65:4).[33] But here it is the opposite: the psalmist is satisfied with suffering. This is like saying today, "I've had it up to here" or "enough is enough." His immanent death comes more sharply into focus in verses 3–5 with repeated pleas for God to rescue him from Sheol (v. 3) the pit (v. 4), and the grave (v. 5). The psalmist echoes this sentiment in verse 11 where he uses "Abaddon," the place of destruction. Sheol, the pit, the grave, and Abaddon are Hebrew synonyms for the realm of death, a deep, dark, and silent realm where God is not. The realm of death is the opposite of the living realm of the Lord.[34] Because the psalmist's life "draws near" to Sheol (v. 3), and he is numbered with those who have already died (vv. 4–5), his own death is a foregone conclusion. He is "as good as dead" or has "one foot in the grave." Because the OT does not present a developed doctrine of the afterlife, people who are nearing death, like the psalmist, do not know what, if anything, lies on the other side of death. As James Mays observes, "In Israel the principle source of imagination about the state of the dead was the grave."[35] Death is final. And as far as the psalmist is concerned, God will forget him when he dies, as the dead are beyond his care.[36] They are "cut off" from the living presence of God (v. 5) in much the same way as the suffering servant of Isaiah, whose tragic death is described as being "cut off" from the land of the living (Isa 53:8).[37] Psalm

32. Zorn, *Psalms*, 149.
33. McCann, *Psalms*, 1028.
34. Eaton, *Psalms*, 315.

35. Mays, *Psalms*, 282. Belcher cites passages like Ps 49:15 and Amos 9:2, which may hint at something beyond Sheol, or, at least God's sovereignty over the grave (*Messiah*, 73). Even so, they do not develop any details of the afterlife. I will speak more on this when commenting on the rhetorical questions of Ps 88:10–12.

36. Longman, *Psalms*, 320.

37. McCann, *Psalms*, 1028. McCann notes that "cut off" also describes the plight

88:3–5 express the lamenter's impending death as the pinnacle experience of his suffering ordeal. He recognizes God's ability to save, and the psalmist cries out for salvation now before his ordeal sends him to the grave, before it is too late.

It would be a mistake to read the psalmist's cry as the natural result of an unfortunate and tragic turn of events or as being a necessary part of the fallenness of the world. His ordeal is not a normal point in the cycle of life, something unavoidable like the expected end of a terminal illness. On the contrary, verses 6–9a insist that *God* is the problem! He is the cause of the psalmist's plight: "*You* have put me (v. 6) . . . *your* wrath (v. 7a) . . . *you* overwhelm (v. 7b) . . . *you* have caused (v. 8a) . . . *you* have made (v. 8b)." Further, the psalmist's complaints in verses 6–9a build on one another and are examples of the heightening effect of Hebrew parallelism. They do not simply repeat with varying phrases the charge that God has afflicted him, but rather *culminate* in his abandonment by his friends. God has put him in the pit; what is more, he has consigned him to the *darkest* regions of the deep (v. 6). God's wrath weighs on him, but it has done even more—it has *overwhelmed* him (v. 7). As if these were not enough, God has caused the psalmist's companions to flee from him so much that he has become a *horror* to them (v. 8). Finally, he is shut in his own prison so that his eyes see only *darkness* instead of light (v. 9a). The heightening is evident: God throws the psalmist into the pit, which culminates in complete isolation from his fellow covenanters.

The psalmist attributes every aspect of his suffering to God; from God's wrath to the psalmist's abandonment by his friends, God is the cause. To be clear, Ps 88 offers no explanation for the outpouring of God's wrath on the poet. He is truly an innocent sufferer. Zorn observers that the psalmist "does not know why it [God's wrath] should be so. Nor why it should be so severe."[38] I appreciate Tremper Longman's title for this section of the psalm in his commentary: "You, God, have ruined my life."[39] Clearly, the lamenter holds God directly responsible for his dismal plight. While some may distinguish between times when God allows suffering (e.g., contracting an illness) and when he causes it (e.g., punishment for sin), the psalmist makes no such distinction. God's "permissive" will is indistinguishable from the direct action of his sovereign will.[40] Even if the psalmist could identify an indirect

---

of the Israelite nation in exile (Ezek 37:11), which fits the corporate interpretation of Ps 88 as a lament of the nation in exile (ibid.).

38. Zorn, *Psalms*, 150.
39. Longman, *Psalms*, 320.
40. Zorn, *Psalms*, 150.

cause for his suffering—such as the wickedness of his enemies, the fallenness of his physical body, or even as the book Job illustrates, Satan—God is sovereign above all and ultimately to blame when crises creep into life. The affirmation of God's sovereignty, so characteristic of the Psalter, demands nothing less than a constant affirmation of that sovereignty in good times as well as bad.[41] We cannot pick and choose which parts of life fall under God's sovereignty. God is the master of the psalmist's misery, but God is also the solution to the psalmist's plight, which is the topic of verse 9b–c.

Verse 9b-c restates the psalm's introductory prayer: "Every day I call upon you, O LORD; I spread out my hands to you." However, the psalmist's prayer for his life to be spared yields nothing but silence. His deepest fears are being realized, as God gives no response to his plea. Not only has God abandoned him, but has caused his friends to shun him as well (v. 8). He is truly alone in his suffering. Granted, the psalmist believes God has the power to act, but he does not act, leaving the psalmist alone and forsaken by all.[42] Therefore, the prayer of verse 9b-c caps the lament of verses 3–8 and also introduces the underlying issue of the rhetorical questions of verses 10–12: God's ability to rescue the dying from the grave. It rounds out the lament as a summary appeal made from a weakened faith, and sets up the probing interrogation of the verses that follow.

The psalmist raises a series of rhetorical questions, each expecting a "no" answer, in verses 10–12. For the psalmist, God does not work his wonders for the dead; those who have died do not sing songs of praise to God; the grave does not declare God's covenant love and faithfulness; the darkness knows not the light of God's wonders; death is the ultimate experience of abandonment because God's goodness is forgotten. The general assumption is that the grave is the apex of isolation from God and the covenant community; the dead lie in the "silence of oblivion."[43] As Derek Kidner explains, "Death is no exponent of His glory. Its whole character is negative: it is the last word in inactivity, silence, the severing of ties,

---

41. For McCann, "The central theological affirmation of the Psalter is this: The Lord reigns!" (*Theological*, 44). Throughout Scripture, God's reign is *inaugurated*; that is, it has begun, yet awaits its full consummation at the end of the ages, when evil and suffering will be eliminated (ibid., 49). This raises the thorny problem of theodicy: God's relationship to the evils of the world, which according to Ps 88, include debilitating illness. The intricacies of this debate are beyond the scope of the book. I only mention it here because the psalmist takes God to task for his suffering, and avoids blaming other "indirect" causes. For the theodicy debate see, Billman and Migliore, *Rachel's Cry*; Carson, *How Long?*; Hicks, *Trust Him*; Tiessen, *Providence*; Zurheide, *Tested*.

42. Belcher, *Messiah*, 73.

43. Eaton, *Psalms*, 315.

corruption (*Abaddon*), gloom, oblivion."[44] The psalmist's fear in the face of death is that he will soon be beyond salvation.[45] The rhetorical questions reflect the common OT belief that there is no afterlife.[46] Granted, there may be slight hints that God's power extends into the grave, but explicit passages are few and far between, and certainly do not reflect the more developed NT conviction of a bodily resurrection. To be clear, we should be cautious of generalizations that propose a uniform OT view of the afterlife, and allow some tension in what seems to be a largely undeveloped concept.[47] Richard Belcher cites Ps 49:15 and Amos 9:2 as OT texts that "affirm" an afterlife.[48] Psalm 49:15 hopes that God will "ransom" the psalmist's "soul" or "life" from Sheol and will "receive" him, presumably to some place beyond the grave, perhaps where God himself dwells. However, this may be read as nothing more than a request for God to rescue the psalmist from death, from going to Sheol in the first place. Similarly, Amos 9:2 describes how God will go to the greatest of lengths to search for and punish rebellious Israel, including reaching down and taking them from Sheol (cf. Ps 139:8). Again, this may simply be poetic language that need not be taken literally. Besides, Job 14:13 shows that some people in the OT period thought of Sheol as a place where one could "hide" from God; Amos's point, then, simply illustrates in the language of the day that no place under the earth is beyond the hand of God.[49]

There may be faint conceptions of the afterlife in the OT, perhaps even a bodily resurrection, though not definitively because the relevant passages may be interpreted figuratively, referring to national restoration from exile (Isa 25:6–9; 26:12–19; 27:12–13; Ezek 37:1–23; Dan 12:2).[50] The most that can be said is that the OT generally conceives of Sheol as a place where God could not be praised (Pss 6:5; 88:10–11), where God was not remembered (6:5), and where God did not remember the dead (88:10a, 12b).[51] Whatever anticipation of an afterlife may exist in the OT, such hope of redemption from the grave is not in the mind of the psalmist

---

44. Kidner, *Psalms 73–150*, 318.
45. Eaton, *Psalms*, 315.
46. Longman, *Psalms*, 320.
47. Alexander, "View," 41–46.
48. Belcher, *Messiah*, 73.
49. Shank, *Minor Prophets*, 290.
50. Ash and Miller, *Psalms*, 308. This brief list does not consider the plethora of OT passages that the NT interprets as evidence of the resurrection (e.g., Pss 16:8–11; 110:1; Hos 13:14; and others).
51. Ibid., 309.

in Ps 88. He fears the opposite: the dead do not, nor cannot, honor and praise God for his acts of mercy.[52]

There are two ways to understand the questions in verses 10–12, which recall a similar scenario in Ps 30:9. The first sees them as appeals to God's good reputation and self-interest to manipulate God into acting of behalf of the psalmist, and thereby uphold God's reputation as the savior of his covenant people.[53] The second interprets them as expressions of the psalmist's desire to continue living a life that praises God.[54] However, the psalmist's life is not exactly a vibrant expression of faith and hope. On the contrary, he loathes his life; he has suffered since his youth (88:14). As Belcher notes, "The fact that darkness permeates this psalm makes it hard to see these questions as positive expressions of faith."[55] Again, this plea for salvation from death comes in the context of a covenant relationship between God and the poet. If God is faithful to bless those who keep covenant, why is the psalmist facing certain death?

Deuteronomy 28 specifies the blessings and curses of the covenant; blessing for obedience and curses for disobedience. The blessings of the covenant are material and tangible, such as protection from enemies (28:7), financial prosperity (28:12), healthy families (28:4, 11), and fruitfulness of the land (28:4, 11), to name a few. The psalmist cannot grasp why he is suffering so severely; there is no confession of sin, so it would be wrong to infer he is being punished for disobedience. On the contrary, what makes Ps 88 so tragic is that the author is indeed an innocent sufferer, like Job, who sees no basis for his suffering. As is, God has cursed him, which is contrary to the covenant relationship that promises blessings for the faithful. Therefore, the rhetorical questions call on God to demonstrate his favor and save the psalmist before it is too late. For Belcher, "Once death comes it will be too late for God to show his favor in this world and too late for the psalmist to offer the appropriate praise to God for his deliverance."[56]

The final section of the psalm begins with a prayer and then continues with a final barrage of lamentation (vv. 13–18). It repeats many of the same motifs that run throughout the previous sections of the psalm, notably "Yahweh" (vv. 1, 9, 13), "cry out" (vv. 1–2, 13) "death" (vv. 5, 10, 15), "wrath" (vv. 7, 16), "flood/waves" (vv. 7, 17), "friends" (vv. 8, 18), and "darkness" (vv. 6, 18). The questions in this final section are more

---

52. Zorn, *Psalms*, 152.
53. Belcher, *Messiah*, 73.
54. McCann, *Psalms*, 1028.
55. Belcher, *Messiah*, 73.
56. Ibid., 74.

personal, focusing on the psalmist himself than those in vv. 10–12: "Why do you cast *my* soul away?" and "Why do you hide your face from *me*?" (v. 14). The problem of the lamenter's abandonment is not an abstract concept, but a personal and practical one. As before, he holds God responsible for his plight: *God* has withdrawn his presence (v. 14); *God's* terrors torment the soul (v. 15b); *God* pours out his wrath (v. 16a); *God* assaults (v. 16b), and *God* has brought abandonment upon the psalmist (v. 18). What is more, *God* has afflicted the psalmist for all or most of his life (v. 15). Again, his suffering is not acute, as if God is momentarily punishing him for sin. Suffering seems to be his lot in life. Whether a chronic illness or another extended trial, the psalmist is no stranger to affliction. God's terrors, which include life-threatening illness and perhaps more, have surrounded and engulfed him like a flood.[57]

As earlier, there is no indication that the psalmist has sinned so that his affliction is God's just punishment. The psalmist honestly asks "Why?" but receives no answer. Unlike Job, who is reassured that God had not forsaken him, the psalmist suffers in silence, alone, with no one to offer him a word of consolation (v. 18).[58] Verse 18 is the darkest, most dismal statement in the psalm, as well as perhaps in the entire Psalter. The last word in the Hebrew text is "darkness" (*makhshakh*). Again, most laments in Psalms end with an expression of hope and faith in the power of God to deliver from distress, but not Ps 88. It literally ends in darkness. It is not simply that the psalmist's friends have deserted him, but that darkness has replaced them as his closest "friend." I appreciate Zorn's literal translation of verse 18: "You have taken from me [my] loved one and friend; my intimate friend is darkness."[59] As Eaton eloquently explains, "The only one that can be relied on to stay is the deadly shadow of Sheol."[60] Seeing that this final, bleak section begins with a prayer, faith may be fading, but all is not lost for implicit is the vital thought that it is God who can change the situation.[61] This is the reality of human faith: it is at times weak, thready, and diminished; it doubts, bemoans, and at times even accuses God for his silence and absence.

Psalm 88 stands as a canonical testimony that dark thoughts and accusatory language are no threat to God's power; it does not hurt God's feelings when we cry out of the depths of our hearts. He can handle it. Lament is not the rejection of faith, but its affirmation. We cry out to the only one who can

---

57. Longman, *Psalms*, 321.
58. Zorn, *Psalms*, 152.
59. Ibid., 153.
60. Eaton, *Psalms*, 315.
61. Ibid.

do anything about our situation. As harsh as our accusations against God are at times, and as severe as our language often becomes, God affirms the truth of our most honest laments (Job 42:7–8).

Christology

Jesus was no stranger to lament. A cursory reading of the passion narratives of the Synoptic Gospels reveals the dark depths of despair that the Son of God feels as he agonized over his impending crucifixion. He was not immune to suffering, and lament was a consistent part of his prayer routine, as the writer of Hebrews declares: "In the days of his flesh, Jesus offered up prayers and supplications, with loud cries and tears, to him who was able to save him from death" (Heb 5:2). Jesus's prayer of anguish in the Garden of Gethsemane, and his cry of abandonment on the cross, make him the biblical paradigm of the innocent sufferer. Luke even records that his agony in Gethsemane was so great that his tears were as "great drops of blood" (Luke 22:44). His cry of abandonment from the cross, "My God, my God, why have you forsaken me?" (Matt 27:46; Mark 15:34) creates a shared experience between himself and the writer of Ps 22:1 so that the psalmist's words, while reflecting his own experience of severe suffering, find their fullest expression in Christ on the cross as the truly innocent sufferer. Jesus therefore empathized with the psalmist because he, too, had his fill of suffering.

However, the words of the psalmist do not verbally predict the sufferings of the Messiah as simplistic and straightforward instances of predictive prophecy; they are instead particularly vivid expressions that evoke Jesus's passion for Christian readers of the psalm. I have used the terminology of "evoke" and "recall" throughout this book as one way of describing how the NT reads the OT as a witness to Christ, and I think it is especially relevant to this discussion of Ps 88 and its christological interpretation. My conviction is that the psalmist's experience in Ps 88 and that of Jesus is an example of biblical typology. Because the entire book of Psalms testifies to Jesus, namely his sufferings (Luke 24:25–27, 44–47), the words of lamentation of the psalmist point to Christ, culminating in his passion experience. The psalmist had his own experience of suffering as the historical analysis indicates, but Jesus also had his own experience that both echoes and exceeds that of the psalmist, as the antitype exceeds the type. Conversely, because Christians read the OT *after* the cross event, the lament psalms illuminate the experience of Jesus. Mays explains how the interpretive current "flows both ways—from psalm to Jesus and from Jesus to psalm. Jesus' passion is a new setting in which the psalm can be understood."[62] Therefore, we may legitimately refer to the psalmists' suffering as a "type" that both anticipate and evoke Christ's suffering, which is the "antitype."

Typology is the study of redemptive-historical correspondences between persons, events, and institutions in the OT with persons, events, and institutions in the NT. That is, OT "types" anticipate later NT "antitypes."[63] Typology is not the same as predicative prophecy, but there is a predictive element involved because God's sovereign control of redemptive history is assumed in both prophecy and typology. In other words, typological correspondences are not mere coincidence; they are "built into" the fabric of redemptive history that is under God's sovereign guidance. One important feature of typology is the NT antitype is greater than the OT type.[64] The type prefigures the antitype, but the latter exceeds it in terms of its importance in redemptive history. For example, Mark Heinemann sees David's experience of suffering and vindication in Ps 22 as typological of Christ's suffering on the cross and vindication in the resurrection:

> Jesus, as David's antitype, became the ultimate example of trusting God in the face of trials. But in Jesus' case, instead of being rescued, He was resurrected. Instead of sparing Jesus' single life, God provided through Jesus' death a glorious resurrection to new life for Him and for all who trust in Him. Also the event of the crucifixion became the antitypical event in which the seemingly exaggerated aspects of David's descriptions of his typical suffering found their literal fulfillment. Likewise David's enemies are types of the enemies of Christ. Those who mocked David prefigured the mockers at Christ's crucifixion. The bulls, lions, and dogs also pre-figured Jesus' enemies—the Jewish leaders who accused Him, the Roman leaders who condemned Him, and the rabble who screamed, "Crucify him!"[65]

62. Mays, *Preaching*, 110–11.

63. McCartney and Clayton, *Reader*, 162–63.

64. Ibid., 167.

65. Heinemann, "Psalm 22," 303. For Ps 22 as a type of Christ's suffering, see Belcher, *Messiah*, 167; Blomberg, "Matthew," 99; Goppelt, *Typos*, 103; Mays, *Psalms*,

Jesus's experiences of suffering and vindication exceed those of David, as the NT antitype exceeds the OT type. In Jesus's suffering, the psalmist's experience is magnified, reaching its pinnacle application. Using Ps 22 as the paradigm for the typological relationship between the psalmist's lament and that of Jesus, I believe the same relationship exists with all the lament psalms, so that even Ps 88, the darkest of the laments, prefigures the suffering of Christ. Jesus, then, becomes the paradigmatic example of the innocent sufferer who pours out his lament before the throne of God. The lament psalms, therefore, do not directly predict Christ's sufferings, but indirectly prefigure them as types.

This typological relationship between Ps 88 and Christ, while not evident at first, arises as a result of the backward reading strategy of the NT's use of the OT. Put simply, Ps 88 evokes for Christians the sufferings of Christ. Because we tend to be deeply familiar with the passion narratives of the Gospels, lament psalms like Pss 22 and 88 sound a lot like what Jesus went through in his final days leading to and including the crucifixion. The psalmist's laments evoke in our minds the sufferings of Christ. When we read of the psalmist being near death in Ps 88, abandoned by his friends and his God, alone in his darkest moments, we recall the sufferings of Christ, his experience of the fear of death and abandonment. That is, when we read the OT from a post-crucifixion perspective, we recognize the sufferings of Christ in the words of the psalmist. Commenting on Jesus's use of Ps 22:1 on the cross, Mays believes that now we can read the psalm as the words of Jesus and understand it in light of his suffering.[66] I believe we can apply a similar reading to Ps 88 by analogy, even though Jesus does not quote it. Similarly, McCann interprets the Christology of the psalm: "Psalm 88 is not a prediction of Jesus' suffering, but it serves to articulate the same experience Jesus would later live out."[67] I would add that it not only articulates, but also *anticipates* the same experience Jesus would later live out based on its typological relationship between the psalmist as the innocent sufferer and Christ as the paradigmatic innocent sufferer.

Psalm 88 evokes the wording and imagery of Jesus's agony in the Garden of Gethsemane and subsequent sufferings on the cross. These connections are not chronological but thematic, and illustrate how Jesus, as the biblical paradigm of the innocent sufferer, experiences and fulfills the psalmist's suffering and lament. The crucifixion of Christ, then, is the

---

106–07. For the lament psalms generally as types of Christ's suffering, see Greidanus, *Preaching Christ*, 35.

66. Mays, *Preaching*, 108.

67. McCann, *Theological*, 99.

climactic moment of darkness and dread anticipated in the psalm. Although John Calvin did not interpret Ps 88 as having any connection to Christ, Augustine interpreted it as the prayer of Christ during his passion.[68] I do not attempt here a verse-by-verse application to Christ, as Augustine does, but instead I want to illustrate how the main message of the psalm points to various aspects of his passion. I will explore seven connections here and leave it to the reader to propose more.

First, in the darkest moment of his life, Jesus still holds on to faith in God's power to deliver, in much the same way as the psalmist, who addresses God as the God of "my salvation" (88:1). Jesus's appeal to God stems from relationship and reveals an "extraordinary sense of intimacy" with God (i.e., "*my* God").[69] Like the psalmist, faith is the bedrock of Jesus's lament. Second, the anxiety of the psalmist also evokes the agony of Christ in the Garden of Gethsemane. As the psalmist has had his fill of "troubles," Jesus is "greatly distressed and troubled" (Mark 14:33) in his soul as he awaits his arrest, trials, flogging, and crucifixion. Third, the primary predicament of the psalmist is his impending death; the psychological struggle of coming to grips with the fact that death looms on the horizon has more or less broken him. This correlates with Jesus's despair in the Garden and his struggle to grasp the will of God, causing him to be "sorrowful unto death" (14:34).

Fourth, the experience of God's wrath is unfathomable for the psalmist, who refuses to concede that sin is the proximate cause of his anguish. On one hand, the Bible affirms that every human being has sinned and fallen woefully short of God's glory (Rom 3:23); therefore, no one can legitimately claim the title of the "innocent sufferer." On the other hand, the psalmist, like Job, maintains his innocence, implied in the fact that the psalm contains no confession of sin. It is a lament psalm not a penitential psalm, and there is no indication whatsoever that the psalmist is trying to hide his sin and suppress it from God's all-seeing eyes.

Jesus is the ultimate example of the innocent sufferer in Scripture. He truly has no sin to confess because he has committed no sin. Yet if we learn anything from the cross of Christ, it is that at that moment he becomes sin, taking upon himself the sins of the nation of Israel and the whole world. By taking the sins of the world on himself, Jesus incurs the wrath of God poured out at the cross. Augustine understood "your wrath lies heavily upon me" (Ps 88:7) as a prophecy of God's wrath poured out on the cross of Christ: "The anger [wrath] of God was not merely roused, but lay hard

---

68. For a rich, christological interpretation of Ps 88, see Augustine, *Expositions* 88. Similarly, Eaton notes that Jerome gives Ps 88 the following heading in the Vulg.: "The voice of Christ: he speaks concerning his Passion to the Father" (*Psalms*, 509).

69. Chouinard, *Matthew*, 495.

upon Him, whom they dared to bring to death, and not only death, but that kind, which they regarded as the most execrable of all, namely the death of the Cross."[70] The NT speaks of Jesus's sacrifice as "propitiation" (1 John 2:2; 4:10), which averts God's wrath from away from sinful humanity, and this is part and parcel of its atoning benefits for the world.[71] Although Jesus himself has committed no sin, he becomes sin on the cross so that his people may follow in his example of cross bearing and may live righteous and upright lives. That is, his sacrifice both atones for sin (2 Cor 5:21) and is the chief example of sacrificial love and living (Mark 10:43–45; 1 Pet 2:21–24). Therefore, Jesus's experience of God's wrath magnifies and multiplies that of the psalmist, being its typological fulfillment.

Fifth, the psalmist laments that his condition has resulted in desertion by his friends. Jesus, too, is shunned by his disciples during the darkest moments of his life, forcing him to endure his trials alone. Matthew associates the flight of the disciples with yet another passion event that has happened in order to fulfill Scripture (Matt 26:56), bearing a striking resemblance to the abandonment of the psalmist and other OT lamenters. Sixth, similar to the wrath typology I mentioned earlier, the psalmist's experience of divine abandonment is typologically related to God's abandonment of Christ on the cross. Because Christ's sacrifice satisfies God's wrath—that is, his holy opposition to sin—diverting it away from sinful humanity and onto himself on the cross, the standard assumption of the doctrine of the atonement is that God must remain wholly separate from sin. God, by definition of his holiness, must "abandon" Jesus on the cross. This is an unfathomable mystery, causing us to ask questions that the biblical text simply does not answer definitively: How can the Father desert the Son for submitting to the Father's will? Did the Trinity really fracture? What kind of relationship exists between the Father and the Son, who is "one" with the Father (John 10:30)? Is the idea of divine abandonment at the cross even accurate at all (John 16:32)? Certainty is elusive regarding the finer points of the relationship between the Father and the Son; the NT does not speak systematically on this. Larry Chouinard admits that we simply "cannot fathom all that it [divine abandonment] might have meant to the relationship between Jesus and the Father."[72] Andreas Köstenberger and Justin Taylor also admit the mystery involved in the cross's impact on Trinity: "In some mysterious way beyond our human understanding, Jesus, the second person of the Trinity, is cut off and separated from God because he is bearing the sin of humanity and

---

70. Augustine, *Expositions* 88, §6.
71. Longman, "Expiation," 549–51.
72. Chouinard, *Matthew*, 495.

enduring God's wrath as a substitute for and in place of sinful humans."[73] The physical pain and torture of the cross pale next to the "terrifying weight of utter separation from God and God-forsakenness."[74]

Whatever we make of sin's impact of on the trinitarian relationship, the reality is that Jesus felt abandoned by God while on the cross, and this is why he quoted the lament of Ps 22:1. The Son had never experienced spiritual separation from the Father to this point. The Gospel of John reminds us of one of the foundational assumptions of the trinitarian relationship: "In the beginning was the Word, and the Word was with God, and the Word was God" (John 1:1). For Jesus to feel abandoned by his Father during the most terrifying moments of his life surely stirred in him feelings of depression and anxiety, causing him to lament the loss of such an intimate relationship. Psalm 88 expresses the same feelings of abandonment, making it a suitable expression of Jesus's desertion by the Father while on the cross.

Finally, the dark tone of Ps 88, which fades to black in the last word of the psalm (i.e., "darkness"), echoes the crucifixion scene. Each of the Synoptic Gospels records that darkness covered the whole land as Jesus was being crucified (Matt 27:45; Mark 15:33; Luke 23:44–45). This was no natural phenomenon, but an unusual darkness symbolizing, among other things, divine judgment on sin (Exod 10:21–23; Isa 13:9–13; Jer 13:16; 15:19; Joel 2:10; 3:14–15; Amos 5:18, 20; 8:9–10).[75] One theory is that because Jesus takes the sin of the world onto himself on the cross, the darkened land symbolizes God's holy opposition (i.e., wrath) to that sin, creating a visual manifestation of the severed relationship.[76] As N. T. Wright has observed, "Part of the whole point of the cross is that there the weight of the world's evil really did converge upon Jesus, blotting out the sunlight of God's love as surely as the light of day was blotted out for three hours."[77] The text is not explicit about the meaning of the darkness; it could illustrate sympathy for the unjust death of a truly righteous sufferer,[78] or God's judgment in general (without pressing the abandonment concept too far).[79] But his judgment saturates the theology of the scene. What is most important to our purpose here is that darkness is yet another example of typology between Ps 88 and

---

73. Köstenberger and Taylor, *Final Days*, 160.
74. Ibid., 161.
75. Ibid., 160.
76. Wilkins, *Matthew*, 902–03.
77. Wright, *Matthew*, 2:190.
78. Keener, *Matthew*, 685.
79. Garland, *Mark*, 591–92.

the passion of Christ; the darkness of the cross is even darker than the misery of the psalmist because of the cosmic implications of God's judgment on sin.

The following table summarizes these numerous points of contact between Ps 88 and the passion of Jesus Christ:

Psalm 88	The Passion of Christ
Lament addressed to God (v. 1)	Lament addressed to God (Mark 15:34)
Soul is full of troubles (v. 3)	Greatly distressed and troubled (Mark 14:33)
Near death (vv. 4–5)	Sorrowful unto death (Mark 14:34)
Wrath (v. 7)	Wrath implied in atoning sacrifice (2 Cor 5:21; 1 John 2:2; 4:10)
Abandoned by friends (vv. 8, 18)	Abandoned by friends (Matt 26:56)
Abandoned by God (v. 14)	Abandoned by God (Mark 15:34)
Darkness is my companion (v. 18)	Darkness over all the land (Matt 27:45)

Table 4 Psalm 88 and the Passion of Christ

Again, typology is the dominant method that allows for a christological interpretation of Ps 88. McCann summarizes the typological relationship between the psalmist's sufferings as those of Christ: "As the psalmist in Psalm 88 suffered, so God's Son suffered life's worst for us."[80]

There is yet another important issue that contributes to a distinctly Christian interpretation of the psalm. As I mentioned earlier, Christians read the OT in light of the cross and resurrection, and while the former is indispensable to the psalm's christological interpretation, the latter provides a hermeneutical lens that alters the main message of the psalm. While we may resonate with the emotions of the psalmist and his feelings of abandonment in the dark recesses of the soul, as we despair over the evils of the fallen world like terminal illness, war, the death of children, injustice, etc., the dilemma of suffering is finally solved in the resurrection of Christ. On one hand, the cross teaches that Christ suffers with us and for us. Bonhoeffer notes that the lament psalms "proclaim Jesus Christ to be the only help in suffering, for in him God is with us."[81] On the other hand, the resurrection is God's answer to the rhetorical questions of Ps 88 as "yes" in Christ: "Do you work wonders for the dead?" Yes! As God raised Jesus from the dead, he pledges to raise also those in him from the grave. "Do the departed rise up to praise you?" Yes! The book of Revelation

---

80. McCann, *Theological*, 99.
81. Bonhoeffer, *Psalms*, 48.

reveals that God's eternal community is a worshiping community. "Is your steadfast love declared in the grave, or your faithfulness in Abaddon?" Yes! The hope of the bodily resurrection gives us the earnest expectation that our loved ones who have died will one day rise again, and we ourselves with them. Although that day is delayed, we eagerly anticipate it. "Are your wonders known in the darkness?" Yes! God's light has invaded the darkest corners of the world. Jesus shines in the darkness, and the darkness has not overcome him. "Is your righteousness in the land of forgetfulness?" Yes! Because of the resurrection, the land of forgetfulness gives way to the land of the living. To be sure, this perspective was not as clearly available to the psalmist as to the Christian, so there is a shift in application from darkness and despair to light and life, resurrection life. Thus, Belcher shows how a christological approach to the psalm emphasizes both the death and resurrection of Christ and transforms how we read the psalm:

> Jesus experienced the darkness and abandonment by God expressed in Psalm 88 as he hung on the cross suffering the judgment of God against sin. His human life ended in darkness, but only for a short time, for on the third day he burst from the grave conquering sin and death. Because Jesus experienced the dark night of the soul we are assured that darkness will not be the last word.[82]

We may very well experience similar depths of despair as the psalmist, but we do so with the conviction that God has not abandoned us; on the contrary, he suffers with us in Jesus Christ. God knows how we feel not simply because he created us, but because he became one of us.

---

82. Belcher, *Messiah*, 76.

Psalm 100

"God's love to sinners was expressed by the gift of his Son to be their Savior."—J. I. Packer

PSALM 100 IS ONE of the most beloved psalms in the Psalter. Its brevity makes it easy to memorize and its wording is ripe for musical expression. It was the inspiration for the Reformation hymn "All People That On Earth Do Dwell," composed by Scottish clergyman William Kethe, and the melody for the hymn "Doxology" is referred to as "Old Hundredth" in commemoration of Ps 100. Its twin themes of thanksgiving and the kingship of Yahweh blend together as the lifeblood of God's people: God's loyal subjects live thankful lives because of the provision and protection of their King. Life is to be rooted in thanksgiving, and our utter dependence on God should permeate every aspect of our being, resulting in the rejection of society's standards of success and the temptation to be "self made." The psalm is first and foremost about God's universal reign as King, in contrast to competing claims to sovereignty of the world's gods. The praise that the psalm calls forth from God's people is relentlessly polemical, as other gods are dismissed as irrelevant and denied any legitimacy.[1] What is more, it is also about the role of God's people as loyal subjects who proclaim his sovereign rule and praise him for his pastoral provisions.

History

Psalm 100 is a call to worship that also sets forth a theology of worship.[2] It invites worshipers into the temple courts to worship Yahweh as the King who provides for his people. However, it is not a static call to worship; there

---

1. Brueggemann, "Psalm 100," 66. Other gods who compete for Israel's loyalty include those of Egypt, Canaan, and Babylon.
2. Mays, *Psalms*, 317.

is a noticeable "movement" at work in the psalm as it takes worshipers on a processional through the "gates" of the temple and through the temple "courts" (100:4), singing the praises of the King, and entering into his very presence.[3] The call to enter into the temple complex for worship naturally raises the question of the date of the psalm's composition. If it was part of the liturgy of Solomon's temple the psalm would be preexilic, but it may equally refer to Zerubbabel's rebuilt temple in the postexilic period.[4] Nevertheless, the precise date of composition does not affect the theology of the psalm.

The structure of Ps 100 is very simple, being composed of three sections that focus attention on the middle section:

> Triple imperative call to worship (vv. 1–2)
> > Central call to *know that the LORD, he is the true God* (v. 3)
> Triple imperative call to worship (vv. 4–5)[5]

The middle section gives the psalm an "explicitly instructional quality," exhorting worshipers to recognize the sovereign kingship of Yahweh.[6] Another structural component involves a string of seven imperatives that progress through the hymn. The psalm-singer exhorts worshipers to "make a joyful noise" . . . "serve the LORD with gladness" . . . "come into his presence" . . . "know that the LORD, he is God" . . . "enter his gates with thanksgiving" . . . "give thanks to him" . . . "bless his name." It is probably not coincidental that seven is the number of perfection in the Bible.[7] This makes Ps 100 a comprehensive call to worship as it proceeds through the seven imperatives. Additionally, while most enthronement psalms are about the kingship of Yahweh, this feature of seven plural imperatives in Ps 100 places a special emphasis on the role of the King's people as loyal subjects.

Psalm 100 is the only psalm in the Psalter with "thanksgiving" in its title, causing many commentators to characterize it as a psalm of thanksgiving.[8] Yet, both its placement in the Psalter and its royal imagery and terminology elevate it above a general song of thanks to more of an enthronement psalm that celebrates the goodness of Yahweh, the King of the world. While the psalm is no doubt theological in that it concerns worship of Israel's covenant God at the temple, it is also political in that its chief concern is the

---

3. Ibid.
4. Zorn, *Psalms*, 236.
5. DeClaissé-Walford, et al., *Psalms*, 735.
6. McCann, *Psalms*, 1078.
7. DeClaissé-Walford, et al., *Psalms*, 736.
8. Bowman, "Routine Words," 30. Mays notes that *todah* can refer to either a thank offering or a liturgical expression of thanksgiving (*Psalms*, 317).

acknowledgement of Yahweh's rightful claim as the sovereign King of all the earth (v. 1). To suggest that it is theo-political is therefore more to the point, balancing a theology of worship with a political affirmation of Yahweh's universal kingship. Craig Bowman summarizes the main theme of the psalm: "Yahweh is the ideal king over all people, therefore come into his presence with thanksgiving, praise, and joy."[9]

The placement of Ps 100 as the conclusion of a series of enthronement psalms (93—100) further underscores its royal connotations. It is debatable whether Ps 100 originally functioned in an enthronement ceremony—it most certainly had some kind of liturgical function—but its placement at the conclusion of the enthronement psalms in Book 4 suggests that its present location in the Psalter serves as a crescendo of praise that began in Ps 93, which declares that Yahweh reigns as King.[10] Psalms 96—99 make up the core of this collection of enthronement psalms, and given the similarities between Pss 95 and 100 (e.g., 95:7; 100:3), these two psalms seem to form a frame around Pss 96—99.[11] And while Ps 100 lacks any specific mention of Yahweh as "King," it shares much of the royal terminology that characterizes the enthronement psalms of Book 4, making it a suitable conclusion to the cluster of psalms.[12] Even so, there is more to this placement because Ps 100 not only concludes the enthronement psalms, but also sits as the heart of Book 4 (90—106). Book 3 laments the apparent dissolution of the Davidic dynasty, concluding with strong accusations against God for abandoning his promises to King David, resulting in the exile of the nation: "How long, O LORD? Will you hide yourself forever? How long will your wrath burn like fire? . . . Where is your steadfast love of old, which by your faithfulness you swore to David? . . . They mock the footsteps of your anointed" (89:46ff). The answers to these laments occur in Book 4 and are as follows: Yahweh is King; Yahweh has been our refuge in the past, long before the monarchy existed, and will be our refuge now in exile since the monarchy is gone; blessed are those who trust in Yahweh for he is the *true* transcendent King, not only of Israel but also the nations.[13] Psalm 100, therefore, with its placement at the end of the enthronement psalms of Book 4, sets forth a final clarion call to worship that echoes the declaration that Yahweh, the Shepherd-King, saves and sustains his people.

---

9. Bowman, "Routine Words," 31.
10. Ibid.,
11. McCann, *Psalms*, 1077.
12. Brueggemann and Bellinger, *Psalms*, 428.
13. Bowman, "Routine Words," 31.

Although Ps 100 lacks some of the more specific royal phrases associated with Yahweh as King like, "The LORD reigns; he is robed in majesty" (93:1), "Great King above all gods" (95:3), "Splendor and majesty are before him" (97:6), "Make a joyful noise before the King, the LORD" (98:6), "He sits enthroned above the cherubim" (99:1), and "The King in his might loves justice" (99:4), it nevertheless contains royal terminology that echoes many of the same themes of the enthronement psalms. Psalm 100 walks a bit of a tightrope in that its language has both cultic and royal connotations at the same time. The worship language is unmistakable as the singer invites worshipers through the gates of the temple and into its courts to praise God, the Shepherd-King. Yet the language equally evokes "royal theology" because the temple was viewed as God's palace in the ancient world. So there is a both/and quality about the psalm that evokes Israel's cult as well as its monarchy, and the two cannot easily be separated. James Mays observes how the terminology of the psalm belongs

> to Israel's cultic vocabulary, and designates the kind of things which Israel (and other peoples of the culture area) were accustomed to do in the public cult. They would form processions before the gates of the sanctuary area, enter its precincts where the deity was believed to dwell or come, all the while lauding him with epithets and affirmations. But cult in Israel's cultural world was not a self-contained and self-defining sphere. All these actions had meaning because they were expressed in the forms by which a people recognized the one who wielded power over them.[14]

In fact, the opening imperative of the psalm, "Make a joyful noise to the LORD," functions not only as the language of worship where the congregation lifts its voice in praise to God, but also has the royal connotations of "shouting joyfully" (*rua*) in reaction to the enthronement of a king or his appearing before his subjects (1 Sam 10:24; cf. 2 Kgs 11:12).[15] The language, therefore, doubles as that of the temple cult and the royal palace.

There is yet another dual connotation of Ps 100, this time in regards to its target audience. With its emphasis on temple worship, the psalm is obviously addressed primarily to the covenant community of Israel. But the psalm also strikes a universal chord given that verse 1 reiterates the universality of Israel's election with an invitation for "all the earth" (i.e., non-Israelites) to make a joyful noise. God's promise to Abraham made it clear that Israel's election was never to be confined to the Jewish nation but

---

14. Mays, "Worship," 321.
15. Greidanus, *Preaching Christ*, 530n10.

was ultimately for the blessing of "all the families of the earth" (Gen 12:3). Walter Zorn notes the universality of the psalm's opening invitation: "The universal appeal is not out of order even though the psalm is addressed primarily to Israel."[16] What is more, the psalm's universal tone is not limited to the opening verse, but extends to all seven imperatives so that they reach out to humanity.[17]

Verse 2 continues the dual-pronged emphasis on liturgy and royalty. On one hand, the second imperative of the psalm, "serve the LORD with gladness," evokes the liturgy of Israel since the word "serve" (*avad*) can be translated as "worship"; thus the NIV, "Worship the LORD with gladness." However, as J. Clinton McCann has pointed out, to render the verb solely as "worship" is unnecessarily constrictive because the term more comprehensively means "to orient one's whole life and existence to a sovereign master—literally, to be 'the servant' or 'slave' of a king."[18] This is confirmed by its customary usage throughout Psalms where it most often occurs in the context of a human or divine king (Pss 2:11; 18:43; 22:30; 72:11; 97:7; 102:22).[19] What is more, this political use of the term occurs repeatedly in the exodus narratives as "serve Yahweh" traditions where it designates leaving Pharaoh's kingdom to go into the wilderness where Israel pledges allegiance to its true King.[20] A transfer of loyalty occurs as Israel leaves behind the old king, Pharaoh, to follow Yahweh anew. This political use of the verb "to serve" continues through Deuteronomy, where serving Yahweh is a polemic against "serving" other gods.[21] Together, these contexts suggest a political and polemical use of "serve" that "excludes slavery to human government or subjection to the power of the gods."[22]

While "serve" no doubt reflects the liturgical act of worship, it also connotes royal theology where service to Yahweh involves political allegiance to him, which necessitates a polemic against other competing kings, both earthy and divine. Similarly, "Come into his presence" (v. 2b) signifies not only entrance into the sanctuary for worship, but also describes how people were given an audience with human kings (1 Sam 10:24; 2 Sam 14:3, 15; 15:2; Esth 4:11, 16; 8:1).[23] Worshipers no doubt engaged in religious

---

16. Zorn, *Psalms*, 236.
17. Mays, "Worship," 320.
18. McCann, *Theological*, 65.
19. Ibid.
20. Mays, "Worship," 322. See Exod 3:12; 4:23; 7:16; 8:1; 10:26.
21. Ibid. See Deut 7:4; 8:19; 11:16; 12:2.
22. Ibid.
23. Ibid.

praise (i.e., "singing") while in the presence of the deity at the temple, but the language is also taken from the political world where audiences shouted acclamation before the king.[24] Therefore, the first two verses of the psalm especially emphasize the political ideology of ancient Israel as a blend of both religious and royal spheres. Given that the king was the earthly representation of God's kingly rule, the two spheres were inseparable.

Verse 3 is the center of the psalm and contains the fourth imperative, "Know that the LORD, he is God!" All the other imperatives in the psalm call for the audience to *do* something, but this one calls for them to *know* something; namely, that the LORD is God.[25] This is a variation on the so-called OT "recognition formula" ("and you will know that I am Yahweh"), which always follows a description of God's redemptive activity on behalf of his people (e.g., Exod 7:5; 8:10; 9:14; 14:4, 18; Deut 4:35, 39; cf. 1 Kgs 8:60; 2 Kgs 19:19; Ps; 46:10; Ezek 5:13; 6:7).[26] The Hebrew concept of knowledge is not primarily head knowledge or intellect, but experience and relationship. Therefore, the psalm is not primarily calling for Israel to cognitively know that Yahweh is God, but to experience the blessings of the covenant relationship with him, recalling his redemptive acts on their behalf, as well as his ongoing protection and provision.

In light of the relentlessly polemical nature of Ps 100, knowing that the LORD is God sounds a loud polemical note over other gods and their competing claims of universal sovereignty. God is not simply Israel's God; he is the true God and reigns supreme over all other rulers, whether human kings or divine beings. Knowing that the LORD is God is a political stance that involves absolute and unadulterated submission to the God of the covenant who redeems his covenant people. Put differently, no other god can call forth the praise and obedience of Israel because their historic redemption comes solely from Yahweh their covenant God. Therefore, knowledge in this context suggests more than knowing about Yahweh, and has more to do with recognizing that the covenant community belongs to him as a result of his redemptive activity on its behalf.[27] Walter Brueggemann offers a helpful contextual frame around the imperative in the context of Ps 100: "The verb 'know' then means to make a decision about one's covenant partner."[28] What is more, the redemptive implications of the recognition formula inform the meaning of the following line: "It is he who made us, and

---

24. Ibid.
25. McCann, *Theological*, 65–66.
26. McCann, *Psalms*, 1078.
27. Brueggemann and Bellinger, *Psalms*, 428.
28. Brueggemann, "Psalm 100," 66.

we are his" or "It is he who made us, and not we ourselves" (Ps 100:3b).[29] However, the precise nuance of "he made us" is hard to determine here. It can refer to the divine act of creation or, alternatively, election as the forming, fashioning, and redeeming of a people (cf. Deut 32:6, 15; Ps 95:6–7; Isa 43:1, 21; 44:2).[30] Thus, the combination of divine activity—creation and election—on behalf of the nation is used as a metaphor for the new creation of a community. Rolf Jacobson observes:

> The phrase "he made us" refers to the Lord's action of claiming Israel as God's priestly nation through the election of Abraham (Gen 12), the redemption of the nation from Egypt (Exod 19), and the return of the people from exile. The verb translated as "made" (*'asah*) is often used for God's redemptive actions in history (1 Sam 12:6; Ps 118:15–16). Thus, based on what God has already done, the psalm exhorts: *Know that the LORD, he is the true God.*[31]

The point hinges on the historical reality that Yahweh, the true God, has a proven track record of redeeming his people. To know that God redeemed Israel, thereby making her a holy nation, involves remembering his mighty deeds performed on her behalf throughout history. Mays explains how "the command to know depends upon and presupposes Yahweh's initiative, that he has acted in such a way as to call for the appropriate corresponding

---

29. This line is notoriously difficult to translate; even ancient scribes struggled with its precise meaning, as evidenced in the MS tradition. In the MT, the Masoretes distinguished between "what is written" (*kethib*), that is, the authoritative and inviolable wording in a MS, and "what is read" (*qere*), which usually refers to marginal notes or variant readings in the MS tradition, often resulting from differences in vowel pointing of the Heb. In the case of Ps 100:3b, the *kethib* reads, "It is he who made us, and not we ourselves," and the *qere* reads, "It is he who made us, and we are his," which is the rendering followed by most Eng. translations. The problem with the *kethib* reading is that the thought of humanity's self-creation was unthinkable in the ancient world. That is not the concern of the Ps 100, but rather Israel's belonging to God (cf. 100:3c), thus, the *qere* reading. I would argue, however, that if the *kethib* is understood to refer not to self-creation per se, but self-sustenance (as in v. 3c), then either reading fits the context of the psalm. It is in this latter sense that Brueggemann ("Psalm 100," 67) notes ancient Israel's repeated temptation to see itself as "self-made" (Isa 45:9–13), and how this fails to acknowledge Yahweh's initiative of Israel's progress as a nation (e.g., Deut 8; Isa 47:9–10; Ezek 28:2; 29:3, 9). For more on *kethib* and *qere*, see Armerding, *Criticism*, 109–10. For a discussion of the vowel pointing of the *kethib* and *qere* in 100:3, see Zorn, *Psalms*, 238–39.

30. McCann, *Theological*, 66. McCann notes that there may be intentional ambiguity here, as Israel did not think of its election apart from an understanding of God's intent for "all the earth" (100:1). See also, Zorn, *Psalms*, 238.

31. DeClaissé-Walford, et al., *Psalms*, 738–39.

response."³² Put differently, knowledge is more than the mere intellectual ascent to the proposition that Yahweh is the true God; it is first and foremost the recognition and recollection of his already-accomplished redemptive actions, which have been repeatedly experienced by his covenant people.

It is this redemptive sense that the poet expresses Israel's relationship to God in terms of belonging: "We are his" (v. 3b). In other words, because God initiates the redemption of a people, they belong to him as subjects belong to a king. The sense of belonging is most profoundly expressed in the last line of verse 3, which uses the popular shepherd-flock metaphor for God's relationship to his people: "We are his people, and the sheep of his pasture" (100:3c).³³ The royal theology of the psalm comes to its fullest and most intimate expression in the last line of verse 3 in the providential care that a shepherd has for his sheep, a royal metaphor commonly used in the ancient world for a king's relationship to his subjects. But the metaphor in the context of Ps 100 reflects not a general concept of pastoring, but a specific memory of being cared for, protected, and fed.³⁴ Verse 3, therefore, affirms both God's kingly, providential, and historic care of his people, as well as their unconditional submission to his sovereignty. Zorn summarizes the royal metaphor of verse 3:

> Human kings were referred to as "shepherds" of their people and so it is here with Yahweh God. He is the sovereign King and Shepherd of his people. He created them, he takes care of them. Israel owes her existence as well as her allegiance to the Creator God of the universe (and so does every human being in a real sense). This is the reason for such worship and service to Yahweh God.³⁵

What is more, this is not a pastoral metaphor that simply provides a picturesque scene of the relationship between God and his people; as with the general tone of the whole psalm its polemical thrust rings loud and clear— those whom Yahweh "shepherds" are to reject the authority of other false shepherds.³⁶

Verse 4 intensifies the invitation of the previous verses for humanity to recognize and recall God's providential care for his people. It also includes the final cluster of imperatives addressed to the flock of the Shepherd-King:

---

32. Mays, "Worship," 323.

33. Greidanus, *Preaching Christ*, 530n10. Greidanus notes the emphatic placement of "his" in the original Heb., which literally reads, "his people we are."

34. Brueggemann, "Psalm 100," 68.

35. Zorn, *Psalms*, 239.

36. Brueggemann, "Psalm 100," 67. Cf. Ezek 34:1–24; Luke 15:2–7; John 10:1–30.

enter, give thanks, and bless. As noted previously, the royal theology is teamed with liturgy as the psalmist invites worshipers to enter into the "gates" and "courts," which signify both temple and palatial precincts where the latter term is where the king's audiences are held.[37] Similarly, the language of "bless" (*barakh*) can also be translated "kneel" (cf. 95:6; 96:2), which obviously has royal connotations, as does the rendering "praise his name" (NIV).[38] Entering the king's presence with thanksgiving and praise are two actions that are not to be sharply distinguished from each other because both are grounded in a concrete action of Yahweh.[39] Once again, this points not as much to a general disposition of worship, but to a response to God's mighty deeds of redemption throughout history.

The final verse essentially states the central confession of the Psalter.[40] It gives the reason why Yahweh should be praised: because of his covenant loyalty to his people, Israel ("For the LORD is good, his steadfast love endures forever, and his faithfulness to all generations"). The verse is saturated with covenantal terminology, which reminds the reader of the character of God expressed in his faithfulness to the covenant. Verse 5a states the matter in what appears at first glance to be a more or less general way: "For the LORD is good." We should not conflate the general use of "good" in English with the use of the Hebrew *tov* in the context of the psalm where it reiterates God's saving acts on behalf of his people, which are born out of his loyalty to the covenant. Good is not simply the opposite of bad; it is an action-oriented term that recalls God's redemptive acts on behalf of his covenant people. In other words, "good" describes what the psalm has affirmed all along: God saves![41]

Similarly, in this context "good" is not a divine attribute of God as morally virtuous, but describes him as "honoring covenant commitments."[42] It is in this same covenantal context that the psalmist uses the unique Hebrew word *khesed*, often translated variously in English as steadfast love, covenant faithfulness, mercy, lovingkindness, loyal love, faithful love, unfailing love, and others. This plethora of possible translations reveals the complex use of the term throughout the OT so that there is no single English word that adequately conveys the sentiment of the Hebrew word. Therefore, Mays

---

37. Greidanus, *Preaching Christ*, 530n10.
38. McCann, *Psalms*, 1078; Greidanus, *Preaching Christ*, 530n10.
39. Brueggemann, "Psalm 100," 68.
40. DeClaissé-Walford, et al., *Psalms*, 740.
41. Mays, "Worship," 328.
42. Brueggemann, "Psalm 100," 69.

concedes that *khesed* is "tantalizingly impossible to reproduce in English."[43] In general, it denotes "the obligation assumed by one person to act on behalf of another, who is usually depending on the aid of the first and helpless to function adequately without it."[44] When placed in the context of Israel's election, including its responsibility to live out the stipulations of the covenant, *khesed* reflects God's continual acts of mercy and grace as he dispenses the blessings of the covenant upon a people who are utterly dependent upon his saving mercies. Seen in the context of God's relationship to Israel, the term is profoundly covenantal, referring to God's "benevolent deeds" for those to whom he was bound together with in covenant.[45]

While verse 5 does not contain the English word "endures" (as in the ESV "his steadfast love endures forever"), a literal translation takes into account the fact that God's steadfast love is coexistent with history.[46] In other words, like the previous mention of "good," it is not simply a divine attribute to be taken in a propositional sense, but a historic and verifiable beneficence that God demonstrates throughout history (i.e., "forever" or "to all generations"). Mays conveys well the historic reality of God's steadfast love: "The knowledge of Yahweh's *favor* comes through traditions of the past, ever renewed by recurrences of that *hesed* in the present. But that knowledge does not call back to the past; it summons to the future."[47] Thus, God's *khesed* is both specific in that he demonstrates it in concrete actions, and repetitive throughout human history.

Finally, steadfast love is often combined with "faithfulness" (v. 5c) in the OT, which further underscores God's unconditional commitment to his covenant people.[48] In fact, the covenantal context of this thanksgiving hymn should not go unnoticed. Psalm 100 does not merely call for a general disposition of thanks on the part of God's people, but instead calls them to give thanks and praise in the context of a covenantal relationship with their Shepherd-King, who sustains them through his commitment to the covenant. It is a covenantal hymn through and through. Therefore, it is not coincidental that this thanksgiving psalm repeats the covenant name of Israel's God, Yahweh, four times in five short verses. Thanksgiving is part and parcel of the covenant relationship.

---

43. Mays, "Worship," 328.
44. Zorn, *Psalms*, 240.
45. Mays, "Worship," 329.
46. Ibid.
47. Ibid.
48. Brueggemann, "Psalm 100," 69.

Christology

Psalm 100 does not at first appear to have a robust christological connection. However, as Mays aptly notes, "The Christian interpreter who works through its measures meets almost no resistance to understanding the gathering of the church through its images and ideas."[49] While it is not a prophecy of the Messiah per se, it is open to future times, and looks forward to future occurrences of God's protection and provision for his people.[50] Of course, Ps 100:1 anticipates the Gentile mission of the church, but nothing more needs to be added here to what was addressed with reference to Ps 67. Additionally, the psalm's shepherd-flock motif obviously anticipates the NT's portrait of Christ as the good shepherd (John 10:1–16), but I have already discussed this motif in connection to Ps 23 and need not repeat it here. Psalm 100 adds another dimension to the shepherd-sheep metaphor that hinges on the sense of belonging, which is so prevalent in verse 3: "Know that the LORD, he is God! It is he who made us, and we are his; we are his people, and the sheep of his pasture." I noted before that this verse is the centerpiece of the entire psalm, evidenced by the psalm's chiastic structure. But verse 3 forms a chiasm of its own, centering on the ownership that the Shepherd has of his sheep. The sequence of the personal pronouns in verse 3 is as follows: *he* is God . . . *he* made *us* . . . *we* are *his* . . . the sheep of *his* pasture.[51] Note the following chiastic structure:

> A He is God
> > B He made us
> > > C We are his
> > B1 His people
> A1 His pasture

This suggests that the flock's sense of belonging to the divine shepherd is the bedrock of its identity. McCann observes how this structure dramatically illustrates how the "question of human identity must begin and end with an understanding of God's identity."[52]

When the apostle Paul confronts unholiness and immorality in the churches, he often appeals to the fact that Christians belong to God, and their identity is bound with his identity as the holy God. In fact, "Christian" (*Christianos*) literally means "belonging to Christ." In continuity with Ps

---

49. Mays "Worship," 316.
50. Ibid.
51. McCann, *Theological*, 66.
52. Ibid.

100's emphases on belonging and worship, Paul exhorts the Corinthians concerning the importance of honoring God with their physical bodies by illustrating their sense of belonging to him as a consequence of the gospel: "Or do you not *know* that your body is a temple of the Holy Spirit within you, whom you have from God? *You are not your own*, for you were bought with a price. So *glorify* God in your body" (1 Cor 6:19–20).[53] While it cannot be proven (or disproven) that Paul alludes to Ps 100, there are nevertheless multiple points of contact between the two passages (note italics). The price that was paid was the death of Christ on the cross, which resulted in the Corinthians' release from sin and the gift of the Holy Spirit as divine empowerment for holy living. Put differently, the Shepherd-King sacrificially lays down his life for his sheep (John 10:11), and this naturally results in praise, thanksgiving, and worship.

While Ps 100 recalls God's great acts of redemption on behalf of the old covenant people, the NT affirms that he accomplishes the ultimate act of redemption in the gospel of Jesus Christ in the new covenant. Therefore, Christians, upon reading Ps 100 in light of the gospel, have a fuller perspective on the psalm's theme of thanksgiving than the psalmist himself. For God demonstrated his *khesed*, his steadfast covenant love and loyalty, most supremely in the gospel of a crucified and risen Savior who now reigns at God's right hand (Acts 7:55–56; Rom 8:34; Eph 1:20–23; Rev 3:21). My logic here reflects a common method of exegesis in the NT known as a "lesser to greater" (*qal wahomer*) argument, which illustrates that what applies in a less important case will certainly apply in a more important case (e.g., Matt 12:12; Heb 2:2–4).[54] Tremper Longman perceives this lesser to greater progression from the psalmist to the Christian in terms of salvation that leads to thanksgiving: "How much more should we be thankful to God for providing his Son as a sacrifice to atone for our sin? As we read the thanksgiving psalms, let our thanks fly to Jesus who suffered and died for our sakes."[55] The redemptive acts of God, which the psalmist recalls (i.e., election, exodus, return from exile), anticipate and reach their ultimate fulfillment in the gospel. Therefore, a christological hermeneutic demands that the seven imperatives of Ps 100 are ultimately addressed to Christians who have experienced the fullness of God's salvation in Jesus Christ. Because of the gospel, Christians confess "The LORD is good; his steadfast love endures forever, and his faithfulness to all generations" (100:5).

---

53. Ibid., 67.
54. Longenecker, *Exegesis*, 20.
55. Longman, *How to Read Psalms*, 72.

In conjunction with the universal reign of Christ is the creation of a people who are his loyal subjects. I have pointed this out in connection with Pss 1, 23, and 46, and the motif is especially prominent here in Ps 100. The center of the psalm affirms, "It is he who made us, and we are his" (100:3), and the gospel is the fullest expression of God's redemption through which he creates a people who belong to him. By using the method of intertextuality—the interconnections between texts—I would like to suggest that 1 Pet 2:9–10 echoes the main themes of Ps 100. To be clear, I am not suggesting that Peter refers Ps 100 per se; in fact, he alludes most clearly to Isa 43 and Exod 19 in 1 Pet 2:9–10. Yet in light of the interpretive conviction that within the context of the Christian canon, no passage exists in isolation from other canonical texts, resulting in resonances between certain passages that often exceed the intentions of the original authors. Put differently, Scripture is a canonical matrix where passages are read in light of each other. As I have noted elsewhere, "A text cannot be read in isolation because it belongs to a web of texts (i.e., a canon of Scripture), which are present whenever it is read or studied."[56] Therefore, I believe 1 Pet 2:9–10 echoes certain themes of Ps 100, which take on added significance for Christians when the psalm is read through a christological lens. These themes include, royal and liturgical imagery, election and creation of a people, possession, and praise for God's mighty deeds: "But you are a *chosen race*, a *royal priesthood*, a holy nation, a people for his own *possession*, that you may *proclaim the excellencies* of him who *called* you out of darkness into his marvelous light. Once you were not a people, but now you are God's people; once you had not received mercy, but now you have received mercy" (1 Pet 2:9–10).

First, for the psalmist, "He made us" (100:3) refers to the redemptive actions of God on behalf of Israel, notably election, the exodus, and return from exile, each signifying the creation of Israel as people. It is therefore likely no mere coincidence that Peter's message to the church alludes to these redemptive events as types of their redemption in Christ. While the NT commonly interprets the exodus and return from exile as typological forerunners of the greater deliverance Christ brings to his people, the combination of these events in 1 Pet 2 is noteworthy. First, 1 Pet 2:9a ("You are a chosen race") alludes to the "chosen people" of Isa 43:20–21, and Peter adopts language that originally referred to Israel's return from exile, and applies it to his new covenant readers. Peter's point is that as God formed a new people in the return from exile, he has now created a new race of people out of the many various ethnicities that make up the churches of the Diaspora (1 Pet 1:1). Karen Jobes explains the many races "constitute a

---

56. Fletcher, *Signs*, 52n111.

new race of those who have been born again into the living hope through the resurrection of Jesus Christ."[57] Hence, Peter emphasizes the creation of a new people in light of God's redemptive activity in the return from exile, something not foreign to the thought of Ps 100:3.

Second, not only does Peter utilize deliverance from exile typology, but also exodus typology in an effort to reiterate the identity of his readers, calling them a "royal priesthood" (1 Pet 2:9b), which he takes from Exod 19:6. The combination of royal theology and liturgy is not unlike the imagery of Ps 100. As is the case with the return from exile typology, the NT frequently interprets Israel's deliverance at the exodus as a type of what God has done in Christ. By alluding to Exod 19:6 ("And you shall be for me a kingdom of priests and a holy nation"), Peter draws on exodus typology to identify his audience, using the same terminology used to identify ancient Israel in the OT. Again, the new creation overtones are present in the very act of redemption. Even more prominent is the blending of royal and liturgical imagery as a description of the church. Again, Jobes notes, "Its faithful consecration to God, the King of the universe, therefore makes its priesthood a royal service."[58] Psalm 100 shares this sentiment as it declares God King of all peoples, who then "serve" or "worship" him as loyal subjects (100:2).

Ancient Israel's holiness as a nation derived from the holy King of the universe, who had cut a covenant with them, binding them to himself, making them not only his subjects but also his sanctified servants (i.e., priests).[59] In conjunction with the royal emphasis of the psalm, Peter's use of the modifier "royal" is apt, for Christians know God as their King, to whom they now owe allegiance.[60] Like Ps 100, Peter combines royal and liturgical imagery, and uses the exodus as an example of deliverance where God created a new people. What is different in Peter's context is that God's pinnacle act of redemption in Christ is the typological fulfillment of the exodus. What is more, election, which obviously contributes to the new creation of a people, is present in Peter's description of the church as being "called out of darkness" (1 Pet 2:9), and the same may be said for being "chosen." As implied in Ps 100:3, God "made" a people through his great acts of redemption, and these include among others election, the exodus, and return from exile. Peter echoes each of these acts as he applies OT terminology to his Christian readers.

---

57. Jobes, *1 Peter*, 159.
58. Ibid., 160.
59. Ibid., 161.
60. Ibid.

Third, another thematic echo can be heard as Peter describes his readers as God's possession: " . . . a people for his own possession . . ." (1 Pet 2:9d), which evokes the psalm's language of "we are his" (Ps 100:3). The phrase comes from Exod 19:5, the same context as the royal priesthood, but Peter has reversed the word order of the original. Part and parcel of Israel's deliverance from Egyptian bondage is their loyalty to their new King, who owns them as a lord owns a vassal, and to whom they belong. The main thought of Ps 100 is that God's acts of deliverance as the sovereign King of the universe demand the loyalty of his subjects; he owns them, and they are his.

Fourth, Ps 100:2 expresses the loyalty of the King's subjects in terms of "service" (or "worship") as the congregation enters the temple courts. Upon entering the temple complex, the congregation sings songs of thanksgiving and praise, blessing the name of the LORD (100:2b, 4). Within the movement of the psalm, this worship experience is undoubtedly the response of the sheep to the protection and provision of their Shepherd, recalling his mighty deeds performed on their behalf. Interestingly, this is where Peter goes next after the description of his readers as God's possession, who "proclaim his excellencies" (or better, his "mighty acts" NRSV)—redemptive events where God has rescued them from darkness, bringing them into his marvelous light. Peter takes the phrase from LXX Isa 43:21, which speaks of the duty of the newly-formed Israelites to declare God's "mighty deeds," "praises," or "manifestations of divine power" (*aretas*).[61] Isaiah 43:21 has a praise and worship tone, and reflects both the poet's and Peter's emphasis on worship as the result of God's mighty deeds. God's reason for delivering Israel from Egyptian bondage and Babylonian captivity is to "constitute a special people who make known what God has done."[62] Recipients of God's redemption do not keep silent but declare his mighty deeds to all peoples. Therefore, both the poet and Peter affirm that deliverance brings ownership, resulting in worship. Put differently, God's mighty acts of election, creation, and redemption are the basis of praise.

All in all, the Christian interpreter can affirm with the psalmist that God has made them and therefore owns them, calling forth praise for his acts of deliverance. They share the same thankful response, but the Christian is even more thankful for God's demonstration of his covenant love demonstrated preeminently in the gospel of Christ. Thus, a christological reading of Ps 100 fills out the praise of the psalmist as "the Christian community declares by its existence, by its liturgy and worship, by the daily lives

---

61. Ibid., 163.
62. Ibid.

of its members the mighty deed of Christ's resurrection, which reveals the praiseworthy character of God."[63]

Psalm 100 also anticipates certain aspects of the new covenant, especially those in Heb 8:10–12. For example, God's ownership of his people, their *belonging* to him, is the substance of the new covenant of Jer 31:33, which is quoted in Heb 8:10 in the context of the contrast of the old and new covenants: "I will be their God, and they shall be my people." Patrick Reardon observes that God is "our God" as a consequence of the new covenant, as distinct from simply "God." And we are "his people," as distinct from just a bunch of folks.[64] This sense of belonging is the source of joy in our psalm,[65] and awaits its full and final consummation in the new heavens and the new earth: "He will dwell with them, and they will be his people" (Rev 21:3). What is more, the *knowledge* of God in Ps 100:3 also finds its fulfillment in the new covenant, as Jeremiah prophesies, "And no longer shall each one teach his neighbor and each his brother, saying, 'Know the LORD,' for they shall all know me, from the least of them to the greatest, declares the LORD" (Jer 31:34; cf. Heb 8:11). I noted before that the Hebrew concept of knowledge is not so much intellectual cognition as it is personal relationship, which is the intent of Jeremiah's prophecy. As J. A. Thompson observes, "*Know* here probably carries its most profound connotation, the intimate personal knowledge that arises from between two persons who are committed wholly to one another in a relationship that touches mind, emotion, and will."[66] To be clear, it is not the case that ancient Israel did not know Yahweh as their covenant God; he had revealed himself to them repeatedly through his mighty acts of revelation and redemption, as Ps 100 confirms. They knew God, but tended to forget him. Through the blood of Christ the new covenant remedies the fractured relationship between God and his covenant partner, Israel, providing "knowledge" that is truly relational and personal. Therefore, the emphasis on knowing God in Ps 100:3 anticipates the personal and intimate relationship between God and his new covenant people. And as Reardon concludes, "This [personal] knowledge of God is that to which we give voice when we 'come into his presence with exultation.'"[67]

---

63. Ibid., 164.

64. Reardon, *Christ*, 197. Reardon also stresses that the new covenant conveys "mutual belonging" because God is *their* God, and they are *his* people.

65. Ibid.

66. Thompson, *Jeremiah*, 581.

67. Reardon, *Christ*, 198.

When read through a christological lens, Ps 100 has a deep structure that reflects multiple facets of the gospel. It looks forward to the new covenant where Christians belong to God as subjects to a king, singing his praises for his acts of deliverance on their behalf, especially Christ's death and resurrection, for which we are supremely thankful. Similarly, the psalm anticipates the new covenant emphasis on knowledge of God as a personal and intimate relationship.

Psalm 119

"The great wonder in the law of God is the revelation of the Lord Jesus Christ."—Dietrich Bonhoeffer

"Inspiring." "Emotional." "Heartfelt." "Picturesque." These words are not usually the first to come to mind after reading Ps 119. Instead, words like "slog," "boring," "tedious," "rambling," "repetitive," and "monotonous" are often how folks describe it. John Calvin even claims that the psalmist himself perceived the need to make the poem "less irksome" to the reader by crafting it as an acrostic where each of its twenty-two stanzas corresponds to a successive letter of the Hebrew alphabet.[1] While I have never been irked by the psalm, I cannot say it was one of my favorites, at least not until now after doing the research for this book. I have a new appreciation for the psalm as the literary masterpiece that it is, and not only for its literary complexity, but also its content, which I hope to show reflects a robust Christology when read in light of the gospel.

To be clear, Ps 119 is not an easy read. It is long; it is sometimes called the "giant psalm," and when the average adult attention span is about twenty minutes, this psalm challenges the mental stamina of many readers. C. S. Lewis likens it to embroidery where there is a pattern woven together stitch by stitch, through long, quiet hours, for love of the subject and for the delight in leisurely, disciplined craftsmanship.[2] Psalm 119 lacks many of the picturesque metaphors associated with other psalms, causing some readers to miss that it nonetheless stems from a troubled heart; it is indeed heartfelt because the poet's overwhelming concern is the expectation that his commitment to God's instruction be rewarded with covenant blessings, not met with the opposition, ridicule, and persecution that characterize his current situation. Put differently, the psalmist sees a disconnect between

---

1. Calvin, *Psalms*, Apple e-book, ch. 119.
2. Lewis, *Reflections*, 58–59.

God's covenant promises of life and blessing and the reality of the psalmist's persecution at the hands of his foes: "I am yours; save me, for I have sought your precepts. The wicked lie in wait to destroy me, but I consider your testimonies" (119:94–95). Far from being 176 propositions on the "law" (*torah*), or even Scripture per se, Ps 119 wrestles with the reality of trials and tribulations *in spite* of torah obedience. It is, therefore, the heartfelt response of the righteous sufferer.

History

Psalm 119 is truly a work of literary artistry, but only the original Hebrew bears this out. Much of the author's literary skill is lost in English translations. Because it is an acrostic (cf. Pss 25; 34; 111; 112; 145; Prov 31:10–31), where each stanza corresponds to successive letters of the Hebrew alphabet, English Bibles print the name of the Hebrew letter as a heading for each stanza so readers can have a sense of the psalm's original literary structure. There are twenty-two stanzas, one for each letter of the Hebrew alphabet, composed of eight lines each for a total of 176 verses. Each verse in the first stanza begins with *aleph*, the first letter of the Hebrew alphabet; each verse of the second stanza begins with *bet*, the second letter, and so on through the whole Hebrew alphabet. Every stanza except one (vv. 9–16) contains at least one occurrence of the Hebrew word *torah*, usually translated into English as "law," making it the main subject of the psalm.[3] In addition to being most likely a memory device,[4] the acrostic structure highlights the comprehensive and all-encompassing nature of torah—it applies to every-

---

3. McCann, *Theological*, 31. Because torah is a way of life in Ps 119, and because the Heb. word *derek* ("way" or "path") is used several times in the psalm, some find "way" to be a meaningful term for describing the essence of the psalm—the delight in walking in God's way. For example, Anthony Ash and Clyde Miller offer a very practical scheme of organizing the psalm around this central theme where "way" occurs in the heading of each St. of the psalm, as follows: the way of blamelessness (vv. 1–8); the way of purity (vv. 9–16); the way of divine counsel (vv. 17–24); the way of faithfulness (vv. 25–32); the way of life (vv. 33–40); the way of liberty (vv. 41–48); the way of obedience (vv. 49–56); the way of fellowship (vv. 57–64); the way of discipline (vv. 65–72); the way of mercy (vv. 73–80); the way of endurance (vv. 81–88); the way of certainty (vv. 89–96); the way of wisdom (vv. 97–104); the way of light (vv. 105–112); the way of fear (vv. 113–120); the way of justice (vv. 121–128); the way of steadfastness (vv. 129–136); the way of righteousness (vv. 137–144); the way of hope (vv. 145–152); the way of vitality (vv. 153–160); the way of rejoicing (vv. 161–168); the way of confession (vv. 169–176). The authors acknowledge that these headings do not exhaust the specific topics covered in each St., and are intentionally broad, useful as basic points of reference (*Psalms*, 386–94).

4. DeClaissé-Walford, *Introduction*, 17.

thing from A to Z (or from *aleph* to *tav*).⁵ Alternatively, the author has said everything there is to say about a subject, having summed it up from beginning to end.⁶ According to C. Hassell Bullock,

> The fact that the poem exhausts the alphabet to describe and praise the Torah would suggest that the poet intended to describe its all-encompassing nature. He has worked over the Torah from "A" to "Z," as it were, and looked at it from the linguistic angle of every single Hebrew letter. This is coupled with the fact that each strophe sustains the same letter in each of its eight verses, intensifying the extensive nature of the Torah. After the alphabet had been exhausted and each letter used as the first letter of eight continuous verses, what more could be said about the Torah! What more need be said!⁷

What is more, every verse except two (vv. 90, 122) contains at least one synonym for torah.⁸ The following table illustrates how frequently the psalm uses torah and its seven synonyms:

Hebrew word	English Translation	Frequency
torah	"law"	25 times
edah	"decree"	23 times
mishpat	"ordinance/rule"	23 times
khoq	"statute"	22 times
dabar	"word"	22 times
mitsvah	"commandment"	22 times
piqqud	"precept"	21 times
imrah	"promise"	19 times

Table 5 Torah and its Synonyms in Psalm 119

5. McCann, *Theological*, 31.
6. DeClaissé-Walford, *Introduction*, 17.
7. Bullock, *Encountering*, 221.
8. Burgess, "Incarnation," 138. Although, there are a few variations like "ways" (vv. 3, 37), "paths" (v. 15), and "faithfulness" (v. 90), not to mention textual variants, all of which makes precise totals elusive. Table 5 follows deClaissé-Walford, *Introduction*, 119. Walter Zorn adds a tantalizing observation that in an effort to compensate for the few verses that lack one of the synonyms, five lines contain two of the key words (vv. 16, 48, 160, 168, and 172) for a total of 177 words, one over the ideal of 176 (22x8). However, textual variants for vv. 48 and 168 reveal the possibility of an excess word in each verse due to dittography, the accidental duplication of a word, letter, or line by a scribe, which brings the total to 175 or 176. The total synonym word count, therefore, is more or less equal to the total number of verses in the psalm (*Psalms*, 374–75).

Because of the repetitious nature of the psalm, and because of its singular focus on torah, each stanza can stand for the whole, but the whole is needed to reach the full effect of the acrostic structure.[9]

The twenty-two stanzas of the psalm have overlapping elements that are repeated throughout the entire psalm, and this makes it difficult to determine its precise genre. These elements include individual lament (v. 107), the song of trust (v. 42), the song of thanksgiving (v. 7), the hymn (vv. 71–72), and the wisdom aphorism (vv. 9, 99).[10] When one considers the whole psalm, it fits quite well into the genre of wisdom psalms (Pss 1, 32, 37, 49, 73, 78, 112, 127, 128, 133), but this can be narrowed even further to include the "torah psalms" (Pss 1, 19).[11] In fact, Ps 119 shares much of the vocabulary of Pss 1 and 19, even to the point where every word of 119:1 occurs in both psalms.[12] Thus, Ps 119 is a natural fit among the torah psalms, which are a subset of the wisdom group. However, the individual lament element of Ps 119 should not be overlooked. When one considers the various genres within the psalm, the elements of the individual prayer for help (i.e., lament) are the most dominant.[13] As James Mays observes, "Petitions, descriptions of trouble with self and others, assertions of trust, and vows of praise compose most of the psalm."[14]

The basic elements of many other lament psalms occur throughout Ps 119, so we should not think in terms of an isolated lament verse here and there, but rather a robust attempt to follow the characteristic movement apparent in most laments. For example, verses 17–24 follows the pattern of other lament psalms: words of petition (vv. 17–18) give way to complaint (v. 19), move on to a description of the oppressors (vv. 21–23), and end with words of trust (v. 24).[15] This continues in the next stanza: complaint—"My soul clings to the dust" (v. 25); petition—"Strengthen me according to your word" (v. 28); and trust—"I cling to your testimonies" (v. 31).[16] Nearly every stanza contains some kind of reference to the suffering of the psalmist. The lament element is so strong that it is possible to see Ps 119 wholly as a lament psalm that moves from complaint to petition (vv. 17–24) to praise and assurance (vv. 169–176). The turning point for the psalmist is the "zenith" of verses

---

9. Mays, *Psalms*, 382.
10. Bullock, *Encountering*, 221.
11. Zorn, *Psalms*, 376.
12. McCann, *Theological*, 31.
13. Mays, *Psalms*, 384.
14. Ibid.
15. DeClaissé-Walford, et al., *Psalms*, 882.
16. Ibid.

89–96, which follows its lowest point in verses 81–88.[17] While it is best not to force Ps 119 into a rigid genre classification, the individual lament proposal is a much-needed corrective to what tends to be an oversimplification of the psalm's type as a wisdom or torah psalm; it also helps protect against a reading of the psalm that focuses on its individual poetic lines, amounting to proof texting at the expense of the psalm's more comprehensive lament context. The reality is more complex because laments are interwoven among the other types of genres so that the psalm is a "montage" of different types, even if individual prayers for help predominate.[18]

The central issue taken up by the psalm is *torah piety*: "diligent adherence to the instructions found in the stories, the laws, and the prophetic words of the Torah, the first five books of the Old Testament."[19] It is unfortunate that in spite of decades of research suggesting the Hebrew word *torah* is not confined to the legal precepts of the Mosaic Law, but also refers more broadly to the "instruction" of the Lord, that most English translations continue to render the word as "law," which often carries a legalistic connotation for modern readers. The NLT, however, stands out in its translation of *torah* as "instructions" in 119:1: "Joyful are people of integrity, who follow the instructions of the LORD."

Although torah in the OT does not refer exclusively to the Pentateuch, it eventually became associated with this literary corpus in Second Temple and rabbinic Judaism.[20] It is important to note that torah designates not only the legal portions of Exodus, Leviticus, Numbers, and Deuteronomy, but also the narratives, ethical exhortations, and genealogies of the first five books of Moses. These serve as "instruction" from the Lord every bit as much as the "law." As Nancy deClaissé-Walford explains, "The Torah is the ancient Israelites' memory of God's total involvement in their life."[21] In other words, it is the *metanarrative* of God's interaction with his people, which ultimately produces a covenantal way of life in them; it is not a legal "system" that assures salvation when performed to the letter. Torah piety,

---

17. McCann, *Psalms*, 1168. McCann is referencing the view of Will Soll, *Psalm 119*. Soll divides the psalm into six sections as follows: Aleph-Beth as the prologue (vv. 1–16); Gimmel-Waw (vv. 17–48); Zayin-Yod (vv. 49–80); Kaph-Samek as the central section (vv. 81–120); Ayin-Tsadhe (vv. 121–144); Qoph-Tav as the concluding section (vv. 145–176). Besides the introduction, each of these sections follows the basic lament pattern of complaint, petition, affirmation of trust, while also containing other characteristics so as not to insist on a rigid pattern. The whole psalm evidences this basic lament pattern.

18. Mays, *Psalms*, 384.

19. DeClaissé-Walford, *Introduction*, 61.

20. Watts, "Torah," 629–30; Longman, "Torah," 1646–47.

21. DeClaissé-Walford, *Introduction*, 61.

therefore, "designates not just a text and its interpretation but also the life of those devoted to its study and to following its precepts, i.e., a life of faithful piety."[22]

The Pentateuch, or literary Torah, is the inscripturated record of the metanarrative of God's total involvement in Israelite life from a literary perspective. However, this is not the sum of the poet's conception of God's torah in Ps 119. In fact, the psalm never actually defines torah nor speaks of its source outside its origin in Yahweh. The psalmist never mentions Moses, Sinai, or the precise content of the Lord's instruction.[23] While he most certainly includes written texts as one source of God's word, he by no means limits divine revelation to written sources.[24] In short, neither the Pentateuch nor any other written source exhausts God's torah. Torah is a way of life that originates in God himself and is manifested in the covenant he has cut with his people.

The psalmist seems to see torah as a "divine hypostasis," like wisdom (*khokhma*) in Prov 8 rather than simply a codification of laws.[25] Torah is not simply a book or body of legislation. The poet recognizes three sources of God's torah in Ps 119. First, torah comes to the psalmist by way of the "received tradition," most notably from his teachers and those of old who have passed it down through the ages: "I have more understanding than all my teachers, for your testimonies are my meditation. I understand more than the aged, for I keep your precepts" (119:99–100).[26] Even if he has now surpassed the insights of his teachers, he nonetheless acknowledges their role in passing down the tradition to future generations. This probably includes both oral tradition and written sources of torah, including the literary Torah. Second, the psalmist sees cosmic or natural law (what we call "natural revelation" today) as a source of torah, given its origin in the Creator: "Forever, O LORD, your word is firmly fixed in the heavens. Your faithfulness endures to all generations; you have established the earth, and it stands fast. By your appointment they stand this day, for all things are your servants" (vv. 89–91).[27] The reference to your "word" in verse 89 (MT *dabar*; LXX *logos*) as one of the synonyms for torah in Ps 119 makes this observation sure. In other words, one can gain insight into God's torah by considering his

---

22. Watts, "Torah," 630.
23. DeClaissé-Walford, et al., *Psalms*, 886.
24. McCann, *Psalms*, 1176.
25. DeClaissé-Walford, et al., *Psalms*, 886.
26. McCann, *Psalms*, 1167.
27. Ibid.

works of creation. Finally, torah comes directly from Yahweh to the psalmist by of unmediated divine teaching:

> My soul clings to the dust; give me life according to your word! When I told of my ways, you answered me; teach me your statutes! Make me understand the way of your precepts, and I will meditate on your wondrous works. My soul melts away for sorrow; strengthen me according to your word! Put false ways far from me and graciously teach me your law. (vv. 26–29)[28]

God is willing to provide direct insight into his "statutes" and "precepts" in order to aid the psalmist's interpretation and application of torah. McCann, therefore, aptly summarizes the sources of torah in Ps 119: "While oral and written tradition were very significant for the psalmist, he or she remained open to God's ongoing instruction, to God's further revelation, to new experiences of the divine Word."[29] For the poet, there is no limit to God's torah; it cannot be put into a box: "Even perfection has its limits, but your commands have no limit" (v. 96 NLT).

Torah piety as a way of life is first and foremost based in the dynamics of the covenantal relationship between God and his people. Walter Brueggemann and William Bellinger explain the covenantal dynamics of torah piety: "It does not consist in the flat response of obedience to a code of commands. Rather, Torah obedience is a full existence of trust in and loyalty to a covenant partner, trust and loyalty that are embodied in obedience to instruction but that bespeak an interpersonal, interactive communion and not simply compliance with a set of rules."[30] Only as a covenantal way of life stemming from the recognition and experience of God's *khesed* could torah be the object of such joy, devotion, and acclaim as shown in Ps 119.[31] In other words, torah piety is not a legalistic system of works righteousness by which one earns God's favor.

I will speak more on the dating on the psalm later, suffice it to say here that most scholars see it as a product of postexilic Judaism, and this naturally raises the issue of the nature of Judaism during this period. We must first recognize that "Judaism" throughout the biblical period was not monolithic. It is a religion that spans thousands of years with different sects, various sacred texts, and multiple theological assumptions. It is not good English to speak of "Judaisms," but this is perhaps the most accurate way of putting it. With that said, each biblical period of Judaism (basically the following:

28. Ibid.
29. Ibid.
30. Brueggemann and Bellinger, *Psalms*, 520.
31. Zorn, *Psalms*, 373.

Patriarchal, Mosaic, monarchy, preexilic, exilic, postexilic/Second Temple) has overlapping as well as unique characteristics, and torah piety is especially prominent in postexilic Judaism and throughout the Second Temple period, notably in the Diaspora. It would be a mistake to characterize torah piety as legalistic, requiring works of human merit that earn God's favor and place one into the covenant. Such was Martin Luther's understanding of ancient Judaism (although not Ps 119 per se—he highly valued it), including that reflected in the NT, as represented by the Pharisees in the Gospels and "Judaizers" in Paul's letters. But Luther's view was rooted in his experience with Medieval Catholicism as a legalistic religion of human works, not in a rigorous historical investigation of the relevant texts from the ancient period, many of which were unavailable to him. Luther viewed the OT as a system of law-works, and the NT as a system of grace.

Although the nature of Second Temple Judaism is hotly debated, the psalmist's perspective in Ps 119 is far from a perfectionistic pursuit of religious performance that earns God's favor, resulting in covenant blessing. The psalmist readily admits his imperfections (vv. 67, 71, 75, 176), and this causes him to rely on God's *khesed* as the basis for the covenant relationship: "In your steadfast love (*khesed*) give me life, that I may keep the testimonies of your mouth" (v. 88; cf. vv. 41, 64, 76, 124, 149). Thus, God's covenant love is the *basis* for the psalmist's obedience: God's grace holds him up and keeps him alive, making his obedience possible. This is far from works righteousness since God's grace comes *before* any action on the part of the psalmist. What is more, the first clause of the final verse of the psalm illustrates the psalmist's outlook on his so-called performance: "I have gone astray like a lost sheep" (v. 176). The psalmist, in other words, is *already* a member of the covenant community; he has been granted salvation as a covenant privilege. Therefore, to label him as trying to "earn" salvation through torah piety misunderstands not only his personal motives but also the nature of Judaism in his day. McCann is adamant that a proper understanding of the psalmist's perspective and postexilic Judaism are indispensable for a proper historical interpretation of Ps 119: "Not infrequently, it has been criticized not only as artificial and tedious, but also as the product of a self-righteous psalmist, who exhibits the legalism that supposedly characterized post-exilic Judaism. The charges against Psalm 119 should be dropped. They are not fair to either the psalm or the psalmist—or to Judaism."[32] Similarly, Gary Burge, Lynn Cohick, and Gene Green conclude, "The characterization of the Jewish faith as nothing more than legalism ignores not only the rich teaching of the OT about the grace and mercy of God but also the many writings of Jews in antiquity who knew that obedience to God could only spring from experiencing his grace."[33] Judaism's self-understanding as the people of God was the covenant made by God with Israel; the covenant was nowhere regarded in Jewish writings as an achievement of human merit.[34] When viewed in this covenantal light, the rescue and redemption of the psalmist are totally in God's hands, and while the poet expresses a robust commitment to torah, he in no way eliminates God's grace as the sole basis for covenant blessing.

While there is no doubt that the psalmist's appeals to his delight and commitment to God's torah, this need not be seen as perfectionism, but as life lived in covenant in view of the covenant's provisions for sin (i.e., offerings, prayers for forgiveness, etc.), what E. P. Sanders calls "covenant nomism."[35] In other words, the reason for the psalmist's confidence regarding his obedience to torah is because he lives within the confines of the covenant by doing what it requires for sin and the maintenance of healthy relationships. These requirements are built into the fabric of the covenant to keep one in the covenant relationship with Yahweh and with his/her fellow covenanters. What is more, the legalistic approach to ancient Judaism tends to emphasize the anxiety and utter frustration at the human inability to keep the law perfectly. But this is nowhere near the psalmist's heart that "delights" in torah piety, and sees it not as a burden but as a blessing because "no pleasure or activity could compare with the life of the Torah."[36] Bullock captures well the joyous life associated with torah piety in the context of the covenant:

32. McCann, *Psalms*, 1174.
33. Burge, et al., *Antiquity*, 264.
34. Dunn, introduction to *Cambridge Companion*, 10.
35. Sanders, *Palestinian Judaism*.
36. Bullock, *Encountering*, 225. The rabbis also saw torah piety as a joyous blessing rather than a burden. Solomon Schechter explains ancient Israel's view of the law: "They [laws] were their very love and their very life." According to later rabbinic literature, "Tremble with joy when thou art about to fulfill a commandment" (Der. Er. Zut., 2). For these, as well as an enlightening commentary on the rabbinic perspective of the joy of torah piety, see Schechter, *Rabbinic*, 148–69.

The purpose of Torah was to build a life lived in accordance with the will of God revealed in his laws, and to build a secure and safe community in which the Torah can be joyfully kept. Yahweh has, therefore, provided a context of love (*khesed*) in which he gave his Torah, and those who keep it find that its benevolent purposes meet life's aspirations and produce human happiness.[37]

Finally, the goal of torah piety is ultimately to know God, the giver of torah. Far from a superficial acquiescence to a system of legal codes, obedience to torah seeks above all a personal and intimate relationship with the God of the covenant. The poet never speaks about the law in the abstract but always in connection to God as the divine originator of torah (i.e., "your law").[38] Therefore, torah never has any independent reality, any existence on its own. The psalm speaks to God about the psalmist's relation to God and his way with his servants, and the word of God is spoken about only in that context.[39] In the effort to learn obedience to torah, the poet's main desire is to be taught by God himself.[40] Psalm 119, therefore, is profoundly relational as the psalmist seeks God and ultimately pleads for God to seek the psalmist (v. 176).

The topic of torah piety potentially impacts the date of composition of Ps 119 because torah piety eventually came to have a certain degree of specificity in Jewish theology. Most scholars agree that the editorial shaping of the Psalter began in the exilic period and reached a fever pitch in the postexilic period. That Ps 119 places such a marked emphasis on torah piety, it is reasonable to conclude that it was composed during the postexilic period when torah piety became the centerpiece of Jewish theology as a description and program of the good life—life in covenant with Yahweh.[41] Bullock even suggests that Ps 119 may be one of the last compositions of the collection.[42] The good life included, among other things, a robust commitment to the study of the literary Torah. The postexilic community seems to have learned the lessons of the exile, including the importance of obedience

---

37. Bullock, *Encountering*, 226.

38. Eaton, *Psalms*, 415.

39. Mays, *Psalms*, 384. As Mays states, "What he [the psalmist] has come to know is that in dealing with the teaching one deals with the teacher."

40. Eaton, *Psalms*, 422.

41. Bullock, *Encountering*, 221. The rabbis, however, thought of David as intensely devoted to the study of torah, even to the extent that all of his sins, notably adultery with Bathsheba, were nullified by his zeal for the study of torah. The rabbis frequently thought of David as the ideal rabbinic scholar (Bassler, "Seasons," 161–62). Therefore, torah piety is not limited to the postexilic period.

42. Bullock, *Encountering*, 222.

to the covenant both as a nation and as individual members of the covenant community. As a marginalized group surrounded by pagan nations, the Jewish community understood itself to be primarily a community of obedience as a consequence of their most recent historical catastrophe (i.e., exile into Babylon).[43] In other words, if disobedience caused the exile, "let's not do this again" was the prevailing wisdom of the day among the postexilic community.

In the absence of the temple and its ministries, which the Babylonians destroyed in 587 BCE, torah piety—intentional life with Yahweh[44]—became the center of Jewish theology as a way to recommit to the covenant and learn the lessons of the past, which provided hope for the future. As I noted previously, torah cannot be limited to written sources in this period, but Israel's primary access to the covenant that they publicly pledged to recommit themselves to was the written Torah (Neh 8:9). In fact, it is not a stretch to suggest that the great moment of the reconstitution of Judaism by Ezra following the exile revolves around the reading of the Torah (Neh 8:1–12), and most scholars believe this reading was of the entire Pentateuch, or at least the Priestly portions of it.[45] The existence of the torah psalms themselves (Pss 1, 19, 119) is evidence for this postexilic torah commitment, which reflects a community whose horizon is defined by the torah, at least in its written form if not other forms as well.[46] What is more, Brevard Childs observes that the theme in the torah psalms of the godly man who desires to "meditate" on God's torah and devotes himself to being obedient to God's commands is parallel to the main thought of Deut 30 and Josh 1, and this reveals "clearly that the commandments of Moses constitute the divine law on which the godly reflect."[47] Childs also observes the function of the canonical placement of Ps 1, a torah psalm, as the introduction to the Psalter: "The Torah of God which is the living word of God is mediated through its written form as sacred scripture. With the written word Israel is challenged to meditate day and night in seeking the will of God. Indeed, as a heading to the whole Psalter the blessing now includes the faithful meditation on the sacred writings which follow."[48] Some scholars have even theorized that an earlier form of the Psalter may have consisted of Pss 1—119, suggesting that torah functions like bookends of the Psalter, serving as both the introduc-

43. Brueggemann, *Theology*, 445.
44. Ibid.
45. Ibid., 591.
46. Ibid., 445.
47. Childs, *Introduction*, 513.
48. Ibid.

tory lens and the summarization of the collection.[49] Intriguingly, that would make the Psalter one grand book about torah piety, which has become virtually synonymous with Scripture piety in the postexilic period. Given this emphasis on torah piety in the Psalter, it is probably not a coincidence that Psalms received its five-book division, which mimics the five books of the Torah, in the postexilic period.[50] Scholars even refer to Psalms at times as "the second Torah."[51] When one considers the postexilic period as a time of intense torah piety, the observation of Brueggemann and Bellinger is appropriate in the context of Ps 119: "The central truth of Torah obedience cannot be said too often."[52]

Another feature of torah piety in the postexilic period is particularly noteworthy in the context of the study of the literary Torah, and has a significant bearing on the place of torah piety in Ps 119. The function of torah piety in the postexilic period is multifaceted: it shapes the identity and ethics of the people of Israel over against the Gentile nations that swarm around them, reinforces commitment to the covenant with Yahweh, and even fulfills certain cultic functions. I have mentioned before that what we call "Judaism" in the biblical period is variegated, depending on the time period and the geographical location of various Jewish groups. For example, diaspora Jews—those who did not return to Palestine at the end of the exile but lived as "dispersed" throughout the Mediterranean world—was in many ways different from that practiced in Palestine, especially Jerusalem. Diaspora Jews did not have a temple, so the literal sacrificial system was more or less irrelevant to them. According to Mark Allan Powell:

> Because Diaspora Jews were often far from Jerusalem (indeed, many never saw the city), the temple system lost some of its relevance and meaning for them. Diaspora Jews tended to look to synagogues rather than to the temple for their religious needs, with the result that, over time, rabbis became more important than priests and obedience to Torah took precedence over the offering of sacrifices (which were allowed only in Jerusalem).[53]

This emphasis on torah took various forms, but arguably chief among them was the intense study of the written Torah, especially in the synagogues, which rose to prominence during this period both in the Diaspora and throughout Palestine. Without the temple, how was it possible for diaspora

49. McCann, *Theological*, 32. This is the view of Westermann, *Praise*, 253.
50. Bullock, *Encountering*, 222.
51. Collett, "Christology," 391.
52. Brueggemann and Bellinger, *Psalms*, 519.
53. Powell, *Introducing*, 32.

Jews to enter the presence of God, which according to Jewish theology was at the temple? The synagogue therefore, functioned as a place of worship where its attendees—both Jews and God-fearing Greeks—could participate in worship apart from the temple. While we do not know much about synagogue worship during this period, a typical service likely contained readings from the Hebrew Scriptures (Torah and Prophets, the latter likely included Psalms as a book of prophecy based on Luke 24:44–47) from the original Hebrew (or from the LXX in Greek-speaking communities). The readings were followed by a translation in Aramaic (primarily in Palestine; cf. Neh 8:1), a brief sermon or word of exhortation, and sometimes the giving of alms.[54] Some ancient sources describe the synagogue service itself primarily in terms of reading and the study of the Scriptures, indicating the prominent place that Jews ascribed to the role of Scripture in the service.[55] Incidentally, it is highly likely that the Psalms featured prominently as formal readings and prayers in the service.[56]

The emphasis on Scripture cannot be easily overstated in connection with the synagogue in both the Diaspora and Palestine, and it is this context that torah piety as Scripture piety rose to prominence in Jewish theology.[57] The practice of reading Torah in the synagogue helped fill a void in diaspora Judaism that lacked a temple; notably the presence of God, which previously was associated with the temple, became accessible to diaspora Jews through fresh reflections on torah, gleaned through the diligent study of the law in the synagogue. As N. T. Wright explains, "By prayerful and obedient study of the Torah, the blessings that one might have had through the 'sacred space' of the Temple could be obtained anywhere at all."[58] In other words, synagogue worshipers all throughout the Diaspora had access to the holy presence, the *Shekinah* glory of God, through the study of Torah. Therefore, in the absence of the literal temple, life in the Diaspora focused on torah observance as a kind of virtual temple so Jews could experience the blessing of the temple remotely:

> A good deal of Torah was about what to do in the Temple, and the practice of Torah in the Diaspora itself could be thought of in terms of gaining, at a distance, the blessings you would gain

---

54. For a more detailed description of the synagogue service, see Ferguson, *Backgrounds*, 576–81.

55. Ibid., 576. E.g., Philo, *Mos.* 2.39.215–16; Josephus, *Ag. Ap.* 2.175.

56. Wright, The *Case for Psalms*, 11.

57. After the composition of Ps 119, Ben Sira (second-century BCE) illustrates the prominence placed on torah piety as Scripture piety (Sir 24:12–23).

58. Ibid., 102.

if you were actually there—the blessing, in other words, of the sacred presence itself, the Shekinah, the glory which supposedly dwelt in the Temple but would also dwell "where two or three study Torah."[59]

We are now in a better position to understand torah piety in the context of Ps 119 as a product of the postexilic community. Torah is not only the written word, but whatever functions as instruction from the LORD. Yet we may reasonably infer, based on the significance placed on torah piety in the postexilic period when diaspora Jews began attending synagogues in order to study their sacred texts (some of which no doubt came to be included in the Hebrew Bible) as a way to enter into the presence of God, that torah piety primarily, but not exclusively, deals with Scripture piety: the interpretation and application of the written record of God's instruction.

Another historical angle that may touch slightly on the date of composition, but more substantially on the political and cultural environment of Ps 119, is the profile of its author, especially given the larger lament context of the psalm. Several hints within the psalm provide insight on the psalmist and his situation. He is most likely a young man (vv. 9, 99, 100) who at one time indulged in youthful passions, but experienced a "conversion" of sorts brought about by "affliction"—possibly an illness—that he attributes to God's hand (vv. 67, 71, 75). He now expresses his commitment to God by delighting in his torah, constantly meditating on it and making it the center of his affection (v. 97). As Bullock summarizes, "So thorough and genuine was his conversion that the Torah came to be his greatest delight . . . and it was more than meditation, it was the driving force of his life."[60] His commitment to torah piety has been ethically transformative, not merely the accumulation of head knowledge. Yet his devotion to torah was not unmolested. He had faced fierce opposition both politically and religiously, being slandered (v. 23), persecuted without cause (v. 161), reproached and ridiculed (vv. 42, 51), and even bound with the ropes of the wicked (vv. 61–62), although this latter description may be symbolic and not literal. What is more, some of his adversaries are none other than "princes" (vv. 23, 161), suggesting perhaps that the psalmist himself may have held a prominent position (it is unlikely that rulers would pursue so persistently the average person of the land).[61] It does not appear that the poet's commitment to torah is the cause of his persecution, but the prevalence of lament throughout the psalm suggests that in the midst of a hostile political

---

59. Wright, *Faithfulness*, 95. Wright adds, "Any place in which Torah was studied might become an alternate Temple" (p. 107).

60. Bullock, *Encountering*, 222.

61. Ibid., 222–23.

and cultural environment torah has been his only companion. His only hope, therefore, is for God to reward torah piety in the context of covenant blessing. Therefore, I would argue that the most prominent theme of Ps 119 is not torah per se, but the lament of the "righteous sufferer," who hopes that God will notice his devotion to torah piety and save him from persecution: "I am yours; *save me, for* I have sought your precepts" (v. 94).

I admit that much of this is a fairly general description of the poet's difficult circumstances and basically reflects the experience of Judah from the exile (586 BCE) to the Hasmonean era (beginning in 142 BCE).[62] Yet the psalm's pointed focus on torah piety remarkably reflects the postexilic period characterized by the governorship of Ezra, which began in 457 BCE.[63] While this historical introduction is more substantive than the others covered in this book, it is necessary for a better understanding of the psalm's contents, especially from a Christian perspective, which often (and unfortunately) reads legalistic notions into the psalm, distorting both the psalmist's personal covenant commitment and the function of the covenant itself as a way of life characterized by torah observance.

Aleph (vv. 1–8)

Psalm 119 begins with the same word that begins the Psalter (*ashrey*), and by stating that those who walk according to God's torah are "blessed," evokes the language of 1:1.[64] *Ashrey* is better translated here as "blessed" rather than "happy," for the latter may give the false impression that God's way is more about happiness than holiness. While the psalmist repeatedly affirms his delight and joy at living according to God's torah, the goal of torah piety is not mere happiness but holiness, a way of life derived from God's covenant. This opening stanza uses the common Hebrew wisdom image of walking along a path, or "way," which also reflects 1:1.[65] Those who walk in God's way are "blameless" and "do no wrong," yet this does not mean sinless perfection, but the wholeness of a heart committed to God's torah in the context of the covenant relationship.[66] "Seeking him [God] with a whole heart" mirrors the terminology of the Chronicler (1 Chr 16:10; 22:19; 28:9; 2 Chr 11:16;

---

62. Ibid., 222.

63. Zorn *Psalms*, 377. Scholars have proposed David, Hezekiah, Josiah, or Jehoiachin as the author of Ps 119, each being devoted to God, yet experiencing opposition from foreign rulers.

64. DeClaissé-Walford, et al., *Psalms*, 882.

65. Longman, *Psalms*, 403.

66. Zorn, *Psalms*, 377–78.

12:14; 15:12, 15; 19:3; 22:9; 30:19; 31:21),[67] who, perhaps not incidentally, also composed his work during the postexilic period when seeking God with the heart was at a premium—a lesson learned from the exile itself. The direct address to the Lord in Ps 119:4 ("you") is in the emphatic position and sustained through the end of the psalm, except for verse 115.[68] The poet humbly admits he is a work in progress in terms of learning obedience, but his intention is good and his commitment resolute. The final line of the first stanza is essentially the petition that permeates the remainder of the psalm: "Do not utterly forsake me!" This prayer, it is already clear, arises from a time of suffering, illustrating the individual lament that recurs so frequently in the psalm. Here it serves as a lens for viewing the psalm's larger context of torah obedience in the midst of opposition. This first stanza contains the elements that make up the remainder of the psalm, and these are repeated throughout.

Beth (vv. 9–16)

This is the only stanza in the psalm where the word *torah* does not appear; however, several synonyms stand in its place (e.g., word, commandments, statutes, ordinances, testimonies, precepts).[69] It is also the only stanza to begin with a question:[70] "How can a young man keep his way pure?" The second line gives the answer: "By guarding it according to your word." This reflects the wisdom tradition of Israel that tends to address the young but is relevant for any age.[71] The "young man" may be a reference to the psalmist himself.[72] As in the first stanza, the second stanza uses the familiar wisdom image of a path that represents one's life; one either walks (i.e., conducts his/her life) on the wise path or the foolish path. This stanza echoes the first as the psalmist resolves to seek God with his heart and to store God's word in his heart. Because the psalm as a whole is ultimately concerned with right behavior, that is, ethics that reflect the covenant relationship with Yahweh, obedience is ultimately transformative, flowing primarily from the heart and cannot be reduced to head knowledge. The poet calls on God's help to enable obedience. Imperatives like "let me not wander" (v. 10) and "teach

---

67. Hicks, *1 & 2 Chronicles*, 26.
68. Eaton, *Psalms*, 416.
69. DeClaissé-Walford, et al., *Psalms*, 882.
70. Longman, *Psalms*, 403.
71. Longman (ibid., 404) notes that the Heb. term *naar* is quite broad, and can refer to a youth (Jer 1:6) or even someone who is about forty years old (2 Kgs 12:10).
72. Ibid.

me" (v. 12) suggest the poet's commitment to God's instruction does not depend upon the poet's own effort, but ultimately relies on God's guidance and grace. Only with God's help can the psalmist learn covenant obedience; diligent and delightful study of God's word is a two-way street—it is relational.

Gimel (vv. 17–24)

The psalmist asks God to illuminate his understanding of torah so that he may live out the Lord's commands. As in the *beth* stanza, the psalmist pleads for God's help, for eyes of faith to see the wondrous things (v. 18) of torah, which probably suggests the need for deliverance.[73] Similarly, the idea of being a sojourner (v. 19) conveys the need for salvation from the present plight.[74] Suffering, which was hinted at before, is now more specific and entails foreign rulers who plot against the psalmist as they heap scorn and contempt upon him. Thus, the psalmist's desire to understand more deeply the wonders of torah comes in the context of opposition, which threatens to cloud his judgment. In other words, torah functions like the psalmist's counselor in the midst of trial. Eaton observes that "if the princes confer and take counsel against him, he has still the comfort and delight of the Lord's testimonies, his words of guidance and assurance, which are [lit.] 'the men of my counsel,' the wise and trusted friends that stay with him to guide and console."[75] It is in this context of persecution that the psalm's lament forms come more sharply into focus and dominate this stanza: petition (vv. 17–18), complaint (v. 19), description of the oppressors (vv. 21–23), and trust (v. 24).[76] In spite of dire circumstances, the poet "delights" in God's torah.

Daleth (vv. 25–32)

The lament intensifies in this stanza, taking on the familiar biblical image of being laid low in the dust (e.g., 22:15; 44:25). It seems as though death is near, given the antithetical parallelism of the first two lines where the first mentions "dust," a symbol of the grave, and the second its opposite—"life." The elements of lament are similar to that in the previous stanza, although the movement is not quite the same: complaint (v. 25), petition (v. 28), and

---

73. McCann, *Psalms*, 1169.
74. Ibid.
75. Eaton, *Psalms*, 417.
76. DeClaissé-Walford, et al., *Psalms*, 882.

trust (v. 31).⁷⁷ The psalmist returns to the familiar wisdom motif of the "way," which in the context of the acrostic naturally calls to mind the Hebrew word *derek* that begins not coincidentally with the letter *daleth*.⁷⁸ In fact, the psalmist uses the word six times in addition to the eight synonyms for torah. God's way and one's adherence to it represent the good life of covenant obedience. Rather than the way of falsehood, the psalmist has chosen the way of faithfulness.⁷⁹

What begins as a complaint concludes with a petition for God to preserve the psalmist from shame, as well as an affirmation of his ongoing commitment to torah obedience. The poet's confidence in the midst of intense suffering is in God's sustaining word. Still, this is problematic because the covenant promises that those who obey God will live and prosper, while those who do not will suffer (Deut 27—28).⁸⁰ This appears to contradict the psalmist's circumstances. In other words, he is not getting what he deserves; death threatens the very fabric of covenant blessings, which are the rewards for faithful obedience. Therefore, he pleads for a deeper understanding of God's torah, for only this will prevent the psalmist from melting away with sorrow (Ps 119:26–28).

He (vv. 33–40)

The lament movement continues as petition dominates this stanza.⁸¹ The psalmist displays yet another example of literary creativity in this stanza. Because his driving assumption is that he cannot keep torah without God's help, the poet illustrates this by using Hebrew's causative verb form for seven of the eight verbs in the stanza, placing a prefixed *he* onto the verbs, which makes them causative: "teach me" (v. 33), "cause me to understand" (v. 34), "cause me to walk" (v. 35), "incline my heart" (v. 36), "turn my eye away" (v. 37), "confirm to your servant" or "fulfill" (v. 38), and "turn away" (v. 39).⁸² I appreciate how Zorn summarizes the main thought behind this construction: "Cause me, by giving me understanding and by your leading, to walk in your way."⁸³ In other words, he delights in God's torah but needs

---

77. Ibid.
78. Zorn, *Psalms*, 379.
79. Eaton, *Psalms*, 417.
80. Longman, *Psalms*, 404.
81. DeClaissé-Walford, et al., *Psalms*, 882.
82. Ibid. Even the final line begins with the Heb. letter *he* (*hinneh*, "Behold"), although the opening verb is not causative (Zorn, *Psalms*, 381).
83. Zorn, *Psalms*, 380.

his guidance on how to live an obedient life. To keep from being tempted and overtaken by the lure of the idols of the world (i.e., "worthless things"), the psalmist relies on God's word for the good life (v. 37). As will become even clearer later in the psalm, God is the main actor—the psalm focuses on his torah—and the psalmist's actions are in response to God's prior activity.

Waw (vv. 41–48)

Because there are so few words in the Hebrew language that begin with the letter *waw*, the psalmist uses his ingenuity to keep the acrostic flowing.[84] He uses *waw* as a conjunction (i.e., the *waw* consecutive) at the beginning of each verse, linking the verses together consecutively, like links in a chain. It basically amounts to placing "and" at the beginning of these verses: "*And* let your steadfast love . . . *and* I shall have an answer . . . *and* take not the word of truth . . . *and* I will keep . . . *and* I shall walk," and so on. The psalmist implies that he is under duress, and the next stanza will make this ever clearer.[85] The opening line in this stanza is a plea for God's saving *khesed* to come to him. Being taunted and tried by his enemies has brought both conviction and concern. His experience of suffering moves him all the more closer to God's torah, giving him the conviction to proclaim God's testimonies before kings (v. 46). Yet there is cause for concern because God's steadfast love, which issues forth to protect his people from their enemies, is the very thing the psalmist prays will come to him.[86] This implies that at present it remains the substance of the opening prayer wish. Even so, the plea moves to assurance in the context of the psalmist's lament. While waiting on God's salvation to come to him, he will continue to hope and walk in God's law, the vastness (i.e., "wide place" in v. 45) of which frees the poet to live the good life. The later targumist insists that "wide place" is none other than torah itself: "And I will walk in the wideness *of the Torah*, for I have sought your commandments" (Tg. Ps. 119:45).[87] In contrast to much of Western Christian thought, torah obedience in the OT is freeing, not constricting.

---

84. Ibid., 381.
85. Longman, *Psalms*, 405.
86. Ibid.
87. Targumic expansion in italics. Eaton takes "wide place" to mean the psalmist's deliverance from the painful pressures of affliction (*Psalms*, 417).

Zayin (vv. 49–56)

The key theme developed in this stanza is remembrance. The word "remember" is powerful and pervasive in the Hebrew Bible, occurring nearly 200 times.[88] It often occurs in lament contexts where the lamenter cries out to God to remember his or her plight. For example, when Hannah cries out to God to make her womb fruitful so that she may bear a son to dedicate to the Lord, she appeals to God: "Remember me and not forget your servant" (1 Sam 1:11). Similar sentiments are found on the lips of other lamenters like Samson (Judg 16:28), Job (Job 10:9), the psalmists (e.g., Pss 25:6–7; 74:2; 89:50; 106:4; 137:7), and the author of Lamentations (Lam 5:1; 6:9), to name a few. This is the meaning here in Ps 119:49. When the psalmist cries out to God to remember his suffering, such remembrance is more than recall, but is also a plea for God to take action. Essentially, the poet exhorts God, "Don't forget about me!"

On one hand, the psalmist takes comfort in the promise of life from God's torah in the midst of suffering (v. 50), on the other hand, appeals to his own obedience to torah as a basis for deliverance. By contrasting his faithfulness with the faithlessness of others (v. 53), the psalmist appeals to God to consider the poet's fidelity to torah and to act on his behalf. As the psalmist calls on God to remember him, he does not forget his own responsibility to remember God. The OT is saturated with admonitions to Israel to not forget what God has done for them. This theme is especially prominent in Deuteronomy (e.g., Deut 4:9, 23; 6:12; 8:11, 14, 19), and unfortunately numerous passages record ancient Israel's repeated failure to remember God and the covenant (e.g., Judg 8:34; Isa 57:11; Ezek 16:22).

Contrary to the deplorable behavior of those around him, the psalmist "remembers" (NIV)[89] God's ancient rules and takes comfort in them in the midst of opposition (Ps 119:52). As Longman notes, God's rules come with promises of blessing for obedience (Deut 27–28), and these provide hope and strength for the psalmist in the face of derision (Ps 119:51).[90] Not only does the psalmist remember God's commands, he sings them (v. 54). John Eaton likens the imagery to that of a weary traveller enjoying rest and music at an inn.[91] The poet refreshes his spirit by chanting God's laws. According to McCann, however, the imagery is even stronger than that of a traveller for "the house of my sojourning" (v. 54) is reminiscent of the "homelessness" of

---

88. DeClaissé-Walford, et al., *Psalms*, 883.

89. The ESV misses the repetition of the verb *zakhar* ("to remember") by translating it "I think" in v. 52.

90. Longman, *Psalms*, 405.

91. Eaton, *Psalms*, 418.

Israel during and after the exile, and this identification would have been particularly meaningful to the exilic and postexilic generations.[92] The image of a sojourner also provides a link with the beginning of the following stanza (v. 57). Finally, not only does the psalmist remember God's commands, but more importantly remembers God himself: "I remember your name in the night, O LORD" (v. 55). By invoking the covenant name of Yahweh God, the psalmist invokes God's covenant loyalty to remember the plight of the psalmist as well as his uprightness, and to deliver him from oppression. After all, torah obedience is ultimately obedience to the God of torah.

Heth (vv. 57–64)

The psalmist continues the theme of homelessness from the previous stanza by using language "The LORD is my portion" in verse 57. The terminology is associated with the gift of land to the Israelites, specifically the allotment given to each Israelite, except the priests and Levites (Num 18:20; Josh 15:13; 18:7; 19:9). Like the language of "sojourning" previously, "portion" would have been especially meaningful to Israel in the exilic and postexilic periods when the Promised Land belonged to someone else. Seen in this context, perhaps the most meaningful profession that a "homeless Israel" could make is that "the LORD is my portion."[93] For the psalmist, despite the current crisis, he is never without a home because he lives in covenant with Yahweh. He continues to pour forth his plea once again: "I entreat your favor with all my heart; be gracious to me according to your promise," while humbly admitting the possibility that his footsteps may waver and go astray (vv. 58–59). However, he eagerly seeks the right path regardless, even when his enemies are like hunters who lay snares (vv. 60–61). As the psalmist is never without a home, he is never without a community because he feels a kinship with all who fear God and keep torah.[94]

Teth (vv. 65–72)

The composer here attributes his moral transformation to a God-given affliction, possibly an illness. While his enemies interpret his affliction as a sign of a great sin deserving of punishment (similar to Ps 30, as well as Job), the psalmist sees it as a positive sign that has brought him back in

---

92. McCann, *Psalms*, 1170.
93. Ibid.
94. All of the words for torah are used in this St. (Zorn, *Psalms*, 383).

line with God's instruction. In contrast to his accusers who are insensitive to God's commands, he now commits his whole heart to torah (vv. 69–70). "Good" (*tov*) is a key word in this stanza; the writer uses it six times (vv. 65, 66, 68 [twice], 71, 72).[95] It describes God's essence throughout the Psalter, frequently in combination with his covenant faithfulness and mercy toward sinners (25:8; 34:8; 73:1; 86:5; 100:5; 136:1; 145:9). This is how the composer uses it here, but also affirms God's goodness and the goodness of torah in the context of despair. In fact, he admits that it was "good" for him to be afflicted (v. 71). Previously, he spurned God's word, but now sees it as the most valuable thing in the world (v. 72) because of its transformative power.

Yodh (vv. 73–80)

The poet draws a connection between God the creator and God the lawgiver. He will return to the creation motif later, but at this point the composer simply declares that God has made him and knows the best way to live life (v. 73).[96] Once again, the writer appeals to God to reveal directly to him an understanding of God's commands (v. 73). In other words, he relies not on his own understanding of torah, but prays to God, the source of torah, for help. The poet once again acknowledges his faults by confessing that his affliction is the result of God's faithfulness to the covenant (v. 75). McCann notes that this, too, creates an analogy between the psalmist and Israel, who repeatedly faltered and was in constant need of God's *khesed*.[97] This also captures well the psychological profile of exilic and postexilic Judah. The psalmist is in dire need of God's *khesed*, which prompts the following pleas: "Let your steadfast love comfort me" and "Let your mercy come to me." Similar pleas for deliverance will reach a new pitch in the following stanza. For the psalmist, the scenario is quite clear: if God shows compassion on him, it will prove devastating to the insolent who slander him.[98] This is important in an honor-shame society such as ancient Israel. The current distress of the psalmist potentially heightens his shame and affirms the honor of his slanderers. That is, if God does not answer his pleas for salvation, then they are proven to be in the right and the psalmist the wrong. However, a great reversal will occur when God answers the poet's prayers, proving him to be honorable and his accusers shameful.

---

95. DeClaissé-Walford, et al., *Psalms*, 883. McCann notes that each of these verses begins with the word "good" (*Psalms*, 1170).

96. Longman, *Psalms*, 406.

97. McCann, *Psalms*, 1171.

98. Zorn, *Psalms*, 384.

Community is not a major theme in Ps 119, but there are hints along the way that the psalmist sees himself as a part of a larger community of faith—a covenant community. For example, he prays to be an example of faithfulness, as one who has received humbly the Lord's discipline, has persevered in his covenant commitment, and has been both fully-tested and enabled to teach God's testimonies to others in the faith community (vv. 74, 79). As Eaton explains, "May he become an example of salvation to gladden believers' hearts."[99] The psalmist has already previously described his torah piety in terms of whole-hearted commitment, not sinless perfection but resolute obedience, which he now requests in terms of being "blameless" (v. 80). Simply put, in the context of maintaining the covenant relationship with God "blameless" means nothing other than to be forgiven (15:).[100] As noted earlier, the OT covenantal system knows nothing of sinless perfection, but has built into it atoning sacrifices and various other means by which a loyal covenanter may find forgiveness for his or her sins, thereby maintaining a right relationship with God.[101]

Kaph (vv. 81–88)

The prayer of lament rises in intensity in this stanza; the psalmist is at his lowest as he contemplates the paradox of his faithfulness and God's slowness to save. By pouring forth urgent questions of faith like, "When?" and "How long?" the psalmist is essentially wasting away with longing for God's salvation (vv. 81, 82). This is the main theme of this section. The imagery of a dried and charred wineskin (not to mention ruined wine!) illustrates the useless feeling of the psalmist (v. 83): for far too long he has been exposed to the taunts and traps of his persecutors. I appreciate John Calvin's explanation of the wineskin simile: "In comparing himself to a bottle or bladder [i.e., "wineskin" ESV], he intimates that he was, as it were, parched by the continual heat of adversities. Whence we learn, that that sorrow must have been intense which reduced him to such a state of wretchedness and emaciation, that like a shriveled bottle he was almost dried up."[102] The psalmist longs for God to take action and rescue him from the metaphorical pits his

---

99. Eaton, *Psalms*, 418.

100. McCann, *Psalms*, 1171.

101. E.g., zealous actions (Num 25:13); thanksgiving (Ps 50:23); repentance (51:9); God's compassion (78:38; 79:8–9); prayer as incense and sacrifice (141:2); steadfast love and faithfulness (Prov 16:6); steadfast love and knowledge of God (Hos 6:6); justice, love, and humility (Mic 6:6–8).

102. Calvin, *Psalms*, Apple e-book, ch. 119.

adversaries have dug for him (v. 85), echoing the language of Jer 18:20–22. As is the case throughout the psalm, the poet ultimately looks to God for life and comfort (Ps 119:88), hoping in God's salvation. Even so, the composer upholds his uprightness in the face of adversity, as he has done so many times before in the psalm. He is truly a model of faith tested, but in the context of the covenant agreement, he implicitly complains that he is not getting what he rightfully deserves. His obedience to God's statutes should bring blessing, not scorn; liberation, not longing. The psalmist is yet another example in the Bible of a suffering servant.[103] His own words best summarize his deteriorating emotional state: "Help me!" (v. 86), while at the same time are an affirmation of faith addressed to the God in whom faith trusts.

Lamedh (vv. 89–96)

This stanza raises torah to new heights, extending it well beyond daily covenantal obedience to a divine law that governs the universe. In doing so it calls to mind the creative capacity of wisdom in Prov 8—like a divine hypostasis—elevating torah to a similar exalted status. In fact, Second Temple Judaism often equated Wisdom with torah. If the previous section represents the low point of the psalmist's emotional state, the pendulum swings upward in this section, which is nothing less than exuberant proclamation of the eternal nature of God's torah.[104] Torah is "firmly fixed in the heavens," and by God's "appointment" (*mishpat*), or better, "ordinances" the earth stands fast (vv. 89–91). God's word stands with him in heaven, and through the divine word the manifold order of creation is established.[105] Here, torah, God's word, functions like the Hebrew concept of Wisdom as the creative capacity of God, echoing of course, the creation accounts of Genesis where God creates by the word of his mouth. While this section highlights the exalted and eternal nature of torah, it does not do so at the expense of its practical function in the life of the poet. Once again, the composer credits God's torah for turning his life around, freeing him from "affliction" (v. 92). It is unclear whether the law saved him by guarding him from sinful behaviors or by motivating him to repent and seek forgiveness.[106] In reality, torah is responsible for both throughout the psalm. Even if exuberance characterizes this section of the psalm, the psalmist has not abandoned his plea for God to save him: "I am yours; save me" (v. 94a). Verse 96 sounds much like

103. McCann, *Psalms*, 1171.
104. DeClaissé-Walford, et al., *Psalms*, 883.
105. Eaton, *Psalms*, 419.
106. Longman, *Psalms*, 406.

a proverb: "I have seen a limit to all perfection, but your commandment is exceedingly broad." Derek Kidner observes that this could well be a summary of Ecclesiastes, where every earthly enterprise has its day and comes to nothing, and only in following God and his commands does humanity get beyond these frustrating limits.[107] Torah obedience is not restrictive, but always relevant and expansive.

Mem (vv. 97–104)

Moving from the lofty paeans of praise for God's eternal law, the psalmist here expresses his heartfelt fondness for torah. If the previous stanza is about the poet's awe at the expansiveness of God's instruction, this one is about his affection for it. McCann observes that the exclamations of verses 97 and 103 are "downright sensual," mirroring some of the terminology of the great Israelite love poem Song of Solomon.[108] The psalmist's "love" (*ahav*) for torah is underscored in that he meditates on it "all the day" (v. 97). When placed in the context of the psalmist's fondness for torah, it would not be a stretch to suggest that he is infatuated with it, not a fleeting emotion but covenantal commitment. In other words, the sensual language of the stanza vividly expresses the poet's commitment to his covenant partner—God. This stanza also utilizes typical Hebrew "wisdom" words to describe torah: "wise" (*khakham*, v. 98), "insightful" (*sakhal*, v. 99 NIV), and "discernment" (*biyn*, vv. 100, 104 NET).[109] The opening declaration, "Oh how I love your law!" (v. 97), sounds somewhat presumptuous to modern ears, yet it exemplifies the righteous one of Ps 1 who delights in God's law.[110] What is more, his boast that he has more wisdom than his enemies, more insight than his teachers, and more understanding than the aged, at first seems the pinnacle of arrogance (119:98–100). While enemies, teachers, and aged may be the same group, it is more likely that they represent the arrogant (vv. 69, 78, 85) who neglect God's law entirely, mere human teachers in contrast to God himself, and those who typify learning and wisdom, presumably through a lifetime of experience and in contrast to the much younger psalmist.[111] Whoever comprises these groups is immaterial, for what matters most to the poet is that his real teacher is God himself ("You have taught me," v.

---

107. Kidner, *Psalms 73–150*, 426–27.

108. McCann, *Psalms*, 1171–72. Song of Solomon often uses *dod* as a synonym for *ahab*; the former is often translated "beloved."

109. DeClaissé-Walford, et al., *Psalms*, 883.

110. Zorn, *Psalms*, 385.

111. Ibid., 385–86.

102); all other teachers pale in comparison. So what appears at first glance to be a vain presumption of wisdom, insight, and discernment, turns out to be an affirmation of trust in God, the source of torah, which so preoccupies the psalmist's affection. This further underscores the theme of the entire psalm: the psalmist's commitment to torah reflects his covenantal commitment to God himself. In other words, the psalm is more about God than torah per se; after all God is the source of torah. Torah piety is not an end in and of itself but a means to an end—covenant life with Yahweh.

Nun (vv. 105–112)

Following the psalmist's affection for God's law, the poet resumes his heartfelt lament for salvation in the face of adversity, which has characterized the psalm in previous stanzas. "Give me life" (v. 107) is yet another iteration of "Save me!" Verse 105 is perhaps the most well known verse in the whole psalm: "Your word is a lamp to my feet and a light to my path." It recalls the familiar wisdom motif of the path of one's life; here, the poet declares that God's word divinely illuminates the direction of his life. Light is a fitting metaphor because God's word reveals his very self, also characterized as light elsewhere in Psalms (4:6; 27:1).[112] Yet, its context here in 119:105 suggests more than the word's role in granting clarity for day-to-day decisions. The well-loved verse occurs in the context of moral decision-making; the "snare" the wicked lays for the psalmist is not so much aimed at his physical wellbeing to cause him harm as much as his moral fiber to cause him to fall: "The wicked have laid a snare for me, *but I do not stray from your precepts*" (v. 110). Therefore, according to Kidner, "This [lighting the psalmist's path] is not convenient guidance for one's career, but truth for moral choices."[113] In spite of the snare of the wicked, God's instructions are the "heritage" (*nakhal*, v. 111) of the psalmist, language that echoes the Israelites' inheritance of the Promised Land.[114] If the land of Canaan brought joy to the Israelites, the psalmist, who lives in a land not his own, rejoices in God's testimonies.

Samekh (vv. 113–120)

This stanza emphasizes the loyalty and whole-hearted commitment of the psalmist to God's torah in contrast to the double-minded evildoers who set

---

112. McCann, *Psalms*, 1172.
113. Kidner, *Psalms 73–150*, 427.
114. DeClaissé-Walford, et al., *Psalms*, 883.

themselves against God's ways. As throughout the psalm, opposition is never far away from the psalmist (vv. 113, 115, 118–119). Contrasts like love and hate, which in Hebrew idiom convey that which one is either for or against, perfuse the poet's thoughts (vv. 113, 115, 118, 119). While this brings nothing new to the psalm to this point, that the psalmist uses the metaphors "hiding place" and "shield" (v. 114) for God are entirely new, evoking imagery found in other places in the Psalter (3:3; 27:5; 31:20; 91:1).[115] The theme of God's judgment on the wicked is also new; because they spurn God's laws, they set themselves against God. The psalmist seeks shelter and security in God, but the wicked leave themselves open to his judgments.

Ayin (vv. 121–128)

The attack of the oppressors on the psalmist is relentless, causing him to once again appeal to his own uprightness over their insolence as the basis of his salvation. The basic movement of lament recurs in this stanza, extending into the following sections, each of which evidences various elements of lament. In general, verses 121–128 form the complaint, verses 129–136 the petition, and verses 137–144 the affirmation of trust.[116] The composer's complaint is rooted in the covenant relationship whereby God promises blessing to his servants. The author expresses impatience with God's slowness to act: "It is time for the LORD to act" (v. 126). Enough is enough; the wicked have endangered the psalmist for too long. The language of verses 121–124 evokes standard covenant terminology in the OT. The bulk of the appeal is to God's "promise" (v. 123) of covenant life, which reflects his own character as "good" (*tov*, v. 122), and in his faithful love (*khesed*, v. 124) to the covenant. For the poet, God's goodness and faithful love are his covenantal attributes that in turn bless those who are "just and right" in their covenant obligations (v. 121). The psalmist's logic is straightforward: "I have upheld my end of the covenant; now it is God's turn to fulfill his promises based on his goodness and faithful love." "Servant" is the psalmist's favorite designation for himself, and its threefold repetition stands out in this section (vv. 122, 124, 125).[117]

---

115. McCann, *Psalms*, 1172.
116. Ibid.
117. Zorn, *Psalms*, 387. E.g., vv. 17, 23, 38, 49, 65, 76, 84, 91, 122, 124, 125, 135, 140, 176.

Pe (vv. 129–136)

On one hand, this stanza comprises the petition portion of the lament pattern that began in the previous section, which was mostly characterized by complaint. On the other hand, it contains the pinnacle of praise for God's torah, noting especially its "wondrous" (*pele*) quality in verse 129: "Your testimonies are wonderful." The Hebrew term *pele* occurs some thirty-three times in the Psalter, and is often used to refer to God's miraculous deeds displayed at the exodus from Egypt (e.g., 105:2, 5; 106:7, 22; 136:4).[118] It often describes "extraordinary phenomena, transcending the power of human knowledge and imagination."[119] In the context of Ps 119 God's torah has a marvelous quality, like miracles.[120] A miracle in the Bible is something that creates abiding astonishment for those who recognize its objective manifestation, yet cannot fathom according to human knowledge, history, or nature its meaning; such persons are capable of receiving (or interpreting) it as miracle.[121] In other words, it is not a figure of the imagination, and is not some "supernatural" or "superhistorical" incident, but simply an act of God, which runs the gamut from his marvelous deeds at the exodus to his day-to-day instruction for covenant living. Simply put, humanity can never plumb the depths of torah nor exhaust its expansiveness. Its marvelousness is beyond human reason; thus, the poet proclaims its divine origin.

Not only does the psalmist wonder at the magnificence of God's torah, he also cannot live without its daily sustenance. He likens his dependence on torah to that of an animal snuffing for water in a drought (v. 131). The imagery is not of a peaceful deer calmly lapping water from a gently flowing stream, but of a parched animal whose very life depends on quickly finding water. For the poet, God's commands sustain his daily existence; without them he would die, especially considering his current distress. What is more, in light of his ordeal the psalmist petitions God for the companionship of his divine presence (v. 135), using the familiar Hebrew terminology of "face" as a metaphor for personal presence. Alluding to the priestly blessing of Num 6:22–27 (i.e., " . . . the LORD make his face to shine upon you and be gracious to you"), the poet longs for the covenantal blessing of God's palpable presence, especially in the midst of suffering.[122] In what may be a surprise to much contemporary Christian thought, which more often than

---

118. DeClaissé-Walford, et al., *Psalms*, 884.
119. Ibid.
120. Eaton, *Psalms*, 420.
121. DeClaissé-Walford, et al., *Psalms*, 884.
122. Longmam, *Psalms*, 407.

not, laments the personal struggles of individual believers, what causes the psalmist the most grief is not his own suffering—although intense—but the observable fact that others show no regard for God's law (v. 136).

Tsadhe (vv. 137–144)

The lament movement of the preceding stanzas culminates, as is the case with most biblical laments, with an affirmation of trust in God in the current stanza (although it also contains petition in v. 144). In general, the scorn of the previous stanza turns into delight. The key word here is *tsedek* ("righteous") and its derivatives ("righteousness," "righteous one"), reflecting the psalm's acrostic structure, which now comes to the letter *tsadhe*. The basic point is summarized in verse 142: "Your righteousness is righteous forever." Because God is righteous, so also are his statutes. The psalm continues to contrast the poet's foes that forget (v. 139) God's words with the poet, who does not forget God's precepts (v. 141).[123] The psalm has repeatedly declared the composer's covenant obedience in spite of his trials, a motif that continues here (vv. 141, 143). In spite of the evidence of his downtrodden life, the psalmist affirms his adherence to torah, which seems to contradict the terms of God's covenant with his people. In short, the poet is not getting what he feels he deserves; instead of blessing for obedience, he receives scorn and ridicule and heartache. His adherence to God's law has brought him trouble instead of success and wealth, and because of this conflicting evidence, he pleads for understanding of God's testimonies, for insight into the relationship between obedience and blessing (v. 144). Perhaps this relationship is not as straightforward as Deut 28 seems to suggest. Herein lies the archetypical biblical suffering servant: the faithful covenanter whose delight is comingled with trouble and anguish, for he exults in God's present reign, yet eagerly awaits its final consummation.[124]

Qoph (vv. 145–152)

The final section of the psalm (vv. 145–176) repeats the basic lament structure of complaint (vv. 145–52) to petition (vv. 153–160) to affirmation of trust (vv. 161–168), culminating in a series of final pleas (vv. 169–176); each lament element is interspersed through each stanza as well.[125] Here,

---

123. Zorn, *Psalms*, 389.
124. McCann, *Psalms*, 1173.
125. Ibid.

the composer's complaint once again centers on the silence of God in the face of persecution (v. 145). Standard lament terminology saturates this stanza: "I cry" (vv. 145a, 147), "answer me" (v. 145b), "I call" (v. 146), "save me" (v. 146), "hear my voice," (v. 149), etc. In spite of his devotion to torah and consistent prayers for relief before dawn and before the night watches, which may reflect set times of prayer,[126] oppression continues unabated. Even though the psalmist faces trial after trial throughout the psalm, and in spite of his repeated pleas for deliverance that God does not seem to notice, the composer declares God's nearness to him, for God's presence is palpable through torah (v. 151). Although the oppressors "draw near" to the psalmist, the reality is that God is nearer. Zorn sees the following paradox: in a "strange twist of events the wicked are 'so near and yet so far away.' And perhaps in the mind of the psalmist (even though he knows better), God seems so near and yet so far away."[127]

Resh (vv. 153–160)

An urgent cry for help dominates this stanza. Its petition is one that is heard throughout the psalm: "Give me life." In fact, it occurs eight times in the psalm as a whole, and three of those instances occur here (vv. 154, 156, 159).[128] The rationale behind the plea in this section is nothing new as the psalmist appeals to God's covenant promise (v. 154), his compassionate nature (v. 156), and his covenant loyalty (*khesed*, v. 159). The language is shot through with covenantal overtones, which implies, of course, not only God's faithfulness to the covenant, but also the composer's obedience. So the poet's appeal to the God of the covenant emphasizes the relational dynamic of the covenant itself where both sides—God and the psalmist—have a responsibility to uphold their respective ends of the covenant. The psalmist, therefore, reminds God of his faithful obedience (v. 153, 157, 158, 159), which serves as an additional rationale for his deliverance, based on the covenant's blessings. Ironically, in spite of undergoing persecution and ridicule, the psalmist confesses that salvation is not ultimately about rescue from his adversaries but in living according to God's torah (v. 156). That is, God's torah brings life, blessing, and peace, which transcend the present circumstances.

---

126. Eaton, *Psalms*, 420.
127. Zorn, *Psalms*, 390.
128. DeClaissé-Walford, et al., *Psalms*, 885.

Sin/Shin (vv. 161–168)

The psalmist affirms his trust in God in this stanza, eagerly anticipating salvation from the present situation: "I hope for your salvation, O LORD" (v. 166). Biblical laments typically conclude with affirmations of faith mixed with praise elements; this stanza is no different. In fact, it begins as a complaint in verse 161 where the poet identifies his persecutors more pointedly here as "princes" than in previous stanzas. Nevertheless, the word "praise" (*halal*) occurs often in Book 5 of the Psalter, and is relatively infrequent in Ps 119, yet it occurs in verse 164. This prepares the reader for the conclusion of the psalm with its twofold occurrence of "praise" (vv. 171, 175).[129] The poet praises God for the wonder and grace of torah, which brings "peace" in the midst of persecution. It is important to note that the psalmist does not praise torah per se, but God, from whom it originates. In other words, the composer does not engage in bibliolatry (i.e., the worship of Scripture) here, but properly focuses his praise on God alone for the gift of torah: "Seven times a day I praise you for your righteous rules" (v. 164). The psalmist knows the difference between God and his word, between God and torah.[130] The term "peace" (*shalom*) is at the very center of this stanza and is a fitting term for the acrostic, which has come to the letter *sin/shin*.[131] "Seven times a day" may be a literal practice as a zealous rule, or more likely, it is figurative, suggesting completion and totality, as is usually the case with the number seven in Scripture (cf. "all day long" in v. 97).[132] The psalmist is totally committed to praising God for his gift of torah and for the peace it brings to his life. Once again, the end-times perspective of the psalm is clear: the one who is persecuted without cause (v. 161) knows simultaneously great peace and security (v. 165).[133]

Taw (vv. 169–176)

The final stanza recapitulates many of the lament elements that have occurred throughout the psalm; especially petition. The psalmist pleads for understanding (v. 169), deliverance (v. 170), help (vv. 173, 175), salvation (v. 174), and life (v. 175), each of which echoes previous petitions in the psalm. Praise also plays a central role in this final stanza (vv. 171, 175). Perhaps what stands out the most is the composer's confession of fallibility in the last

---

129. McCann, *Psalms*, 1174.
130. Zorn, *Psalms*, 392.
131. Ibid., 391.
132. Longman, *Psalms*, 408.
133. McCann, *Psalms*, 1174.

verse of the psalm, which seems at first to contradict his confident claims of obedience throughout the psalm. But the astute reader will recall a similar confession in verse 67. Again, covenant obedience does not imply moral perfection. McCann keenly observes as 119:1 echoes the first verse of Ps 1 ("blessed"), 119:176 echoes the last verse of Ps 1, especially regarding those who "perish" (1:6; cf. "lost" in 119:176).[134] In short, the poet feels like a lost sheep and prays to God, the Shepherd, to seek and find him (v. 176). One can easily argue, therefore, that the psalm's central purpose is a cry from the heart, a desperate supplication for salvation.[135] Because there is no resolution to the poet's plight, the psalm ends with a cliffhanger: will the Shepherd search for his lost sheep?

Christology

While Ps 119 does not contain predictive prophecies of the Messiah, its Christology is nonetheless rich and robust. Reading the psalm in light of the gospel, that is, with christological lenses that are provided as a result of Christ's finished work, reveals multiple facets for viewing the main message of the great psalm in relation to the incarnation of Christ. For example, I have noted previously the messianic end-times trajectory of the Psalter, and Ps 119 anticipates this same outlook with the poet's anticipation of an ever-increasing measure of wisdom and knowledge of God's word and the experience of salvation. Clearly there is something more to be gained in the poet's covenant obedience that transcends his present situation, which is characterized by suffering. According to Hilary of Poitiers (c. 315–367 CE), when read in light of the christological fulfillment of Jesus Christ, the composer of Ps 119, while ignorant of the fuller implications of his end-times understanding, "hopes in fact for eternity, he hopes for the kingdom of heaven, he hopes for the kingdom of God, he hopes for the spiritual blessings given in heaven in Christ."[136] Such a reading occurs only after the gospel has given clarity to the christological character of the OT. That Ps 119 preaches Christ is seen only *from the faith of the gospel*, in hindsight, and not from supposed "predictions" from the pen of the prophet.[137]

Patrick Reardon proposes two additional angles from which to read Ps 119 christologically. First, one can read it as a prayer of Christ, the suffering servant, who strengthens his covenant commitment in the face of oppression,

---

134. Ibid.
135. Eaton, *Psalms*, 421; cf. Calvin, *Psalms*, ch. 119.
136. Burgess, "Incarnation," 160.
137. Ibid., 142.

obeying torah from the heart and resolving to live faithfully while patiently awaiting his deliverance. Finding strength and sustenance from Scripture, Christ reveals the covenant blessings of seeking God's torah, especially in hard times. McCann explains how the psalmist "clearly reminds us of figures like Jeremiah and Elijah, who suffered as a result of their faithfulness to God's word and will. Christian readers of Psalm 119 will also inevitably be reminded of Jesus."[138] He becomes, then, the model and author of our own faith.[139]

I showed before that torah in Ps 119 should not be limited to written Scripture, but certainly includes it among other revelatory motifs. Inasmuch as Scripture is God's torah in written form, the life, ministry, and death of Christ reveals that his heart was soaked in God's inscripturated word. The psalmist's commitment to discerning God's word and to doing his will anticipates the life and ministry of Jesus.[140] Steve Moyise notes, "Jesus was a Jew, and like other Jews he was brought up to believe that the Scriptures of Israel were not simply human wisdom but a gift from God."[141] The four Gospels show Jesus quoting nearly sixty different verses of Scripture throughout his ministry, many of which are from Psalms.[142] What is more, he alludes to Scripture at least twice as often, although "allusions," "echoes," and general references are more difficult to quantify than direct quotations. Precise statistics are problematic because of exceedingly complex criteria as to what constitutes a "quotation" or an "allusion/echo" in the scholarly literature on the topic of the NT use of the OT. Nevertheless, no one debates the centrality of Scripture for the life, ministry, and death of Jesus in the Gospels. However, the issue here is two-fold. First, from the perspectives of the evangelists, each goes to great lengths to interpret Jesus in light of Jewish Scripture. Every major aspect of his identity and mission is grounded in God's word. In other words, there are no surprises regarding Jesus's identity and mission because the Scriptures point to him in every conceivable way regarding his life, ministry, and death. From his virgin birth to his resurrected body, nothing is left to chance.

Second, not only do the evangelists seek to establish Jesus's identity and mission according to Scripture, they also highlight the importance of Scripture to Jesus himself throughout his earthly ministry, showing how Scripture permeates his thoughts and actions, much like the composer of Ps 119. For example, the Gospel of Luke presents Jesus as a young boy in the temple discussing spiritual matters with the scriptural experts, that is, the "teachers"

---

138. McCann, *Psalms*, 1175.
139. Reardon, *Christ*, 238.
140. McCann *Psalms*, 1175.
141. Moyise, *Jesus and Scripture*, 1.
142. Ibid., 3–4.

(Luke 2:42–51). He amazes them with his "understanding" (2:47), while continuing to grow in "wisdom" (2:52); phrases that echo those of the psalmist (Ps 119:98–100). Similarly, the temptation of Christ prior to his public ministry illustrates his commitment to Scripture, which strengthens and guides him during the devil's opposition. Jesus responds to each of the devil's temptations, which are distortions of the Scriptures, with passages that mirror the testing of the Israelites in the wilderness (Luke 4:1–13 and pars.; cf. Deut 8:3; 6:13, 16). This invites comparison with the poet in that by constantly affirming that he lives by the word of God, the psalmist anticipates Jesus's articulation of the motive for his faithful, hopeful obedience to God in the midst of adversity: "One shall not live by bread alone, but by every word that comes from the mouth of God."[143] Also, a prophetic passage of Scripture serves as a table of contents for the inauguration of Jesus's earthly ministry during his sermon in the synagogue in Nazareth (Luke 4:18–30; cf. Isa 61:1–2). Not only does he read the liberating passage of Isa 61 to his audience but proclaims, "Today this Scripture has been fulfilled in your hearing" (Luke 4:21). For Luke, Scripture itself chronicles the details of Jesus's mission.

Even in Jesus's darkest moment on the cross, Scripture functions for him as an expression of his emotional pain, as well as his hope and trust in his Father to save. For example, the cry of Jesus from the cross comes from Ps 22:1 as the cry of the innocent sufferer (Matt 27:46; Mark 15:34). Luke does not record the cry of abandonment but records instead a prayer of trust: "Into your hands I commit my spirit" (Luke 23:46; cf. Ps 31:5). The Gospel of John records neither the cry of abandonment nor the prayer of trust, but the evangelist implies that Jesus's statement, "I thirst" (John 19:28), is more or less a quotation (or at least a very strong allusion) of the OT, although it is not clear what passage he has in mind. Most likely, it is in accordance with the rejected king motif cited elsewhere in reference to Jesus's passion (e.g., Ps 69:4, 9, 21).[144] Other examples of Jesus's pervasive use of Scripture can be multiplied, but these help to show Jesus's devotion to God's word and illustrate how his heart and will are completely committed to God's instruction. Like torah for the psalmist, God's word for Jesus is the compass that directs the trajectory of his life, and the lamp that lights his path, even in the darkest of times when God's voice is silent.

The second angle that Reardon proposes for reading Ps 119 in light of the gospel is to view it as a psalm *about* Jesus himself, where each of the psalm's testimonials to God's word, or torah, refers to him of whom the law itself prophecies and in whom it is fulfilled. Therefore, every observation

---

143. McCann, *Psalms*, 1175.
144. Thompson, *John*, 400. Other candidates are Pss 22:15; 42:2; 63:1.

about torah ultimately speaks of Jesus.[145] I will not attempt a line-by-line analysis here, but will briefly isolate four of the most salient features of torah and describe how the NT defines them in relation to Christ as their fullest expression. First, the psalmist sees God's torah as the means through which one learns of and experiences God's "way," which is shorthand for covenant obedience as a manner of life that reflects the righteousness of God and nourishes a vibrant covenant relationship with him. While not one of the eight synonyms for torah, "way" (*derek*) is nonetheless frequently associated with God's instruction, so that by adhering to God's commands, one is assured of living the way of covenant obedience, eschewing the way of wickedness (119:1, cf. 119:9, 14, 27, 30, 32, 33, 101, 104, 128). For the psalmist, God's torah is also "truth" in the sense of it being the standard of truth, even truth itself (119:142, 151, 160).[146] And, as a consequence of torah being the truth of God, torah obedience brings "life," covenant life with Yahweh (119:25, 37, 40, 50, 93, 107, 156, 159). The terms "way," "truth," and "life" are frequently combined in OT wisdom literature (16:11; 86:11; Prov 15:24),[147] and in the context of Ps 119, refer to torah and the covenant benefits of torah obedience. In the OT and in Second Temple literature, "the way(s) of truth" is a life lived in conformity with the law (e.g., "I have chosen the way of faithfulness; I set your rules before me," 119:30; cf. Tob 1:3; Wis 5:6).[148] In other words, the language is familiar to the OT where the "way" is usually associated with God's law and God's wisdom.[149]

Given the Gospel of John's emphasis on Jesus as the climactic revelation of God, truth incarnate, the fulfillment of torah (more on this later), it is not a coincidence that Jesus is "the way, the truth, and the life" (John 14:6). Gary Burge calls this verse the "premier expression" of the theology of the Fourth Gospel.[150] To be sure, John develops each of these terms to fit his unique Christology, so there is not a simplistic correlation between 14:6 and Ps 119 regarding the words themselves. But as Raymond Brown notes, the OT provides the "raw material" for interpreting John's use of these terms in a Jewish context.[151] Delving into the multifaceted details of "way," "truth," and "life" in the Johannine context is beyond the scope of the current study, but suffice it to say, John alludes to and transforms the torah terminology

---

145. Reardon, *Christ*, 238.
146. Bullock, *Encountering*, 224.
147. Köstenberger, *John*, 429n38.
148. Ibid., 429.
149. O'Day and Hylen, *John*, 145.
150. Burge, *John*, 392.
151. Brown, *John 13—21*, 630.

of the OT into christological titles, illustrating that Jesus is the point of access to God ("way"), the pinnacle revelation of God as the incarnate Son ("truth"), and the embodiment of eternal life ("life"). Andrew Lincoln summarizes John's Christology of the way, the truth, and the life:

> Jesus' claim to be the way is the primary one and the claims to be the truth and the life clarify how and why he is the way. He is the way to the Father because he is the truth as the revelation of God. His mission has as its purpose to bear witness to the truth, and his life, death, resurrection and exaltation embody that truth. Jesus is the way to the Father because he is the life as the means of participating in the life of God.[152]

Second, the claim of Jesus's unique revelation as the "way" should be interpreted in relation to similar claims in the OT (notably Ps 119) for torah. For John, Jesus does not oppose the OT concept of torah; he is the true torah of the messianic era, the fulfillment of the end-time hope of torah to bring righteousness and life to God's people. Christ is preeminently the new torah, God's Word in human flesh (John 1:1), his fullest and final revelation. All that torah sought to accomplish—to bring life and righteousness through a covenant relationship with God and to reveal the nature and will of God—Christ now accomplishes more fully and finally. For John Pryor, Jesus "is the hope and focus of eternal life being in his very person all that the Jews thought of the Torah: the true revelation of God."[153] Second Temple Judaism anticipated the renewal of torah in the messianic era based on an interpretation of Isa 2:3, which states, "For out of Zion shall go the law, and the word of the Lord from Jerusalem." Old Testament end-times expectation anticipates that at an unspecified time in the future, Israel will be restored and the nations (Gentiles) will be incorporated into the covenant people of God. A new covenant will be inaugurated where God's law will be written on the hearts of the people (Jer 31:31–34), and the Spirit will be poured out, which will enable God's people to obey the law (Ezek 36:25–27). A consequence of this end-times expectation was the renewal of torah in the messianic era. The Messiah will inaugurate a new era of obedience to torah. Given the end-times expectations of Isaiah, Jeremiah and Ezekiel, it is reasonable to believe that Jewish Christians in the first-century CE may have expected a renewal of torah in the messianic era, an era inaugurated by Jesus the Messiah.[154] Jesus was, then, the supreme revelation of God: the torah had gone out from Zion.[155]

---

152. Lincoln, *John*, 390–91.
153. Pryor, *Evangelist*, 123.
154. Keener, *John*, 1:359.
155. Ibid., 1:363.

In the context of John's Gospel, Jesus as the new torah is most clearly associated with the prologue, which presents him as the preexistent "Word" (*logos*) that became flesh and dwelled among humanity (John 1:1–18), revealing the essence of the Father. Pryor explains that in its OT context, the word of God "becomes associated both with his Wisdom and his Torah—indeed, word, wisdom, and Torah come to refer to essentially the same aspect of the revelation of God to his covenant people."[156] Many scholars have rightly pointed to the resonances between John's prologue, regarding the creative capacity of the Word and divine Wisdom as the agent of creation in the OT (Prov 8:22–31; Sir 24:3–12; Wis 7:22–30).[157] However, God's word, or torah, and his Wisdom are not mutually exclusive in the OT, the former being the consummate expression of the latter.[158] As Craig Keener remarks, "Playing on the link between Torah and Wisdom, the Fourth Gospel presents the Logos of its prologue as Torah."[159] The creative capacity of the Word in John 1:3 also calls to mind that of torah in Ps 119:89–91. After all, what the OT ascribes to Wisdom it also ascribes to torah. "In the beginning" (John 1:1) is an obvious allusion to Gen 1:1 ("In the beginning God created . . ."), which recounts God's creation of the world simply by the *word* of his mouth (e.g., "And God *said*, let there be . . ." 1:3ff.) John's prologue, therefore, declares that Jesus is the climactic and unique revelation of God, the Word through whom God creates, sustains, and enlightens all things, thereby further illuminating the thought of the Hebrew creation narrative.

Third, the main point of John's prologue is not simply to give a christological commentary on the Genesis creation narrative, but also to establish that Jesus, the preexistent Word, is the premier expression and explanation of God to humanity, a role previously occupied by torah. As T. F. Glasson comments, "We thus have in the Prologue a transference to Christ of what has been ascribed to the Torah."[160] Given that Ps 119 uses "word" twenty-

---

156. Pryor, *Evangelist*, 8.

157. Notably Witherington, *Wisdom*, 47–59.

158. Ibid., 52. Withering notes that the apocryphal book Wisdom of Solomon uses "wisdom" and "word" synonymously: "O God of my ancestors and Lord of mercy, who have made all things by your word, and by your wisdom have formed humankind to have dominion over the creatures you have made" (Wis 9:1–2 NRSV).

159. Keener, *John*, 1:360.

160. Glasson, *Moses*, 88. Glasson notes that not only does John reference torah here, but also the OT wisdom tradition, esp. Prov 8 and Sir 24, which describe Wisdom as a divine hypostasis that was present at creation and the means through which God created all things. John's prologue alludes to both torah and Wisdom; but these two are not distinct in Jewish thought; they are one and the same (p. 87). Pryor (*Evangelist*, 8) cites the later rabbis who equated hypostatic Wisdom as the agent of creation in Prov 8 with torah: "Through the beginning God created the heaven and the earth; the 'beginning' is

two times as one of the eight synonyms for torah, the association of Jesus the Word and torah is a natural one; especially considering the lofty description of the word in 119:89–91: "Forever, O LORD, your word is firmly fixed in the heavens. Your faithfulness endures to all generations; you have established the earth, and it stands fast. By your appointment they stand this day, for all things are your servants."

Fourth, not only does the Word in John's prologue call to mind the creative capacity of God's torah in Ps 119, but also its practical, ethical, and instructional nature where God's word teaches the psalmist the way of righteousness and covenant life. Jesus, too, brings "life" and "light" to humanity (John 1:4; 8:12), both of which are also associated with torah in Ps 119:25, 105, 130, and others. The major difference between torah in the OT and Jesus the new torah is where the former is a divine hypostasis, like Wisdom, an impersonal force that reveals God's will, the latter is a personal being—Jesus of Nazareth. As Glasson observes about John's prologue, "It is the *person* of the Logos which holds the central place."[161] What is more, where torah offers covenant life in Ps 119, the "good life" in the present but that ends at the grave, Jesus offers "eternal life"—the present and future experience of an intimate relationship with the Father and the Son (John 17:3), an experience of life that begins now and continues for eternity. Thus, there is a typological relationship between covenant life through obedience to God's word in Ps 119 and eternal life in the new covenant through God's Word, Jesus Christ.

In light of the nature of typology, which has a "lesser to greater" progression, it is a mistake to interpret John as simply suggesting that Christ the Word is simply to be equated with torah, for in reality the whole point of John's prologue is to emphasize the superiority of the Word's revelation that exceeds that of torah (cf. Heb 1:1–2). The prologue shows that the interpretive key to the divine will "is not to be found merely in an identity of wisdom and torah, but in the incarnation of Jesus Christ in whom both the wisdom and law of God is united."[162] The OT type (torah) anticipates and is fulfilled in the NT antitype (the Word). To be clear, the Word does not oppose or contradict torah, as Jesus does not contradict Moses (John 5:45–47; cf. Matt 5:17); however, the Word exceeds the revelatory capacity of torah. In other words, the torah reveals God; the Word *is* God. The first torah describes God, while the second shows him. Put differently, the law reveals the nature

---

nothing other than the Torah, as it says in Prov 8:22, 'Yahweh created me at the beginning of his way'" (Gen. Rab. 1:1). I would note here a major difference between Wisdom in Prov 8 and the Word in John's prologue is that the former is created by God while the latter is preexistent (i.e., God does not create the Word).

161. Glasson, *Moses*, 94. Italics added.
162. Childs, *Canon*, 137.

of God as "grace and truth" (Exod 34:6); the Word *is* grace and truth (John 1:17). The former deals with indirect revelation; the latter with direct revelation. When seen through the christological lens provided by the Gospel of John, especially identifying Jesus as the way, the truth, and the life, and the Word, Ps 119 becomes much more than the composer's reflections on Scripture; it becomes an end-times expectation of Christ, God's Word in the flesh of Jesus of Nazareth, the new torah, who fully reveals the Father. It is difficult to do better than Eaton:

> The strengthening references to the Lord's word here [Ps 119] become related to Christ the Word, and all the light of guidance and salvation given through him. He is the Word established forever in the heavens, the thought and true expression of God, eternal and boundless, yet close in his grace as teacher, counselor, comforter, shepherd, lamp, fountain of hope and joy. The psalm becomes a prayer through this Word, built on him, and offered for all his suffering ones.[163]

A final important correlation remains between the Jesus and the psalmist. In that torah in Ps 119 at least includes written Scripture, the poet and Jesus both agree that Scripture does not point to itself, but to God. I mentioned previously the psalmist does not engage in bibliolatry—the worship of Scripture—but properly sees Scripture as a means to an end, not an end in and of itself. The goal of Scripture for the psalmist is to come to an intimate knowledge (in the Hebrew sense of relationship, not mere head knowledge) of God and his will. As Eaton observes about the psalm, not the commandments themselves but the "guiding, teaching *Lord* comes to dominate the mind of the one reciting the psalm."[164] God is above all the object of the psalmist's affection; his devotion to Scripture serves the goal of nurturing a covenant relationship with Yahweh. Jesus teaches the same in John 5:39–40 when he warns the Jewish leaders about the shortsightedness of their approach to Scripture, which was more about external obedience to rules than relationship: "You search the Scriptures because you think that in them you have eternal life; and it is they that bear witness about me, yet you refuse to come to me that you may have life." Jesus makes it clear that Christology is the center of the OT.

To be clear, Jesus does not chastise the Jewish leaders for diligently studying Scripture, but rather for failing to take such study to its logical conclusion: a life-giving relationship with Jesus Christ to whom Scripture points. In other words, the goal of knowing Scripture is to cultivate and

---

163. Eaton, *Psalms*, 422.
164. Ibid., 415. Italics added.

nourish a relationship with Christ. There is nothing intrinsically life-giving about studying the Bible.[165] It is possible to miss the life-giving power of the Scriptures that comes only through recognition that the biblical word bears witness to Jesus.[166] The NT declares that Jesus is the goal and summation of Israel's Scriptures (Luke 24:25–27, 44–47), as he is the goal and summation of torah in general. Scripture never points to itself as the definitive revelation of God, but to Christ, the Word, as God's climactic revelation to humanity. N. T. Wright quips, "When John declares that 'in the beginning was the word,' he does not reach a climax with 'and the word was written down' but 'and the word became flesh.'"[167] Point being, in all our admiration of the Bible as the inspired word of God, it is not the pinnacle revelation of God to humanity; Jesus is. The Bible serves the goal of bringing humanity into a covenantal relationship with God through Christ.

Jesus is the goal of Israel's Scriptures, not in the sense of fulfilling a few "messianic" passages scattered throughout the OT, but as the focal point of the *narrative* of Scripture. The OT is a comprehensive witness to the gospel, and the whole is more "messianic" than its parts. In other words, the gospel of Christ is the pinnacle moment in Israel's history and is the event to which the entire OT leads. Peter Enns explains, "The Old Testament is a story, compiled over time, that is going somewhere, which is what the apostles are at great pains to show. It is the Old Testament as a whole, particularly in its grand themes, that find its *telos*, its completion, in Christ."[168] All the mighty deeds of God in the OT point to Christ as their complete fulfillment: creation (John 1:3), the covenant with Abraham (Gal 3:16), the Passover and the exodus (Last Supper and passion narratives of the Gospels; 1 Cor 5:7), the tabernacle of God's presence (John 1:14), the covenant of Moses (Heb 9:15), the miraculous food and drink in the wilderness (John 6:35; 1 Cor 10:4), the uplifted serpent (John 3:14), the monarchy (Matt 2:2), the temple (John 2:21), the return from exile (Mark 1:3), to name a few. As Willem VanGemeren aptly observes, "*The center of the Bible is the incarnate and glorified Christ, by whom all things will be renewed.* All the acts of God, all the revelation of his promises and covenants, all the progression of his kingdom, and all the benefits of salvation are *in Christ*."[169] The psalmist's devotion to God's word in Ps 119 calls to mind the centrality of the Word, Jesus Christ, to Israel's Scriptures, as well as the covenant relationship that his disciples have with God through him.

---

165. Carson, *John*, 263.
166. Moloney, *Signs and Shadows*, 23–24.
167. Wright, *Scripture*, 22.
168. Enns, *Inspiration*, 154.
169. VanGemeren, *Progress*, 27.

Psalm 127

"Unless the LORD builds the church, they labor in vain who build it."—James L. Mays

History

PSALM 127 SEEMS AT first to be a very simple and straightforward psalm about God's involvement in the day-to-day activities of our lives. Our homes, cities, and children flow from the hand of God, and we should reflect on his mercies and how underserving we are of them, rejecting any thought that they are the work of our own hands. This is, by and large, the main message of Ps 127, but pressing into the details of its background and structure reveals anything but a simple composition. It is intentionally ambiguous in its use of words like "house," "city," and "sons," which tends to tilt its interpretation in either of two directions, although these are not necessarily mutually exclusive. On one hand, this is the language of ordinary life—fruitful work and fruitful families. On the other hand, it is the language of King David's dynasty, which includes King Solomon, and alludes to God's covenant with David in 2 Sam 7.[1] David wanted to build a "house" for God, which is obviously a reference to the temple (7:2). But the prophet Nathan relates to David the converse: God will establish a "house" for David (7:11). Here, "house" means "dynasty." David's son, Solomon, would in fact build God's house/temple and will also be the beginning of a "house" for David, a "dynasty." What is more, "He shall build a house for my name" (7:13) may be a double use of the word "house" in that it may refer to either the temple that Solomon would build or it may mean "dynasty"—the dynasty of David as God's vice regent in Israel for the sake of his name. Additionally, "build a house" (*banah bayit*) in the Hebrew Bible can also refer to creating a family (Deut 25:9; Ruth 4:11) or the literal dwelling place of a family, and the verb "build," even when not linked to the noun "house," can refer to having

---

1. This discussion follows Zorn, *Psalms*, 419–20; Miller, "Psalm 127," 123.

children or building a family line (Gen 16:2; 30:3). The meaning of "house" and "build" are multivalent, depending on context. Similarly, "sons" (Ps 127:3–5) can refer to male children, children in general, or more specifically to heirs of the throne (2 Sam 7:14). How one interprets these terms effects the interpretation of Ps 127.

I will return to the ascription "of Solomon" (*lishlomoh*) later, but at this point it is important to recognize Ps 127 as a "Song of Ascents," which is a collection of pilgrim psalms (120—134) sung by worshipers on their way to the holy city, Jerusalem, in order to worship at various religious festivals, including Passover, the Feast of Weeks, and the Feast of Tabernacles.[2] John Eaton believes the topics of Ps 127 are relevant in the autumn festival—toil and produce, fertility and blessing the family, and the annual autumn pilgrimage to the "house" (temple) and "city" (Zion).[3]

Read by itself as a stand-alone psalm, Ps 127 appears to be a wisdom psalm, exhorting the reader to consider God's role in both civic and family life. One should be careful not to think that human ingenuity and intelligence is anything apart from the providence of God. God makes both work and womb fruitful, and the recognition that his will guides these efforts helps protect against pride and self-reliance. No one is "self-made." However, it begs the question whether or not Ps 127 should be read in isolation, especially given its placement in the Ascents collection, not to mention its sister psalm, Ps 128, which echoes many of the same themes as Ps 127: blessedness, labor, children, house, and Zion/Jerusalem. Upon comparing the two, Patrick Miller observes that Ps 127 describes work as being in vain when undertaken apart from the recognition of God's providence, and Ps 128 mirrors a more holistic outlook on work: "here is a positive kind of labor that is blessed by God, the work of those who fear him, who walk in his ways. To labor apart from Yahweh, in a frantic, ceaseless manner, is to experience the painful toil, the vain labor."[4] James Mays notes that fruitful work and fruitful family as the blessing of the LORD is the topic of both Pss 127 and 128; therefore, "the two psalms should be read together as a mutually interpretive context. Work and family were the two constitutive dimensions of ordinary life in Israel."[5] But, these were not always certain since work did not always come to fruition and marriage

---

2. DeClaissé-Walford, et al., *Psalms*, 917. The superscript may also be translated "a song of the steps," which may refer to the steps leading up to the Jerusalem temple used by religious pilgrims, or even the psalm's step-like parallelism, which is characteristic of many of the psalms in this collection (pp. 887–90).

3. Eaton, *Psalms*, 435.

4. Miller, "Psalm 127," 129.

5. Mays, *Psalms*, 401. For a more precise discussion of the commonalities between Pss 127 and 128, see Miller, "Psalm 127," 129; Bullock, *Encountering*, 211.

did not always produce children. Psalm 127 is grounded in the fundamental trust in God's providence as the "decisive factor in all human life."[6] This has a profound impact on life in the early postexilic period, where God has given his people the opportunity to start afresh as a society that looks upward rather than inward, trusting in his gracious provision rather than in its own autonomy. As a community that has come through the horrible experience of the exile, the early postexilic period is characterized by rebuilding both land and life. This seems to be the most basic theme of the psalm, highlighting its practical dimension.

However, in the Psalms of Ascents, "house" frequently refers to the temple or Davidic lineage, "sons" to the Davidic dynasty, and "city" to Jerusalem/Zion.[7] In the context of the Ascents as pilgrim psalms, which were likely composed and compiled into the present collection during the Persian period (ca. 537–332 BCE) when Jews reinstituted temple worship after the exile, the emphasis on the rebuilt temple and city coincide with the concerns of each psalm in the collection.[8] The worshipers of the postexilic community might have thought of the temple and its repair, as well as those of Jerusalem, upon hearing the opening of the psalm: "Unless the LORD builds the house, those who build it labor in vain. Unless the LORD watches over the city, the watchman stays awake in vain" (127:1). Does Ps 127, therefore, interrupt the pilgrimage motif of the collection as a stand-alone psalm about God's involvement in the construction of cities, homes, and families, or should it be read in light of the concerns of the Psalms of Ascents? To be clear, the language of Ps 127 is non-specific, referring simply to "house," "city," and "sons," and could refer to a literal house or family, any city, and children in general. More than likely, the terminology is intentionally ambiguous, reflecting both the pilgrimage theme as well as civic and family life. Brueggemann and Bellinger explain this poem about daily work and family has been included in a collection tied to pilgrimage to Jerusalem and thus interpreted in that light when read in the context of the Ascents collection.[9]

---

6. Mays, *Psalms*, 401.

7. Brueggemann and Bellinger, *Psalms*, 542. Mays offers the following statistics: Jerusalem or Zion occurs twelve times in eight of the collection; "house of the LORD" in two of the eight, with a possible allusion in another (Ps 127:1); "Israel" occurs nine times in the collection (*Psalms*, 386).

8. Zorn, *Psalms*, 394. As Elie Assis explains, "The Psalms of Ascents were written in the exile after the destruction of the Temple in the year 587 BCE, and they reflect the thoughts and feelings at the beginning of the exile, and at the time of the return to Yehud [Judah], at the commencement of the renewed settlement of the Land of Israel." See Assis, "Psalm 127," 262. Of course, they may have been composed prior to the exile, and reflect the pilgrimages to Jerusalem during the monarchy period.

9. Brueggemann and Bellinger, *Psalms*, 542.

It also provides a practical focus on the family as one of God's blessings celebrated during the pilgrimage.

Again, the Psalms of Ascents likely reflect the Persian period and take up the concerns of rebuilding Israelite society after the exile. Beyond this, it is exceedingly difficult to determine the historical backdrop to Ps 127. Its placement in the middle of the Ascents collection makes it a bridge between Pss 120—126, which are fairly negative in tone, appealing to God's mercy to restore the fortunes of his people, and praying for "help" from the LORD, etc., and 128—134, which are more positive.[10] The first psalm in the collection, Ps 120, probably reflects the experience of exile, speaking mostly of the psalmist's distress in the midst of a hostile people, even describing his situation as a "sojourn" (120:5). The remainder of the collection refers more specifically to the pilgrimage context with themes like the Davidic king, the temple, and Jerusalem. While this likely refers to religious pilgrimages to the temple during the Persian period and the reinstitution of the kingly dynasty, it would be a mistake to think this time in Judah's "restoration" was altogether pleasant. Simply because they had been restored to the land, the city of Jerusalem had been fortified with walls, and the temple had been rebuilt, they were still a subservient people. The Persian ruler, Cyrus, most likely for political reasons than sheer goodwill, had simply permitted the people of "Yehud" (i.e., Judah) to practice their religion upon their return to their homeland (2 Chr 36:22-23; Ezra 1:1-11).[11]

The pilgrim psalms reflect the reinstitution of Israel's temple worship and religious festivals during this period. Psalm 127, therefore, falls in the middle of the collection as a transitional piece, moving away from the negative tone of the first half of the collection to the more celebratory tone of the second half, which speaks more often of blessing, the temple, unity, etc. It should be pointed out, however, that pleas for mercy do occur in the second half (e.g., Ps 130) as celebration occasionally occurs in the first (e.g., Ps 123). The categorization of the two halves of the collection is not airtight but is generally the case. As a whole, the theme of *blessing* unifies the collection as pilgrims to Jerusalem/Zion go to the sacred city seeking God's blessing.[12]

The two parts of Ps 127 reflect the emphases in terms of "house," "city," and "sons," but how the two sections relate to each other is more complex. As I mentioned, one can read the psalm through a lens of building a city and

---

10. McCann, *Psalms*, 1197.

11. Iain Provan, et al., *History*, 287. Thus, the archeological discovery of the "Cyrus Cylinder" in 1879, which alludes to Cyrus's policy of allowing conquered peoples to return and rebuild their homelands. See Arnold and Beyer, *Encountering*, 258, 268.

12. Brueggemann and Bellinger, *Psalms*, 543-44.

family generally, or through a temple, Jerusalem, Davidic dynasty lens. The structure of Ps 127 is simple, consisting only of two sections:

The house (vv. 1–2)
The children (vv. 3–5)[13]

The question remains as to the relationship between the two sections. Are they two separate psalms altogether, where the first addresses the building of families and the second temple and city construction? If so, have they been haphazardly fused together into one psalm with contrasting topics? Or, are they united by mutually illuminating themes, making them a single composition?[14] Interpretations of this short psalm run the gamut of the proposals, and more; a brief look at the psalm's postexilic background may help work toward a solution regarding the relationship of the two sections.

The postexilic period was marked by three significant elements, and each are reflected to some degree in Ps 127.[15] First, under the direction of Zerubbabel in the late 520s BCE, the reconstruction of the temple foundation and the altar of burnt offering began (Ezra 3:1–6). However, the temple itself was unfinished for several years because of opposition from the "enemies" (i.e., Samaritans) of Judah (4:1–5), and perhaps even the peoples' lack of interest, but it was completed at the exhortations of Haggai (Hag 1—2; cf. Ezra 3:7–13; 5:6—6:15) and Zechariah (Zech 4:9) in 515 BCE, again, under the leadership of Zerubbabel (and the priest, Jeshua).

---

13. DeClaissé-Walford, et al., *Psalms*, 917.

14. Assis, "Psalm 127," 256–72. Assis believes Ps 127 was composed during the period when the temple remained unfinished. The two sections of the psalm present a "dichotomy" between what Judah should avoid doing (i.e., rebuilding the temple at this time) and what they should do (i.e., build their families instead). Considering this to be a national and religious crisis, Assis theorizes that Ps 127 addresses this crisis by reminding the people that only through *God's* will would the temple be rebuilt (v. 1), and in its absence they should focus their energy not on fretting about the absence of the temple, but on building families and raising up the next generation of Israelite leadership, for this also is the will of God (vv. 3–5). In other words, building families substitutes for building the temple. This historical reconstruction is speculative, to be sure, assuming there was indeed a "crisis" among the people about the rebuilding of the temple, and draws too sharp a wedge between the two parts of the psalm, even if the point of his article is to read the psalm as a single composition. What is more, Assis fails to consider the building of the city in verse 2, which occurred ca. 445 BCE, at least fifty years after the rebuilding of the temple, although he considers verses 1–2 to be a unity that conflicts with the remainder of the psalm (pp. 256–57). However, I appreciate the effort to explain how the two sections interpret one another within the larger context of postexilic Judah, even if his dating of the psalm is too precise.

15. This brief discussion of the early postexilic period loosely follows Provan, et al., *History*, 286–302.

The second major event in the postexilic period was the rebuilding of the walls of Jerusalem under Nehemiah (Neh 3:1—7:4), which aimed to resurrect the glory of the city devastated by the Babylonians. It, too, occurred in the face of opposition by the Samaritans (Ezra 4:6–23), leaving the city without sufficient defenses. This might be part of the background to "building" and "guarding" the city in Ps 127:2. According to Bill Arnold and Bryan Beyer:

> Nehemiah had enemies all around him. But he constantly encouraged the people to keep working and praying. Half his crew worked construction, while the other half stayed armed and ready to defend the city (Neh 4:16). His method of dealing with opposition was prayer followed by suitable action (4:9), and he always gave God credit for successes. (4:15)[16]

The third significant element of the postexilic period was Zerubbabel's role in governing the people of Judah, especially his role in rebuilding the temple and uniting the people in the faith of Yahweh. The language of the prophets Haggai and Zechariah indicate that Zerubbabel is more than a mere "governor" of the people of Judah (Hag 1:1). Through the prophets he receives a divine commission for his task of rebuilding the temple as God's "servant," a title not casually thrown around in the OT: "I will take you, O Zerubbabel my servant, the son of Shealtiel, declares the LORD, and make you like a signet ring, for I have chosen you, declares the LORD of hosts" (2:23). Being God's signet ring suggests divine authority, and being called God's "servant" places him among the ranks of the greatest leaders of Israel, including Moses, Caleb, Joshua, David, Elijah, Hezekiah, and Nehemiah (Num 12:7; 14:24; Josh 24:29; 2 Sam 3:18; 2 Kgs 10:10; 2 Chr 32:16; Neh 1:11). His commissioning in Zechariah's vision reflects the sovereign authority of the LORD:

> Then he said to me, "This is the word of the LORD to Zerubbabel: Not by might, nor by power, but by my Spirit, says the LORD of hosts. Who are you, O great mountain? Before Zerubbabel you shall become a plain. And he shall bring forward the top stone amid shouts of 'Grace, grace to it!'" Then the word of the LORD came to me, saying, "The hands of Zerubbabel have laid the foundation of this house; his hands shall also complete it. Then you will know that the LORD of hosts has sent me to you. For whoever has despised the day of small things shall rejoice, and shall see the plumb line in the hand of Zerubbabel." (Zech 4:6–10)

---

16. Arnold and Beyer, *Encountering*, 269.

Zechariah then captures the symbolism of Zerubbabel's divinely-ordained status where he is one of the two olive branches beside the two gold pipes that pour oil onto the lampstand in Zechariah's vision (4:7–8).[17] Last but not least for the postexilic community, he is part of the family lineage of King David (1 Chr 3:19), being "a royal actor in the temple rebuilding ceremony."[18] Surely his leadership, divine commission, and royal ancestry sparked a renewed messianic hope in the restoration of David's dynasty among the returnees. Therefore, we can be sure that many people thought that the restoration of the Davidic throne was immanent.[19]

The Psalms of Ascents, therefore, echo the fever-pitch hopes of Judah after the return from exile, speaking often of God's "house," the "city" Jerusalem/Zion, and the Davidic dynasty (i.e., "sons"). As Mays observes, "When the terms are read in light of these associations, the whole question of the building (and rebuilding) of city and temple and the continuity of the Davidic kingship looms as a setting in which to read the psalm."[20] This makes the ascription of Ps 127 to Solomon all the more interesting. Not only is he the son of David and the third king of Israel, he is noted for building the temple and expanding the borders of the kingdom to their largest in ancient history. Thus, the ascription to Solomon is a major clue to how the psalm was understood when included in the collection. Solomon is a builder of the temple (1 Kgs 3:1–2) and cities (2 Chr 8:1–6) . . . In the LORD's covenant with David, the promise is that the LORD would build David's house, and David's successor would build the LORD's house.[21] Similarly, Miller sees the ascription to Solomon as a lens through which to approach the psalm: "If one wants to know specifically what verse 1 has in mind, look at Solomon, the master builder of houses (1 Kgs 3:1–2; 7:1ff.; 8:13; 9:1), and cities (2 Chr 8:1ff.). One cannot build a house for oneself or God without God's help. And one cannot protect it or ensure the security of the human community, even Jerusalem, without the Lord watching over it."[22]

What is more, Solomon is also God's "beloved," which is the word from which Jedidiah, his personal name from God was formed (2 Sam 12:24–25; cf. 7:15), suggesting yet another connection with the psalm (Ps

---

17. Provan, et al., *History*, 289.

18. Ibid.

19. Ibid. It is ironic, however, that upon completing the task of rebuilding the temple, Zerubbabel disappears from the biblical text, perhaps suggesting he was not the final answer for the people of God (ibid., 290).

20. Mays, *Psalms*, 402.

21. Ibid.

22. Miller, "Psalm 127," 128.

127:2).[23] The first two verses of Ps 127 clearly evoke Solomon, although not necessarily the rest of the psalm. In fact, as Derek Kidner aptly notes, the lessons of the psalm were largely lost on Solomon: his building became reckless (1 Kgs 9:10–19), his kingdom a ruin (11:11ff.), and his marriages a disastrous denial of God (11:1ff.).[24] But these are not the focus of the psalm; it is more likely that achievements in life, even those of Solomon, the archetypal builder-king and son of David, are "in vain" without Yahweh's participation.[25] Therefore, we can fairly speak of a Davidic thread that runs through the psalm with a timely message of God's providence during the postexilic period consistent with the other psalms in the Ascents collection. Again, its placement next to Ps 128 suggests a practical emphasis on ordinary life—building homes and cities and bearing children—even if the Davidic thread runs underneath the surface of the psalm.

Perhaps the best way to approach the historical exegesis of Ps 127 is to consider verses 1–2 together and 3–5 together as the two major sections of the psalm. The first two verses, while focused specifically on house building and city defenses, set the overriding theme of the psalm—blessings from God. This theme, which is prevalent in the Psalms of Ascents, ties both of the psalm's sections together, making it a wisdom psalm. The point is both simple and substantive: any effort that humanity undertakes should properly be seen in light of God's gracious provisions. From house building—be it family or temple—to the construction and protection of the city—be it Jerusalem or any city—the acknowledgement of God's providence should permeate every endeavor. What is more, efforts that refuse to acknowledge God's hand are meaningless, empty, void of substance, and doomed to failure. The workings of humanity are not autonomous from God. From the smallest segments of society (the family unity), to the largest (the city), God is actively involved as his work intertwines with that of his people.

Verse 2 magnifies the point by clarifying the type of toil indicted in verse 1—anxious toil—a striving and straining kind of work that never stops to reflect on God as the sole provider for his people. The latter part of verse 2 is notoriously difficult to translate, although the two resulting interpretations are not mutually exclusive; both fit the theme of the psalm. Most English translations interpret the Hebrew verb (*shena*) as "to sleep," yielding something like, "For he gives to his beloved sleep." While his beloved toils on and on, God provides for those he loves when they least expect it—during sleep! Losing sleep in order to obtain food is a waste of time; God grants

23. Kidner, *Psalms 73–150*, 440.
24. Ibid.
25. Brueggemann and Bellinger, *Psalms*, 542.

sleep (and food) to those he loves.²⁶ To be clear, this does not mean people can just sit at home (cf. Prov 6:6–11; 10:4–5), expecting God to provide in their slumber, but makes the point that no matter how intense our efforts, success comes only from the hand of God.²⁷ The other translation of *shena* takes it to mean something like "esteem" or "honor."²⁸ As Miller explains, "The first part of the verse refers to those who seek to attain wealth or high position by the drive of their own achievements, presumably without looking to God for help or placing their labors in his hands. Such activity and efforts are in vain. Yahweh is the one who gives wealth and honor."²⁹ Taken as a whole, verse 2 builds on the thought of verse 1, suggesting a frantic, racing, ceaseless involvement in work, is completely useless because God gives his prosperity or his honor, his grace.³⁰

At first glance, verses 3–5 seem to address very different concerns than verses 1–2. I noted previously that this might suggest the psalm is not a single composition, but a combination of two smaller psalms or proverbs. Yet not only is there a unifying theme in God's blessings generally between the two sections, they are bound together by their beginning with two key Hebrew words that have different meanings but similar sounds: *banah* ("build" in v. 1) and *banim* ("sons" in v. 3). And, the house that is built in verse 1 is likely related to the sons that are the heritage of Yahweh in verses 3–5.³¹ Not only do these internal factors weigh in favor of the psalm's unity, there is also an external factor that suggests the same. There is an ANE parallel account in the hymn to the Sumerian goddess Nisiba. The hymn mirrors the themes and progression of Ps 127 by noting the goddess's providence in fruitful work and womb:

> Nisaba, where you do not ordain it, man builds no (house), he builds no city, he builds no palace, he appoints no king, he does not take care of the purification cults of the gods. Nisaba, where you are not near, he builds no fold, he makes no pen, the shepherds's heart does not rejoice in playing the shawm. Nisaba, when your heart impels you, you make everything broad, let everything extend itself, you order the ponds like the heavenly pond, you order the sanctuaries, pouring out brightness (over them). The Lady, who gives the heart's joy, are you, you put

26. Longman, *Psalms*, 426.
27. Ibid.
28. Miller, "Psalm 127," 125–26.
29. Ibid., 126.
30. Ibid., 127.
31. Ibid., 121.

good seed in the womb, let the fruit grow in the womb, give the mother love for the child.[32]

Miller observes not only the similarity in content but also the order of the elements themselves: "The hymn can and does move from the goddess's role as ordainer and builder of things to her role as giver of fertility to women."[33] Therefore, because similar hymns existed in antiquity, there is no compelling reason to reject the unity of Ps 127.

If the Davidic context continues through this section, "sons" in verse 3 would refer to royal heirs, like Solomon. However, sons in general were highly prized in the ancient culture, providing blessing and security for the family. The imagery of sons as arrows in a quiver (vv. 4–5) illustrates their role as providing security for the family in the face of adversity. For the ancients, the larger the family, the less vulnerable it was; having many sons might even convey a small army, standing with the "warrior" (v. 4) to defend the home front. Even in the midst of a male-dominated society like ancient Israel, daughters, too, could be sources of security and strength to a family (Ruth 4:15; Job 42:15).[34] Therefore, given the larger context of family blessing and God's providence, the thought of these verses is that *children are the gift of God*, a "heritage" (v. 3a) from him and represent life, security, and future blessing.[35] In ancient Israelite society, children born to a young couple became a great support and strength as their parents aged.[36]

The poet also describes the gift of children as a "reward" (v. 3b) from God for faithfulness. The reader should not miss the allusion to God's promise to Abram to provide an abundance of offspring for him to secure his lineage for the ages as a "reward" for faithful obedience (Gen 15:1, 5).[37] Given the unifying theme of divine blessing in the psalm, as house building and city building are ultimately the works of God, so also is bearing children. Patrick Reardon explains as God gives us the fruits of our anxious labor while we are sleeping, so also with the gift of children, for they are conceived "in bed," having more to do with human rest that with human

---

32. Ibid.
33. Ibid., 122.
34. Eaton, *Psalms*, 436.
35. McCann, *Psalms*, 1198. McCann notes that the Heb. word for heritage (*nakhala*) is the same used in Joshua to describe God's gift of the Promise Land to Israel (Josh 14:3). DeClaissé-Walford, et al., observes that the term occurs at least thirty-seven times in Joshua (*Psalms*, 918).
36. Eaton, *Psalms*, 436.
37. Ibid.

toil.[38] In the context of the psalm, there is no room for a "planned parenthood" strictly speaking because children are conceived in the context of rest, they are purely the gift of God.[39] The psalm concludes with yet another benefit of children: their presence at the city gate brings safety and security during a trial. The city gate was the gathering place where the community leaders settled disputes, rendered judgments, and made important decisions in the community. It is not clear, however, how having children present at a dispute would provide a sense of stability for the family. Mays proposes, "When a man had to face his adversaries in a legal conflict that ended up in the court convened in the gates of the city, it helped greatly to appear accompanied by a platoon of strapping boys."[40] Such fathers are "blessed" (*ashrey*, v. 5a); the use of this wisdom word helps identify the poem as a wisdom psalm.[41] Whether one reads the psalm through the pilgrimage lens of the end-times hopes of the postexilic community or through the lens of God's involvement in every day life, both are meaningful and contribute to a well-rounded historical interpretation of the psalm. Both views essentially make the same point but from different, though not contradictory, angles:

> Psalm 127 encompasses the most fundamental of enterprises— the building and founding of human structures, the securing and protecting of community, the work and vocation of men and women, the building of home and family. The word of the Psalm is that unless such enterprises become God's enterprises as those who build, watch, and labor seek his will and way and invoke his presence and purpose in these activities, then there is an emptiness to them. They are without purpose or effect. When, however, the Lord is at the center of such endeavors, then those who so live may see the good of Jerusalem and their children's children.[42]

Christology

In our frantic, fast-paced society that tends to idolize career, unfortunately often elevating it above faith and family, the message of Ps 127—that all blessings come from the hand of God—is especially timely. The ever-present

---

38. Reardon, *Christ*, 254.

39. Ibid.

40. Mays, *Psalms*, 401. Zorn adds that the presence of sons in court could testify to their father's character. This hardly fits the warrior imagery of the context, but a change in the imagery is possible (*Psalms*, 424).

41. DeClaissé-Walford, et al., *Psalms*, 919.

42. Miller, "Psalm 127," 130.

temptation today is to see ourselves as "self made," pulling ourselves up by our own bootstraps, which all too often leads to either burnout or functional workaholism—a never-ending cycle of toil and frustration. Psalm 127 demolishes the idol of self-sufficiency by calling us back to the reality of God's role in our lives, reminding us that all advancement, be it career, society, or family, is due to God's gracious blessings. Brueggemann and Bellinger explain the perspective of Ps 127 is that human endeavors do not succeed from "autonomous human effort but from work in the context of the gift of the creator."[43] What is more, in our society of "militant consumerism," the psalm challenges us to think again about our approach to life, work, and family; Ps 127 exhorts us to reject the foolishness of autonomy from God.[44] Its exhortation against anxious toil should comfort those who feel trapped in a web of work to the point of not enjoying life because of constant worry about their stability and sustenance in a world that keeps these things at arm's length. The message of the psalm is not to cease our labors altogether, but to put them into proper focus by looking upward rather than inward, recognizing that the best of our efforts accomplish nothing apart from the providential hand of God.

Like Ps 127, Jesus teaches the importance of depending on God in the Sermon on the Mount, exhorting his listeners against the anxious life that frets about lacking the necessities of life (Matt 6:25–34). God graciously provides all we need in spite of our anxious toiling on and on. We can rest peacefully, knowing that God blesses the work of our hands and provides for us while we are sleeping, or, alternatively, exalts us in spite of our ceaseless toiling (Ps 127:2). James also evokes the main thought of the opening lines of the psalm when he warns against the futility of undertaking human endeavors apart from recognizing the will of God in our endeavors:

> Come now, you who say, "Today or tomorrow we will go into such and such a town and spend a year there and trade and make a profit"—yet you do not know what tomorrow will bring. What is your life? For you are a mist that appears for a little time and then vanishes. Instead you ought to say, "If the Lord wills, we will live and do this or that." As it is, you boast in your arrogance. All such boasting is evil. So whoever knows the right thing to do and fails to do it, for him it is sin. (Jas 4:13–17)

To be clear, James does not warn against planning, as the psalm does not reject work; but he warns against the mindset that does not acknowledge God's role in bringing our plans to fruition. Making plans apart from God's

---

43. Brueggemann and Bellinger, *Psalms*, 543.
44. Ibid., 544.

will, as if one's livelihood were solely in his or her own hands, is as arrogant, sinful, and vain, as building a home or guarding a city without relying on God's blessing.

Psalm 127 places children among the blessings of God, mirroring the ministry and message of Jesus. In many ancient cultures, children were often viewed as more of a burden than a blessing, at least until they were old enough to work and help support the family. The psalm, in contrast, describes children as gifts from God, as rewards for faithfulness. Israelite society integrated children into all facets of life, especially home and nation, at an early age where they were valued for their potential roles: contributing to the material wellbeing of the family, carrying on the family name, perpetuating the covenant nation's unique identity and purpose from one generation to the next.[45] But they were both valuable and vulnerable, being blessings from God yet subject to the cruelties of the fallen world in terms of power (children typically had none), prestige (only royal children had any at all), and physical wellbeing (infant mortality rates were high; an estimated sixty percent of the children in the first-century Mediterranean society were dead by the age of sixteen).[46] Jews and Christians, in contrast to their pagan neighbors, deplored practices like abortion, exposure of newborns, and infanticide for economic and other reasons.[47]

It is no wonder then, that Jesus has a special place in his heart for children who, as among the lowliest in Greco-Roman society, are special recipients of his blessings. Far from viewing children as bothersome, he declares their value as humble, trusting recipients of the kingdom, and defends their vulnerability against the power brokers of the day. Nowhere in the NT is this more evident than in Jesus's rebuff of his disciples, who rebuked the crowds for bringing little children to him (Mark 10:13–16 and pars.). The perception of the disciples is that Jesus is too busy or important to have to deal with kids, and so the disciples "rebuke" the people for bringing small and insignificant children to Jesus.[48] But Jesus will have none of it, and uses the situation as a teaching moment to explain the dependence of

---

45. Gundry-Volf, "Child, Children," 588.

46. Longman, "Family," 574.

47. Gundry-Volf, "Child, Children," 589. Everett Ferguson references a papyrus from 1 BCE from Alexandria, Egypt that conveys the general pagan view of infants: "I beg and entreat you, take care of the little one, and as soon as we receive our pay I will send it up to you. If by chance you bear a child, if it is a boy, let it be, if it is a girl, expose it" (*P. Oxy.* 744). See Ferguson, *Backgrounds*, 81.

48. Luke adds to Mark's account that the people "even" (*kai*) brought "infants" (*brefē*) to Jesus, capturing the absurdity of the moment in the eyes of the disciples and the prevailing culture (Luke 18:15).

children, who cannot support themselves but expect and receive their support from parents, as a metaphor for entering the kingdom of God.[49] For Jesus, children are model disciples in the way they receive the kingdom as a gift from God, and are ever-present reminders of the reign of God, which knows nothing of the worldly notions of power, prestige, prominence, and promotion. Each of the Synoptic Gospels records Jesus's interaction with the children, but only Mark mentions that the disciples' actions made Jesus "indignant" (Mark 10:14), and only in Mark does Jesus "bless" the children (v. 16).[50] I am not suggesting that Ps 127 per se informs the background of this Synoptic episode, but the two passages mutually interpret one another by their emphasis on the blessedness of children and their special status before God.

From a more specific christological perspective, Ps 127 calls to mind several interrelated NT images relating to Christ as the new temple, and the church as both the house of God and his children. To the extent that the opening line of Ps 127 is in some sense connected with the temple as the "house"—whether Solomon's or Zerubbabel's—the Gospel of John proclaims that Jesus is the true temple, fulfilling all ritualistic activities associated with the temple (e.g., sacrifice, burning of incense, festivals, etc.), as well as its most important function as the dwelling place of God's presence among humanity. Craig Koester summarizes the function of the temple in Second Temple Judaism: "The temple in Jerusalem was the place where God made his name or glory to dwell. Although God's presence was not confined to the temple, it was generally understood that the sanctuary was, in some sense, God's dwelling place."[51]

While all of the Gospels mention the cleansing of the temple by Jesus when he drives out the moneychangers, only John offers an explicit christological interpretation of the event. Pilgrimages to Jerusalem are prominent in John's Gospel (2:13, 23; 5:1; 7:2, 14; 11:55–56; cf. 10:22), and it is not a coincidence that the event takes place during a pilgrimage to the Passover feast. It is entirely possible that Jesus and those traveling with him would have sang Ps 127 and the other Ascent Psalms on their way "up" to Jerusalem from Galilee (John 2:13). After the Jewish authorities question Jesus after he had cleared the temple, he replies: "Destroy this temple, and in three days I will raise it up" (2:19). John follows immediately with an interpretation of Jesus's words, which turn out to be a prophecy of his crucifixion in the context of John's Gospel: "He was speaking about the temple of his

---

49. Williamson, *Mark*, 179.
50. Ibid., 178.
51. Koester, *Symbolism*, 88.

body" (v. 21). It is clear that for John, God's presence and glory would be manifested not in a building, but in a person—Jesus Christ. By placing the temple cleansing at the beginning of his Gospel, John gives his readers an interpretive lens through which to read the remainder of the narrative: Jesus and his body are the new temple only by passing through temporary destruction and being raised again on the third day (2:20).[52]

By the time of John's christological reflections in the late first-century CE, Judaism, in spite of its doctrinal diversity and variegated sects (e.g., Sadducees, Pharisees, Essenes, Zealots), had developed the anticipation that the messianic era would be characterized, in part, by a reconstructed and purified temple (Tob 14:5; 1 En. 90:28; 91:13; Jub. 1:17, 27, 29; 25:21; 11Q19 29.8–10; 4Q174).[53] Stemming from OT passages like Zech 6:12 ("Behold, the man whose name is the Branch: for he shall branch out from his place and he shall build the temple of the LORD" cf. Ezek 40—46), the Jewish literature of the period echoes the prophetic hope that the Messiah, David's kingly heir (2 Sam 7:10–14), would build the new temple in the messianic era. The Gospel of John leaves no doubt who the Messiah is—Jesus Christ (John 20:31)—as well as his divinely-appointed role of the rebuilding the temple, for his indestructible body is the temple, the dwelling place of God among humanity. Marianne Meye Thompson puts a fine point on Jesus as the new temple:

> John's account reflects both the conviction that the temple is the dwelling of the holy God, or of God's glory and name, and the hope, found in Jewish literature of the time, for a new temple that would replace the temple in Jerusalem. Jesus himself is a temple that, like the Jerusalem temple, will be destroyed; yet he will be raised up—and in three days. In John, the risen Jesus is the new, purified, and indestructible temple that is truly the dwelling of God.[54]

What is more, Rev 21:22 reveals the ultimate christological fulfillment of this new temple theme in its description of the heavenly Jerusalem: "And I saw no temple in the city, for its temple is the Lord God the Almighty and the Lamb." Given that the temple housed the glory of God in the OT, it is significant that the new Jerusalem does not have a physical sanctuary.

---

52. Köstenberger, *Theology*, 195. Köstenberger observes how John, in a way, "robs the narrative of all suspense" by placing the temple incident near the beginning of the story (p. 197).

53. The rabbis believed that the Messiah himself would be the builder of the new temple (Tg. Zech. 6:12–13; Tg. Isa. 53:5).

54. Thompson, *John*, 68–69.

Glory permeates the city because God and the Lamb are there, replacing and perfecting the main function of the temple—divine presence. As Grant Osborne notes, "With God and the Lamb physically present, there is no need for a literal temple."[55] The physical structure yields way to the indestructible presence of God manifested in the indestructible body of Christ. Put differently, the symbol of God's presence gives way to the reality of his presence.[56] The gospel, therefore, illuminates the temple imagery of the pilgrimage context of Ps 127 and the Accent Psalms: Jesus fulfills the postexilic, messianic hopes of a rebuilt and renewed "house."

I noted earlier that given Zerubbabel's "disappearance" from the biblical record after constructing the temple, he was obviously not the final answer to messianic hopes of the postexilic community. The NT leaves no doubt about who is the final answer to the messianic hopes of Israel—Jesus Christ. Not only is Jesus the "builder" of the eschatological temple (of his body), he is also the archetypal son of David, a fact that the genealogies of both Matthew and Luke make clear (Matt 1; Luke 3), forming a typological fulfillment with the (Davidic) "sons" of Ps 127. Considering Ps 127's dual emphasis on house building and sonship against the background of God's covenant with David in 2 Sam 7:13, which was only provisionally fulfilled by both Solomon and Zerubbabel, these messianic expectations culminate in Jesus Christ. He is the culmination of Israel's monarchy, the archetypal son of David, and builder of the temple of his body in the messianic age.

Nowhere in the NT do the words "builder," "house," and "son" occur is such close proximity in a christological context than in Heb 3:1–6. This makes it ripe for christological reflection in relation to Ps 127:

> Therefore, holy brothers, you who share in a heavenly calling, consider Jesus, the apostle and high priest of our confession, who was faithful to him who appointed him, just as Moses also was faithful in all God's house. For Jesus has been counted worthy of more glory than Moses—as much more glory as the builder of a house has more honor than the house itself. (For every house is built by someone, but the builder of all things is God.) Now Moses was faithful in all God's house as a servant, to testify to the things that were to be spoken later, but Christ is faithful over God's house as a son. And we are his house if indeed we hold fast our confidence and our boasting in our hope. (Heb 3:1–6)

Having already established Christ's superiority to angels (Heb 1), the preacher of Hebrews now aims to establish Christ's superiority to Moses.

---

55. Osborne, *Revelation*, 760.
56. Mounce, *Revelation*, 395.

Hebrews 3:1–6 illustrates this superiority by explaining the respective roles of Moses and Christ in God's house, which the preacher uses metaphorically for the people of God. Because the context compares Moses and Jesus, the preacher most clearly alludes to Num 12:7 ("He [Moses] is faithful in all my house"), not Ps 127; my observation here is that Ps 127 and Heb 3:1–6 nevertheless mutually illuminate each other in the larger context of the Christian canon of Scripture, regardless of the original intent of the human authors. Canonical connections exist between the two passages, which, when read in light of each other, contribute to a christological interpretation of the psalm. Besides, we cannot rule out a secondary allusion to God's covenant with David in 1 Chr 17:10–14 (cf. 2 Sam 7:11–16), which must also be considered in understanding the full implications of Heb 3:2.[57]

Psalm 127 and Heb 3:1–6 share the terminology of "house," "builder," and "son," and I showed earlier that one can legitimately interpret "house" as lineage, or even dynasty, in addition to a literal house or temple. Hebrews develops the former in this context, speaking of Jesus and God—as one—as the builder of the house (3:3–4), the faithful messianic community (v. 6). The comparison between Moses and Jesus is not a contrast per se, at least not one where Jesus contradicts Moses. In fact, fidelity to God's house is what joins them; so there is no putdown of Moses in this comparison, as though Jesus were faithful but Moses unfaithful.[58] The author compares the respective status of Moses and Jesus in God's house: the former as a "servant" *in* the house and the latter as a "son" *over* the house. The fact that Moses is a servant does not diminish him; in fact, it gives him an even greater role than angels, as indicated in later Jewish tradition.[59] However, Jesus's status as son gives him a greater *rank* than Moses, and this is the heart of the comparison: both Jesus and Moses were "faithful, but Jesus has a superior ranking as Son in comparison with Moses's status as servant."[60] George Guthrie summarizes:

> The sphere of Moses' ministry was "in all of God's house," meaning that his authority and leadership extended over all God's people at that time. He, however, was a part of that house as a servant rather than an heir. The purpose of his role was to point to later revelation, anticipating the fullness of God's revelation in the Son. Christ, on the other hand, was "over God's house," not in it. Servants have an obligation to faithfulness, but sons have

---

57. Ellingworth, *Hebrews*, 210.
58. Craddock, *Hebrews*, 46.
59. Lane, *Hebrews*, 58.
60. Ibid., 59.

a special, vested interest in and authority over the house. Jesus displayed a filial kind of faithfulness as the Lord and founder of his house, the new covenant people of God.[61]

This is especially relevant when considering "sons" in Ps 127 as Davidic royal heirs and the messianic hope associated with the restored monarchy in the postexilic period. Hebrews goes to great lengths to establish the doctrine that Christ, as a son, reigns over the house of God, that is, his people. The preacher, however, is not content to simply declare the authority of Christ as a son over God's house, apart from application for his audience. Once he has demonstrated the faithfulness of both Moses and Jesus and the superiority of the latter over the former, the preacher exhorts his hearers to mirror the faithfulness of both, while upholding Christ as the founder of their faith, who has by his status as Son more authority than even Moses. They would be foolish to return to the domain of the servant in the old era once the Son has been given all authority in the new. The following table summarizes the comparison of Moses and Jesus as well as the resulting application, stemming from the greater authority of the Son:[62]

Moses	Jesus
Faithful to God (v. 2b)	Faithful to God (v. 2a)
Faithful as a servant (v. 5)	Faithful as a Son (v. 6a)
A servant *in* God's house (v. 5a)	A Son *over* God's house (v. 6b)
Conclusion: *We* are his house if we prove faithful (v. 6b)	

Table 6 Servant, Son, and God's House

It is probably not in passing that the writer of Hebrews draws attention to the construction of the house of God, where both Jesus and God are said to be the builder, evoking the opening phrase of Ps 127:1 ("Unless the LORD builds the house..."). The architectural imagery builds on the "house" of Heb 3:2. This draws out the comparison between Moses and Jesus even more by indicating that Jesus's authority is no arbitrary accident of a blind universe; design logically presupposes a designer.[63] The recipients of the letter should see the progression of their covenantal relationship from Moses, the servant in the old era, to Jesus, the Son in the new, as divinely ordained.

---

61. Guthrie, *Hebrews*, 128.
62. Lane, *Hebrews*, 60.
63. Girdwood and Verkruyse, *Hebrews*, 114.

Even more, because Jesus is the builder of the house, he is functioning at the level where God functions.[64] Looking at a magnificently constructed building may inspire awe and wonder, but praise belongs ultimately to the builder rather than the building. The implication here is that Moses is a part of the house that Jesus built; because Jesus, as God, has made Moses, a member of the people of Israel, and Jesus, as creator, is worthy of more honor and glory than one of his creatures.[65] In the final analysis, Ps 127 and Heb 3:1–6 have very different contexts, to be sure. The psalm is not about Moses's servanthood, but it does point to Jesus's sonship and authority over God's house. Hebrews masterfully draws out the full implications of the psalm's family dynamic in the Moses-Jesus context of the preacher and his audience, illustrating a sonship Christology and its practical effects of exhorting faithfulness in the family of God, a house built by God. Another way of describing this is to speak of God's people as a family, which is, of course, consistent with the language of Ps 127 where building the house is synonymous with building a family. For example, Paul describes the church as a family of faith composed of Jews and Gentiles from all strata of society, which recalls God's covenant with Abraham (Gal 3:28–29), a covenant that is ultimately fulfilled in Jesus Christ (3:16).[66]

Similarly, for the preacher of Hebrews, "house" clearly refers to the messianic community, the household of faith, and this language is consistent with Ps 127, where God's house is a metaphor for either David's dynasty or a family unit in general. Yet the metaphor is not limited to Hebrews, but is also prominent throughout the NT (Gal 6:10; Eph 2:19–22; 1 Tim 3:15; 1 Pet 2:5; 4:17).[67] The NT builds on the metaphor, describing the messianic community as a "spiritual house" (1 Pet 2:5), a temple, in whom God dwells

---

64. Ibid., 115.
65. Guthrie, *Hebrews*, 128.
66. Longman, *Psalms*, 427.
67. The theology of God's people as a holy temple is not unique to Christianity. The Qumran community thought of itself as the true temple, in contrast to the corrupt temple system in Jerusalem: "The Community council shall be founded on truth, like an everlasting plantation, a holy house for Israel and the foundation of the holy of holies for Aaron, true witnesses for the judgment and chosen by the will [of God] to atone for the earth and to render the wicked their retribution" (1QS 8.5–7). They also believed the temple of the end times would be "sanctuary of man," not a literal building per se: "And he commanded to build for himself a temple of man, to offer him in it, before him, the works of thanksgiving" (4Q174 1.7). This section in the scroll is speaking about a sanctuary of the last days that God, not humans, will build; it will not be a building, but a spiritual house, a community of faith. For the desert community, the Lord's end-times sanctuary will be like the Qumran community, or perhaps even equal to it. For the translations, see Martínez, *Dead Sea Scrolls Translated*, 12, 136. On the Qumran community as a temple, see VanderKam, *Dead Sea Scrolls Today*, 51.

through his Spirit. According to Karen Jobes, the primary attribute of a temple in first-century thought was its holiness.[68] The NT echoes this sentiment when it applies the temple metaphor to the church. For example, Peter applies the Jewish interpretive method of typology to illustrate a degree of continuity between the old covenant people of God and the new, describing his Gentile audience in terms reminiscent of ancient Israel, namely, that God is building them into a spiritual house for his own sanctified purposes:

> You yourselves like living stones are being built up as a spiritual house, to be a holy priesthood, to offer spiritual sacrifices acceptable to God through Jesus Christ. For it stands in Scripture: "Behold, I am laying in Zion a stone, a cornerstone chosen and precious, and whoever believes in him will not be put to shame."
> . . . But you are a chosen race, a royal priesthood, a holy nation, a people for his own possession, that you may proclaim the excellencies of him who called you out of darkness into his marvelous light. Once you were not a people, but now you are God's people; once you had not received mercy, but now you have received mercy. (1 Pet 2:5–10)

The Christian community plays the role of the continuing people of God in history by being a sanctified house/temple built by God, which includes being a priestly community that offers spiritual sacrifices like holy living and doing good deeds on behalf of the world (2:11–12). Here is a prime example of the NT indicative-imperative logic where identity fuels behavior: God's people are a temple, a royal and priestly nation, so their ethics should reflect that holy identity. As Eugene Boring exclaims, "Who you *are* is basic to what you are to *do*."[69] As God's presence sanctified the temple in Jerusalem, he now sanctifies the messianic community. The Christian church is not primarily a social organization, but the new temple where the transformed lives of believers are offered as sacrifice to the glory of God.[70]

Similarly, when the apostle Paul exhorts the Corinthians toward unity, warning against divisions and factions that threaten to destroy the church, he uses the temple metaphor to illustrate the fact that together they are a corporate body of believers in whom God's Spirit dwells: "Do you not know that you are God's temple (*naos*) and that God's Spirit dwells in you?" (1 Cor 3:16). The personal pronouns are plural ("you all"), so the emphasis is not on each individual Christian being a temple, but the community as whole. The point being, the church already exists as a unified building, so Christians

---

68. Jobes, *1 Peter*, 149.
69. Boring, *1 Peter*, 102.
70. Jobes, *1 Peter*, 149.

must seek to maintain that unity as a single structure and not reduce it to rubble. Even more, the community is not just any building, but in fact the temple of God, the place where God's Spirit dwells.[71] As holiness was a key attribute of a temple throughout the biblical period, so was divine presence. The temple sanctuary (*naos*) was the holiest place on earth because the very presence of God dwelled there. It was the one place on earth where God dwelled in holiness among an unholy people, who had to perform ritualistic acts of purity in order to come before his presence. For Paul, God's presence no longer resides in a building built by the covenant community, but in the community itself by the indwelling Holy Spirit (cf. Ezek 36:25–27; 2 Cor 6:16). The Spirit of God is present in the community, and it is now the place where praise and worship are rightly offered up to God. The Spirit of God no longer can be localized in a sacred building; it is to be found in the Christian community. Pneumatology, therefore, is bound together with ecclesiology; God's chosen mode of dwelling among his people is in the community itself through his Spirit, and, for Paul, those who interfere with his chosen mode of presence will incur judgment.

Even so, Paul does not stop here. When he exhorts the Corinthians against sexual immorality, he speaks of the bodies of individual Christians as being the temple (*naos*) of God: "Do you not know that your body is a temple of the Holy Spirit within you, whom you have from God?" (1 Cor 6:19). The context clearly concerns individuals and their behaviors, and is an extension of the church's corporate identity as the temple of the holy God. What Christians do with their physical bodies matters because they house the Holy Spirit of God. They have been made holy, as Paul reminds the Corinthians when he refers to them as "sanctified in Christ Jesus, called to be holy people" (1:2), so they must live out the implications of their sanctification by living holy lives, avoiding especially sexual immorality. Arguably, the Corinthians struggled with holiness more so than any other church that Paul writes to in the NT, yet he refers to them as "saints," illustrating not only their identity in Christ, but also their being the temple of the Holy Spirit, in spite of appearances to contrary. Finally, the beautiful architectural imagery of the people of God that he builds into a spiritual house as both a household of faith and a temple, comes to its fullest expression in Eph 2:19–22, calling to mind the language of Ps 127:

> So then you are no longer strangers and aliens, but you are fellow citizens with the saints and members of the household of God, built on the foundation of the apostles and prophets, Christ Jesus himself being the cornerstone, in whom the whole

---

71. Hays, *First Corinthians*, 56.

structure, being joined together, grows into a holy temple in the Lord. In him you also are being built together into a dwelling place for God by the Spirit.

The context is different than in 1 Corinthians and concerns the status of Gentiles as full members of God's family—with all the rights and privileges thereof—built by God into a temple to house his Holy Spirit. In other words, the house of Israel is now simply the house of God, composed of both Jews and Gentiles, in whom the Spirit of God dwells. Frank Thielman keenly observes how the architectural imagery calls to mind the rebuilding of the temple for the postexilic community and is pregnant with end-times expectations: "Paul's readers are the carefully shaped and fitted building blocks presently being added to the building. The way in which Paul describes this temple recalls the OT expectation of a rebuilt temple in which Israel and the nations would join together in the worship of God."[72] For Paul, God is even now building the end-times temple, made of both Jews and Gentiles, as a result of the work of Christ.

The NT takes all of this imagery from the OT and applies it to the church as a consequence of Christians being *in Christ*. The imagery is both transformed and transferred to the new covenant people as a result of Christ's work as the cornerstone of the new temple (1 Pet 2:6). Because of his resurrection from the dead, he is the "living stone" (2:4) on which God builds the remainder of his house. Thus, inasmuch as Ps 127 uses "house" to encompass both the literal temple as well as the people of God, the NT evokes similar language and fleshes out the full implications of the metaphor: the church is the both the house of God, his people, a household of faith, as well as the temple of the Holy Spirit. We can shout a resounding "Amen" to Mays: "Unless the LORD builds the church, they labor in vain who build it."[73]

---

72. Thielman, *Ephesians*, 185.
73. Mays, *Psalms*, 402.

Psalm 137

"Jesus Christ himself requests the execution of the wrath of God on his body, and thus leads me back daily to the gravity and the grace of his cross for me and all the enemies of God."—Dietrich Bonhoeffer

History

CERTAIN PSALMS, OFTEN CALLED "imprecatory psalms" (from Lat. *imprecc-ari* "to invoke, to pray to") or "cursing psalms," invoke God's righteous wrath and call down curses on the enemies of his people, asking him to openly condemn and destroy the wicked (e.g., Pss 35, 55, 59, 69, 109, 137, 140). However, imprecatory is not a type of psalm per se because all psalms are made up of various elements. The curses occur primarily in laments, making them a subcategory of lament psalms. Cursing psalms can be among the most difficult to interpret for Christians because Jesus teaches us to love our enemies and to pray for those who persecute us (Matt 5:44).

C. S. Lewis said that the "spirit of hatred" in the imprecatory psalms strikes us in the face, like the heat from a furnace mouth.[1] For him, they are "terrible," "contemptible," even "devilish."[2] Here are a few examples of the vitriolic language directed against the poets' enemies: "Let their way be dark and slippery . . . let destruction come upon him when he does know it" (Ps 35:6, 8); "Destroy, O Lord . . . let death steal over them; let them go down to Sheol alive" (55:9, 15); "Consume them in wrath" (59:13); "Let their eyes be darkened, so that they cannot see, and make their loins tremble continually. Pour out your indignation upon them, and let your burning anger overtake them. May their camp be a desolation; let no one dwell in their tents" (69:23–25). Even more severe and tortuous to our sensibilities are the prayers against the enemy's wife and children: "May his children be fatherless and his wife a widow! May his children wander about and beg, seeking

---

1. Lewis, *Reflections*, 20
2. Ibid, 20–22.

food far from the ruins they inhabit . . . let there be none to extend kindness to him, nor any to pity his fatherless children" (109:9–10, 12). And perhaps most shocking is the wish for physical violence against innocent children in our current psalm: "Blessed shall he be who takes your little ones and dashes them against the rock" (137:9), a passage of which Kenton Sparks asks an honest and pointed question: "What will one committed to the gospel of God's love do with this horrifying image of judgment?"[3] The curses against the children insult our sensibilities, especially in light of our earlier discussion of the high value placed on children in Ps 127. For Dietrich Bonhoeffer, every attempt to pray these psalms seems "doomed to failure."[4]

As I will show, these curses are at times so vile that many ancient commentators turned them into allegories of spiritual truths rather than address them as the "dark side" of the Psalter. In a biblical book known for its picturesque metaphors about the caring love of God and his eagerness to forgive sinners, reading passionate pleas for his vindictive wrath strikes a confusing and controversial tone. We have several interpretive options for dealing with them, but none, in my humble opinion, are very helpful if we have a high view of Scripture as the inspired word of God. As Walter Brueggemann and William Bellinger summarize, "Some suggest that the blessing on vengeance is so abhorrent that it should not be considered as part of the revelation of Scripture. Others would find quick support for acting in vengeance on their enemies. Neither of those perspectives appreciates the full sense of the psalm."[5] There are a host of perspectives that lie between these two extremes. First, we can ignore them, bury our heads in the sand, and pretend they are not part of sacred Scripture. But the fact that Jesus's mind and language were clearly steeped in the Psalter, which in its entirety is in some sense about him (Luke 24:25–27, 44–47), prevents us from ignoring these controversial passages.[6] Second, we can explain them away as somehow being good and pious simply because they are in Scripture, even if their piety remains a mystery to us.[7] But this ignores the contextual nature of the Bible itself; it did not fall out of heaven, but grew out of the soil of humanity as it were, warts and all, and reflects ancient cultures and expressions that are quite foreign, even offensive, to modern readers. As Lewis describes, "The poets [as well as all the biblical authors] lived in a world of savage punishments, of massacre and violence, of blood sacrifice

3. Sparks, *God's Word*, 324.
4. Bonhoeffer, *Psalms*, 56.
5. Brueggemann and Bellinger, *Psalms*, 575.
6. Lewis, *Reflections*, 22.
7. Ibid.

in all countries and human sacrifice in many."[8] Of course, one could argue that our world has not changed very much—the savagery simply looks different with bombs, machine guns, and nuclear weapons replacing swords and spears—but this is a topic for another book. It does no good to confess the divine nature of Scripture apart from its human nature because God is a God of history; his mighty acts of redemption and revelation (including Scripture) occur on the stage of human history, not in a heavenly vacuum.

Third, we can relegate the offensive parts to a dispensational, pre-Christian, lower ethic, using a form of "progressive revelation" where NT ethics are higher and nobler than those in the OT. In other words, the psalmists use vitriolic language because they are not "Christian," and that is apparently okay, presumably because they did not know any better, being ignorant of Jesus's love ethic. But the NT itself applies some of these same cursing psalms, most notably in Acts 1:20 where Luke quotes from Pss 69 and 109 (the latter being arguably the most severe imprecatory psalm in the Psalter), applying them to Judas after his betrayal of Jesus. Richard Belcher, then, rightly emphasizes the continuity of the OT and NT: "Any view that sets up a dichotomy between the Old Testament and New Testament on this issue in order to question the legitimacy of these psalms is to be rejected."[9] Not only does this potentially create a Marcionite[10] division in Scripture, but does not even square with the OT itself, which commands Israel to be kind and compassionate to all people, including their enemies (Lev 19:17–18; Exod 23:4–5; Prov 24:17).

Jesus repeatedly reinforced, continued, refined, and sublimated Judaic ethics, and very rarely introduced a novelty.[11] Put differently, Jesus's love ethic comes from the OT, even if he demonstrates it more perfectly than anyone previously or since.[12] Fourth, we can do as many church fathers, even Lewis in

---

8. Ibid., 23.

9. Belcher, *Messiah*, 77.

10. Marcion was a second-century Christian heretic who rejected the OT due to God's seemingly violent and vengeful nature, which Marcion viewed as incompatible with God's love in the NT.

11. Lewis, *Reflections*, 26–27.

12. I recognize, however, tensions exist in Scripture among "lower" and "higher" ethical standards. For example, Exod 21:20 allows masters to beat their slaves, and this contrasts sharply with Jesus's love ethic, as well as the NT admonition for masters to be gentle to their slaves (Eph 6:9). Further, there are tensions within the NT itself: Paul preaches against racial divisions (Gal 3:28), but also promotes racial prejudice by affirming, "Cretans are always liars, evil beasts, lazy gluttons" (Titus 1:12–13). Granted, one could argue Paul is using hyperbole; obviously, Cretans are not "always" wicked, gluttonous, liars because Paul's letter to Titus deals with Cretan *Christians* (1:5). Even so, if Jesus's love ethic and racial reconciliation engendered by the gospel really held

our own time, and allegorize the vicious language, diluting it so that it refers to something hidden beneath the surface of the text. In the case of smashing the infants against the rock, Origen writes, "For 'the little ones' of Babylon (which signifies confusion) are those troublesome sinful thoughts that arise in the soul, and one who subdues them by striking, as it were, their heads against the firm and solid strength of reason and truth, is the person who 'dashes the little ones against the stones'; and he is therefore truly blessed."[13] When taken this way (i.e., "little ones" are evil thoughts, not literally children), we can certainly agree with Lewis who said we should "knock the little bastards' brains out."[14] However, Geerhardus Vos observes about such allegorizing:

> This amounts to an attempt to find an easy way out of the difficulty by boldly explaining away the statements of Scripture. It is perfectly obvious that the wicked persons whose doom is prayed for in the Imprecatory Psalms are not temptations, sinful tendencies in human nature, nor even demonic powers. They are human beings, who may, indeed, have been under the influence of demonic powers, but who were nonetheless human.[15]

Therefore, we can soften the terminology so that it refers not to the human persecutors of the psalmists, but to the wicked actions of the persecutors, as in "love the sinner; hate the sin."[16] But this, too, does not do justice to the plain sense of the passage where evil *people* (e.g., "May *his* children be fatherless") cause the vicious victimization of God's covenant community.

Another view takes the imprecations merely as predictions of the fate of wicked people and not as a personal desire, or prayer, for his or her doom. That is, the curses foretell the fate of such individuals, but do not refer to anyone in particular. But the language of imprecation in the Psalter is that of a prayer-wish addressed to God, not general prediction per se.[17] Finally,

---

sway, Paul's comment would have been better left unsaid.

13. Origen, *Against Celsus* 7.22 in Wesselschmidt, *Psalms*, 379–80. Both Ambrose (p. 380) and Augustine allegorized 137:12 in the same way as Origen. See Augustine, *Expositions* 137, §12.

14. Lewis, *Reflections*, 136.

15. Vos, "Ethical Problem," 126–27.

16. Lewis, *Reflections*, 32. I am reminded of Paul's strong words in Galatians, wishing that the agitators would "emasculate themselves" (Gal 5:12). He does not wish this upon their false teaching alone, but also the false teachers themselves (cf. 1:8–9). In other words, his rhetoric only works if it refers to actual male human beings. Therefore, not even the NT is isolated from imprecations involving physical violence.

17. Vos, "Ethical Problem," 126. One may raise the issue of the so-called "predictive" application of Pss 69 and 109 to Judas in Acts 1:20, but this is an isolated incident. At no other point does the NT cite the fulfillment of an imprecatory psalm to a person.

we can view them simply as vindictive human words, divorcing them completely from the divine author of Scripture.[18] But this does not work if we believe in the inspiration of Scripture where the text somehow functions as divine revelation from God to humanity. Granted, the doctrine of biblical inspiration is exceedingly complex and beyond the limits of this book, but unless we have a simplistic and pre-critical understanding of the process whereby God simply tells the writers what to write—something that Scripture never actually says—we have to ask how these malicious passages *function* in the context of inspired Scripture. I think it best to affirm the divine and human natures of Scripture as a sacred mystery, but humbly accept that God has not given us a clean and tidy text, free of theological problems. The Bible is both sacred and broken in that it is inspired by God's Spirit—even if we cannot work out all of the implications of so-called "terrible texts" like the imprecatory psalms, the genocide of the exodus conquest, slavery, etc.—and reflects the fallenness of sinful humanity because all of its human authors see in a mirror dimly and have a limited perspective (1 Cor 13:12). Sparks eloquently reminds us of "one of the great mysteries of faith that God's redemptive activity is carried out successfully and beautifully through the agency of fallen men and women."[19] And, "in Scripture, God speaks to us through the finite and fallen perspectives of human authors and, thereby, through the limited and fallen horizons of human cultures and audiences."[20]

Inasmuch as human authors composed the Bible, it participates in their limited horizons, so that whatever the divine inspiration of Scripture is or involves, it does not run roughshod over the humanity of the biblical authors in order to protect and insulate them from the limitations of their perspectives and judgments.[21] As Sparks explains, we have to wrestle with the question of

> whether God somehow protected or insulated their [human authors of Scripture] biblical words from their human fallenness. If he did so, it should be easy to recognize. Scripture would reflect a single, coherent, and consistent God-given view of morals

---

18. Ibid., 127.
19. Sparks, *Sacred Word*, 54–55.
20. Ibid., 59.
21. Sparks, *God's Word*, 227. This is similar to the doctrine of "accommodation" where God accommodates, or condescends, to the spiritual and/or intellectual limitations of human beings, and "adopts" their words as Scripture. Sparks prefers a nuanced and more proactive model of *providential adoption*: "In adopting human texts as his own, [God] was involved both in the production of the texts and in their canonical adoption as sacred Scripture" (*Sacred Word*, 55). For more on accommodation, see Sparks, *God's Word*, 229–59; Pinnock and Callen, *Scripture Principle*, 122–27.

and ethics from Genesis to Revelation. Its words would be free of the sinful vagaries of human authors and would give us the one and only universal ethic of Christ's teaching.[22]

Instead, in the production of Scripture, including the terrible psalms, God adopted human authors as his covenant communicators and, in doing so, permitted them—fallen as they were—to write the sorts of things that ancient, fallen people would write about their enemies.[23] It would be a strange, foreign, unrecognizable, and therefore meaningless revelation from God if Scripture were void of the brutality, blood sacrifice, racism, genocide, gender inequality, slavery, polygamy, and other troublesome attributes that characterized ancient cultures. The contextual nature of Scripture is not simply that the Bible was written in specific historical contexts but that it also reflects those historical contexts warts and all. Peter Enns captures this contextualization, nothing that the Bible "belonged in the ancient worlds that produced it. It was not an abstract, otherworldly book, dropped out of heaven. It was *connected to* and therefore *spoke to* those ancient cultures . . . God's word reflects the various historical moments in which Scripture was written."[24]

Perhaps another angle from which to look at the inspiration of the cursing psalms is to think through the raw human emotions themselves where the Spirit approves of their inclusion in Scripture, permitting the psalmist to utter the sentiments of his own heart (cf. Eccl 2:1).[25] To feel nothing in the face of vicious victimization is far worse than feeling white-hot anger. The fact that the psalmists deplore evildoers says something about the moral fiber of the lamenters themselves. The utterance of these cruel curses give their authors an outlet for the anger they feel against those who oppose God, and it staves off emotional neurosis, a Stoicism that is indifferent to pain.[26] Let's be honest; I would be willing to bet upon looking at images of Adolf Hitler, Osama Bin Laden, ISIS, Boko Haram, and others who have committed atrocities throughout history, you are not flooded with warm and fuzzy feelings of love and forgiveness. In fact, downright hatred, seething anger, and the eager anticipation for God to pour out a bowlful of his wrath on such wickedness is often at least our *initial* response to evil incarnate in our world. In the wake of the terrorist attacks on September 11

---

22. Sparks, *God's Word*, 226. Sparks continues, "The real question is why a book written by God would ever assume lower ethical standards in one instance and higher standards in another" (226n24).

23. Sparks, *Sacred Word*, 54.

24. Enns, *Inspiration*, 17–18.

25. Tesh and Zorn, *Psalms*, 62.

26. Ibid., 63.

and in the subsequent rise of militant groups like ISIS, I have heard some U. S. politicians and faithful Christians alike cheering the battle cry to go after the families of the terrorists! This is not any different than the cursing psalms, especially those that include curses on the innocent children of the evildoers. We have to remember that Psalms reflects the entire gamut of human emotions and provides God's people with the language to express the feelings of their hearts, even if that language is at times venomous. Since God created us and knows our hearts, honesty with him, rather than attempting to hide our emotions from God, is the best policy.

God's faithful people have always been the minority in a world of evil and wickedness. Persecution is nothing new to the people of God. Luke reminds us that entrance into the kingdom comes through many trials (Acts 14:22), and as Paul reminds Timothy, "All who desire to live a godly life in Christ Jesus will be persecuted" (2 Tim 3:12). Given the exilic and postexilic editing of the Psalter, the oppression and persecution of God's people takes center stage in many psalms, especially the so-called "community lament" psalms. The authors not only lament the trials and tribulations of the whole nation—not to mention complaining about God's seeming absence during suffering—but also appeal to his justice and judgment upon wicked persecutors. All of this is part and parcel of an oppressed people, like Israel during the exile, and upon their return to a foreign-occupied Promised Land in the years following. In spite of the poets' vitriolic language, one constant affirmation of the imprecatory psalms is that judgment belongs to God alone. Venting their anger to God allows the psalmists to turn the matter over to him for his justice to take effect. Vengeance belongs to God, not the psalmists; they take no action of their own but leave the matter to God (cf. Deut 32:35; Rom 12:17–19). Because only God is truly just, the psalmists give to him not only their lament about their desperate situations, but also the right to judge their wicked oppressors, who cause the desperation of God's people in the first place. Feelings of hot anger and hatred, even the desire for vengeance, are natural emotions in the face of malevolent mistreatment, and the imprecatory psalms give expression to these feelings before giving the matter *wholly* to God. Simply put, imprecatory psalms do not ask God for the resources and opportunity to take vengeance on our enemies; they ask God to do so and acknowledge his freedom to act or not act as he sees fit.[27] Responding in kind to their persecutors with bloodshed and retribution only perpetuates the cycle of violence in a way that misuses "eye for eye, tooth for tooth" so that it translates into "do unto to others as they have done to you." Thus, the singers, even in the midst of these prayers to God for

---

27. Longman, *Psalms*, 52.

his vehement revenge, break the cycle of violence, as their words in and of themselves become acts of non-violence.[28] I will offer another fruitful angle for viewing the *function* of the Bible's cursing psalms and other terrible texts in the Christology section later in this chapter. For now, a closer look at the historical and literary contexts of Ps 137 is in order.

While the imprecatory language of Ps 137:8-9 is severe, the psalm itself is a community lament, although it does not follow the typical lament pattern.[29] Instead of ending on a note of trust or reorientation, it ends with a graphic curse on the enemies of God's people. The psalm's imprecatory element occurs only in the last two verses, whereas the majority of the song is a lament about Zion or Jerusalem. This, in combination with the use of the Hebrew word for "ascend" (*alah*) in verse 6, likely connects it in some way to the "Psalms of Ascent" (120—134), perhaps as an "appendix" (135—137) to the collection about "going up" to Jerusalem.[30] In the larger context of Books 4 and 5 of the Psalter, which relate to the crisis of the exile, Ps 137 echoes the crisis, and anticipates the next collection of Davidic lament psalms (138—145), especially Ps 138 with its reference to the temple, singing, and enemies (138:2, 5, 7).[31]

Although Ps 137 is about the horrors of the exile, it was not written during the experience itself, but afterward by one who experienced it firsthand and remembers its atrocities, possibly while back in Jerusalem (v. 5). It is difficult to be more precise than this about the setting of the psalm's composition, but the use of "there" (*sham*) in verses 1 ("*there* we sat down and wept"), 2 ("*there* we hung up our lyres"), and 3 ("for *there* our captors . . .") suggests the memory of one looking back on the miserable experience in Babylon while in a new context.[32] The singer does not appear to be a typical Israelite, but one of the religious leaders, perhaps a Levite or temple musician—hence, "our lyres" (v. 2)—who was actively involved in the cult before the exile (2 Chr 25:1-8; Ezra 2:40-42). This would have made him and his guild of Levitical singers special targets of their captor's cruel humor, stemming from a religious polemic that touted the victory of the Babylonian gods over Yahweh.[33] Estimates of the number of Israelites taken into captiv-

---

28. McCann, *Psalms*, 1127, 1228.
29. Brueggemann and Bellinger, *Psalms*, 573.
30. Zorn, *Psalms*, 470.
31. Brueggemann and Bellinger, *Psalms*, 573.
32. Zorn, *Psalms*, 466. Zorn (p. 467) theorizes that the date of composition could be early in the return before the temple was rebuilt (ca. 537-515 BCE), or perhaps later before the rebuilding of the walls of Jerusalem (ca. 537-445 BCE). Whatever the precise date of composition, the memory of the exile was fresh for the singer.
33. Mays, *Psalms*, 421.

ity vary, reaching upward of 200,000; many of these included those from the elite class like politicians and religious rulers. This probably resulted in less than 25,000 "people of land," that is, common folk, remaining in the Palestinian region.[34]

The main theme of Ps 137 is "remember," and the singer composes the song around this central theme:

> Remember Zion in Captivity (vv. 1–4, in the past)
>
> Remember Jerusalem in the Land (vv. 5–6, in the present)
>
> Remember the Day of Jerusalem (vv. 7–9, in the future)[35]

The importance of memory is pervasive throughout the psalm, both literarily and conceptually.[36] For the postexilic community in Jerusalem, remembering the past experience of exile was important as the community struggled to maintain their identity in a new world.[37] The exiles in the poem "cannot sing, but they could and must and did remember."[38]

Psalm 137 begins with a definite historical reference, which is exceedingly rare in the Psalter, recalling the terrible experience of exile in Babylon. We have seen in many of the psalms covered so far in this book hints of the exilic experience of Israel, but here it is much more specific. The singer recalls weeping "there" beside the "waters of Babylon" (v. 1), and this is an apt description because of Babylon's many rivers, notably the Tigris and Euphrates, tributaries, and canals; hence, the Greek reference to the Babylonian territory as Mesopotamia ("the midst of the rivers").[39] These were essential to the mercantile economy of the Babylonian Empire.[40] The cause of the weeping of the singer and his community was, of course, their vivid remembrance of the destruction of the beloved city, Zion, by the Babylonians in 587 BCE. The musicians hung their lyres on the willow trees beside the waters as a symbol of dejectedness (v. 2). The imagery may be metaphorical, yielding a sad picture of silence, of instruments not being plucked, and muted of music—the opposite of their intended purposes. However, it is likely that the Babylonians required the temple musicians to bring their instruments with them during the siege of Jerusalem as a mocking gesture of the recently razed temple complex. Indeed, the psalmist paints a gloomy

---

34. Zorn, *Psalms*, 466.
35. Adapted from ibid., 2:468, Mays, *Psalms*, 421, and McCann, *Psalms*, 1227.
36. McCann, *Psalms*, 1227.
37. DeClaissé-Walford, *Introduction*, 124.
38. McCann, *Psalms*, 1227.
39. Reardon, *Christ*, 273. This region today is essentially southern Iraq.
40. Ibid.

portrait of silent singers dejected to the point where even their instruments are muted and untouched. One might think that a picturesque setting of shady willows beside flowing waters would be an ideal location to inspire creative songs of praise, soothing the Levites' dejected minds, but it only inspires tears for their homeland. John Calvin captures the despondent spirits of the musicians in contrast to the serene setting:

> When willows are mentioned, this denotes the pleasantness of the banks, which were planted with willows for coolness. But the Psalmist says that these shades, however delightful, could not dispel a grief which was too deeply seated to admit of common consolations or refreshment. As they sat upon the banks of the rivers covered with the shadows of the trees, this was just the place where they might have been tempted to take up their harps, and soothe their griefs with song; but the Psalmist suggests that their minds were too heavily wounded with a sense of the displeasure of the Lord to deceive themselves with such idle sources of comfort.[41]

What is more, to add insult to injury, the "captors"[42] command the Levites to raise their voices in song, taking up their lyres in praise of Zion (v. 3), perhaps performing one of the "Psalms of Zion" (Pss 46, 48, 76, 84, 87, 122). As Brueggemann and Bellinger paraphrase verse 3: "We want to hear you sing one of your famous songs of Zion now while you are defeated captives in this land of exile."[43] Yet James Mays keenly reminds us that the real issue here is not music, but faith.[44] This is no request for entertainment, much less a call to worship. Instead, the captors, in an attempt at cruel humor, mock not only the now silent Levitical singers, who normally sang sacred songs at the Jerusalem temple, but ultimately Israel's defeated God, Yahweh.[45] In the minds of the Babylonians, their gods had defeated Yahweh, which was symbolized by the razing of the city of Zion and its temple. In other words, because Zion was the dwelling place of Yahweh, its destruction marked both a geopolitical and religious victory for Babylon and her gods.

---

41. Calvin, *Psalms*, Apple e-book, ch. 137.

42. The Psalms Targum calls them "despoilers" (Ps. Tg. 137:3), referencing how the Babylonians plundered the temple, taking its vessels and treasures, as well as the wealth of the king and other elite leaders of Judah as spoils back to Babylon (2 Kgs 25:9–19; 2 Chr 36:18–19; Jer 52:12–23).

43. Brueggemann and Bellinger, *Psalms*, 574.

44. Mays, *Psalms*, 422.

45. Brueggemann and Bellinger, *Psalms*, 574.

It is ironic that the singer laments the impossibility of singing of Zion while in a foreign land (v. 4), but then goes on to do so in verses 5 and 6, vowing to never forget Jerusalem's former glory, as well as longing for the completion of its future restoration.[46] What matters most for the singer is not his own personal wellbeing, but that of Jerusalem. What is more, verses 5–6 form the centerpiece of the psalm, emphasizing even more the crucial activity of remembering, as evidenced in the following chiastic arraignment:

A If I *forget you*, O Jerusalem,
   B let *my right* hand wither!
   B1 Let *my tongue* cling to the roof of my mouth,
A1 if I do not *remember you* . . .[47]

The poet addresses this song within a song to Jerusalem ("If I forget *you*, O Jerusalem . . .") and invokes a self-imprecation if he ever forgets Jerusalem. The vivid imagery of a musician's withered right hand and unresponsive tongue is a powerful one. For this Levite, failing to remember Jerusalem results in the inability to perform his divinely appointed task as a temple musician. The hand would no longer be able to play the lyre, and the tongue unable to sing the Songs of Zion. Indeed, the scenario is worse than at the opening lines of the psalm where the musicians could theoretically sing and perform songs of praise, but instead, out of choice, sat weeping with their instruments hanging on the willows. The scene in verses 5–6 is more dreadful—the psalmist, should he forget Jerusalem, would lack even the *ability* to perform a song of Zion: a withered hand and paralyzed tongue cannot perform songs of Zion.

Astonishingly, he puts the memory of Jerusalem before his own physical wellbeing in this self-curse because memory is a powerful weapon and can be sustained over the long haul and fuel resistance.[48] While the captors can control the worship practices of the exiles, effectively silencing their voices from praising Yahweh in a foreign land, they cannot control the memory and imagination of this community of exiles.[49] The final line of verse 6 is notoriously difficult to translate, but most likely expresses the idea that Jerusalem is the source of their highest joy.[50] Belcher expresses the true motivation of the community's lament as the wellbeing of Jerusalem: "Jerusalem is important not just because it is the capital of the nation, but because

---

46. Reardon, *Christ*, 274.
47. McCann, Jr., *Theological*, 118.
48. Brueggemann and Bellinger, *Psalms*, 574.
49. Ibid.
50. Longman, *Psalms*, 449.

it represents the purposes of God and the glory of his name. Here the cause of God is placed above the situation of the community in exile. They are not ultimately concerned about their situation but about the honor of God's name."[51] After all, Zion is first and foremost the city of God.

Verses 7–9 contain the psalm's imprecation, evoking a curse of the enemies of Judah—the Edomites and the Babylonians. The Edomites were the descendants of Esau, and the Israelites of Jacob; in spite of being blood relatives, the two became bitter enemies, their conflict reaching back to the wilderness wanderings when the Edomites refused passage through their land via the King's Highway to Moses and the Israelites (Num 20:14–21). Even still, Moses commanded the Israelites to not hate their Edomite relatives (Deut 23:7–8). However, continual conflicts occurred during various reigns of Israelite kings like Saul (1 Sam 14:47), David (2 Sam 8:13–14), and Uzziah (2 Chr 26:6–7), and Ahaz (28:17). More relevant to the exilic context of Ps 137 is the fact the several OT prophets condemn Edom for its passivity during the siege of Jerusalem at the time of the exile. Although the details are few and far between, numerous prophets condemn Edom for mocking the people of Judah by cheering on the Babylonian destruction of Jerusalem and for failing to intervene on behalf of their brothers (Isa 34:5–9; Jer 49:17; Lam 4:21; Ezek 25:12–14; 35:15; Amos 1:11–12; Obad 10–15). For Obadiah, Edom "stood aloof" and "gloated" as the Babylonians sacked Jerusalem, and by doing so were complicit with the violence done to their brethren. What is more, Edom apparently took advantage of the siege and looted the city along with the Babylonians. The psalmist in Ps 137:7 echoes the prophetic oracles of judgment upon the Edomites, calling for God's vengeance upon them: "Remember, O LORD, against the Edomites the day of Jerusalem, how they said, 'Lay it bare, lay it bare, down to its foundations!'"

The theme of memory that pervades the first six verses of the psalm continues even into the imprecation stanzas. The curse reaches a fever pitch in verses 8–9, but is addressed to the "daughter of Babylon," which may be a way of describing Edom's complicity with the Babylonian siege or a reference to Babylon itself; either way it personifies the nation as an individual.[52] In the eyes of the singer they are one and the same, so it is best to see the targets of the curse in verses 7–9 as both Edom and the Babylonians for the vicious violence against Jerusalem.

Given the prophetic oracles previously mentioned, which eagerly anticipate God's repayment of Edom, as well as those that foretell of his retribution against Babylon (Isa 13:17–10; Jer 50; 51:62–64), the psalmist refers

51. Belcher, *Messiah*, 79.
52. Zorn, *Psalms*, 471.

to God as "blessed" (e.g., "blessed shall *he* be who repays . . .") in anticipation of his day of wrath and "repayment" on the enemies of Israel (Ps 137:8). The imagery of the final verse graphically describes the "repayment" of the previous verse as smashing infants against the rock. This was apparently the experience of Judah during the siege. This last verse reflects the barbaric world of the period where a victory on the battlefield was not complete until the next generation of potential warriors, i.e., the children of the defeated nation, were destroyed (2 Kgs 8:12; Isa 13:16; Hos 10:14; 13:16; Nah 3:10).[53] Many adults might be spared to serve various capacities for the conquerors as spoils of war, but the infants were killed to end the community's future.[54] For the psalmist, the "little ones" are the future of an oppressive empire.[55] The singer, therefore, expresses his desire for the cultural practices of the day to play against his enemies, and in a way calls for the principle of "eye for eye, tooth for tooth" (Exod 21:24) to take effect in the name of strict divine justice.[56]

One important disclaimer here is that the singer does not enact vengeance himself, but submits his anger to God's actions to repay or not to repay. He takes his fierce anger and "gives it to God," so to speak. This is evident where the singer addresses God directly in the imprecatory section ("Remember, O LORD"). In other words, personal vengeance is not in view here, and quite probably eliminates the need for the singer to enact actual, physical revenge on the enemy.[57] While the language is both jolting and revolting, the singer expresses a brutally honest cry of unrestrained faith in the justice of God upon evil. Bellinger notes about the severity of the curse: "Its brutal candor makes us flinch, but this speaker has no inhibitions in expressing to God the rawest of hopes."[58] Even still, one wonders why the sentiment could not have been expressed without the apparent gleeful attitude of the singer, especially if one translates the Hebrew *ashrey* as "happy" or "blessed."[59] While we can debate the appropriateness or inappropriateness of the poet's expression of his desire for divine vengeance, we should not forget that this prayer for God's retributive justice was in fact answered

---

53. Brueggemann and Bellinger, *Psalms*, 575.
54. Eaton, *Psalms*, 455.
55. Brueggemann and Bellinger, *Psalms*, 576.
56. Zorn, *Psalms*, 471–72.
57. McCann, *Theological*, 119.
58. Bellinger, "Psalm 137," 14.
59. Ash and Miller, *Psalms*, 423. With Nancy deClaissé-Walford, et al., *Psalms*, 956, it is probably best to translate *ashrey* in this context as "content," conveying a sense of peace that results from God's judgment on Israel's enemies.

in the Babylonian destruction of Edom and the Babylonian Empire at the hands of the Persians in 539 BCE.[60]

Christology

I want to begin my christological reflections by first considering the broader implications of the presence of imprecatory psalms and other terrible texts in the Christian canon, and then work toward more refined reflections on the Christology of Ps 137. In light of the earlier discussion of the manifold mysteries surrounding inspiration generally and the imprecatory psalms and other terrible texts specifically, it seems to me productive to speak of their inspiration in terms of canonical *function*, which is not to give us divine authority to curse our enemies, enact holy wars, etc., but to call to our minds the gospel of Jesus Christ who redeems the fallenness evidenced in terrible texts. We should take such passages not in isolation, but in the larger context of the Christian canon where they, like all other biblical texts, ultimately point to redemption in Christ. I appreciate the view of Sparks who explains that this "canonical effect is really cumulative, so that any one text, if taken alone as the final voice of Scripture, might seriously lead us astray."[61] When taken as a canonical whole, passages—even tyrannical and terrible ones—direct us and push us in appropriate directions, i.e., toward Christ and his redeeming words and works. For Sparks, "Ultimately, the redemption of both testaments, and of the cosmos and humanity, is accomplished by the death, burial, resurrection, ascension, and return of Jesus Christ. Until that final day arrives, we will continue to struggle with the problems of pain and suffering, and with the problems in Scripture."[62] Therefore, I would argue the most important aspect of the inspiration of Scripture, which includes terrible texts, is its *function*, which is both to testify to the redeeming power of Jesus Christ (John 5:39–40) and to instruct God's people toward righteousness, transforming them into the image of Christ (2 Tim 3:15–17).

Therefore, when we as Christians read problematic passages that speak of bashing babies against a rock or praying that the children of an enemy would be starving, begging orphans in the streets, we should be morally repulsed, but at the same time reminded of the forgiving love of Christ that redeems such fallenness. In other words, if upon reading them we do not recall Jesus's radical love ethic and seek to apply it in our daily lives, especially unto our enemies, we have misread them as isolated proof texts and

60. Zorn, *Psalms*, 472.
61. Sparks, *Sacred Word*, 113.
62. Ibid., 71.

not as contributions to a comprehensive canon of Scripture, whose chief end is to guide us to Jesus Christ's redeeming love. Therefore, the canonical function of the imprecatory psalms is to lead us to Christ's radical love for his enemies, evoking his call for us to demonstrate the same love for ours.

There is no way to harmonize the psalmists' contempt for their enemies with Jesus's radical love for his (Luke 23:34), as well as the command to his followers to demonstrate the same kind of love in concrete ways (6:27–36). Eaton eloquently calls us to recognize the clearer vision of the larger biblical witness on a given topic, specifically imprecatory psalms, as opposed to interpreting them as propositions in and of themselves as we navigate the relationship between the cursing psalms and their counterparts:

> The bitter words must at last be washed over by streams of mightier teaching: "Seek the peace of the city (Babylon) whither I have caused you to be carried away captive, and pray to the Lord for her (Jer 29:7)"; "If your enemy be hungry, give him bread to eat . . . (Prov 25:21)"; "Love your enemies, and pray for those who persecute you . . ." (Matt 5:44)[63]

For Christians, for those who believe and live by the redeeming and reconciling power of the gospel of Christ, the imprecatory psalms—with all their vitriol and vengeance—call to mind the merciful gospel of Christ, which proclaims the opposite of the curses found in the psalms.

While the theology of the imprecatory psalms is exceedingly complex, their basic request is really quite simple: that God would openly condemn wickedness and execute his holy wrath against it. This is precisely what occurred on the cross of Christ. Not only do the imprecatory psalms point canonically to the love of Christ for his enemies, they also reach their most climactic *application* at the cross where God condemned sin and wickedness by funneling the sins of both Israel and the whole world onto Jesus. His death on the cross was the public display of God's curse and wrath against sin (Gal 3:13; cf. Deut 21:23). This pouring out of God's wrath on sin lies behind the NT description of Jesus's sacrifice as the "propitiation" for sin (Rom 3:25; Heb 2:17; 1 John 2:2; 4:10), diverting God's wrath away from sinners and pouring it out onto Christ on the cross. God's vengeance, his righteous repayment for sin and wickedness, did not strike the sinners— that is, the targets of the imprecatory psalms—but the one sinless man who hanged in their place, namely, God's own Son.[64] Jesus Christ bore the wrath of God, for the outpouring of which the imprecatory psalms pray. Thus, the cross was the goal of the imprecatory psalms as God's wrath was meted

---

63. Eaton, *Psalms*, 456.
64. Bonhoeffer, *Psalms*, 58.

out on sin—on Jesus Christ, who became sin (2 Cor 5:21). Jesus himself prayed for the execution of God's wrath upon evil when he prayed in the Garden of Gethsemane, "Not my will, but yours, be done" (Luke 22:42). As we read the imprecatory psalms, we should see them not only in the larger canonical context of Christian Scripture where Jesus's love ethic corrects the vulgarities of the psalmists, but also in the larger context of redemptive history where Jesus is the man on whom God executes his judgment. While the curses are bound tightly to the historical experiences of the poets, they nonetheless go beyond the ancient contexts and find fuller application in the victorious death of Jesus on the cross.

There is yet another christological angle from which to view the cursing psalms, which, in addition to pointing to God's public judgment of sin and wickedness, point ultimately to the love of God, which forgives enemies ("Father, forgive them . . .").[65] The imprecatory psalms do not represent the conclusion or goal of our anger, for that would be to seek personal vengeance, even physical harm, on our enemies; as we have seen, this is contrary to the gospel of Christ. Instead, they represent the first step in a larger process of healing, which culminates in forgiveness. Again, we must be honest with ourselves and confess that forgiveness is not usually our first response to monstrous evil, white-hot anger is. The imprecatory psalms allow us to vent our anger, direct it toward God, forgive our enemies, and wait for his righteous judgment. McCann argues, I believe convincingly, that the cursing psalms point ultimately to the cross because "vengeance submitted to God results eventually in forgiveness and compassion."[66] Then, and only then, after giving the matter wholly to God can we forgive our enemies.

One of the thorny questions we must ask is, "Can Christians pray these psalms, given Jesus's command to love our enemies and seek their wellbeing?" I would argue the answer is a cautious "yes," but only as the *first* step of a larger process of healing from the wrongs others have done to us and to our community. However, because of the more comprehensive witness of the biblical canon, especially Jesus's radical application of his love ethic, these prayers must be followed by genuine requests for God's forgiveness of our enemies, spoken with the recognition of our own sin and need for forgiveness, and culminate in concrete acts of love and reconciliation. Only then can peace-seeking followers of Christ begin to break the cycle of violence. By praying these psalms as part of this larger process of healing, they highlight our own

---

65. Ibid., 58–59.
66. McCann, *Theological*, 120.

finitude and fallenness, causing us to submit ourselves to God as we begin a journey that transforms grief and anger into compassion.[67]

Certain elements of the Lord's Prayer (Matt 6:9–13; Luke 11:2–4), or better, the Disciples' Prayer (because Jesus teaches his disciples how to pray), can help take us through the process of healing. To be clear, I am not suggesting the prayer specifically and systematically conveys this process, but some of its elements address the process by way of application. First, the prayer for God's kingdom to come is an indirect imprecation and an appeal for God's judgment on evil. God's kingdom has its roots in OT theology, and while the phrase "kingdom of God/heaven" never occurs in the OT, the idea of God as king, as we have seen from this brief study of Psalms, certainly does. "Your kingdom come" reflects the OT teaching that the final Day of the Lord, the inbreaking of God's reign into human history, will be not only a day of joy for God's people, but also a day of judgment on their enemies. Simply put, the salvation of God's people will not occur without the condemnation of God's enemies. As Vos understands, "God's kingdom cannot come without Satan's kingdom being destroyed. God's will cannot be done in earth without the destruction of evil. Evil cannot be destroyed without the destruction of men who are permanently identified with it . . . the glory of God demands the destruction of evil."[68] Scot McKnight explains the Jewish conception of the consummation of God's kingdom on the Day as a time when God steps in to end what is wrong and to establish what is right in the world.[69] The King executes his retributive justice on evil while at the same time exercising his compassionate covenant love for his people, dwelling among them for eternity.

"Your will be done, on earth as it is in heaven" is a parallel idea to the coming of God's kingdom in the context of Jesus's prayer; it expresses the same wish for God's kingdom, his will, to be made manifest in the fallen world as it is already manifest in heaven. God's sovereign power extends over all the cosmos, although not all persons and powers in the universe yet acknowledge that fact. For Jesus, God's kingdom advances where his will is accomplished, which includes the eradication of evil. When we pray with Jesus, "Your kingdom come, your will be done, on earth as it is in heaven," we are praying among other things for the "redemption of the world; for the radical defeat and uprooting of evil."[70] We recognize that the world in its

---

67. Ibid., 121. Belcher observes: "Those who have not lost that much have trouble with these psalms, but those who have been victimized and plundered understand the expressions of curse in these psalms" (*Messiah*, 78).

68. Vos, "Ethical Problem," 138.

69. McKnight, *Kingdom*, 183.

70. Wright, *Prayer*, 31.

fallenness is not right. We mourn with the singer of Ps 137 when we lament similar atrocities against humanity throughout history: the Crusades, the Holocaust, genocide, terrorism, war, gun violence, and everything else that opposes God's kingdom. Put simply, we ache for the judgment of God on evil, anticipating the final and full execution of his retributive justice. As McKnight describes:

> The future kingdom is a utopian vision of justice, peace, the end of suffering, joy in safety and health, the reconciliation of fractured relationships, a society marked by love and wisdom and joy ... Many today long for those days, but for those days to come, the injustices, broken relationships, betrayals, pain, suffering, and tragedies of this world have to be named for what they are—sinfulness, systematic evils, satanic manifestations—and done away with through judgment.[71]

Second, after a simple declaration of faith in the daily providential care of God for his people ("Give us this day our daily bread") comes the forgiveness clause of the prayer, "And forgive us our debts." As we pray for an end to sin, we reflect on the sin in our own hearts, confessing that we are sinners so that we may continually submit our lives to God's reign. Yet the forgiveness of our faults is correlate with the forgiveness we extend to those who sin against us: "As we also have forgiven our debtors." The point is not that we earn God's favor by forgiving others, but that we live as loyal subjects of God's kingdom where forgiveness is the central blessing of that kingdom.[72] Finally, when we pray with Jesus, "Deliver us from evil," we confess the fallenness of the present world and the desire for God to purge evil from it, along with the sin in our hearts. N. T. Wright unpacks these words so that they encompass the entire realm of evil in our world:

> Deliver us from the horror of war! Deliver us from human folly and the appalling accidents it can produce! Let us not become a society of rich fortresses and cardboard cities! Let us not be engulfed by social violence, or by self-righteous reaction! Save us from arrogance and pride and the awful things they make people do! Save us—from ourselves ... and Deliver us from the Evil One.[73]

In the meantime, we wait for God's ultimate deliverance of his people from all forms of evil, and we wait for Jesus to fully destroy wickedness, even as

71. McKnight, *Kingdom*, 200.
72. Wright, *Prayer*, 55.
73. Ibid., 75.

he has begun to do so on the cross. We pray the imprecatory psalms with the recognition that the fallen world has not yet reached God's goal of total kingdom saturation. We pray these psalms as we weep with those who weep and anticipate the renewal of all things, including ourselves.

All in all, Ps 137 is a song of two cities: Babylon and Jerusalem.[74] Within the larger canon of Scripture the former represents idolatry, chaos and oppression, the latter covenant loyalty, freedom, and peace. Both cities become symbolic of the conflict between good and evil, especially in the book of Revelation, where the thoughts and ideas of Ps 137 come to full expression. This psalm, then, looks forward to the final destruction of Babylon, the archetypal wicked city. Where the psalmist exults at how God will repay Babylon for her atrocities, so also Revelation rejoices at God's retribution on the last day when he vanquishes evil:

> Pay her back as she herself has paid back others, and repay her double for her deeds; mix a double portion for her in the cup she mixed. As she glorified herself and lived in luxury, so give her a like measure of torment and mourning, since in her heart she says, "I sit as a queen, I am no widow, and mourning I shall never see." For this reason her plagues will come in a single day, death and mourning and famine, and she will be burned up with fire; for mighty is the Lord God who has judged her . . . Rejoice over her, O heaven, and you saints and apostles and prophets, for God has given judgment for you against her! Then a mighty angel took up a stone like a great millstone and threw it into the sea, saying, "So will Babylon the great city be thrown down with violence, and will be found no more; and the sound of harpists and musicians, of flute players and trumpeters, will be heard in you no more, and a craftsman of any craft will be found in you no more, and the sound of the mill will be heard in you no more." (Rev 18:6–8, 20–22)

The vision eerily evokes the silence of the Levitical musicians in Ps 137 as the silence comes full circle; "Babylon" is now void of music (cf. Isa 24:8; Ezek 26:13). Consistent with the imprecatory nature of Ps 137, there is great rejoicing at the justice of the vengeance that has taken place when Babylon falls in the NT (Rev 19:1–3).[75] Although this victory over "Babylon" symbolizes God's victory over Rome in the original setting of Revelation, its larger canonical function is a metaphor for God's final victory over the forces of evil.

---

74. Reardon, *Christ*, 274.
75. Belcher, *Messiah*, 82.

What is more, Jesus is the judge on the final Day of the Lord in the NT (Matt 25:31–46; John 5:22–30; Acts 10:42; 2 Cor 5:10; Rev 19:11–21).[76] In Revelation, he destroys all the enemies of God in a scene that culminates in the gory supper of Rev 19:11–21.[77] While the imagery is vivid, even grotesque (see the Christology of Ps 46), it is not literal, but figurative. It is meant to illicit a strong emotive response at the repulsive rhetoric. Once again we are reminded that as we pray for the return of Christ to set the world to rights, this joyous event brings with it the dreadful destruction of evil. God's people will indeed rejoice, worship, and dine at table with Christ, while the wicked will be slaughtered by the sword of his mouth and their corpses devoured by scavenging birds. The full and final destruction of evil occurs when Satan is thrown into the lake of fire and his armies "consumed" by fire from heaven (20:9–10). The scene is swift; the text devotes only two verses to the most climactic battle in all of Scripture.

Not only does Ps 137 look forward to the judgment of the enemies of God and his people, but also the new Jerusalem as the restored city of God on the last day (Rev 21—22). A full description of the city is beyond our purposes here, and we have already discussed the divine presence aspect of the new Jerusalem in connection with Ps 46 earlier. In short, as the singer of Ps 137 yearns to sing of Jerusalem while in Babylon, Christians also long for the new Jerusalem, heaven itself, as we are mindful that we are not yet "home" with God.[78] In the new Jerusalem, all accursed things have been done away with, and worship erupts at the eternal riddance of all wickedness (Rev 22:3). As Grant Osborne observes, "Life in the New Jerusalem is one long experience of worship."[79] God eradicates all that caused the psalmist's mourning and pain: "He will wipe away every tear from their eyes, and death shall be no more, neither shall there be mourning, nor crying, nor pain anymore, for the former things have passed away" (21:4). With the psalmist, we, too, eagerly await the city where singing and harps are heard forever, where God's people worship him unopposed and out of exile.[80] God has answered the pleas of Ps 137 to avenge the suffering of the community and return them to their rightful home—the holy city— and he has done so in Jesus Christ.

---

76. McKnight, *Kingdom*, 184–85.
77. Belcher, *Messiah*, 82.
78. Longman, *Psalms*, 449.
79. Osborne, *Revelation*, 49.
80. Reardon, *Christ*, 274.

Psalm 148

"And raised up a horn of salvation for us in the house of his servant David."—Zechariah (Luke 1:69)

History

THE FINAL PSALM I want to examine from a christological angle is appropriately a song of praise. We usually refer to the grand corpus of poetic praise in the Bible as the book of Psalms based on its title in the LXX, which simply means "songs" (*psalmoi*), but its title in the Hebrew text is more specifically "Book of Praises/Hymns" (*sepher tehillim*), reflecting its use in worship.[1] The Psalter in the Hebrew Bible closes with five praise psalms, each beginning and ending with "hallelujah." This concluding doxology is sometimes called the "Final Hallel."[2] Psalm 148 inspired the poem "The Song of the Brother Sun" by Francis of Assisi (d. 1226), which was later put to music by William Draper in the song "All Creatures of Our God and King." Psalm 148 is usually classified as a creation psalm, along with Pss 8, 19, 65, and 104; each praising the Creator of all things and basking in the beauty of his creation.[3] For Duane Warden, "Praise shines through Psalm 148. Like a rainbow, it enters the consciousness in an overarching burst of grandeur."[4] Praise is clearly the main theme of psalm with the verb "to praise" (*halal*) occurring twelve times in the psalm.[5] This poetic strategy of repetition of the praise theme to the point of sheer saturation of the psalm leads readers and hearers to the overpowering sense of the summons of all things—animate and inanimate—to praise Yahweh.[6] What is more, the psalm's place

1. Arterbury, et al., *Engaging*, 107.
2. DeClaissé-Walford, et al., *Psalms*, 1002.
3. Ibid.
4. Warden, "Praise Him," 101.
5. DeClaissé-Walford, et al., *Psalms*, 1002.
6. Brueggemann and Bellinger, *Psalms*, 614.

in the concluding doxology of the book focuses attention on the praise theme in a unique way. Psalm 147 presents two alternating spheres of God's activity—creation and deliverance—and Ps 148 focuses more on the former by summoning all creation to praise God, reserving only the final verse of the psalm for deliverance (of God's people). The final verse of Ps 148, then, anticipates Israel's deliverance as the dominant sphere of God's activity in Ps 149, setting up the grand doxology of Ps 150 as the pinnacle of praise that concludes the Hebrew Psalter.[7] The kingship of Yahweh is a major theme of Book 5, and while it may not be a major component of Ps 148, it is nevertheless present. First, the psalm's placement at the end of Book 5 contributes to the Psalter's overwhelming emphasis on Yahweh's kingship after the collapse of the Davidic monarchy and the exile. Neither Ps 147 nor 148 contain the word "reign" or "king," but they are bracketed by two psalms that do (146:10; 149:2); the effect, then, is that Pss 147 and 148 declare God's universal sovereignty.[8] Second, the psalm proclaims God's royal majesty in verse 13 as being above both earth and heaven, and this is certainly consistent with God's reign not only in Book 5, but throughout the whole Psalter.[9]

It is impossible to date the composition of Ps 148 with any precision. The content is general enough to have been written quite early, perhaps as early as the monarchy period or sometime prior to the exile. But given the emphasis in Book 5 on the restoration of Israel after the exile and their commitment to Yahweh as their rightful king, the placement of the psalm calls forth the rebirth of the nation, inviting all creation, including Israel (v. 14), to share in the praise of such a wonderful God.[10] While not adding much in the way of specifics on the date of the psalm's composition, the Additions to Daniel in the LXX, notably, The Song of the Three Jews, which is a legendary account of the prayer of Shadrach, Meshach, and Abednego while in the fiery furnace (Dan 3:8–30), seems modeled on Ps 148. The content of the prayer follows much the same sequence as the psalm, calling on creation—heaven, sun, moon, stars, angels, waters above the heavens, followed by various elements and formations on the earth, etc.—to praise the Lord (Sg Three 35–68).[11] David deSilva notes that while the first addition to Daniel, the Prayer of Azariah, is likely from the Hellenistic period (approx. 332–167 BCE), the Song of the Three Jews could be considerably older than the rest

---

7. McCann, *Psalms*, 1270.
8. Ibid.
9. Mays, *Psalms*, 444.
10. Zorn, *Psalms*, 528.
11. Reardon, *Christ*, 297.

of Daniel, which dates from the Persian period (approx. 537–532 BCE).[12] All of this to say Ps 148 is older than the Song of the Three Jews.

If the content of the Song of the Three Jews reflects Ps 148, the psalm itself mirrors the creation account of Genesis.[13] The elements of creation in Ps 148 resemble many of those in Gen 1:1—2:4, although not in exactly the same order, as illustrated in the following table:

Genesis 1—2	Psalm 148
Created (1:1, 21, 27)	Created (v. 5)
Deep (v. 2)	Deeps (v. 7)
Hosts (2:1)	Hosts (v. 2)
"And God said . . ." (1:3, 6, 9, 11, 14, 20, 24, 26)	"He commanded . . ." (v. 5)
Sun, moon, and stars (vv. 14–19)	Sun, moon, and stars (v. 3)
Fruit trees (v. 11)	Fruit trees (v. 9)
Heavens and waters above the heavens (vv. 6–8)	Heavens and waters above the heavens (v. 4)
Sea creatures (v. 20)	Sea creatures (v. 7)
Flying birds (v. 20)	Flying birds (v. 10)
Livestock, creeping things, and beasts (vv. 24–25)	Beasts, livestock, and creeping things (v. 10)
Human beings (vv. 26–27)	Human beings (vv. 11–12)
Earth and heaven (2:4b)	Earth and heaven (v. 13)

Table 7 Creation in Genesis 1—2 and Psalm 148

In contrast to Israel's ANE neighbors, whose creation stories were chaotic and violent, Ps 148 reflects the peaceful and orderly account of Genesis where God creates all things by the word of his mouth, culminating in the crown of creation—humanity. The emphasis in the psalm is that the created order continues day-to-day; when God brought order from of chaos "in the beginning" he "established" that order (148:6), decreeing it so that chaos is forever tamed.

The psalm's structure is easy to identify because it consists of two clear sections, calling the heavens to declare the praise of God in the first and the earth in the second:

> Praise the LORD from the heavens (vv. 1–6)
>
> Praise the LORD from the earth (vv. 7–14)[14]

---

12. DeSilva, *Introducing*, 227.

13. McCann, *Psalms*, 1271. For parallel accounts to the Genesis creation narrative, see Job 28:23–28; 38—41; Sir 43.

14. DeClaissé-Walford, et al., *Psalms*, 1002.

What is more, the psalm follows the pattern of a typical praise hymn with a summons to praise followed by a reason for praise; but Ps 148 is different in that the author spends an inordinate amount of attention on the summons rather than the reason.[15] The effect of this unbalanced structure is to produce an overwhelming sense of praise, saturating the psalm from beginning to end with "Praise the LORD" (*halelujah* in vv. 1, 14).

The psalm opens with dizzying heights of praise "from the heavens" (v. 1), and in many ways reflects the ANE cosmology shared between Israel and her neighbors. The poet calls for all the inhabitants of the heavenly realms, both angels and hosts to lead a chorus of praise to God (vv. 1-2). "Hosts" amplifies "angels" so that praise extends from God's messengers and includes the totality of heavenly beings, being innumerable.[16] This illustrates not strictly speaking "synonymous" parallelism where angels are equal to hosts, but conveys a heightening and intensifying effect that broadens God's praise to all inhabitants of the heavenly realms. The use of angels and hosts to describe heavenly beings reflects the ANE idea of a heavenly society that is parallel to earthly societal structures.[17] What is more, the sun, moon, and stars, as inhabitants of the heavenly realms, are included in this paean of praise (v. 3). Other ANE peoples considered these to be individual gods worthy of worship. The psalmist insists, however, they are simply elements of God's creation, integral to the establishment of earth's order, but not divine in and of themselves (cf. Job 31:26-27). The great lights and stars are not gods to be worshiped, but objects that worship God, their creator and sustainer.[18]

The terminology of "highest heavens, and you waters above the heavens" in Ps 148:4 most likely mirrors ANE cosmology that believed there was a vast fresh-water ocean—the so-called supercealian sea—above the sky.[19] The ancients believed the sky was essentially a stretched out solid piece of material—held up by the mountains—that protected the earth from being flooded by this sea. Rainfall, for its part, resulted when windows were opened periodically to allow the fresh water above to fall through.[20] To be clear, rain resulted not from the accumulation of water droplets in the clouds, as in modern meteorology, but from the ocean far above the earth,

---

15. Brueggemann and Bellinger, *Psalms*, 612.
16. Zorn, *Psalms*, 528.
17. DeClaissé-Walford, et al., *Psalms*, 1003.
18. Ibid.
19. Zorn, *Psalms*, 528-29n309. DeClaissé-Walford et al. adds that the ancients also believed in "waters below" the earth (or better, "dome"), which were the source of springs, rivers, and seas (*Psalms*, 1003-04).
20. Ibid.

which separated the "highest heavens" (i.e., realm of the gods) from the "heavens" (i.e., sky).

Verse 5 offers the first reason for praise in the psalm: "For he commanded ... he established ..."). Not only did God speak the heavens and heavenly bodies into existence (v. 5), he also established their respective roles, which they perform faithfully from day-to-day (v. 6), and this is in and of itself worthy of praise. The poet calls for the heavenlies to praise the "name of the LORD" (v. 5), that is Yahweh, the covenant God of Israel, who is the one true creator of all things. Praising his name is a summons to praise his character and purposes, which represent his very being, and in the context of Ps 148 includes his creative and covenantal fidelity.

The second half of Ps 148 concerns the ongoing praise of God's creation "from the earth" (v. 7). Following the general order of the Genesis creation narrative, the psalm moves from the heights of heavens to the depths of the sea, with the praise of the Creator continuing as the psalm's central theme. The poet exhorts representative creatures from every domain of creation to join in the chorus of praise. "Great sea creatures and all deeps" (v. 7) recalls the Genesis creation account where God's Spirit tames the waters, which represent primordial chaos (Gen 1:2). As a result, God creates all the great creatures of the sea (1:20–21). The psalmist's reflection on the sea and its creatures here in Ps 148 suggests that God's taming of the abyss was firmly established and still stands.[21] Verse 8 contains an additional element of the natural world not included in the original Hebrew creation account, namely, weather patterns. This verse looks back to 147:15–18, which conveys the same notion as our current psalm: God commands and the elements obey. In this context "fire" is likely how the ancients referred to what we call "lightning" today. Hail, snow, mist, and stormy winds represent other weather phenomena; but for the poet, these are not mere natural occurrences, but rather aspects of the created world that fulfill God's word. In other words, they are fully obedient to their Creator's command. John Calvin captures this sense of the weather's obedience to God's word:

---

21. "Great sea creatures" may recall God's primordial victory over the great mythical sea dragon, Leviathan, before the creation of the earth could occur (Zorn, *Psalms*, 529). Scripture sometimes refers to Leviathan in a mythical fashion, representing primordial chaos (Ps 74:13–14; Isa 51:9), as in other ANE accounts. At other times, the Bible seems to imply that Leviathan is an actual earthly creature (Job 41:1–11; Ps 104:26; Isa 27:1). In the latter instances, "Leviathan is not a fearsome, mythic monster to be conquered, but is just another creature of the Lord" (DeClaissé-Walford, et al., *Psalms*, 777). God subdues Leviathan in both instances.

> Unless perchance it be unknown to us in whose power it lies to sustain this infinite mass of heaven and earth by his Word: by his nod alone sometimes to shake heaven with thunderbolts, to burn everything with lightnings, to kindle the air with flashes; sometimes to disturb it with various sorts of storms, and them at his pleasure to clear them away in a moment; to compel the sea, which by its height seems to threaten the earth with continual destruction, to hang as if in mid-air; sometimes to arouse it in a dreadful way with the tumultuous force of winds; sometimes, with waves quieted, to make it calm again! Belonging to this theme are the praises of God's power from the testimonies of nature.[22]

For the poet, no aspect of God's creation is immune from praise, not even inanimate objects like mountains and trees (v. 9). Evoking the creation narrative of Genesis, representative creatures from the animal kingdom contribute their own unique voices in this grand chorus of praise to the Creator (v. 10). Before moving to the final section, which focuses on human praise for God, it is worth asking how the representative creatures listed in vv. 1–10, including inanimate objects, who lack the volition to worship their Creator, answer the call to praise? Simply put, they do so by existing and by fulfilling their God-ordained roles according his divine command (vv. 5–6, 8). For example, the stormy winds praise God by being stormy winds and obeying God's creative decree.[23] James Mays explains that in the context of the psalm, "the creation and the creatures praise in their very being and doing, by existing and filling their assigned place."[24]

The first section of the psalm focuses on the natural world, God's good creation, which points not to itself, but to the Creator. Calvin rightly observes that God discloses himself in the whole workmanship of the universe: "The Lord began to show himself in the visible splendor of his apparel, ever since in the creation of the universe he brought forth those insignia whereby he shows his glory to us, whenever and wherever we cast our gaze."[25] I have commented on similar "natural" theology earlier in Ps 29, the main point being that for biblical thought, nature is part of God's creation and not to be identified in any way with deity, as in Pantheism, where the natural world displays divine attributes. In the Bible, creation testifies to the Creator, never pointing to creation itself as divine, but always to the supreme Maker of heaven and earth. Psalm 148 is yet another example of creation recognizing

---

22. Calvin, *Institutes* (1.5.6), 59.
23. Mays, *Psalms*, 445.
24. Ibid.
25. Calvin, *Institutes*, (1.5.1), 52.

its proper place in the grand scheme of God's cosmos, as creatures who do the bidding of the Creator, according to the Creator-creation distinction that runs throughout the Bible. Thus, Warden correctly understands the psalm in light of the Bible's doctrine of the natural world: "Psalm 148 offers neither praise nor glory to natural forces and objects as such; they merely reflect the glory of the God who made them. This Psalm is an implicit condemnation of any understanding of the universe that results in the worship of mere created objects as if they were divine beings capable of reasoning and acting."[26]

As in Gen 1, the focus of God's creation in Ps 148 is the culmination and crown of creation—humanity. All kinds of human beings from all walks of life join with the rest of creation to answer the summons of praise (vv. 11–13). From kings to young children, all people acknowledge the reign of God, declaring the second reason in the psalm for proclaiming his praises: for his name alone is exalted and his kingly majesty is over all things (v. 13). Now the whole creation joins together, lifting their unique voices to praise God and to declare his reign through the entire universe.[27]

The psalm takes a different turn in the final verse, shifting the focus from the representatives of all classes of humanity in the previous verses to the nation of Israel. In light of the creation emphasis in the psalm, Israel becomes the premier "creation" of the Creator, being the recipients of his covenant blessings. This leads naturally to the final summons of "Praise the LORD." "Horn" in verse 14a is a common metaphor in the Bible, usually symbolizing strength.[28] The imagery is probably intended to call to mind a bull, whose horns are a source of pride and power.[29] The phrase "to raise up a horn" (v. 14a) often occurs in contexts of praise, resulting from what God has done on behalf of someone. It can express victory over one's enemies (2 Sam 22:3; Pss 18:2; 75:4–5; 92:10; Jer 48:25). When considering the postexilic shaping of the Psalter and an emphasis in Book 5 on God's deliverance of Israel from exile, the idea in Ps 148 would be that Yahweh, their true king, has restored military strength (i.e., "raised a horn") to Israel, assuring victory over its enemies.[30] However, this runs aground here because the liturgy of the psalm calls the nation to exercise power not in a political or militaristic fashion, but through praise.[31] What is more, Israel's military

26. Warden, "Praise Him," 103.
27. Zorn, *Psalms*, 530.
28. Brueggemann and Bellinger, *Psalms*, 613.
29. Longman, *Psalms*, 474n32.
30. Schmutzer and Gauthier, "Identity," 183.
31. Longman, *Psalms*, 474.

status on the world stage was anything but fearsome after the return from exile. They remained a heavily taxed and subservient people even after God restored them to their land. C. Hassell Bullock correctly observes that at the end of Book 5, Israel had finally learned not to trust in military prowess and power, but on their sovereign God:

> For a people whose armies had been humiliated and their kings deposed, the powerful weapon of praise would accomplish the task of vengeance which the military and monarchy could never do. At last the people of Israel had turned to their sovereign Lord and left vengeance in his hands. At last they had learned not to trust in horses and military hardware. At long last they had come to David's conclusion in Book 1: "Some trust in chariots and some in horses, but we trust in name of the LORD our God." (Ps 20:7)[32]

"To raise a horn" can also occur in contexts where God rescues someone from personal calamity, as in the case of Hannah, who praises him for exalting her horn by opening her barren womb to conceive the prophet Samuel (1 Sam 2:1). It can also describe the security and wellbeing of the righteous in contrast to the misery of the wicked (Ps 112:9). However, neither use fits the community context of Ps 148. Finally, the phrase sometimes describes the strength of God's anointed king, especially in Davidic contexts, portraying the king as delivering the nation (2 Sam 2:10; Pss 89:17, 24; 132:17; Ezek 29:21). This gives the phrase a messianic ring in certain contexts.

The rabbis understood "horn" as referring to the future messianic deliverer, according to the fifteenth benediction of the great prayer called the *Shemoneh Esreh* ("Eighteen Benedictions"): "The offspring of David Thy servant speedily cause to flourish, and let his horn be exalted in Thy salvation; for Thy salvation do we hope daily. Blessed art Thou, O Lord, who causest the horn of salvation to flourish."[33] Even so, this does not seem to coincide with the creation–praise–salvation–praise movement of Ps 148, which speaks not a word of the earthly king in the *original historical* context, but instead proclaims the "majesty" of Yahweh (v. 13). Again, this is consistent with Book 5 as a whole, which stresses the universal kingship of Yahweh over a failed Davidic monarchy. What is more, it is none other than David who leads the nation in celebrating the God who created, sustained, and guided them throughout their history: "I will extol you, my God and King,

---

32. Bullock, *Encountering*, 71.
33. Schürer, *History*, 87.

and bless your name forever" (145:1).[34] Therefore, the reference to "horn" in verse 14a appears to be broader in terms of the covenant community.[35]

What is the horn of the community, then, if it is not the restoration of the Davidic dynasty after exile? The liturgical context of Ps 148 is the best clue for making sense of the relationship of the poetic lines: "He has raised up a horn for his people" // "praise for all his saints . . ." The parallelism suggests that the horn of the people is their worshipful praise of (*le*) Yahweh. "Praise *for* (*le*) his saints" is none other than God's gift of worship given to Israel.[36] The LORD has given his faithful praise as their dignity and power so that now upon being restored to the land, their purpose and place in life is to praise Yahweh's universal kingship.[37] Mays summarizes the thought of verse 14 as the conclusion of the psalm: "In the praise of the people of the LORD, the name that is the truth about the entire universe is spoken on behalf of all the rest of creation."[38] Considering the historical circumstance of the return from exile evidenced in Book 5, and in light of the concluding doxology of the Psalter, the horn of praise in verse 14 affirms that Israel must no longer rely upon human strength and power for its deliverance; rather, its worship and praise of Yahweh will be Israel's true source of strength and power. The psalm, therefore, calls forth creation's praise for the Creator, while summoning the redeemed people of God to add their voices to creation's chorus, worshiping Yahweh for his nearness and salvation.

Christology

Psalm 148 is a paean of praise to God for his role as the creator of all things in heaven and on earth. With its consistent call for the created world to praise the name of the Creator, it stands tall among the creation psalms. The psalm repeatedly reminds creation that is owes its very existence to God's command; his word as the agent of creation. I noted earlier in connection with Ps 119:89–91, which also speaks of God's word as the means of creation, Jesus's fulfillment of this thought in John 1, as God's Word incarnate, through whom all things came into being. That connection is also valid here in Ps 148, and for the same reason: Jesus as the Word is the creative capacity

---

34. DeClaissé-Walford, *Introduction*, 142.

35. Brueggemann and Bellinger, *Psalms*, 613.

36. Although the phrase "praise for his people" may indicate God's praise for Israel (Warden, "Praise Him," 107), this interpretation goes against the sense of the psalm, which centers exclusively on creation's praise for God.

37. Mays, *Psalms*, 445.

38. Ibid.

of God (John 1:3). However, to avoid repeating that discussion I refer the reader to the earlier treatment of Ps 119:89–91 and the Christology associated with it.

I noted in the history section that the language "he has raised up a horn" in 148:14 probably does not have a messianic meaning in the original context. Even so, we must remember that as Christians we do not read the psalm from the same perspective as its original audience. According to the NT, Christians occupy a unique place in redemptive history as the messianic community "in the fullness of time" (Gal 4:4; Eph 1:10). A distinctly Christian interpretation of the OT is a christological one, a "backward" reading from a post-resurrection perspective that sees Jesus as the culmination of the Jewish Scriptures, the climax of the entire biblical narrative. As J. Scott Duvall and J. Daniel Hays note:

> We read and interpret the Old Testament as Christians. That is, although we believe that the Old Testament is part of God's inspired Word to us, we do not want to ignore the cross and thus interpret and apply the literature as if we were Old Testament Hebrews. We affirm that we are New Testament Christians, and we will interpret the Old Testament from that vantage point.[39]

Therefore, a christological interpretation of Ps 148 gives "he has raised up a horn" a decidedly messianic ring, anticipating Jesus Christ as the "horn of salvation" for God's people (Luke 1:69). Additionally, the Greek translation changes the verb tense of the Hebrew from past (i.e., "he has raised . . .") to future (i.e., "he will raise . . ."), which opens a host of theological interpretations, including messianic ones, that go beyond the original context of the psalm.[40] According to the Hebrew text, the psalmist speaks of what God has already accomplished by raising up a horn for his people. However, the LXX leaves the same verse open to future possibilities by using the future tense—"he will raise up a horn for his people."

While the NT does not quote this verse per se, there is evidence in the NT that the Greek translation of the OT provided fodder for the church's messianic application of some passages over against their Hebrew originals, which, presumably, did not lend themselves as readily to future fulfillments. This exegetical strategy appears in Acts 2:27 where Luke describes the resurrection of Christ as a fulfillment of Ps 16:10. Where the Hebrew speaks of God having rescued David from Sheol: "For you did

---

39. Duvall and Hays, *Grasping*, 331.

40. Schmutzer and Gauthier, "Identity," 166–67, 180. The authors correctly note, however, that this change in verb tense in the LXX is common, and probably not theological motivated.

not give me up to Sheol" (Ps 16:10), the Greek renders this as a future hope: "For you will not abandon my soul in Hades" (15:10). For Luke, the Greek translation provides a clearer statement of a future expectation of bodily resurrection than the Hebrew original. When commenting on this verse, he explains that David was a "prophet," who had in fact died and was buried and whose body still remains in the tomb; thus, he "foresaw" the resurrection of Christ (Acts 2:30–31). The appeal to the LXX instead of the MT has the effect of shifting the meaning from "avoiding death" to "surviving death."[41] Applying similar christological exegesis, therefore, places a premium on the future expectation that God "*will* raise up a horn for his people," pointing to Jesus Christ. This appeal to the LXX of Ps 148:14 need not be our only recourse for a messianic application of the term "horn" because the Hebrew text speaks of it in specifically Davidic contexts, anticipating the future deliverance in the messianic era (1 Sam 2:10, Pss 89, 132). I offer this example from LXX because it relates concretely to the current psalm, and provides an exegetical basis that is consistent with methods of exegesis practiced elsewhere in the NT, helping to establish a christological interpretation of the psalm.

I noted earlier the rabbinic association of "horn" with the end-times Messiah, and this association is equally as strong in Christianity, beginning in the NT itself, notably in the Gospel of Luke. Zechariah, the father of John the Baptist, raises his newfound voice in a Spirit-inspired, prophetic song of praise to God for the redemption of his people in the so-called *Benedictus* (Luke 1:68–79). In many ways this prophecy lays out the "messianic thrust" of Luke's Christology in the very first chapter of his Gospel, where Zechariah proclaims that God "has raised up a horn of salvation for us in the house of his servant David" (v. 69).[42] The association of the horn with the house of David shows that Zechariah is not speaking here of his son, but of the promised Messiah.[43]

Zechariah is a pious Jew in the first century, and his messianic expectation reflects the view of most Jewish sects at that time that the Messiah, as a son of David, would primarily be a military and political ruler, sent by God to liberate the Jewish people from their enemies, notably Rome (v. 71). Consequently, for Zechariah, "horn of salvation" has militaristic overtones where it symbolizes the strength and vigor of the Messiah and his ability to defeat his opponents. Even so, it would be a mistake to limit Zechariah's

---

41. There are other nuances at work in Luke's quotation of LXX Ps 15:10 that contribute to his christological interpretation, notably the change from "me" to "my soul" and from "Sheol" to "Hades" (Moyise, *Later Writings*, 15–16).

42. Bock, *Theology*, 154.

43. Garland, *Luke*, 107.

song to national deliverance; he speaks also to the ultimate goal of messianic liberation as unfettered worship, serving God without fear and in righteousness and holiness (vv. 74–75).[44] As R. Alan Culpepper concludes, "The true end of God's redemption is not merely deliverance from political domination—as important as that is—but the creation of conditions in which God's people can worship and serve God without fear."[45] Luke's purposes, however, go beyond the messianic expectations of Zechariah the priest. Frequently in the Gospels, characters say and do more than they know, speaking and acting "prophetically" without fully understanding all of the implications of their words and actions (e.g., Mark 8:27–33; Luke 9:33; John 11:50–51; 12:1–7). Again, for Zechariah, the Messiah, the horn of salvation, inaugurates an era of deliverance from human enemies, namely Rome. Luke's Christology, however, goes well beyond the messianic expectations of first-century Judaism and Zechariah. When considered in the larger context of Luke's Gospel, the scope of salvation in the *Benedictus* is broader than mere political liberation:

> The Promised One from David's house has power than extends beyond political forces that sit over Israel. God has "raised up" this significant figure onto the world's stage. The Son of David (God's "servant," v. 69) will become a servant himself. He will take on the cosmic forces that oppress humanity and bring pain and suffering into the world. When liberation comes through his ministry, sin and Satan will lead the enemy lines.[46]

Zechariah's song in the larger context of Luke's Christology provides a canonical lens for reading Ps 148 messianically, extending it beyond the confines of the return from exile and the worship of Israel to include a more comprehensive understanding of God's horn and salvation. For the psalmist, God had liberated Israel from Babylonian exile, returning them to their land so that they may worship him there, uncontested. For Luke, God's horn is none other than Jesus Christ, and the deliverance given to God's people—both Jew and Gentile—as a result of Christ's work, naturally results in the praise of his name. The horn of salvation, Jesus Christ, brings salvation to his people, but it is more than life in the land or deliverance from earthly enemies:

---

44. The Gk. for "to serve" in v. 74 is *latreuō*, which is used exclusively in the NT of service given in a religious context (e.g., 2:37; 4:8; Rom 1:25). See Bock, *Luke*, 76.
45. Culpepper, *Luke*, 59.
46. Bock, *Luke*, 76.

Salvation is also the coming of the kingdom of God, then, the coming of God's reign of justice, to deconstruct the worldly systems and values at odds with the purpose of God. Salvation also entails membership in the new community God is drawing together around Jesus, a community into which all—especially the previously excluded for reasons of sin, and its corollary, despised status—are invited to participate in the blessings of the kingdom as well as to share in its service.[47]

Church history reveals more christological interpretations of "horn," most likely stemming from the *Benedictus* in Luke as well as in fulfillment of OT instances. For example, when commenting on the Greek text of Ps 148 as a sunrise prayer, Augustine refers to Jesus as the horn of the people, reflecting on Christ's sufferings and resurrection as the grounds for the resurrection of believers on the last day. He uses an allegory of a dead vine in the winter, symbolizing the reality that believers die physically in this world; yet summer follows as a time of life, representing the bodily resurrection:

> Now the "horn of his people" is humble in afflictions, in tribulations, in temptations, in beating of the breast; when will He "exalt the horn of his people"? When the Lord has come, and our Sun is risen . . . Summer will come, the Lord will come, our Splendour, that which was hidden in the stock, and then "He shall exalt the horn of his people," after the captivity wherein we live in this mortal life.[48]

Similarly, when debating the deity of Jesus Christ, Gregory of Nyssa (ca. 335–394) compiles various titles for God from Psalms, such as "rock," "fortress," "refuge," "deliverer," "God-helper," "hope," "buckler," "horn of salvation," and "protector," concluding that the "Only-begotten Son" is also all of these to humanity.[49]

In the original context of Ps 148, the poet summons creation to praise God for his mighty acts of creation, and Israel joins the chorus, praising God for his mighty acts of salvation. For the psalmist and his audience, the return from exile was the pinnacle experience of God's redemption of his people to that time. However, a Christian interpretation of the psalm recognizes the redemptive-historical distinction between ancient Israel in the pre-messianic era and the church in the messianic era, especially in terms of salvation. Christians have a fuller experience of the salvation of God than either the psalmist or the postexilic community because of where Christians

---

47. Green, *Theology*, 94.
48. Augustine, *Expositions* 148, §10.
49. Gregory of Nyssa, *Against Eunomius*, §I.24

stand in the fullness of time of redemptive history—the last days. God has sent Jesus the Messiah, who has inaugurated the kingdom of heaven and manifested its blessings and benefits on the earth. Simply put, the return from Babylonian exile was not the end of the story for God's people.

The heart of the gospel is that the Creator of heaven and earth has created a new humanity, a new covenant people who, based on their identity in Christ, inherit the blessings of the new covenant, namely, the gift of the indwelling Holy Spirit, the forgiveness of sins, eternal life, which begins now and continues through eternity; as well as a new community, composed of Jews and Gentiles—people of all classes, nations, races, men, women, and children, with whom God is near. Warden perceives the newness of the good news of Christ anticipated in 148:14: "After the coming of Christ, and because of Christ, God today has a people of his choosing who come from every kindred and tongue. Today there is a new Israel, a new chosen people (Rom 2:29; Eph 1:4; Phil 3:3). For those washed in the blood of the Lamb, God has raised a horn of strength. Sin and death have flown away."[50] Praise flows naturally from the recognition that God has raised up a horn for his people in Jesus Christ. Praise the Lord!

---

50. Warden, "Praise Him," 107–08.

Conclusion

ATHANASIUS (CA. 295–373 CE) wrote a letter to his dear friend Marcellinus who, while suffering from a severe illness, devoted his leisure time to diligently studying the Scriptures, especially Psalms. In the letter, Athanasius set forth what he believed was a simple, yet spiritually nourishing method for understanding the "inner force and sense" of the various psalms. He wrote, "For a soul rightly ordered by chanting the sacred words forgets its own afflictions and contemplates with joy the things of Christ alone."[1] For Athanasius, reading Psalms was not primarily to sooth one's suffering soul, or to identify with the various plights and praises of the psalmists, but rather to encounter the subject of Psalms, Jesus Christ, and the joys of having a relationship with him. In this book, I have highlighted ways that seemingly "non-messianic" psalms can point to Christ, both anticipating and evoking various aspects of his person, purpose, and passion. According to the NT, this is the primary purpose of Psalms, as well as the entire OT.

Psalms is a treasury of human emotions, and the empathy Christians often feel with the psalmists is not imaginary; we find great comfort in their words, thoughts, and emotions. From the dizzying heights of praise to the darkest lament, the language of Psalms reflects how we feel at any given moment, and the book functions as a mirror of the soul, displaying the full range of human emotion. Jesus quoted from Psalms out of the severe emotional and physical trauma of the cross, drawing consolation from the words of the psalmists, while at the same time venting his own anxiety and feelings of abandonment: "My God, my God, why have you forsaken me?" (Matt 27:46 and pars.; Ps 22:1). When reflecting on the trials of his apostolic ministry, Paul lamented to God with the words of the psalmist: "I believed, and so I spoke" (2 Cor 4:13; Ps 116:10). The expressions of the psalm singers resonate with readers in a variety of ways, and we find consolation in their songs, albeit in different circumstances and contexts.

---

1 Athanasius of Alexandria, *Letter to Marcellinus*, para. 30.

Even so, the book of Psalms is ultimately about Jesus Christ, who is the point from which the whole circle of the Psalter is drawn.[2] He is the culmination of the story of redemption that runs throughout the Bible, and the summation of the history of Israel. The entire biblical narrative moves toward Jesus Christ, finding in him the climax of the story. Jesus's fulfillment of Israel's story is evidenced in the editorial shape of the Psalter, which looks forward to the universal kingship of God. Because Psalms was shaped in the Second Temple period of Jewish history when messianic expectations flourished, it is reasonable to expect that messianism is a dominant theme of Psalms.[3] By the time of the redaction of the Psalter, the Davidic dynasty had collapsed, and so we must ask why the editor(s) included Davidic psalms? Was it simply to convey historical information, highlighting the failure of the Davidic covenant, or did it refer to a Davidic "scion" yet to come?[4] It is difficult to hear the language "of David," the king, or the Lord's anointed in Psalms without hearing messianic reverberations.

While the story of the Hebrew Psalter does not end with an explicit messianic hope per se, either in the concluding doxology or the final psalm, its retelling of Israel's history calls forth the end-times anticipation of the final and full realization of the kingdom of God, inaugurated by a Davidic heir, an earthly king who manifests God's reign of justice and peace on the earth. This kingdom is unfulfilled at the end of Psalms. The following paragraphs trace in very general terms the story of the Psalter, noticeably its messianic trajectory. Aided by the editorial superscripts, which help to illustrate the messianic undercurrent that flows through its five main divisions, the story anticipates the universal kingship of Yahweh through the rule of his Messiah.

Book 1 (Pss 1—41) recalls the "golden age" of Israel's history when a king of God's choosing sat on the throne in Jerusalem, who was devoted to God's faithful instruction (*torah*), and testified to the universal kingship of Yahweh. Devotion to torah (Pss 1 and 19) and dedication to the reign of God (Ps 2) are ideal commitments of the king, including David, whose presence dominates Book 1. James Mays summarizes the prominent role of the Davidic psalms in this book: "David was the sweet psalmist of Israel. The songs that came out of his life as shepherd and warrior, as refugee and ruler, were the inspired expression of a life devoted to God in bad times and good,

---

2. This is very near a quotation by Martin Luther where he speaks of Christ as the center of the OT; I have adopted it here because of its obvious relevance to Psalms. Cited in Grant and Tracy, *History*, 94.

3. Mitchell, "Remember David," 529.

4. Ibid., 528. The end of the Gk. Psalter, however, ends with Ps 151, a psalm of David, ripe with messianic overtones (Reardon, *Christ*, 303–04).

and therefore the guiding language for all who undertook lives of devotion. He was the chosen of the Lord, the messiah."[5] Thirty-nine of the forty-one psalms in Book 1 are "of David," and illustrate different facets of his life, including his victories and shortcomings.

Book 2 (Pss 42—72) continues to recount the life of David, evoking especially his sufferings, as indicated by the high number of lament psalms (twenty out of thirty-one psalms: sixty-five percent).[6] Davidic psalms are relatively few in this book—only eighteen—and their superscripts reveal not a triumphant and glorious king, but a very human one, whose tribulations are on full display.[7] David's reign comes to an end in Book 2, and the kingdom is placed in the hands of his descendent, King Solomon. David's hopes are high at the end of this Book (Ps 72), as he prays for Solomon a "vision of enduring kingship" of a rule that in many ways commemorates that of his own: hope for a just rule, desire for an enduring reign, plea for worldwide dominion, hope for compassionate justice, and desire for a prosperous kingdom, proclaiming the glory of God.[8] The messianic hope could not be higher, as Solomon becomes God's earthly king.

David's hopes for Solomon's glorious reign are shattered in Book 3 (Pss 73—89). The splendor of Solomon's reign is short-lived, as the kingdom is torn in two under his son, Rehoboam. Book 3 recounts the disastrous times of the divided kingdom in Israel, the subsequent obliteration of the northern kingdom by the Assyrians, and the destruction of the southern kingdom by the Babylonians.[9] By the end of Book 3, the Davidic dynasty is no more, and the despair of the exile is acute. David is noticeably absent in this book, having only one psalm, a lament, attributed to him. Yet even in the midst of this bleak book, God has chosen David's kingdom of Judah "to be the shepherd of his people Jacob" (78:71). Messianic hope remains.

Book 4 (Pss 90—106) recalls the horrors of the Babylonian exile. Zion and the temple lay in ruins, and the Davidic dynasty comes to an unglorious end. Stripped bare, humiliated, and horrified at the murder of young and old, women and children, and many prominent leaders in Judah, God's people must learn to cope with the losses, and survive in a new wilderness experience. Moses, therefore, in Ps 90 exhorts Israel to remember a time in their past when God, not an earthly king, was their only sovereign. In the formative years of Israel's history, they had to rely solely on God's provision

---

5. Mays, "David," 145.
6. DeClaissé-Walford, *Introduction*, 75.
7. Ibid., 78.
8. Wilson, *Psalms*, 985.
9. DeClaissé-Walford, *Introduction*, 85.

and protection in a hostile environment; now they must learn to do so again in exile. Memory is powerful. Reminders and recitals of the past help to correct the errors of past, provide identity in the present, and hope for the future. As Walter Brueggemann and William Bellinger observe, "Recitation is more than a description of the past; it is a rehearsal of the past so that the present and the future might be wondrous."[10] Israel's story to this point in history follows a pattern: God graciously provides, Israel obeys for a time, rebels, yet God is always faithful to his covenant (Pss 105—06).[11] The majority of psalms in Book 4 are enthronement psalms, declaring the universal sovereignty of Yahweh, and these serve to remind Israel that he is king, despite the deplorable circumstances surrounding them. Enthronement psalms help to cultivate a sense of eager expectation for the earthly reign of God through his Messiah over evildoers who oppress his people.

Yahweh's future reign over a renewed and restored Israel is the topic of Book 5 (Pss 107—150). The exile is over; Zion is rebuilt, and the temple once again functions as the center of the Jewish faith. The story recounts God delivering the Israelites from captivity and returning them to their own land. At the same time, the miseries of the exile are not forgotten. Because the Davidic kingdom had not been restored, the people had to learn to apply the lesson of Book 4: to trust in Yahweh alone as their king going forward into an unknown future; a future that included both problems (Israel was occupied by the Persians) and possibilities (the fullness of the kingdom remained a future hope). Interestingly, David reappears in Book 5, after being greatly diminished in Books 3 and 4, to lead the community once again to celebrate God as king.[12] Through David, Israel's most decorated and devoted king, Book 5 takes the reader from the despair of exile to new life in the land of Israel with God as king and the torah as the guide for life.[13] In spite of Persian rule over Israel, the future looks bright at the end of the Psalter, as Israel's greatest king summons the nation to submit to God's reign, which awaits its final and full consummation. To be sure, God has not broken his covenant with David. Book 5 implicitly confirms God's promise to David's house: "David's family continues to possess an eternal promise, yet their leadership is not physically evident at this time. Their eternal glory is a promise whose fulfillment is deferred but which must come to pass. This

---

10. Brueggemann and Bellinger, *Psalms*, 341.
11. DeClaissé-Walford, *Introduction*, 110.
12. Ibid., 142.
13. Ibid., 128.

delay forces the psalms beyond immediate worship concerns to the embracing of long-term, eschatological hope."[14]

The story of the Psalter is the story of ancient Israel, and its anticipation for the fullness of the kingdom of God. However, the story is unfinished at the end of Psalms, awaiting the climactic in-breaking of the kingdom where justice, peace, and covenant love reign supreme. Beginning with the birth announcements in the Gospels of Matthew and Luke, the arrival of the good news of the kingdom of God in Mark, and new creation by God's eternal Word in John, the NT emphatically declares that the story of Israel culminates in Jesus Christ, who is the long-awaited messianic king because of his crucifixion, resurrection, and eternal reign (Acts 2:22–36). Consequently, a Christian reading of Psalms results from a heart-felt conviction of the truth of the gospel—Jesus reigns! His first arrival on the world stage, and his current presence in the church through the Holy Spirit, manifests the blessings of the kingdom—peace, justice, forgiveness, compassion, community, radical love, holiness, divine presence, new creation, etc.—provisionally now, in eager expectation of the full arrival of the kingdom at his second coming. The story of the Psalter is the story of Jesus Christ, Israel's son of David in the last days, who fulfills the trials and triumphs of the psalmists, preeminently in his crucifixion and subsequent resurrection, ascension, and enthronement. This is not a story that only a handful of "messianic" psalms tell, but the summation of the story of the whole Psalter.

---

14. House, *Theology*, 422.

Bibliography

Alexander, Desmond. "The Old Testament View of Life After Death." *Themelios* 11 (1986) 41–46.
Armerding, Carl E. *The Old Testament and Criticism*. Grand Rapids: Eerdmans, 1983.
Arnold, Bill, and Bryan Beyer. *Encountering the Old Testament: A Christian Survey*. 2nd ed. Grand Rapids: Baker Academic, 2008.
Alter, Robert. *The Art of Biblical Poetry*. NY: Basic Books, 1985.
Arterbury, Andrew E., et al. *Engaging the Christian Scriptures: An Introduction to the Bible*. Grand Rapids: Baker Academic, 2014.
Ash, Anthony, and Clyde Miller. *Psalms*. Living Word Commentary on the Old Testament. Austin: Sweet, 1980.
Assis, Elie. "Psalm 127 and the Polemic of the Rebuilding of the Temple in the Post Exilic Period." *Zeitschrift für die alttestamentliche Wissenschaft* 121 (2009) 256–72.
Athanasius of Alexandria. *The Life of Antony and The Letter to Marcellinus*. Translated by Robert C. Gregg. New York: Paulist, 1980. http://www.athanasius.com/psalms/aletterm.htm.
Augustine of Hippo. *Expositions on the Psalms*. In *Nicene and Post-Nicene Fathers*. Vol. 8. Edited by Philip Schaff. Translated by J. E. Tweed. Buffalo, NY: Christian Literature, 1888. http://www.newadvent.org/fathers/1801088.htm.
Barber, Michael. *Singing in the Reign: The Psalms and the Liturgy of God's Kingdom*. Steubenville, OH: Emmaus Road, 2001.
Bassler, Jouette. "A Man for All Seasons: David in Rabbinic and New Testament Literature." *Interpretation* 40 (1996) 156–69.
Beale, G. K. *Handbook on the New Testament Use of the Old Testament: Exegesis and Interpretation*. Grand Rapids: Baker Academic, 2012.
―――, ed. *The Right Doctrine From the Wrong Texts? Essays on the Use of the Old Testament in the New*. Grand Rapids: Baker Academic, 1994.
Beale, G. K., and D. A. Carson, eds. *Commentary on the New Testament Use of the Old Testament*. Grand Rapids: Baker Academic, 2007.
Belcher, Richard P. *The Messiah and the Psalms: Preaching Christ from All the Psalms*. Geanies House, Fearn, Ross-shire, Scotland: Mentor, 2006.
Bellinger, William H. Jr. "Psalm 137: Memory and Poetry." *Horizons in Biblical Theology* 27 (2005) 5–20.
Berding, Kenneth, and Jonathan Lunde, eds. *Three Views on the New Testament Use of the Old Testament*. Grand Rapids: Zondervan, 2007.

Billman, Kathleen D., and Daniel L. Migliore. *Rachel's Cry: Prayer of Lament and Rebirth of Hope*. Cleveland: United Church Press, 1999.

Black, David Alan. *It's Still Greek to Me*. Grand Rapids: Baker, 1998.

Black, Mark. *Luke*. College Press New International Version Commentary. Joplin: College Press, 1996.

Blaising, Craig A., and Carmen S. Hardin, eds. *Psalms 1—50*. Ancient Christian Commentary on Scripture 7. Downers Grove: InterVarsity, 2008.

Blomberg, Craig L. *Matthew*. New American Commentary 22. Nashville: Broadman, 1992.

———. "Matthew." In *Commentary on the New Testament Use of the Old Testament*, edited by G. K. Beale and D. A. Carson, 1–109. Grand Rapids: Baker Academic, 2007.

Bock, Darrell L. *Luke*. New International Version Application Commentary. Grand Rapids: Zondervan, 1996.

———. *A Theology of Luke and Acts: God's Promised Program, Realized for All Nations*. Grand Rapids: Zondervan, 2012.

Bonhoeffer, Dietrich. *Psalms: The Prayer Book of the Bible*. Minneapolis: Augsburg, 1970.

Boring, Eugene M. *1 Peter*. Abingdon New Testament Commentaries. Nashville: Abingdon, 1999.

Bowman, Craig. "More Than Routine Words: A Reflection on Psalm 100." *Christian Studies* 20 (2004) 29–32.

Boyd, Gregory A. *Cross Vision: How the Crucifixion of Jesus Makes Sense of Old Testament Violence*. Minneapolis: Fortress, 2017.

Brendsel, Daniel J. *"Isaiah Saw His Glory": The Use of Isaiah 52—53 in John 12*. Beihefte zür Zeitschrift für die newtestamentliche Wissenschaft 208. Berlin: De Gruyter, 2014.

Brown, Raymond E. *The Gospel According to John 13—21*. Anchor Bible 29A. New York: Doubleday, 1970.

Bruce, F. F. *The Epistle to the Galatians*. New International Greek Testament Commentary. Grand Rapids: Paternoster, 1982.

Brueggemann, Walter. "Psalm 100." *Interpretation* 39 (1985) 65–69.

———. *Theology of the Old Testament: Testimony, Dispute, Advocacy*. Minneapolis: Fortress, 1997.

Brueggemann, Walter, and William H. Bellinger, Jr. *Psalms*. New Cambridge Bible Commentary. New York: Cambridge University Press, 2014.

Bryant, Beaufort H., and Mark S. Krause. *John*. College Press New International Version Commentary. Joplin: College Press, 1998.

Bullock, C. Hassell. *Encountering the Book of Psalms: A Literary and Theological Introduction*. Grand Rapids: Baker Academic, 2001.

Burge, Gary M. *John*. New International Version Application Commentary. Grand Rapids: Zondervan, 2000.

Burge, Gary, et al. *The New Testament in Antiquity: A Survey of the New Testament Within Its Cultural Contexts*. Grand Rapids: Zondervan, 2009.

Burgess, Rebecca Eaton. "The Law Preaches the Incarnation: Reading the Law in Hilary of Poitiers' Commentary on Ps 119." *Phronema* 30 (2015) 137–67.

Campbell, Alexander. *The Christian System*. Nashville: Gospel Advocate, 1835; repr., Nashville: Gospel Advocate Restoration Reprints, 2001.

Calvin, John. *Commentary on Psalms*. New Zealand: Titus Books, 2013. Apple e-book.
———. *Institutes of the Christian Religion*. Book 1. Edited by John T. McNeill. Translated by Ford Lewis Battles and Philip Schaff. Louisville: Westminster John Knox, 1960.
Carson, D. A. *How Long, O Lord? Reflections on Suffering and Evil*. Grand Rapids: Baker, 1990.
———. *The Gospel According to John*. Pillar New Testament Commentary. Grand Rapids: Eerdmans, 1991.
Carson, D. A., and H. G. M. Williamson, eds. *It is Written: Scripture Citing Scripture: Essays in Honour of Barnabas Lindars*. New York: Cambridge University Press, 1988.
Childs, Brevard S. *Biblical Theology of the Old and New Testaments: Reflections on the Christian Bible*. Minneapolis: Fortress, 1992.
———. *Introduction to the Old Testament as Scripture*. Philadelphia: Fortress, 1979.
———. *The New Testament As Canon: An Introduction*. Valley Forge, PA: Trinity Press International, 1994.
Chouinard, Larry. *Matthew*. College Press New International Version Commentary. Joplin: College Press, 1997.
Clowney, Edmund P. *Preaching Christ in All of Scripture*. Wheaton: Crossway, 2003.
———. *The Unfolding Mystery: Discovering Christ in the Old Testament*. 2nd ed. Phillipsburg, NJ: P&R, 2013.
Cole, R. Dennis. *Numbers*. New American Commentary 3B. Nashville: Broadman & Holman, 2000.
Collett, Don. "The Christology of Israel's Psalter." *Currents in Theology and Mission* 41 (2014) 390–95.
Craddock, Fred B. *The Letter to the Hebrews*. New Interpreter's Bible 12. Edited by Leander E. Keck. Nashville: Abingdon, 1998.
Culpepper, R. Alan. *The Gospel of Luke*. New Interpreter's Bible 9. Edited by Leander E. Keck. Nashville: Abingdon, 1995.
Dahood, Mitchell. *Psalms 1—50*. Anchor Bible 16. Garden City, NY: Doubleday, 1966.
Daly-Denton, Margaret. *David in the Fourth Gospel: The Johannine Reception of the Psalms*. Boston: Brill, 2000.
Davidson, Benjamin. "*Ashrey*" in *The Analytical Hebrew and Chaldee Lexicon*. Peabody: Hendrickson, 2000.
Davis, Christopher A. *Revelation*. College Press New International Version Commentary. Joplin: College Press, 2000.
DeClaissé-Walford, Nancy L. *Introduction to the Psalms: A Song from Ancient Israel*. St. Louis: Chalice, 2004.
DeClaissé-Walford, Nancy L., et al. *The Book of Psalms*. New International Commentary on the Old Testament. Grand Rapids: Eerdmans, 2014.
DeSilva, David A. *Introducing the Apocrypha: Message, Context, and Significance*. Grand Rapids: Baker Academic, 2002.
Duguid, Iain M. *Is Jesus in the Old Testament?* Phillipsburg, NJ: P&R, 2013.
Dunn, James D. G. Introduction to *The Cambridge Companion to St. Paul*, edited by James D. G. Dunn, 1–15. New York: Cambridge University Press, 2003.
———. *New Testament Theology*. Nashville: Abingdon, 2009.
Duvall, J. Scott, and J. Daniel Hays, *Grasping God's Word: A Hands-On Approach to Reading, Interpreting, and Applying the Bible*. 3rd ed. Grand Rapids: Zondervan, 2012.

Eaton, John. *The Psalms: A Historical and Spiritual Commentary with an Introduction and New Translation.* New York: Continuum, 2005.

Ellingworth, Paul. *The Epistle to the Hebrews.* New International Greek Testament Commentary. Grand Rapids: Eerdmans, 1993.

Enns, Peter. *The Bible Tells Me So: Why Defending Scripture Has Made Us Unable to Read It.* New York: HarperOne, 2014.

———. *Inspiration and Incarnation: Evangelicals and the Problem of the Old Testament.* Grand Rapids: Baker Academic, 2005.

Evans, Craig A. *Ancient Texts for New Testament Studies: A Guide to the Background Literature.* Peabody: Hendrickson, 2005.

Fletcher, Daniel H. "Seeking Solace in the Sanctuary: The Canonical Placement of Psalm 27." In *Hebrew and Beyond: Essays in Honor of Rodney E. Cloud,* edited by David Musgrave, 97–119. Montgomery, AL: Amridge University Press, 2017.

———. "From Covenant to Constitution: Alexander Campbell's Dispensational Hermeneutic and Adult Baptism." *Restoration Quarterly* 57 (2015) 1–17.

———. "Nicodemus and LXX Numbers: Johannine Intertextuality." ΠΝΕΥΜΑΤΙΚΑ 1 (2013) 111–32.

———. *Signs in the Wilderness: Intertextuality and the Testing of Nicodemus.* Eugene, OR: Wipf and Stock, 2014.

Ferguson, Everett. *Backgrounds of Early Christianity.* 3rd ed. Grand Rapids: Eerdmans, 2003.

Garland, David E. *Luke.* Zondervan Exegetical Commentary on the New Testament. Grand Rapids: Zondervan, 2011.

———. *Mark.* New International Version Application Commentary. Grand Rapids: Zondervan, 1996.

George, Timothy. *Galatians.* New American Commentary 30. Nashville: Broadman & Holman, 1994.

Girdwood, Jim, and Peter Verkruyse. *Hebrews.* College Press New International Version Commentary. Joplin: College Press, 1997.

Glasson, T. Francis. *Moses in the Fourth Gospel.* Studies in Biblical Theology 40. Eugene, OR: Wipf & Stock, 2009.

Goheen, Michael W. *A Light to the Nations: The Missional Church and the Biblical Story.* Grand Rapids: Baker Academic, 2011.

Goldsworthy, Graeme. *Preaching the Whole Bible as Christian Scripture: The Application of Biblical Theology to Expository Preaching.* Grand Rapids: Eerdmans, 2000.

Goppelt, Leonhard. *Typos: The Typological Interpretation of the Old Testament in the New.* Translated by Donald H. Madvig. Grand Rapids: Eerdmans, 1982.

Gowan, Donald E. *Eschatology in the Old Testament.* Edinburgh: T. & T. Clark, 2000.

Grant, Robert M., and David Tracy. *A History of the Interpretation of the Bible.* 2nd ed. Minneapolis: Fortress, 1984.

Green, Douglas J. "'The Lord is Christ's Shepherd': Psalm 23 as Messianic Prophecy." In *Eyes to See and Ears to Hear: Essays in Memory of J. Alan Groves,* edited by Peter Enns, et al., 33–46. Phillipsburg, NJ: P&R, 2010.

Green, Joel B. *The Theology of the Gospel of Luke.* New York: Cambridge University Press, 1995.

Gregory of Nyssa. *Against Eunomius.* In *Nicene and Post-Nicene Fathers.* Vol. 5. Edited by Philip Schaff and Henry Wace. Translated by William Moore and Henry Austin

Wilson. Buffalo, NY: Christian Literature, 1893. http://www.newadvent.org/fathers/290101.htm.

Greidanus, Sidney. *Preaching Christ From the Old Testament: A Contemporary Hermeneutical Method*. Grand Rapids: Eerdmans, 1999.

———. *Preaching Christ From Psalms: Foundations for Expository Sermons in the Christian Year*. Grand Rapids: Eerdmans, 2016.

Grenz, Stanley J. *Theology for the Community of God*. Nashville: Broadman & Holman, 1994.

Gundry, Stanley, et al., eds. *Three Views on the New Testament Use of the Old Testament*. Grand Rapids: Zondervan, 2007.

Gundry-Volf, Judith M. "Child, Children." In *NIDB* 1:588–90.

Gunn, George A. "Psalm 2 and the Reign of the Messiah." *Bibliotheca Sacra* 169 (2012) 427–42.

Guthrie, George H. *Hebrews*. New International Version Application Commentary. Grand Rapids: Zondervan, 1998.

Hays, Richard B. "Christ Prays the Psalms: Israel's Psalter as Matrix of Early Christology." In *The Conversion of the Imagination: Paul as Interpreter of Israel's Scripture*, 101–18. Grand Rapids: Eerdmans, 2009.

———. *Echoes of Scripture in the Letters of Paul*. New Haven: Yale University Press, 1989.

———. *First Corinthians*. Interpretation: A Bible Commentary for Preaching and Teaching. Louisville: John Knox, 1997.

———. *The Letter to the Galatians*. New Interpreter's Bible 11. Edited by Leander E. Keck. Nashville: Abingdon, 2000.

———. *Reading Backwards: Figural Christology and the Fourfold Gospel Witness*. Waco: Baylor University Press, 2014.

Hays, Richard B., and Joel B. Green. "The Use of the Old Testament by New Testament Writers." In *Hearing the New Testament*, 2nd ed., edited by Joel B. Green, 122–39. Grand Rapids: Eerdmans, 2010.

Heinemann, Mark H. "Exposition of Psalm 22." *Bibliotheca Sacra* 147 (1990) 286–308.

Hicks, John Mark. *1 & 2 Chronicles*. College Press New International Version Commentary. Joplin: College Press, 2001.

———. *Come to the Table: Revisioning the Lord's Supper*. Orange, CA: New Leaf Books, 2002.

———. *Yet Will I Trust Him: Understanding God In a Suffering World*. Joplin: College Press, 1999.

Hicks, John Mark, et al. *Embracing Creation: God's Forgotten Mission*. Abilene, TX: Abilene Christian University Press, 2016.

Hirsch, E. D., Jr. *Validity in Interpretation*. New Haven: Yale University Press, 1967.

House, Paul R. *Old Testament Theology*. Downers Grove: InterVarsity, 1998.

Jacobson, Rolf A., ed. *Soundings in the Theology of Psalms: Perspectives and Methods in Contemporary Scholarship*. Minneapolis: Fortress, 2010.

Jobes, Karen H. *1 Peter*. Baker Exegetical Commentary on the New Testament. Grand Rapids: Baker Academic, 2005.

Juel, Donald H. "Interpreting Israel's Scriptures in the New Testament." In *A History of Biblical Interpretation: The Ancient Period*, edited by Alan J. Hauser and Duane F. Watson, 283–303. Grand Rapids: Eerdmans, 2003.

Just, Felix. "Quotations from the Old Testament in the New Testament." http://catholic-resources.org/Bible/Quotations-OT-NT.htm.
Keener, Craig S. *A Commentary on the Gospel of Matthew*. Grand Rapids: Eerdmans, 1999.
———. *The Gospel of John*. Vol. 1. Peabody: Hendrickson, 2003.
———. *Revelation*. New International Version Application Commentary. Grand Rapids: Zondervan, 2000.
Kidner, Derek. *Psalms*. 2 vols. Tyndale Old Testament Commentaries. Downers Grove: InterVarsity, 1973.
Koester, Craig R. *Symbolism in the Fourth Gospel: Meaning, Mystery, Community*. 2nd ed. Minneapolis: Fortress, 2003.
Köstenberger, Andreas J. *John*. Baker Exegetical Commentary on the New Testament. Grand Rapids: Baker Academic, 2004.
———. *A Theology of John's Gospel and Letters*. Grand Rapids: Zondervan, 2009.
Köstenberger, Andreas J., et al. *The Cradle, the Cross, and the Crown: An Introduction to the New Testament*. Nashville: B&H Academic, 2009.
Köstenberger, Andreas J., and Justin Taylor, *The Final Days of Jesus: The Most Important Week of the Most Important Person Who Ever Lived*. Wheaton: Crossway, 2014.
Köstenberger, Andreas J., and Richard D. Patterson, *Invitation to Biblical Interpretation: Exploring the Hermeneutical Triad of History, Literature, and Theology*. Grand Rapids: Kregel, 2011.
Kriegshauser, Laurence. *Praying the Psalms in Christ*. Notre Dame: University of Notre Dame Press, 2009.
Kugel, James L. *The Idea of Biblical Poetry: Parallelism and Its History*. Baltimore: The Johns Hopkins University Press, 1981.
Lane, William L. *Hebrews: A Call to Commitment*. Peabody: Hendrickson, 1985.
Lea, Thomas D., and Hayne Griffin, Jr. *1, 2 Timothy, Titus*. New American Commentary 34. Nashville: Broadman, 1992.
Lewis, C. S. *Reflections on the Psalms*. New York: Harcourt Brace Jovanovich Publishers, 1958.
Lincoln, Andrew T. *The Gospel According to John*. Black's New Testament Commentaries. New York: Continuum, 2005.
Longenecker, Richard N. *Biblical Exegesis in the Apostolic Period*. 2nd ed. Grand Rapids: Eerdmans, 1999.
Longman, Tremper III, ed. "Day of the Lord." In *BIBD* 573–75.
———, ed. "Expiation." In *BIBD* 549–51.
———, ed. "Face." In *BIBD* 562–63.
———, ed. "Family." In *BIBD* 573–75.
———. *How to Read the Psalms*. Downers Grove: InterVarsity, 1988.
———, ed. "Korahites." In *BIBD* 1020.
———. *Psalms*. Tyndale Old Testament Commentaries. Downers Grove: InterVarsity, 2014.
———, ed. "Torah." In *BIBD* 1646–47.
Longman, Tremper III, and J. Alan Groves. Foreword to *After God's Own Heart: The Gospel According to David*, by Mark Boda. Phillipsburg, NJ: P&R, 2007.
Longman, Tremper III, and Daniel G. Reid. *God is a Warrior*. Grand Rapids: Zondervan, 1995.

Luther, Martin. *A Complete Commentary on the First Twenty-Two Psalms: Vol. 1.* Translated by Rev. Henry Cole. London: W. Simpkin and R. Marshall, 1826. Apple e-book.

———. "A Mighty Fortress is Our God." http://www.hymnary.org/text/a_mighty_fortress_is_our_god_a_bulwark.

Manning, Gary T. *Echoes of a Prophet: The Use of Ezekiel in the Gospel of John and in Literature of the Second Temple Period.* Journal for the Study of the New Testament Supplement Series 270. London: T. & T. Clark, 2004.

Margalit, Baruch. *The Ugaritic Poem of Aqht: Text, Translation, Commentary.* Beihefte zür Zeitschrift für die alttestamentliche Wissenschaft 182. Berlin: De Gruyter, 1989.

Martínez, Florentino García. *The Dead Sea Scrolls Translated.* 2nd ed. Grand Rapids: Eerdmans, 1996.

Mays, James L. "The David of the Psalms." *Interpretation* 40 (1985) 143–55.

———. *Preaching and Teaching the Psalms.* Louisville: Westminster John Knox, 2006.

———. *Psalms.* Interpretation: A Bible Commentary for Preaching and Teaching. Louisville: John Knox, 1994.

———. "Worship, World, and Power: An Interpretation of Psalm 100." *Interpretation* 23 (1969) 315–30.

McCann, J. Clinton Jr. *The Book of Psalms.* New Interpreter's Bible 4. Edited by Leander E. Keck. Nashville: Abingdon, 1996.

———. *A Theological Introduction to the Book of Psalms: The Psalms as Torah.* Nashville: Abingdon, 1993.

McCartney, Dan G. "The New Testament's Use of the Old Testament." In *Inerrancy and Hermeneutic: A Tradition, A Challenge, A Debate,* edited by Harvie M. Conn, 101–16. Grand Rapids: Baker Book House, 1988.

———. "Should We Employ the Hermeneutics of the New Testament Writers?" Paper presented at the annual meeting of the Evangelical Theological Society, Atlanta, GA, November 19–21, 2003. http://www.bible-researcher.com/mccartney1.html.

McCartney, Dan, and Charles Clayton. *Let the Reader Understand: A Guide to Interpreting and Applying the Bible.* 2nd ed. Phillipsburg, NJ: P&R, 2002.

McKnight, Scot. *Galatians.* New International Version Application Commentary. Grand Rapids: Zondervan, 1995.

———. *Kingdom Conspiracy: Returning to the Radical Mission of the Local Church.* Grand Rapids: Brazos, 2014.

Milgrom, Jacob. *Numbers.* Jewish Publication Society Torah Commentary. Philadelphia: Jewish Publication Society, 1989.

Miller, Patrick D. "Psalm 127: The House That Yahweh Builds." *Journal for the Study of the Old Testament* 22 (1982) 119–32.

Mitchell, David C. "Lord, Remember David: G. H. Wilson and the Message of the Psalter." *Vetus Testamentum* 56 (2006) 526–48.

———. *The Message of the Psalter: An Eschatological Programme in the Book of Psalms.* JSOTSup 252. Sheffield: Sheffield Academic Press, 1997.

Moloney, Francis J. *Signs and Shadows: Reading John 5—12.* Eugene, OR: Wipf & Stock, 2004.

Moo, Douglas J. *Galatians.* Baker Exegetical Commentary on the New Testament. Grand Rapids: Baker Academic, 2013.

Mounce, Robert H. *The Book of Revelation.* Rev. ed. New International Commentary on the New Testament. Grand Rapids: Eerdmans, 1998.

Moyise, Steve. *Evoking Scripture: Seeing the Old Testament in the New*. New York: T. & T. Clark, 2008.

———. *Jesus and Scripture: Studying the New Use of the Old Testament*. Grand Rapids: Baker Academic, 2010.

———. *The Later New Testament Writings and Scripture: The Old Testament in Acts, Hebrews, the Catholic Epistles, and Revelation*. Grand Rapids: Baker Academic, 2012.

———. *Paul and Scripture: Studying the New Testament Use of the Old Testament*. Grand Rapids: Baker Academic, 2010.

O'Day, Gail R., and Susan E. Hylen. *John*. Westminster Bible Companion. Louisville: Westminster John Knox, 2006.

Osborne, Grant R. *Revelation*, Baker Exegetical Commentary on the New Testament. Grand Rapids: Baker Academic, 2002.

Perkins, Pheme. *The Gospel of Mark*. New Interpreter's Bible 8. Edited by Leander E. Keck. Nashville: Abingdon, 1994.

Pinnock, Clark H., and Barry L. Callen. *The Scripture Principle: Reclaiming the Full Authority of the Bible*. 2nd ed. Grand Rapids: Baker Academic, 2006.

Powell, Mark Allan. *Introducing the New Testament: A Historical, Literary, and Theological Survey*. Grand Rapids: Baker Academic, 2009.

Poythress, Vern S. *The Retuning King: A Guide to the Book of Revelation*. Phillipsburg, NJ: P&R, 2000.

———. "What Does God Say Through Human Authors?" In *Inerrancy and Hermeneutic: A Tradition, A Challenge, A Debate*, edited by Harvie M. Conn, 81–99. Grand Rapids: Baker, 1988.

Provan, Iain, et al. *A Biblical History of Israel*. Louisville: Westminster John Knox, 2003.

Pryor, John W. *John: Evangelist of the Covenant People: The Narrative and Themes of the Fourth Gospel*. Downers Grove: InterVarsity, 1992.

Reardon, Patrick Henry. *Christ in the Psalms*. Ben Lomond, CA: Conciliar, 2000.

Sanders, E. P. *Paul and Palestinian Judaism*. Philadelphia: Fortress, 1977.

Schaff, Philip, ed. *Nicene and Post-Nicene Fathers: First Series*. Vol. 8. Translated by J. E. Tweed. Buffalo, NY: Christian Literature, 1888.

Schaff, Philip, and Henry Wace, eds. *Nicene and Post-Nicene Fathers*. Vol. 5. Translated by William Moore and Henry Austin Wilson. Buffalo, NY: Christian Literature, 1893.

———. *Nicene and Post-Nicene Fathers: Second Series*. Vol. 6, Translated by W. H. Fremantle, G. Lewis, and W. G. Martly. Buffalo, NY: Christian Literature, 1893.

Schechter, Solomon. *Aspects of Rabbinic Theology: Major Concepts of the Talmud*. Peabody: Hendrickson, 1998.

Schmutzer, Andrew J., and Randall X. Gauthier. "The Identity of 'Horn' in Psalm 148:14a: An Exegetical Investigation in the MT and LXX Versions." *Bulletin for Biblical Research* 19 (2009) 161–83.

Schleiermacher, Friedrich. *Hermeneutics: The Handwritten Manuscripts*. Edited by H. Kimmerle. Translated by J. Duke and J. Forstman. Missoula, MT: Scholars, 1977.

Schürer, Emil. *A History of The Jewish People in the Time of Jesus Christ*. Second Division. Vol. 2. Translated by Sophia Taylor and Rev. Peter Christie. Peabody: Hendrickson, 1998.

Scott, Matthew. *The Hermeneutics of Christological Psalmody in Paul: An Intertextual Enquiry*. New York: Cambridge University Press, 2014.

Seibert, Eric A. *The Violence of Scripture: Overcoming the Old Testament's Troubling Legacy*. Minneapolis: Fortress, 2012.

Shank, Harold. *Minor Prophets: Hosea—Micah*. College Press New International Version Commentary. Joplin: College Press, 2001.

Silva, Moisés. "The New Testament Use of the Old Testament: Text Form and Authority." In *Scripture and Truth*, edited by D. A. Carson and John Woodbridge, 147–65. Baker Book House, 1992.

Snodgrass, Klyne. "The Use of the Old Testament in the New." In *Interpreting the New Testament: Essays on Methods and Issues*, edited by David Alan Black and David Dockery, 209–29. Nashville: Broadman & Holman, 2001.

Soll, Will. *Psalm 119: Matrix, Form, and Setting*. Catholic Biblical Quarterly Monograph Series 23. Washington, DC: Catholic Biblical Association, 1991.

Sparks, Kenton L. *God's Word in Human Words: An Evangelical Appropriation of Critical Biblical Scholarship*. Grand Rapids: Baker Academic, 2008.

———. *Sacred Word, Broken Word: Biblical Authority and the Dark Side of Scripture*. Grand Rapids: Eerdmans, 2012.

Subramanian, Samuel J. *The Synoptic Gospels and the Psalms as Prophecy*. New York: T. & T. Clark, 2008.

Tannehill, Robert C. *Luke*. Abingdon New Testament Commentaries. Nashville: Abingdon, 1996.

Tesh, S. Edward, and Walter D. Zorn. *Psalms*. Vol. 1. College Press New International Version Commentary. Joplin: College Press, 1999.

Thielman, Frank. *Ephesians*. Baker Exegetical Commentary on the New Testament. Grand Rapids: Zondervan, 2010.

Thomas of Celano. "That Day of Wrath." https://hymnary.org/text/that_day_of_wrath_that_dreadful_day_when.

Thompson, J. A. *The Book of Jeremiah*. New International Commentary on the Old Testament. Grand Rapids: Eerdmans, 1980.

Thompson, Marianne Meye. *John*. New Testament Library. Louisville: Westminster John Knox, 2015.

Tiessen, Terrence. *Providence and Prayer: How Does God Work in the World?* Downers Grove: InterVarsity, 2000.

VanderKam, James C. *The Dead Sea Scrolls Today*. Grand Rapids: Eerdmans, 1994.

VanGemeren, Willem. *The Progress of Redemption: The Story of Salvation from Creation to the New Jerusalem*. Grand Rapids: Baker, 1988.

Virkler, Henry A., and Karelynne Gerber Ayayo. *Hermeneutics: Principles and Processes of Biblical Interpretation*. 2nd ed. Grand Rapids: Baker Academic, 2007.

Vos, Johannes Geerhardus. *Biblical Theology: Old and New Testaments*. Carlisle, PA: The Banner of Truth Trust, 1978.

———. "The Ethical Problem of the Imprecatory Psalms." *Westminster Theological Journal* 4 (1942) 123–38.

Walker, Andy. "The Kerygmatic Function of Retelling Israel's History in Poetic Sections of the Hebrew Bible." PhD diss., Amridge University, 2015.

Walters, Stanley D. "Finding Christ in the Psalms." In *Go Figure! Figuration in Biblical Interpretation*. Princeton Theological Monograph Series 81, 31–47. Eugene, OR: Pickwick, 2008.

Waltke, Bruce K. "Christ in the Psalms." In *The Hope Fulfilled: Essays in Honor of O. Palmer Robertson,* edited by Robert L. Penny, 26–46. Phillipsburg, NJ: P&R, 2008.

———. *The Psalms as Christian Worship: An Historical Commentary.* Grand Rapids: Eerdmans, 2010.
Warden, Duane. "All Things Praise Him (Psalm 148)." *Restoration Quarterly* 35 (1993) 101–08.
Watts, James A. "Torah." In *NIDB* 5:629–30.
Wenham, Gordon. "Towards a Canonical Reading of the Psalms." In *Canon and Biblical Interpretation*, edited by Craig G. Bartholomew, et al., 333–51. Grand Rapids: Zondervan, 2006.
Wesselschmidt, Quentine F., ed. *Psalms 51—150.* Ancient Christian Commentary on Scripture 8. Downers Grove: InterVarsity, 2007.
Westermann, Claus. *Praise and Lament in the Psalms.* Translated by Keith R. Crim and Richard N. Soulen. Atlanta: John Knox, 1981.
Wilkins, Michael J. *Matthew.* New International Version Application Commentary. Grand Rapids: Zondervan, 2004.
Williams, Michael. *How to Read the Bible Through the Jesus Lens: A Guide to Christ-Focused Reading of Scripture.* Grand Rapids: Zondervan, 2012.
Williamson, Lamar Jr. *Mark.* Interpretation: A Bible Commentary for Preaching and Teaching. Louisville: John Knox, 1983.
Wilson, Gerald H. *Psalms.* Vol. 1. New International Version Application Commentary. Grand Rapids: Zondervan, 2002.
Witherington, Ben III. *John's Wisdom: A Commentary on the Fourth Gospel.* Louisville: Westminster John Knox, 1995.
Wright, Christopher J. H. *Deuteronomy.* New International Biblical Commentary 4. Peabody: Hendrickson, 1996.
———. *Knowing Jesus Through the Old Testament.* Downers Grove: InterVarsity, 1992.
———. *The Mission of God's People: A Biblical Theology of the Church's Mission.* Grand Rapids: Zondervan, 2010.
Wright, N. T. *The Case for the Psalms: Why They Are Essential.* New York: HarperOne, 2013.
———. *The Lord and His Prayer.* Grand Rapids: Eerdmans, 1996.
———. *Matthew for Everyone.* 2 Vols. Louisville: Westminster John Knox, 2004.
———. "On Becoming the Righteousness of God." In *Pauline Theology.* Vol. 2, edited by D. M. Hay, 200–08. Minneapolis: Augsburg Fortress, 1993.
———. *Paul and the Faithfulness of God.* Minneapolis: Fortress, 2013.
———. *Scripture and the Authority of God: How to Read the Bible Today.* San Francisco: HarperOne, 2013.
Xu, Ying. "From the Lament of David to the Prayer of Christ in His Passion: A Canonical Process Approach to Psalm 3." PhD diss., Westminster Theological Seminary, 2012.
Zorn, Walter D. *Psalms.* Vol. 2. College Press New International Version Commentary. Joplin: College Press, 2004.
Zurheide, Jeffry R. *When Faith is Tested: Pastoral Responses to Suffering and Tragic Death.* Minneapolis: Fortress, 1997.

www.ingramcontent.com/pod-product-compliance
Lightning Source LLC
Chambersburg PA
CBHW050437240426
43661CB00055B/2417